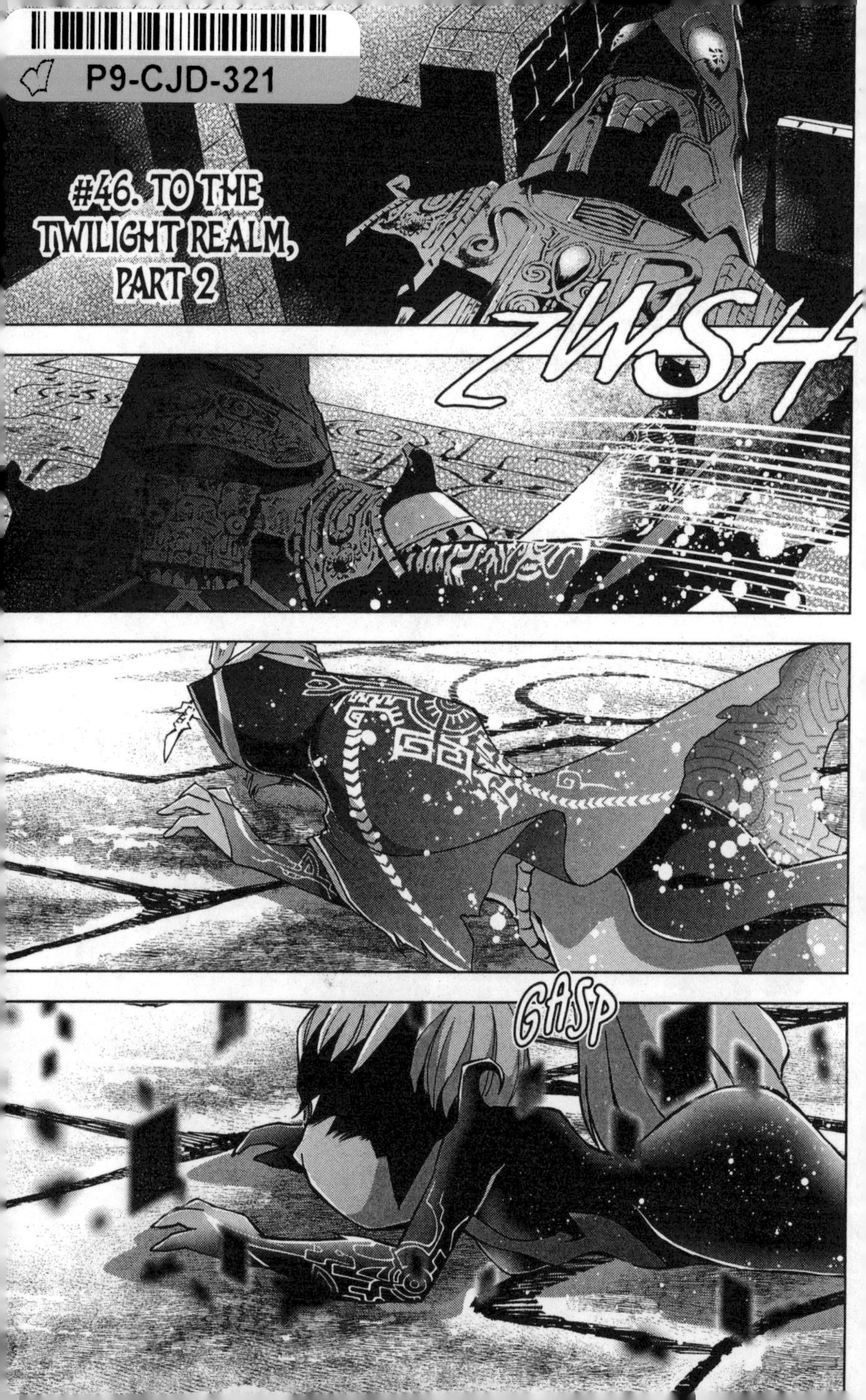
#46. TO THE
TWILIGHT REALM,
PART 2
ZWSH
GASP

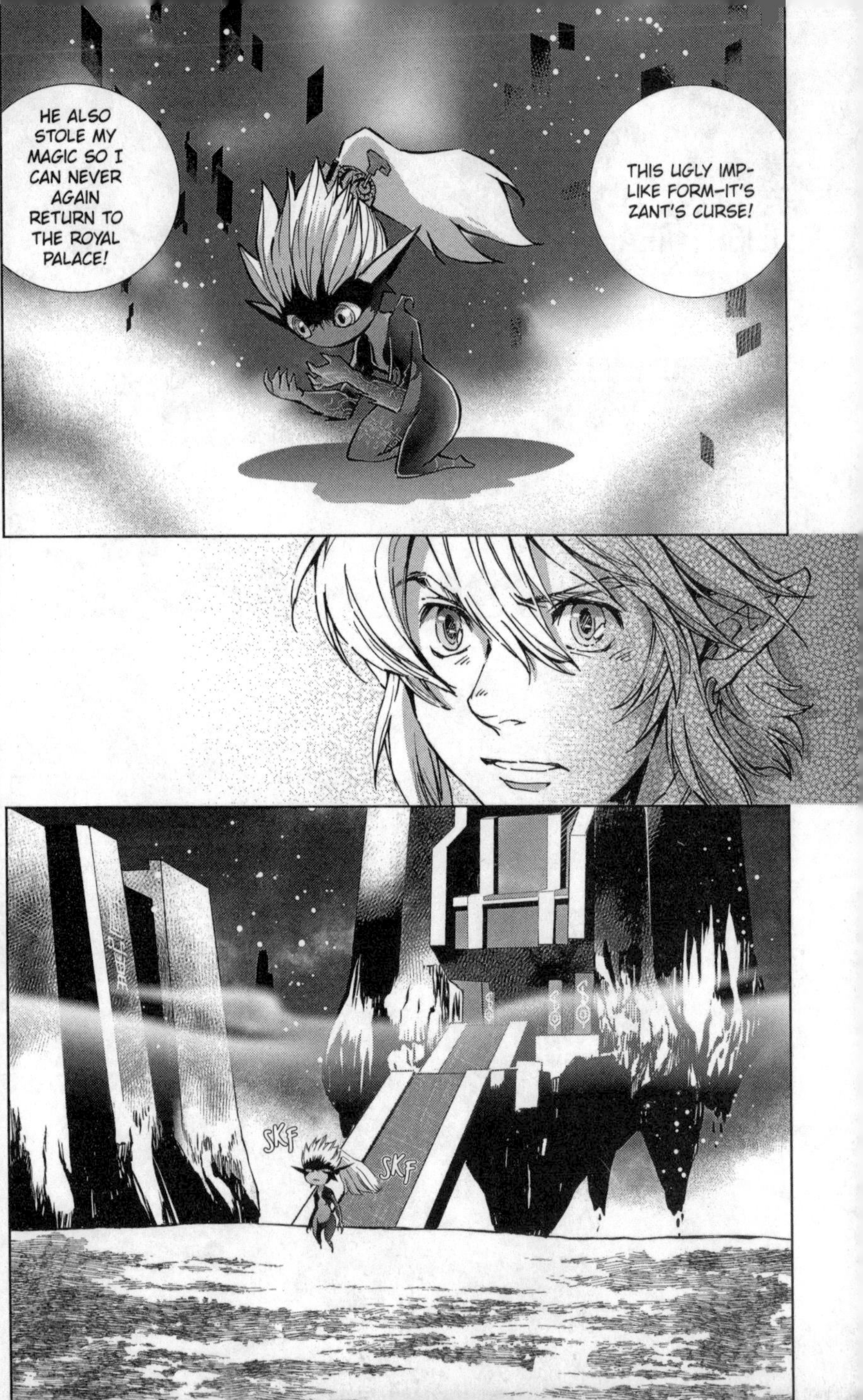
THIS UGLY IMP-LIKE FORM—IT'S ZANT'S CURSE!
HE ALSO STOLE MY MAGIC SO I CAN NEVER AGAIN RETURN TO THE ROYAL PALACE!
SKF
SKF

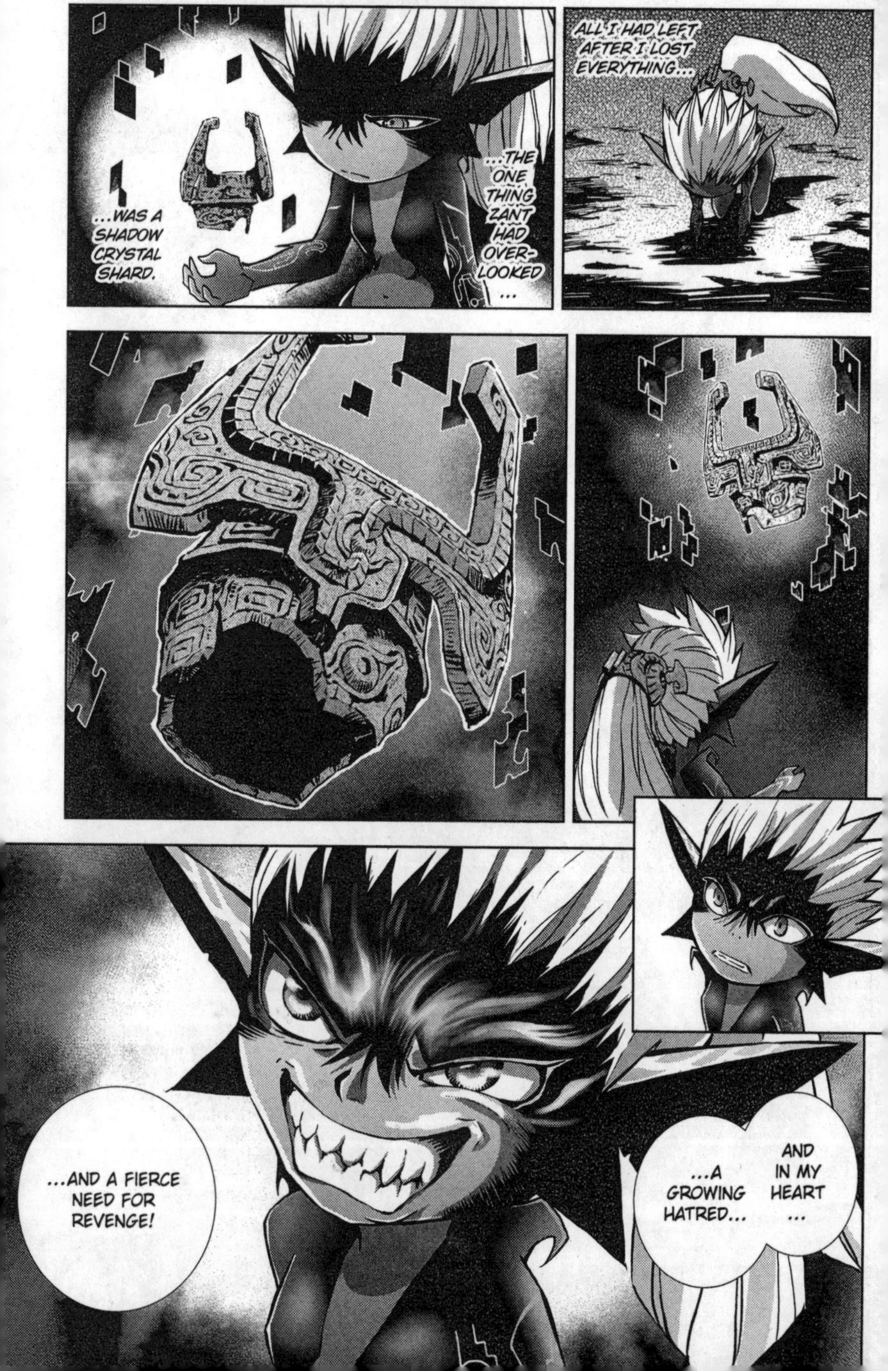
ALL I HAD LEFT AFTER I LOST EVERYTHING...
...THE ONE THING ZANT HAD OVER-LOOKED ...
...WAS A SHADOW CRYSTAL SHARD.
AND IN MY HEART ...
...A GROWING HATRED...
...AND A FIERCE NEED FOR REVENGE!

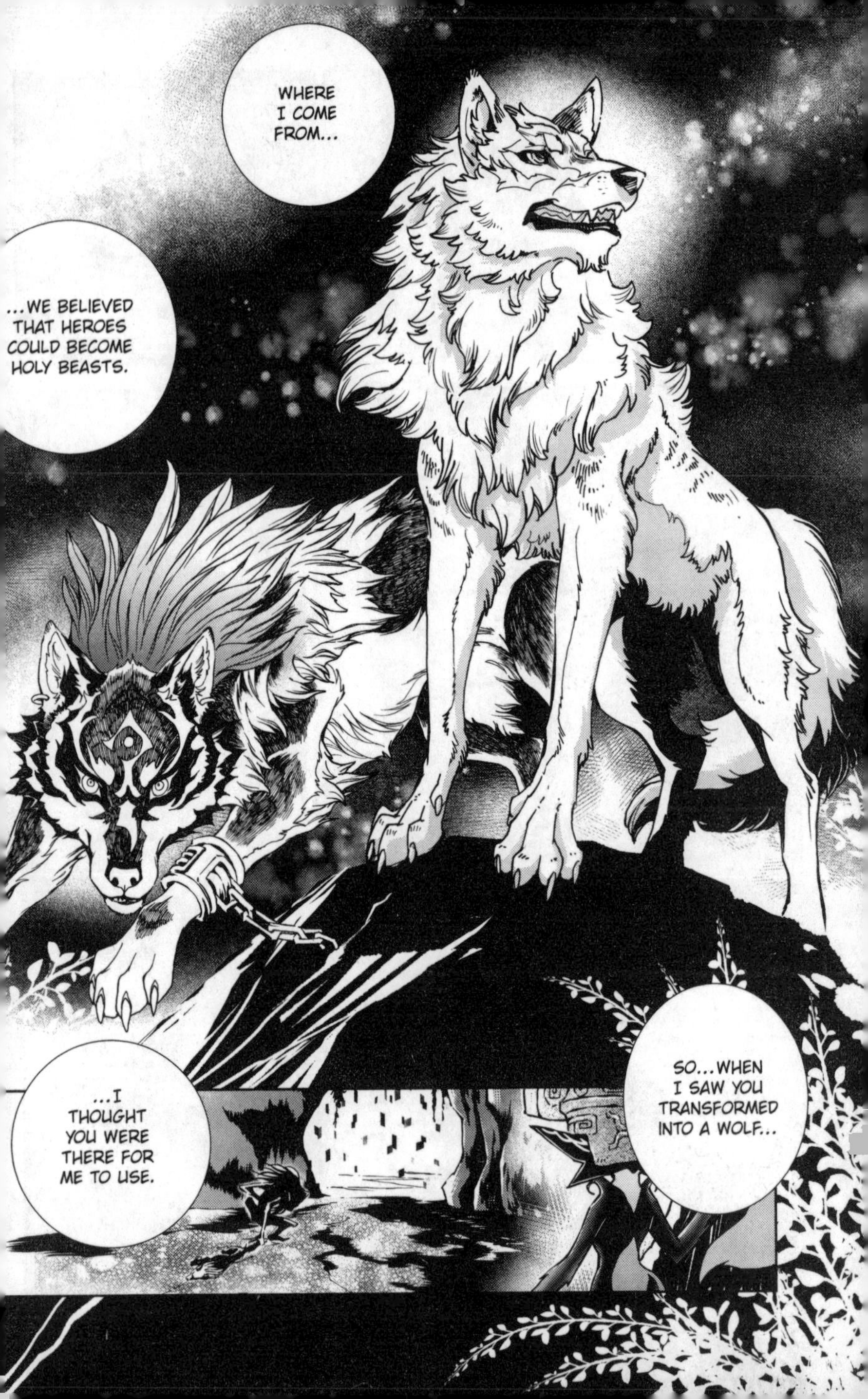
WHERE I COME FROM...
...WE BELIEVED THAT HEROES COULD BECOME HOLY BEASTS.
SO...WHEN I SAW YOU TRANSFORMED INTO A WOLF...
...I THOUGHT YOU WERE THERE FOR ME TO USE.

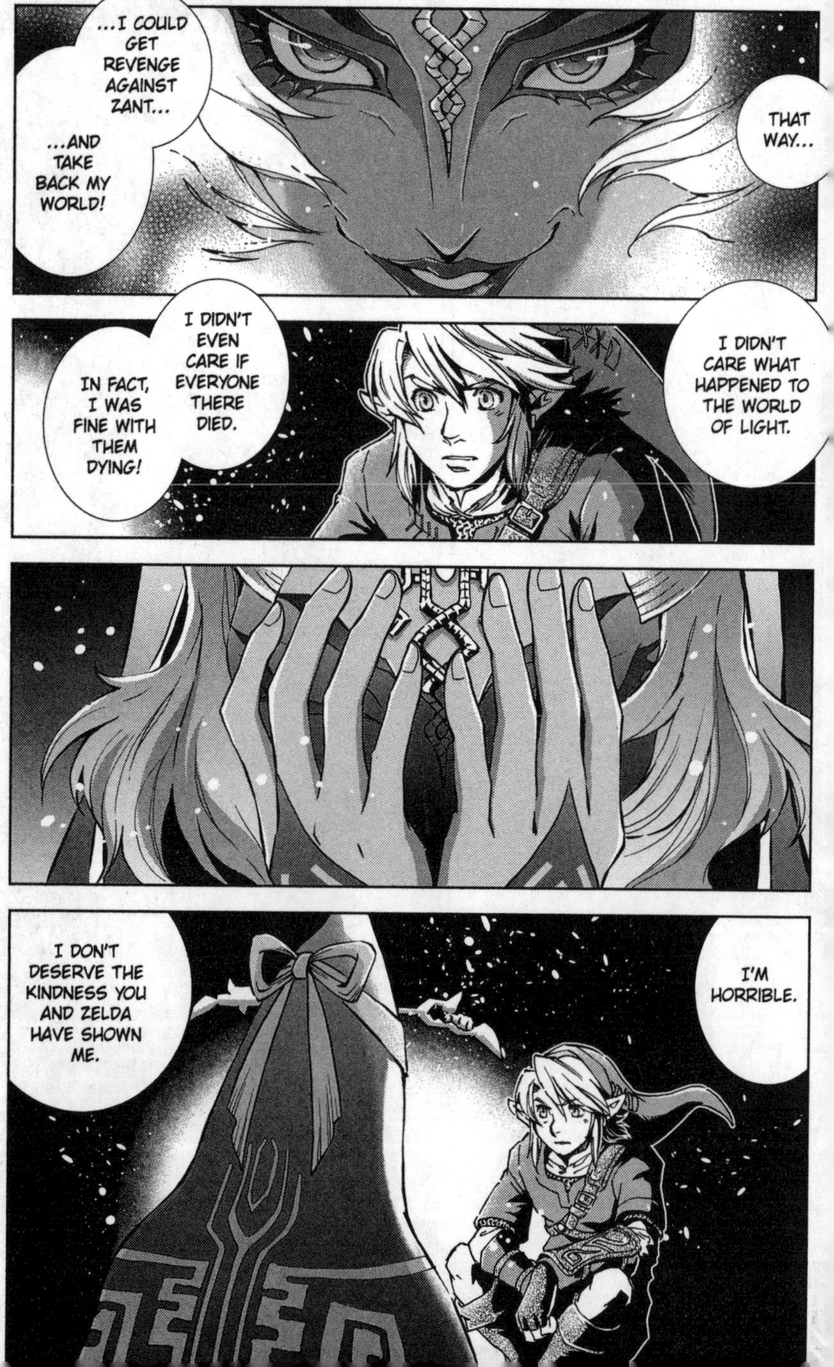
THAT WAY...
...I COULD GET REVENGE AGAINST ZANT...
...AND TAKE BACK MY WORLD!
I DIDN'T CARE WHAT HAPPENED TO THE WORLD OF LIGHT.
I DIDN'T EVEN CARE IF EVERYONE THERE DIED.
IN FACT, I WAS FINE WITH THEM DYING!
I'M HORRIBLE.
I DON'T DESERVE THE KINDNESS YOU AND ZELDA HAVE SHOWN ME.

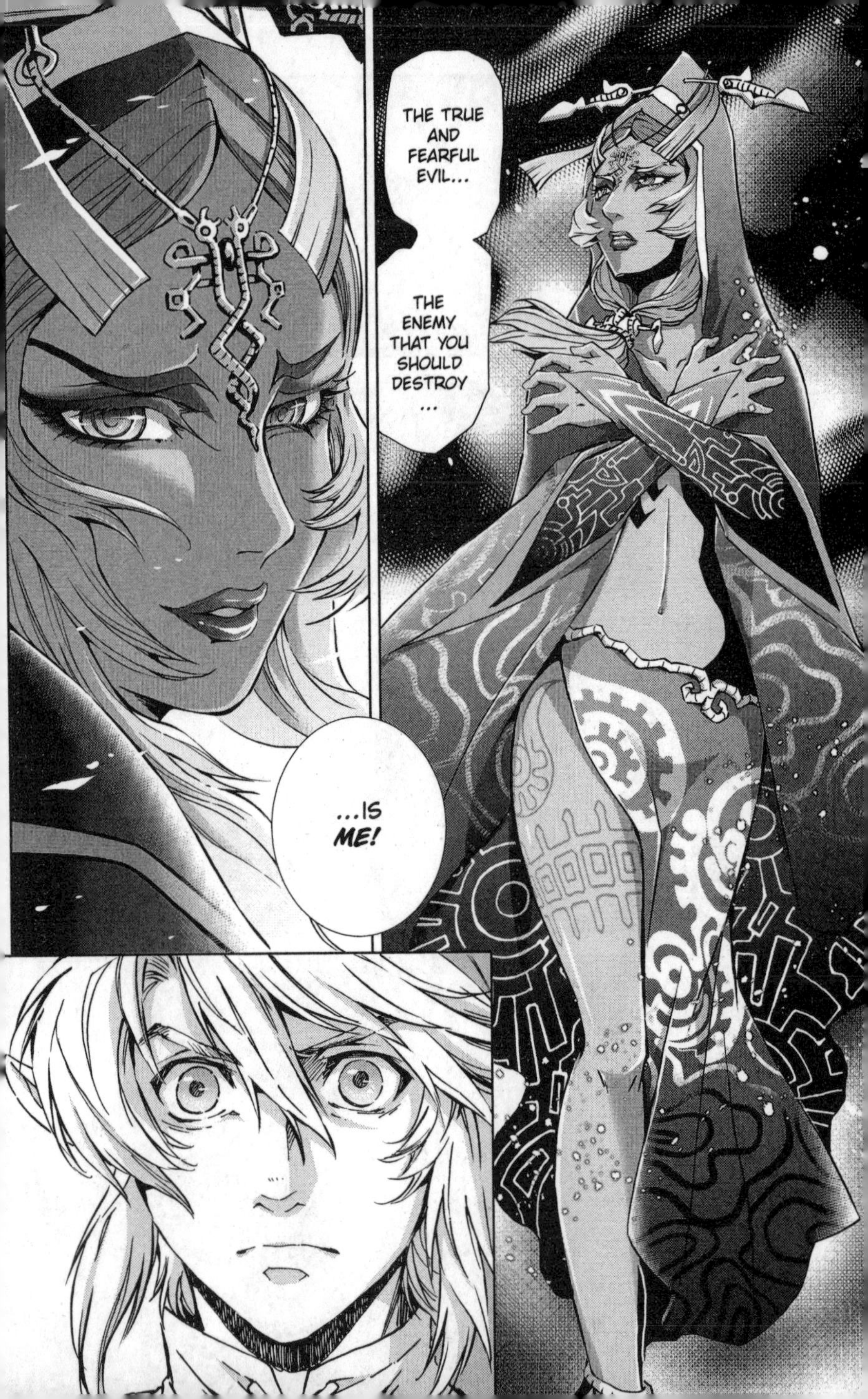
THE TRUE AND FEARFUL EVIL...
THE ENEMY THAT YOU SHOULD DESTROY...
...IS ME!

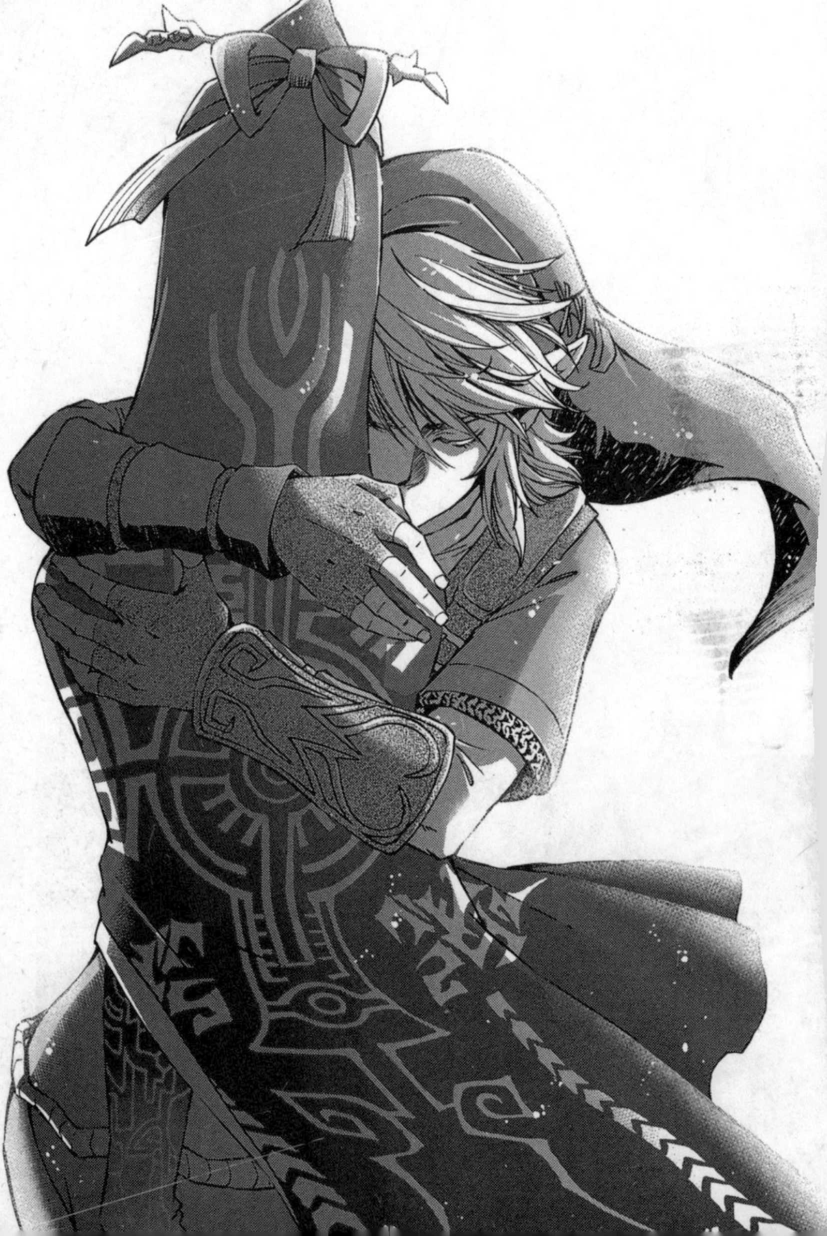

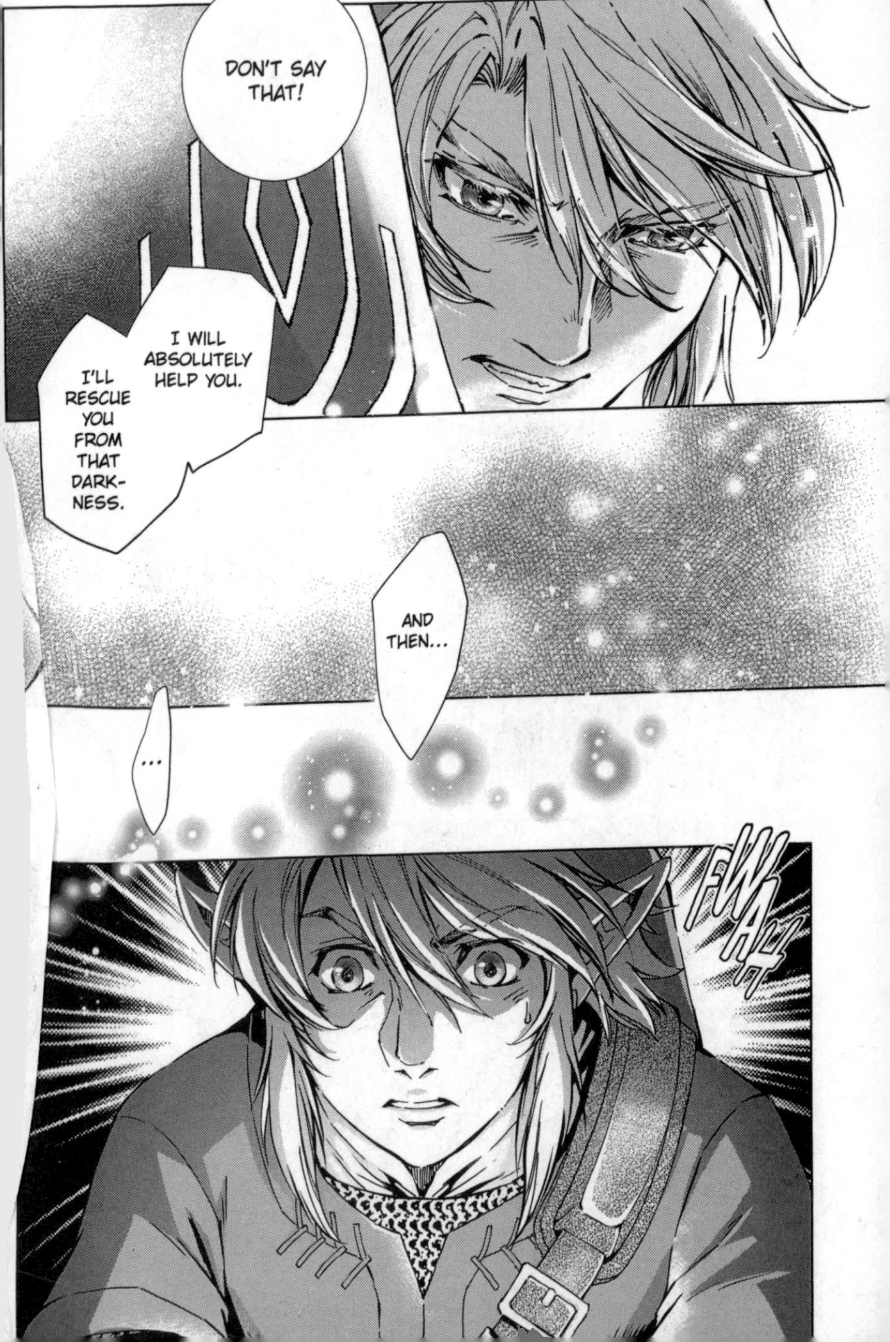
DON'T SAY THAT!
I WILL ABSOLUTELY HELP YOU.
I'LL RESCUE YOU FROM THAT DARKNESS.
AND THEN...
...
FWAH

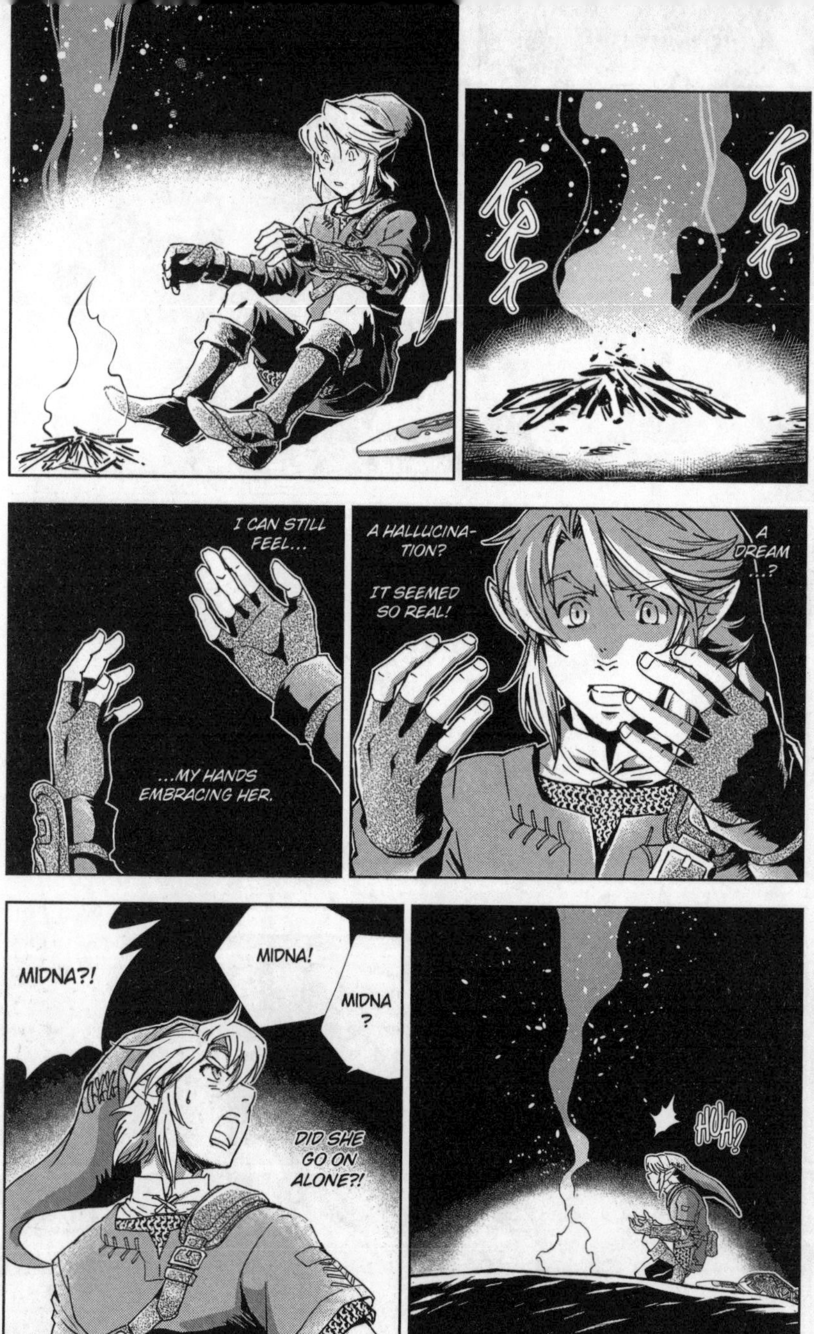
KRK
KRK
A DREAM...?
A HALLUCINATION?
IT SEEMED SO REAL!
I CAN STILL FEEL...
...MY HANDS EMBRACING HER.
HUH?!
MIDNA?
MIDNA!
MIDNA?!
DID SHE GO ON ALONE?!

I'M NOT GOING TO...

...DISAP-PEAR.

YOU AREN'T A LOST CHILD SEARCHING FOR HIS MOTHER.

STOP SHOUTING.

SO, SHALL WE GO?

PARTNER?

YEAH!

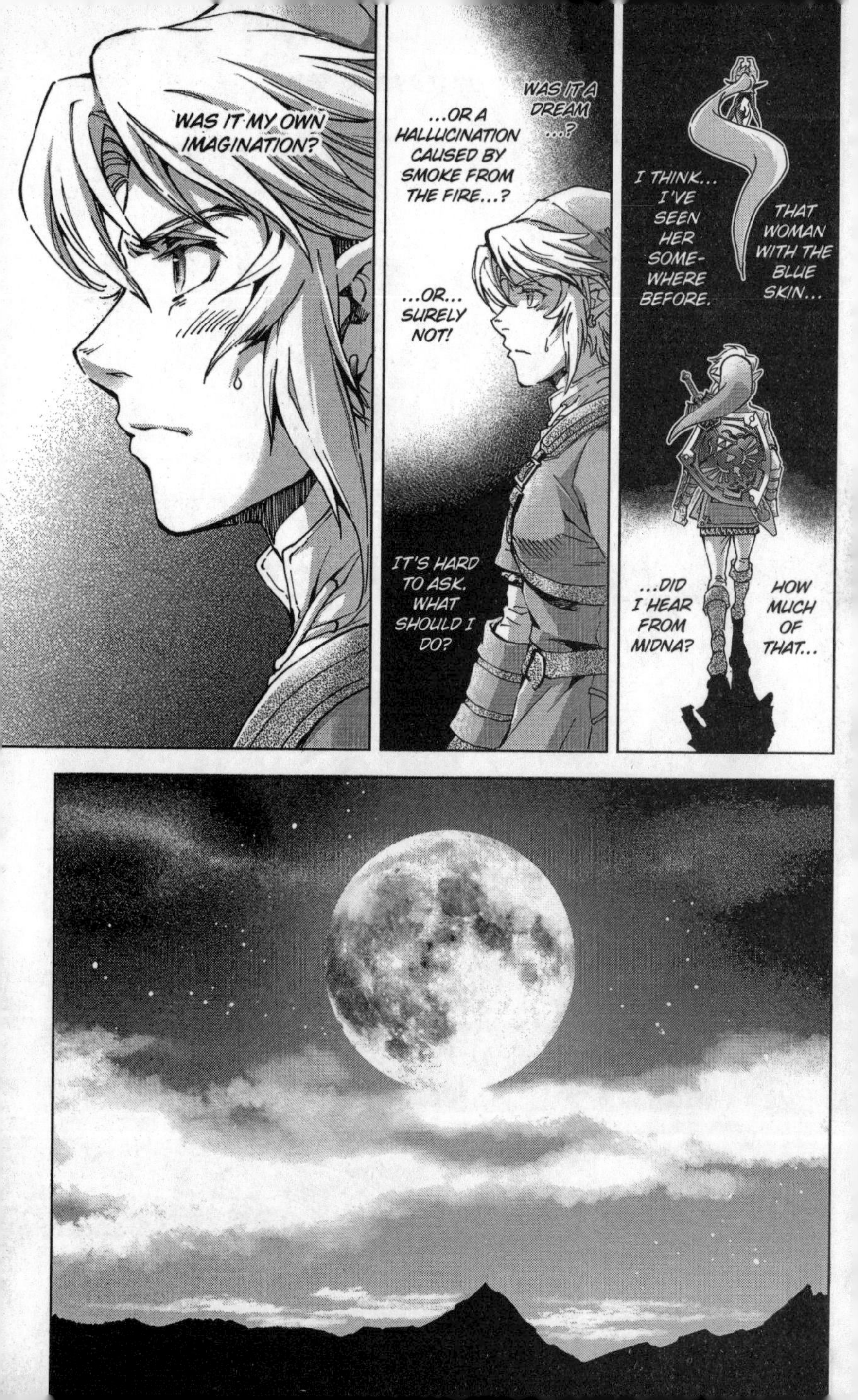
THAT WOMAN WITH THE BLUE SKIN...
I THINK... I'VE SEEN HER SOME-WHERE BEFORE.
HOW MUCH OF THAT...
...DID I HEAR FROM MIDNA?
WAS IT A DREAM ...?
...OR A HALLUCINATION CAUSED BY SMOKE FROM THE FIRE...?
...OR... SURELY NOT!
IT'S HARD TO ASK. WHAT SHOULD I DO?
WAS IT MY OWN IMAGINATION?

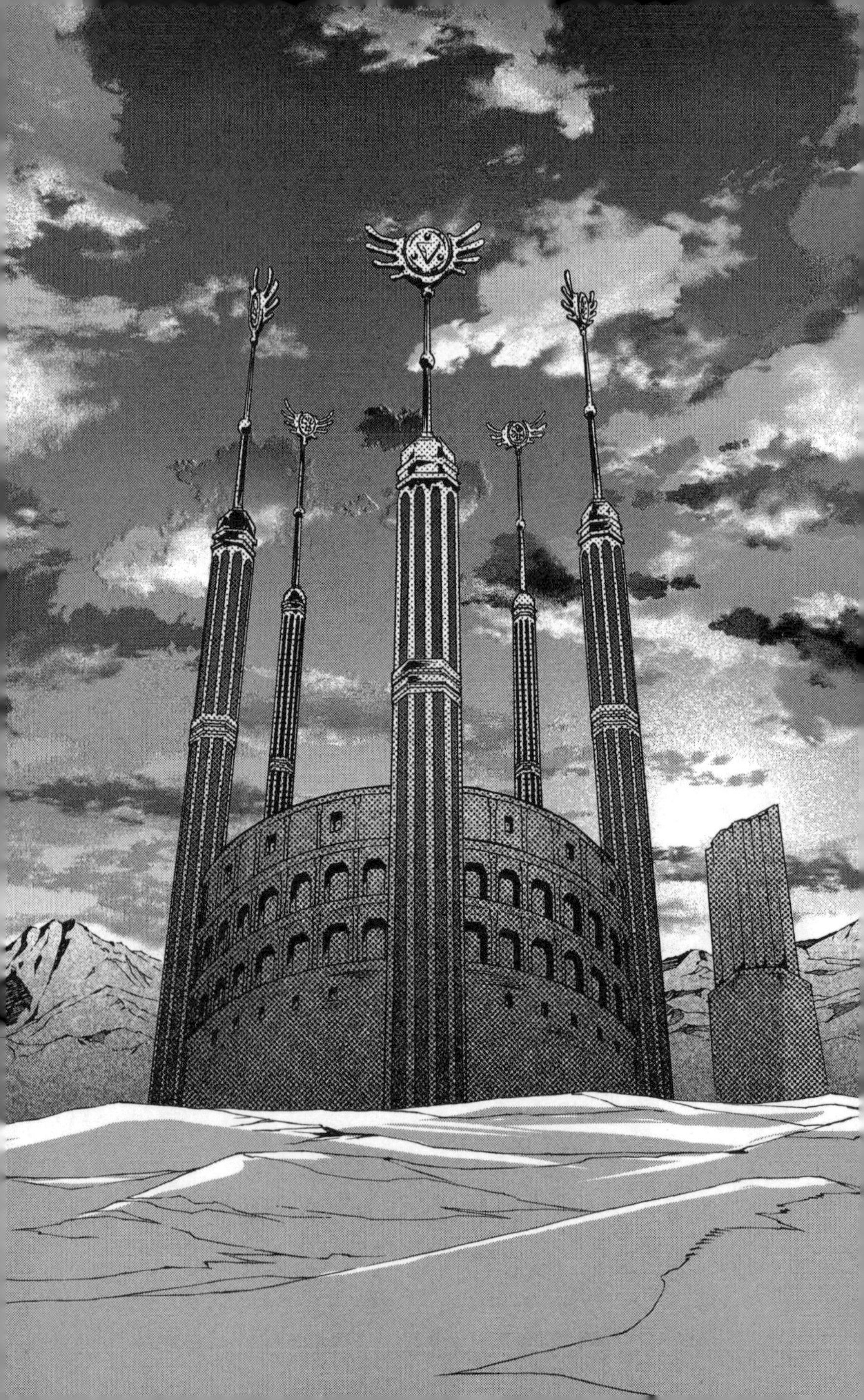

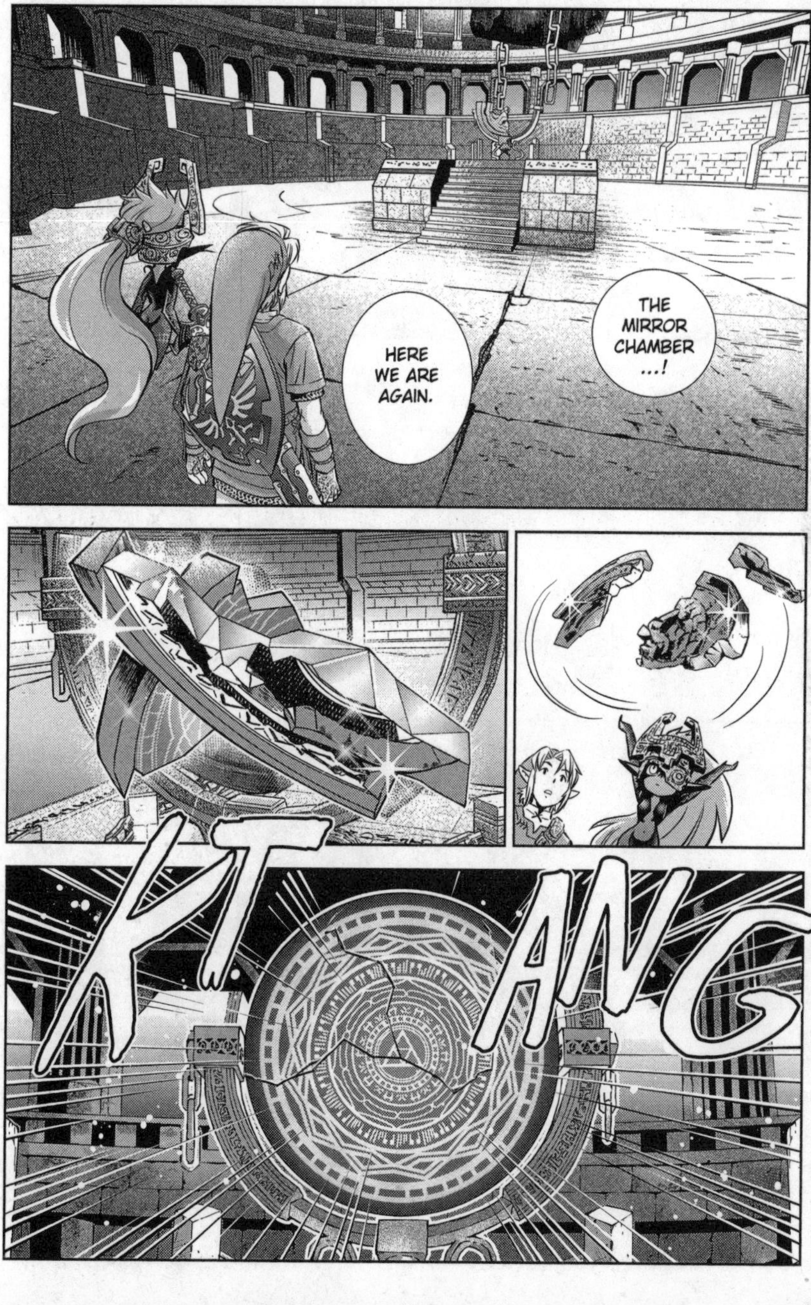
THE MIRROR CHAMBER ...!
HERE WE ARE AGAIN.
KT ANG

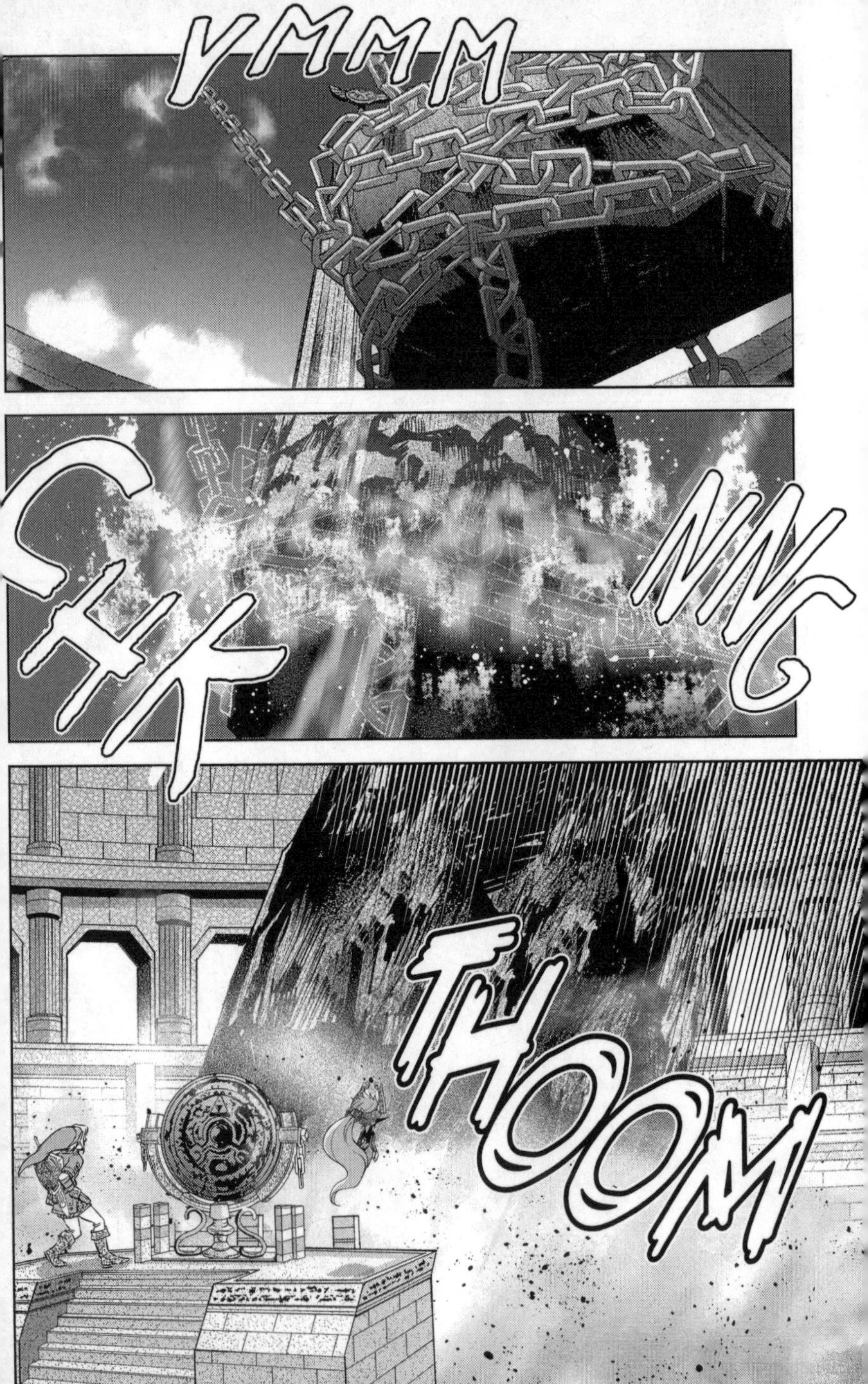
YMMM
CHK
NNG
THOOM

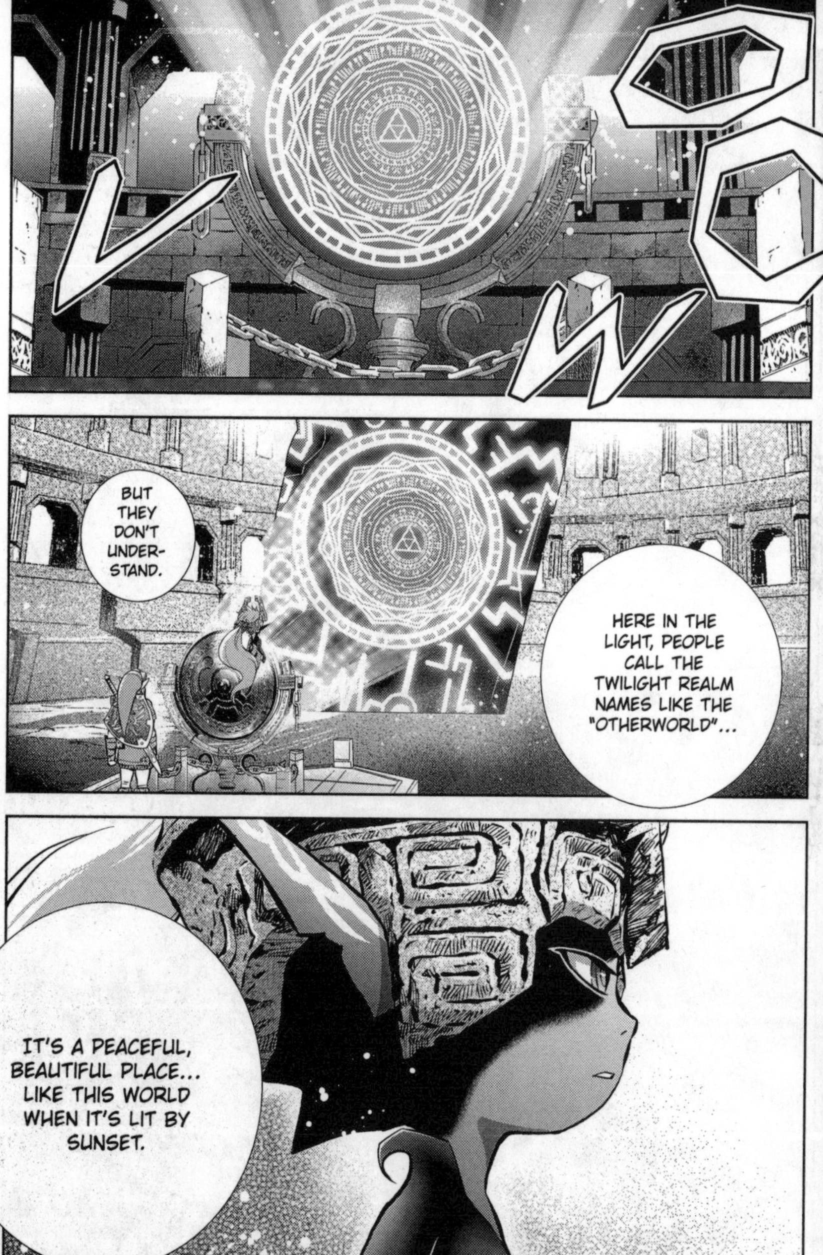
VWOO
HERE IN THE LIGHT, PEOPLE CALL THE TWILIGHT REALM NAMES LIKE THE "OTHERWORLD"...
BUT THEY DON'T UNDER-STAND.
IT'S A PEACEFUL, BEAUTIFUL PLACE... LIKE THIS WORLD WHEN IT'S LIT BY SUNSET.

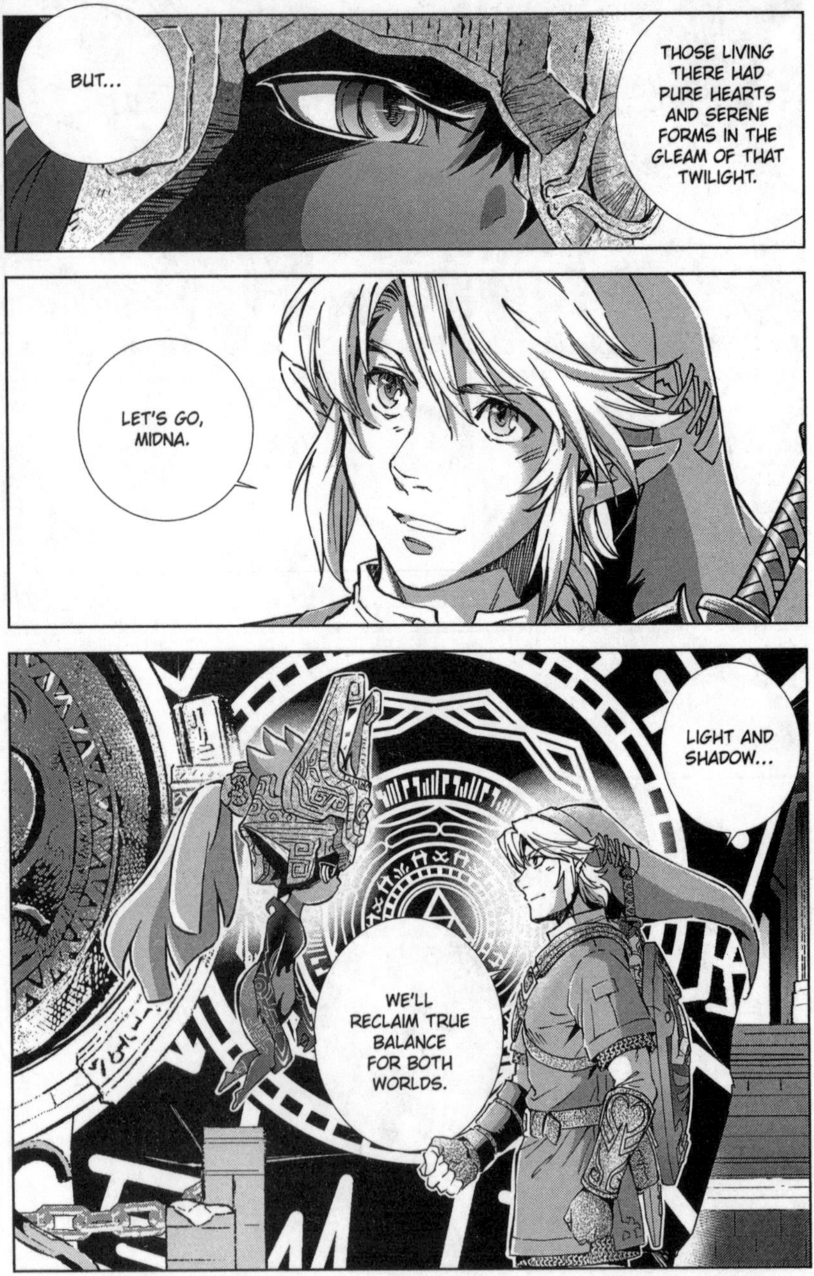
THOSE LIVING THERE HAD PURE HEARTS AND SERENE FORMS IN THE GLEAM OF THAT TWILIGHT.
BUT...
LET'S GO, MIDNA.
LIGHT AND SHADOW...
WE'LL RECLAIM TRUE BALANCE FOR BOTH WORLDS.

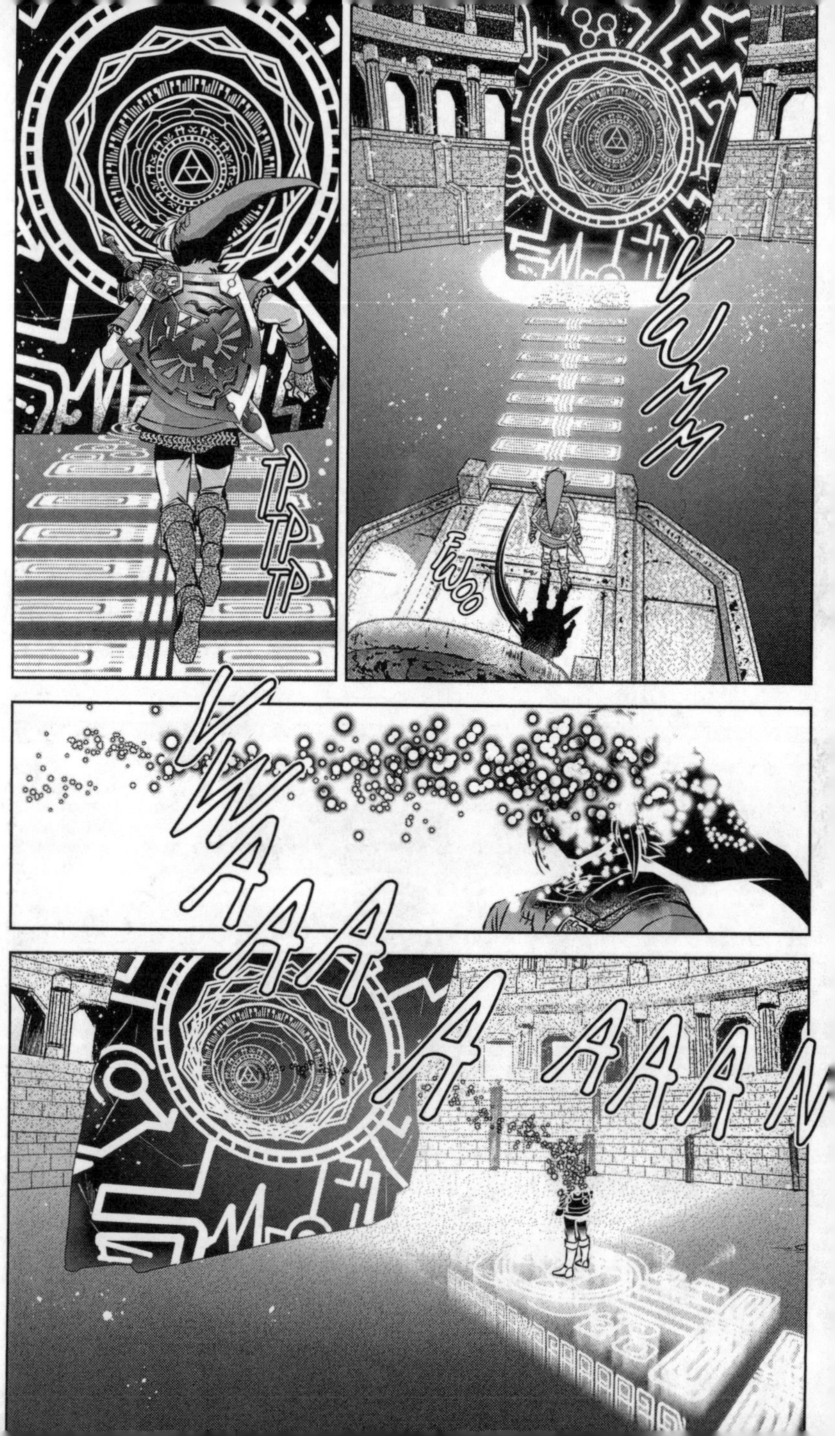
VUMM
Fwoo
TPTPTP
VWAAA
A
AAAN

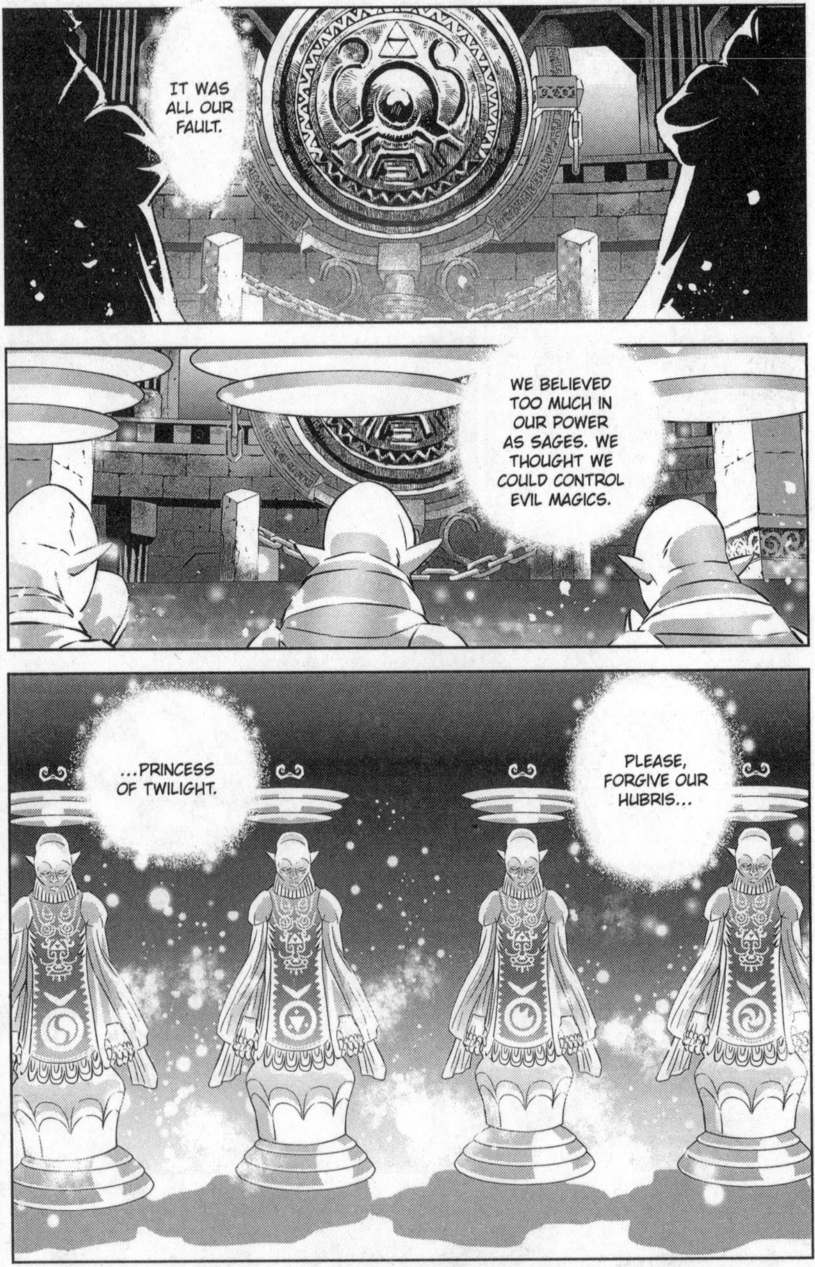
IT WAS ALL OUR FAULT.
WE BELIEVED TOO MUCH IN OUR POWER AS SAGES. WE THOUGHT WE COULD CONTROL EVIL MAGICS.
PLEASE, FORGIVE OUR HUBRIS...
...PRINCESS OF TWILIGHT.

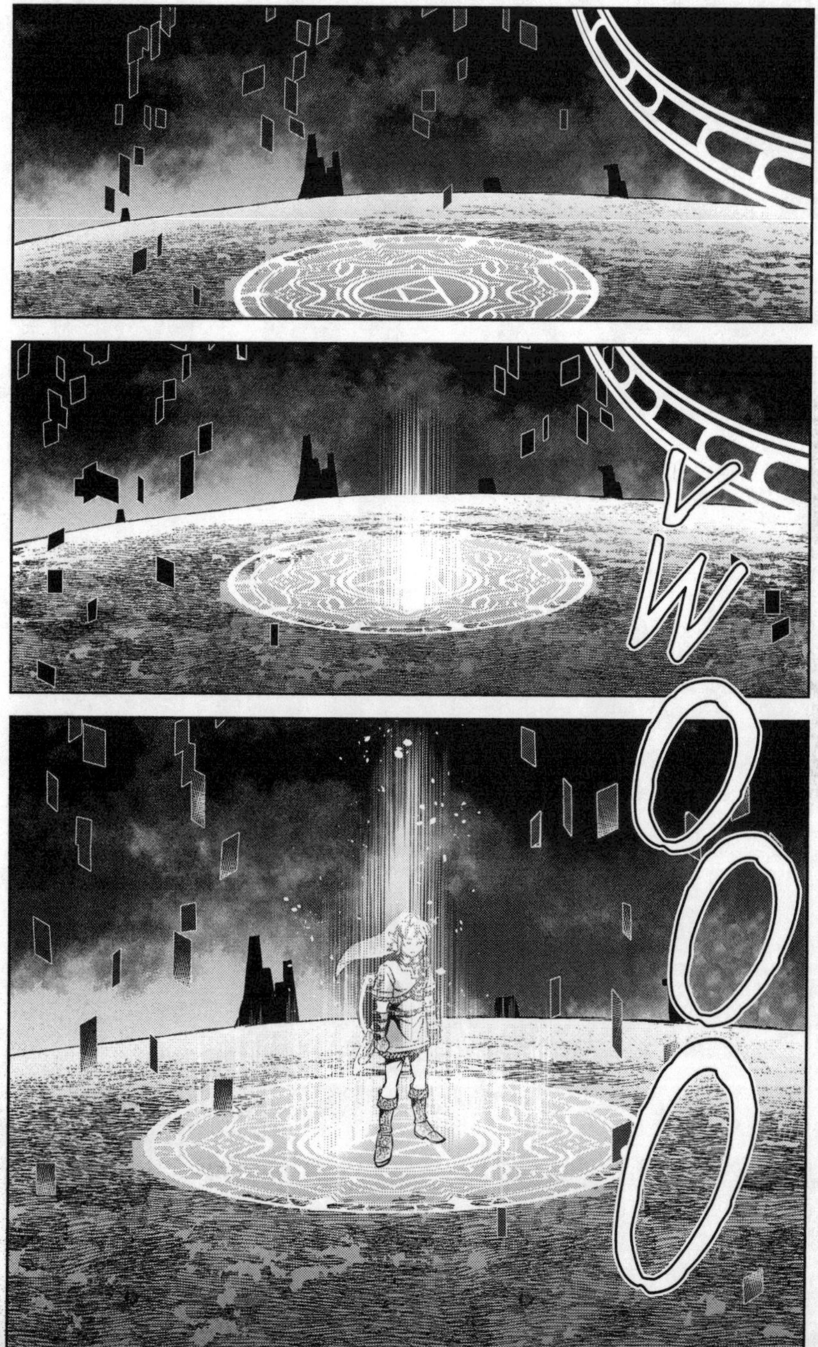
VWOOO

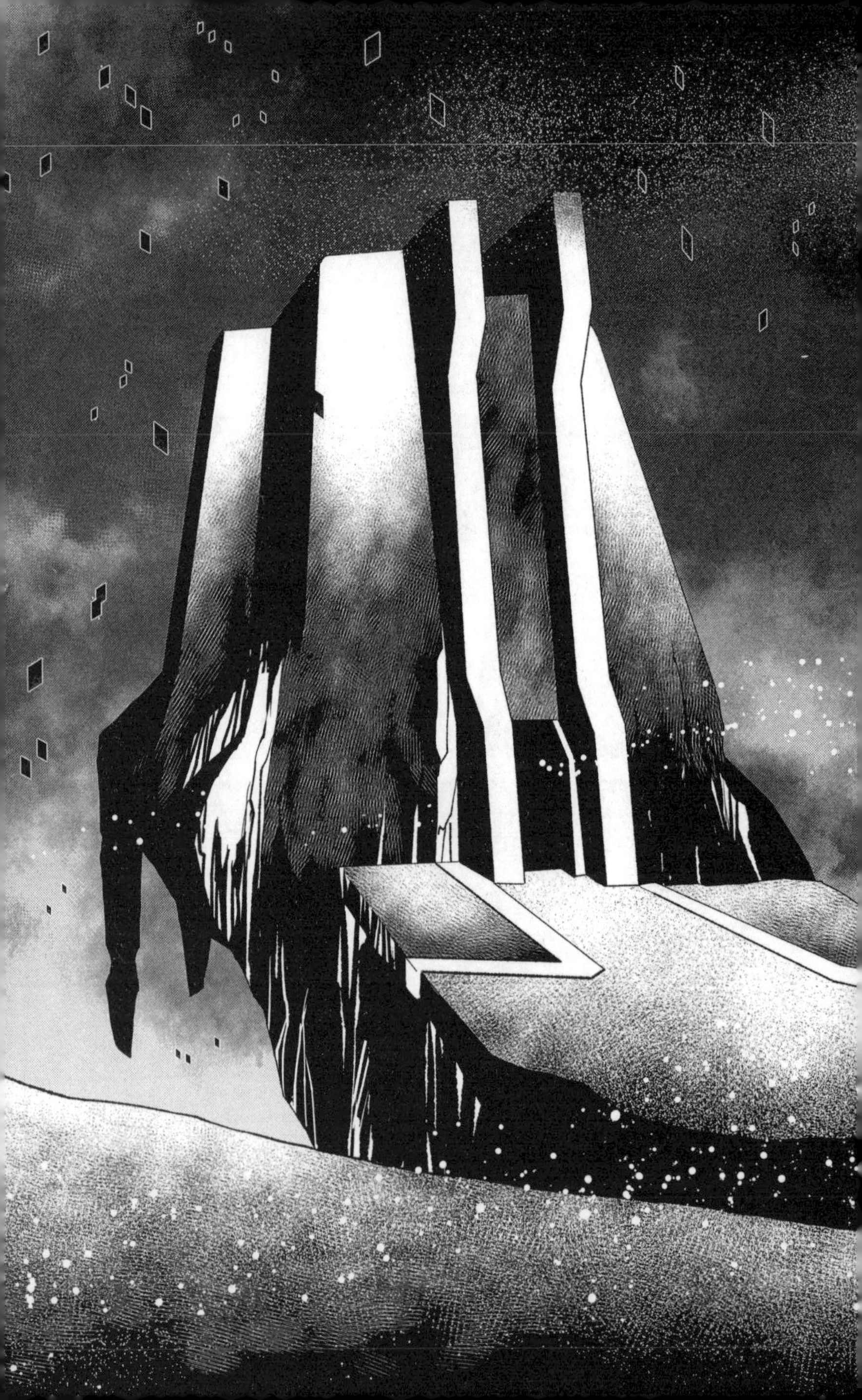

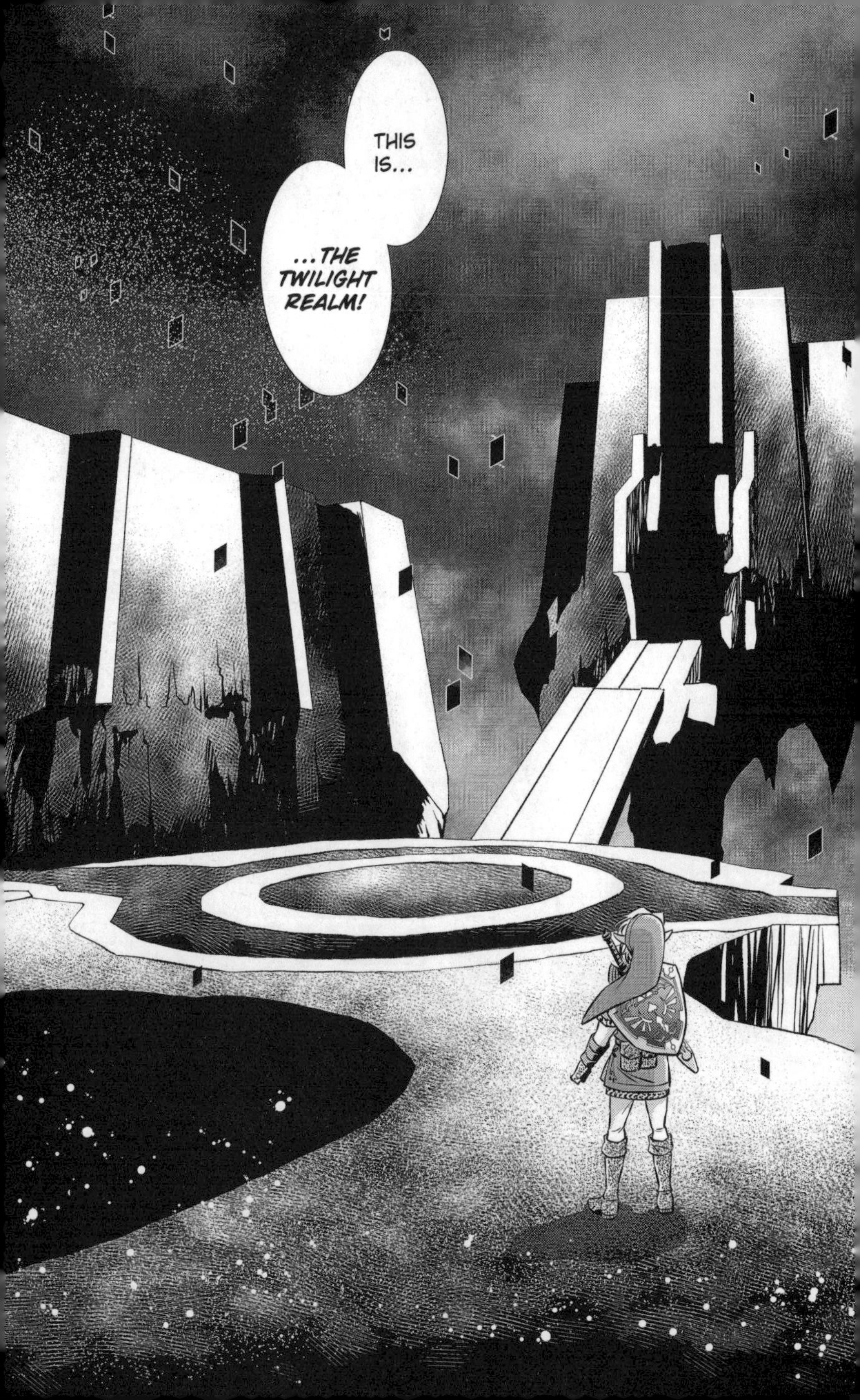
THIS IS...
...THE TWILIGHT REALM!

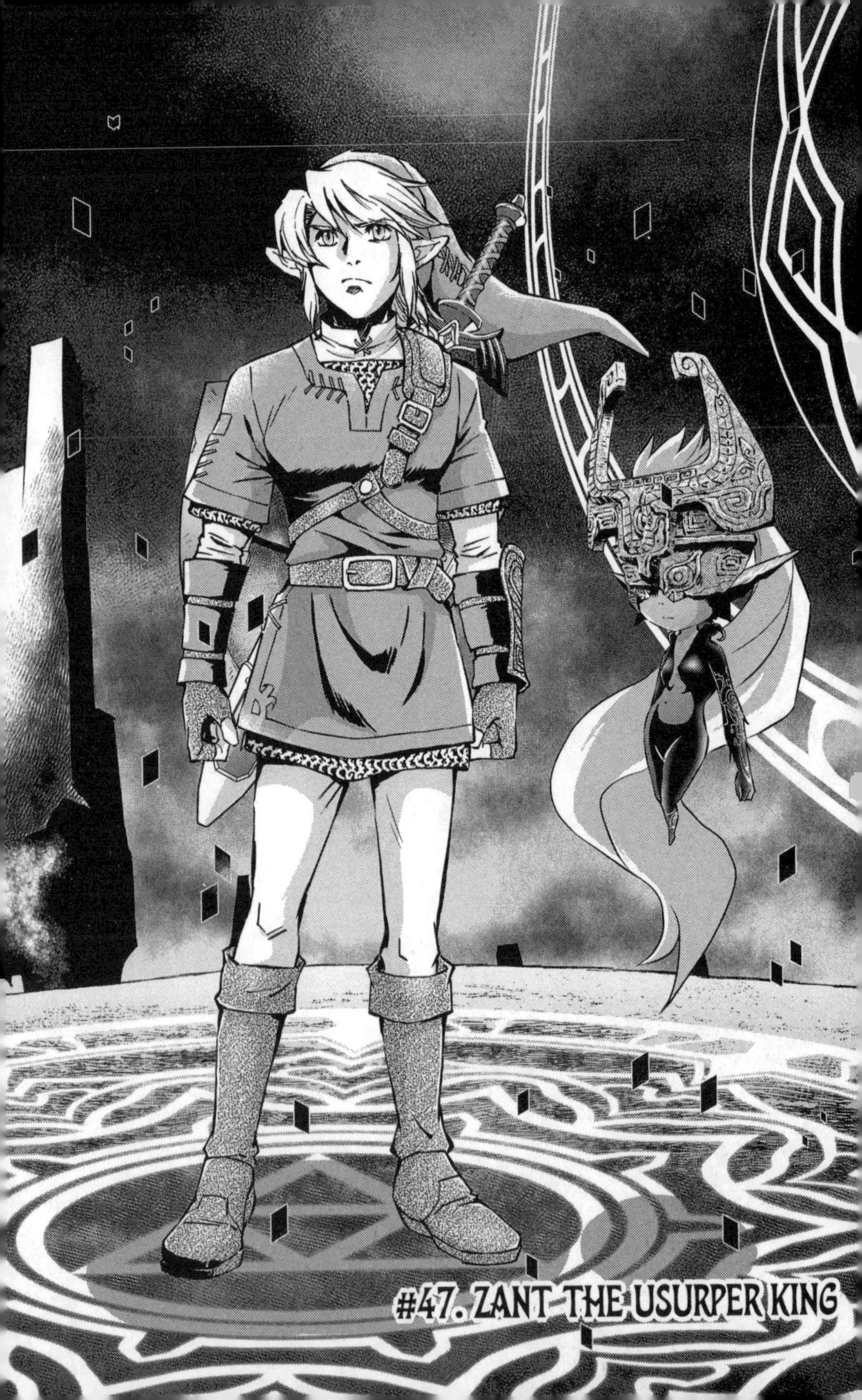
#47. ZANT THE USURPER KING

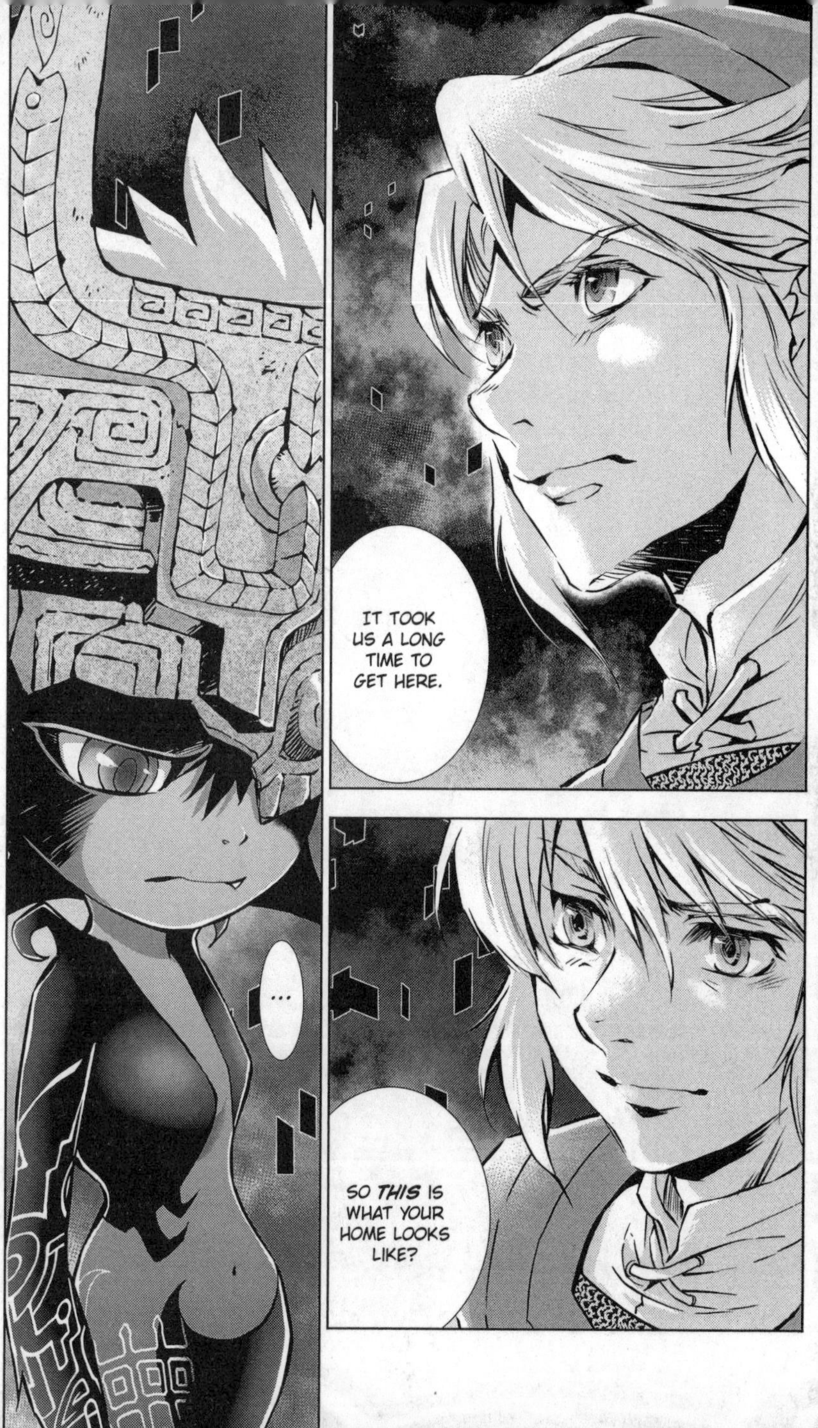
IT TOOK US A LONG TIME TO GET HERE.
SO *THIS* IS WHAT YOUR HOME LOOKS LIKE?
...

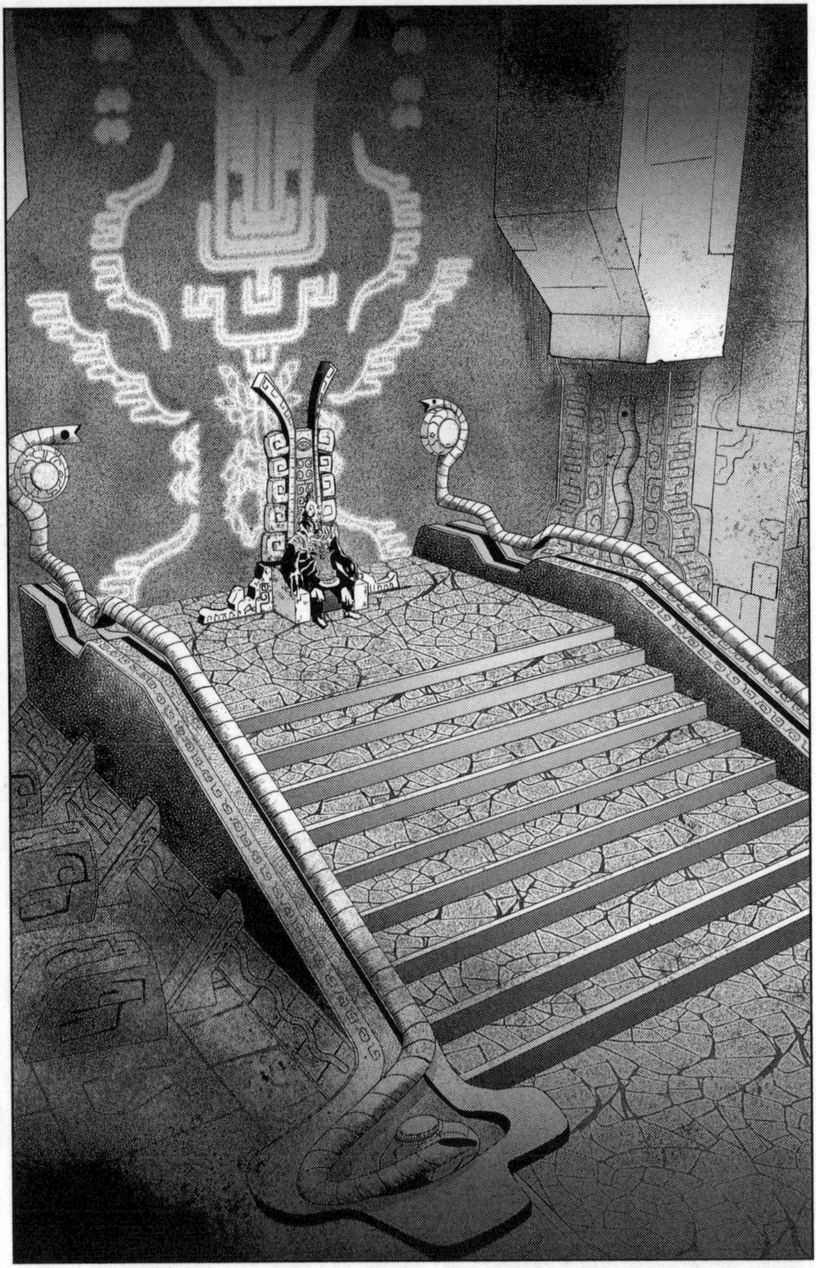

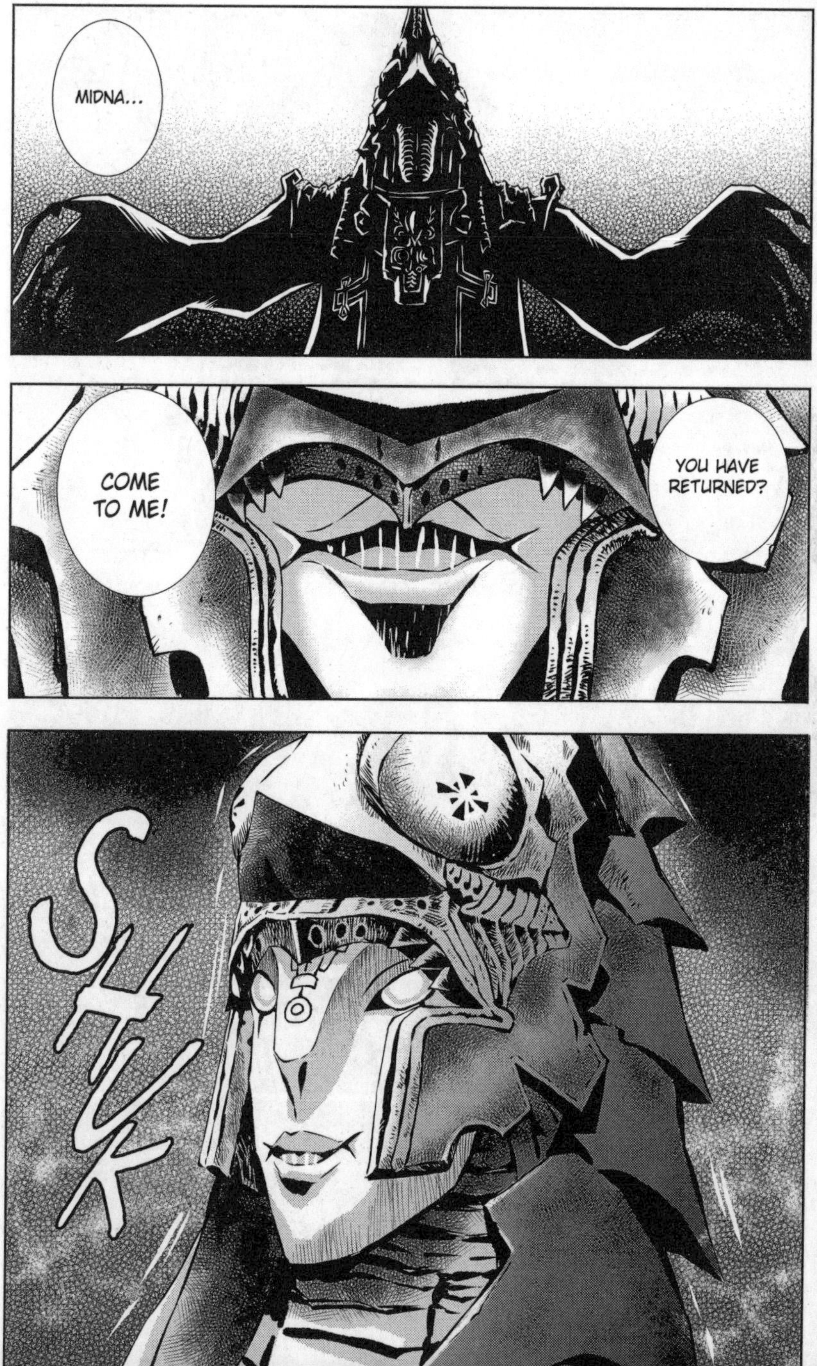
MIDNA...
YOU HAVE RETURNED?
COME TO ME!
SHUK

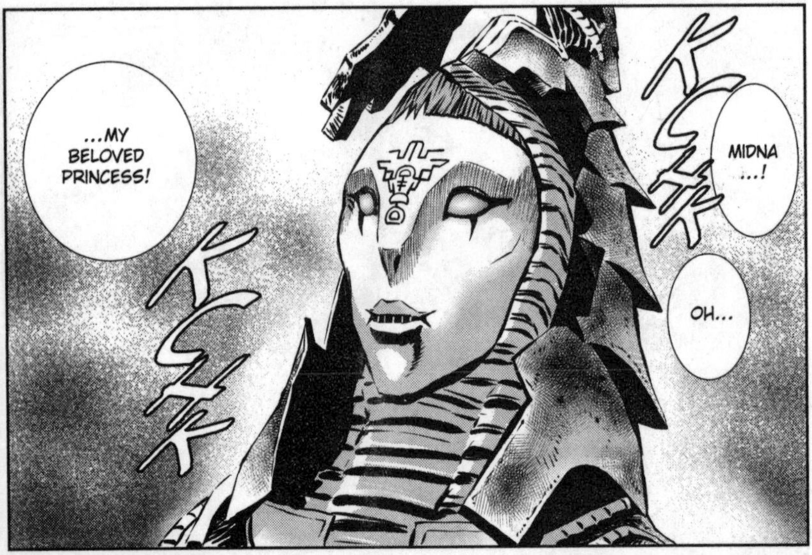
KCHK
MIDNA ...!
OH...
KCHK
...MY BELOVED PRINCESS!

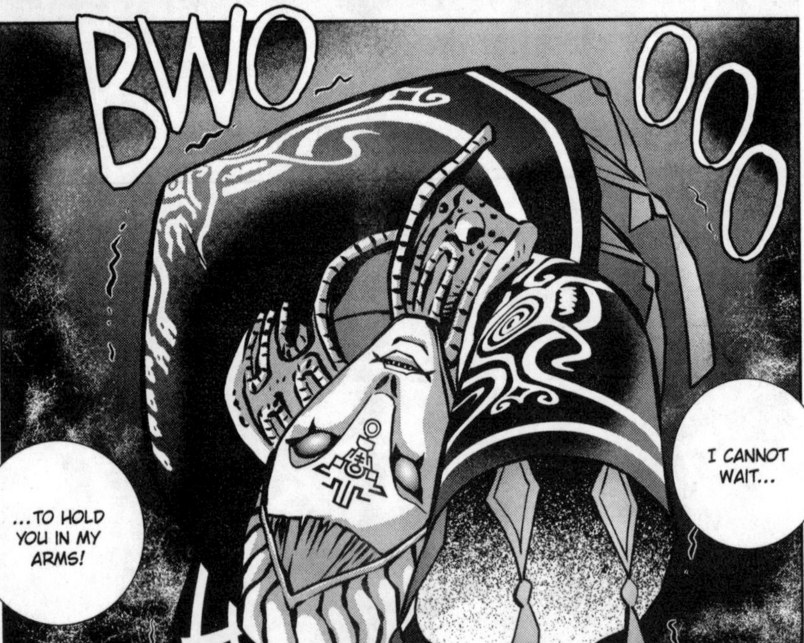
BWOOOOH
I CANNOT WAIT...
...TO HOLD YOU IN MY ARMS!

...WE SHALL BE ONE.

AT LONG LAST...

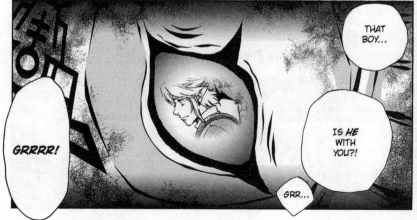

THAT BOY...

IS *HE* WITH YOU?!

GRRRR!

GRR...

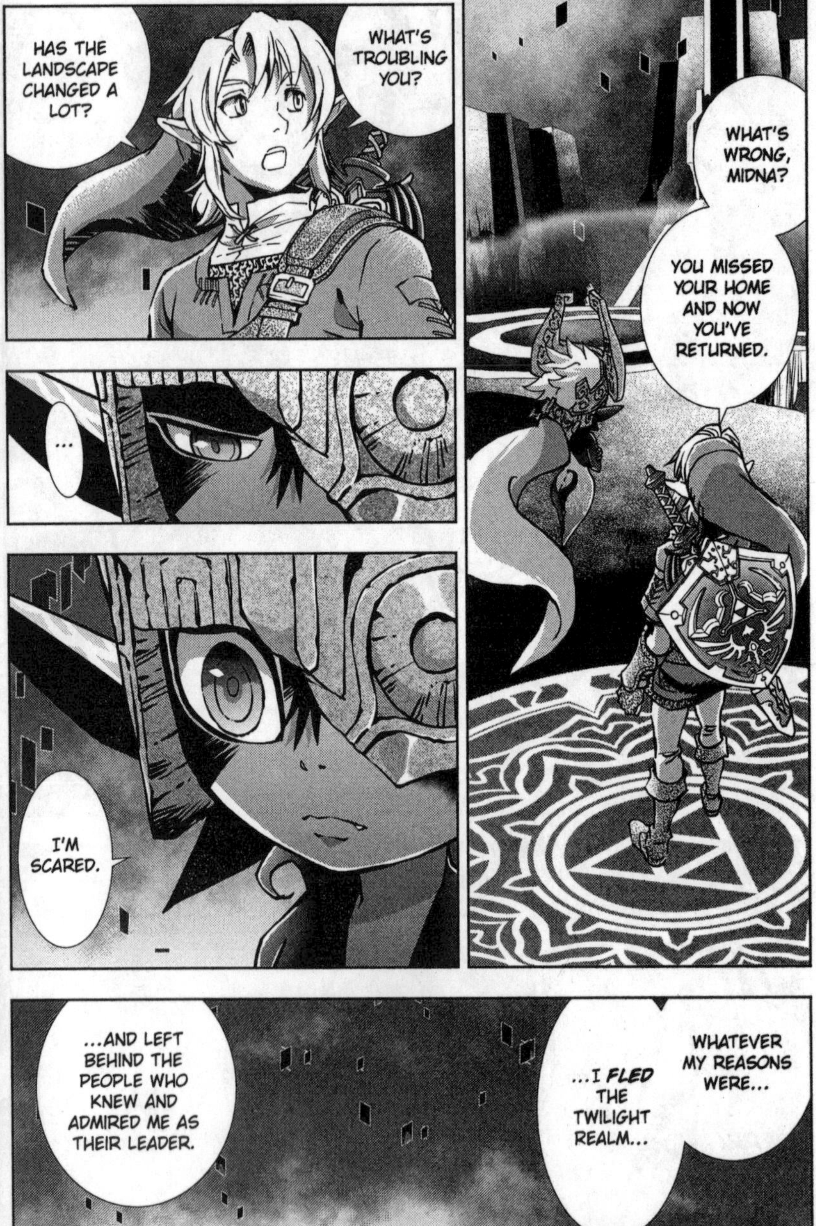
WHAT'S WRONG, MIDNA?
YOU MISSED YOUR HOME AND NOW YOU'VE RETURNED.
WHAT'S TROUBLING YOU?
HAS THE LANDSCAPE CHANGED A LOT?
...
I'M SCARED.
WHATEVER MY REASONS WERE...
...I *FLED* THE TWILIGHT REALM...
...AND LEFT BEHIND THE PEOPLE WHO KNEW AND ADMIRED ME AS THEIR LEADER.

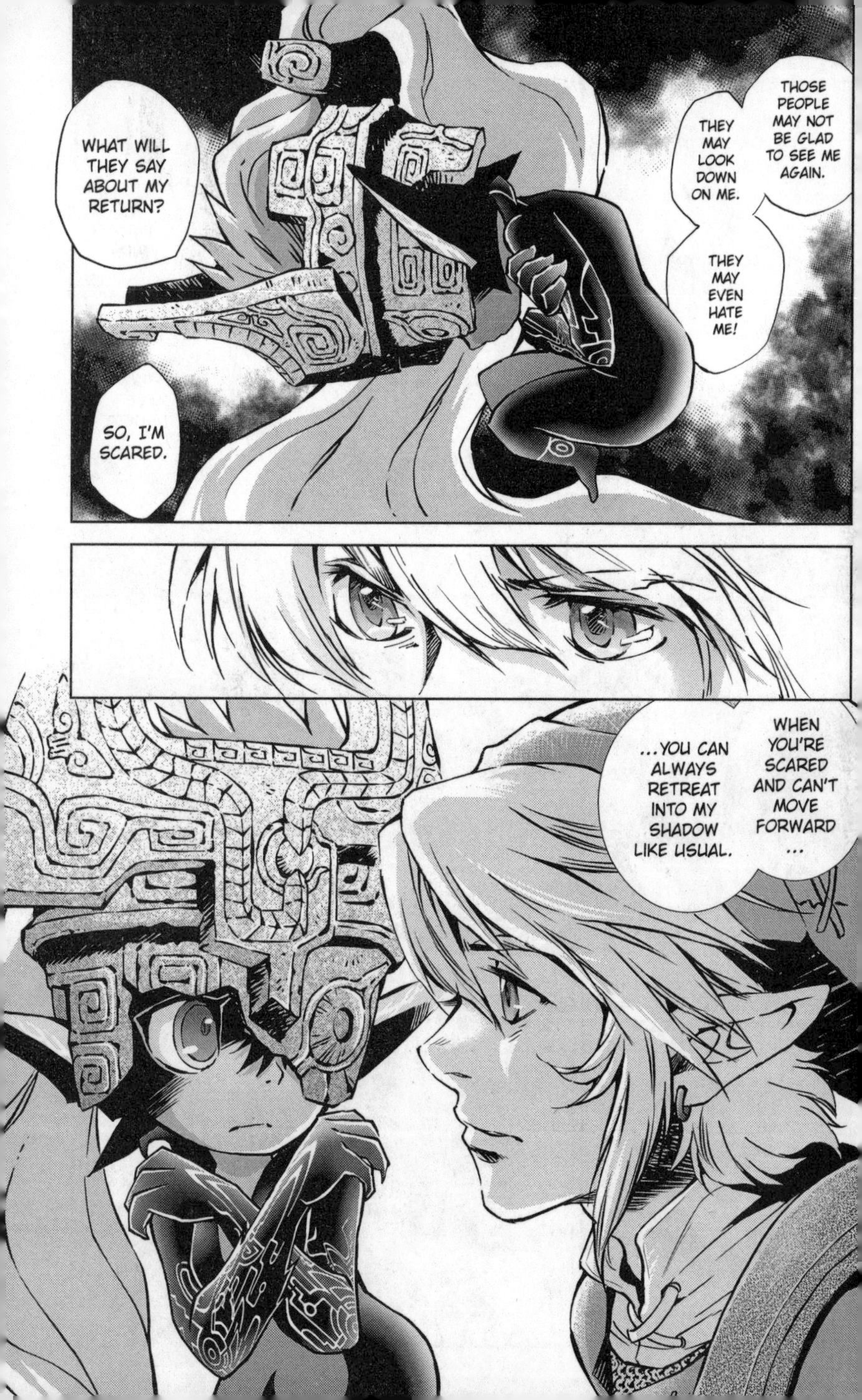
THOSE PEOPLE MAY NOT BE GLAD TO SEE ME AGAIN.
THEY MAY LOOK DOWN ON ME.
THEY MAY EVEN HATE ME!
WHAT WILL THEY SAY ABOUT MY RETURN?
SO, I'M SCARED.
WHEN YOU'RE SCARED AND CAN'T MOVE FORWARD ...
...YOU CAN ALWAYS RETREAT INTO MY SHADOW LIKE USUAL.

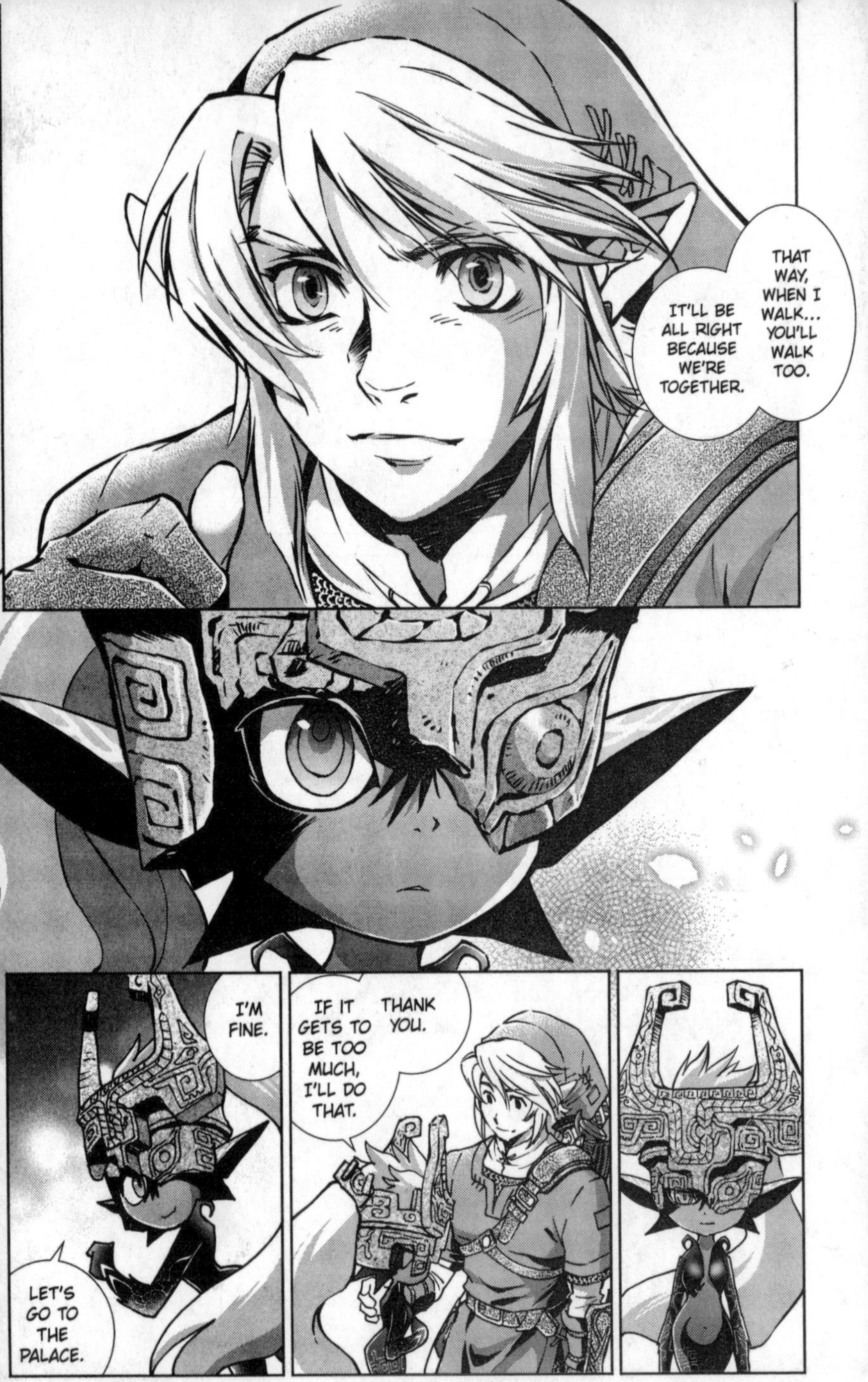
THAT WAY, WHEN I WALK... YOU'LL WALK TOO.
IT'LL BE ALL RIGHT BECAUSE WE'RE TOGETHER.
THANK YOU.
IF IT GETS TO BE TOO MUCH, I'LL DO THAT.
I'M FINE.
LET'S GO TO THE PALACE.

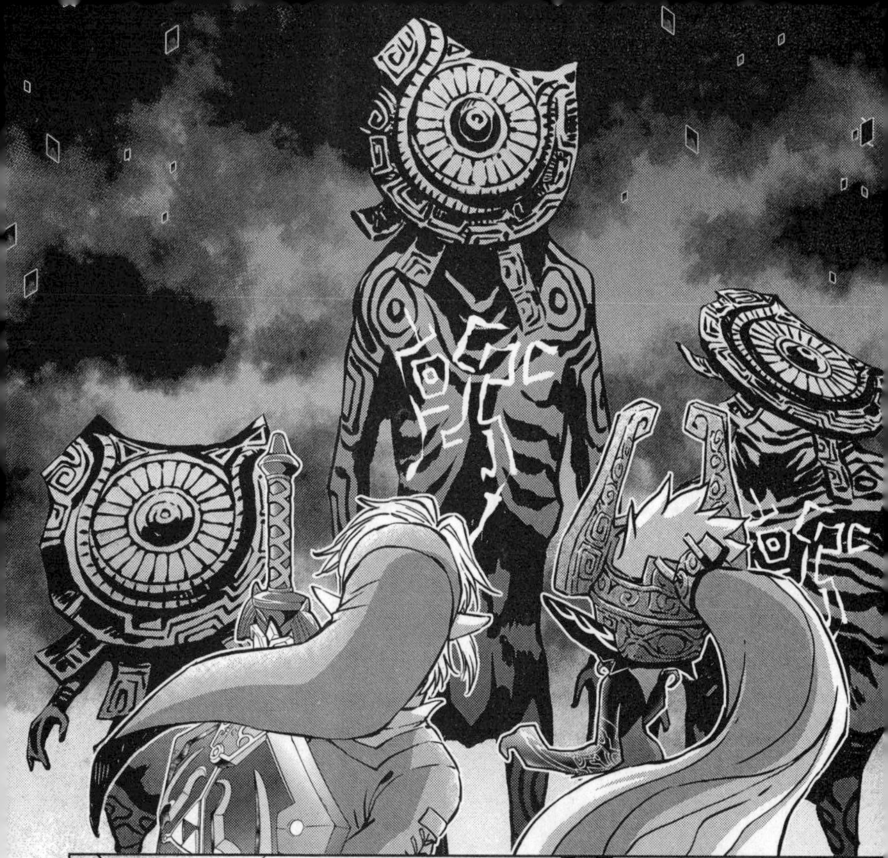

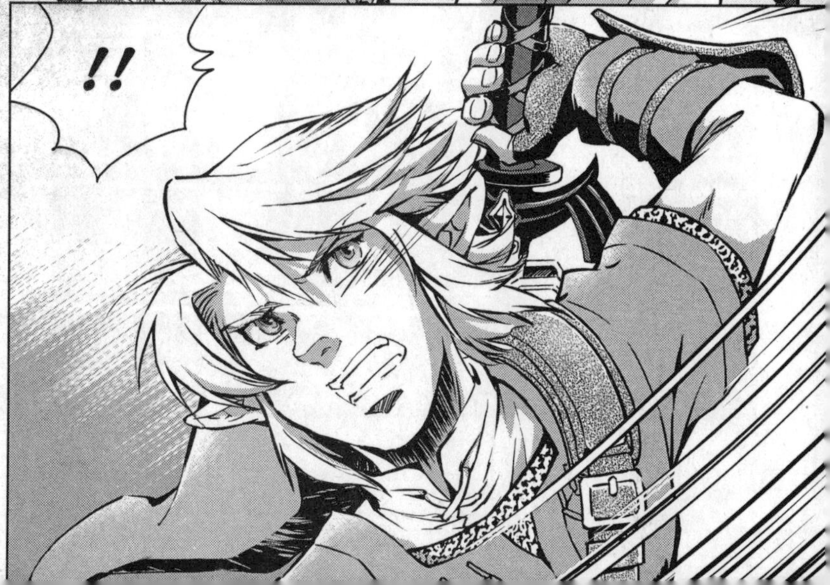
!!

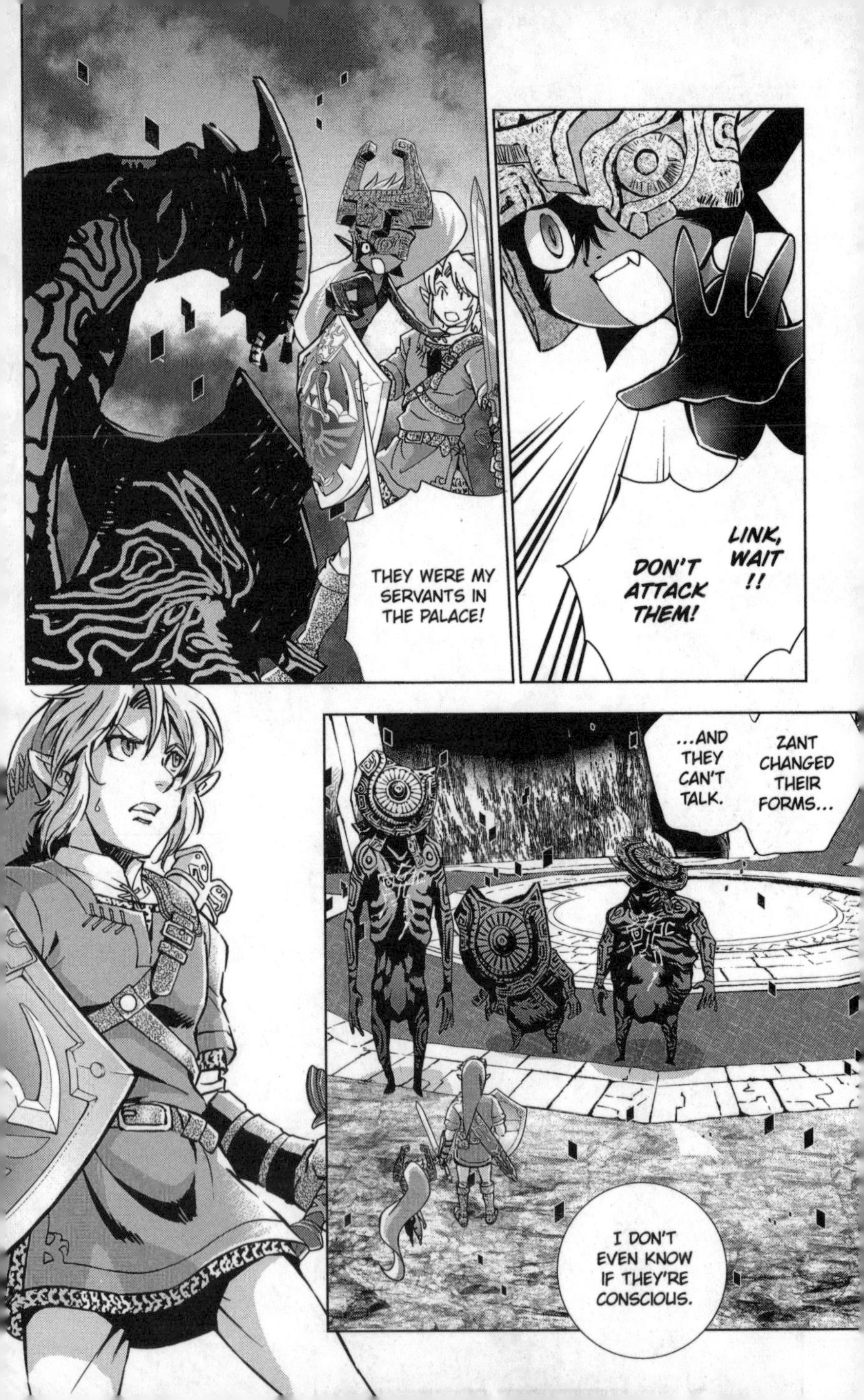
LINK, WAIT !!
DON'T ATTACK THEM!
THEY WERE MY SERVANTS IN THE PALACE!
ZANT CHANGED THEIR FORMS...
...AND THEY CAN'T TALK.
I DON'T EVEN KNOW IF THEY'RE CONSCIOUS.

I'M SORRY...

I SIMPLY WASN'T STRONG ENOUGH!

MIDNA...

WOBBLE
SWAY

WOBBLE
WOBBLE

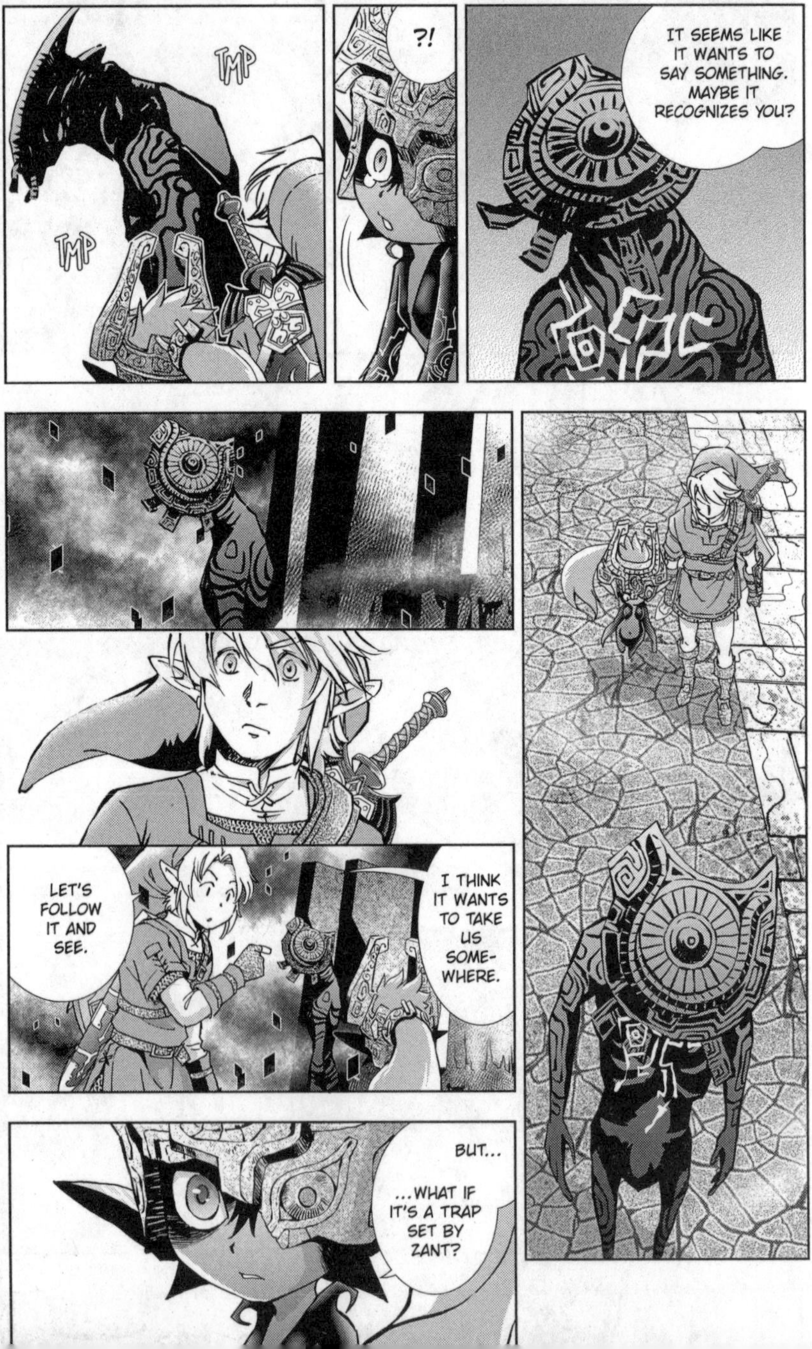
IT SEEMS LIKE IT WANTS TO SAY SOMETHING. MAYBE IT RECOGNIZES YOU?
?!
TMP
TMP
I THINK IT WANTS TO TAKE US SOME-WHERE.
LET'S FOLLOW IT AND SEE.
BUT...
...WHAT IF IT'S A TRAP SET BY ZANT?

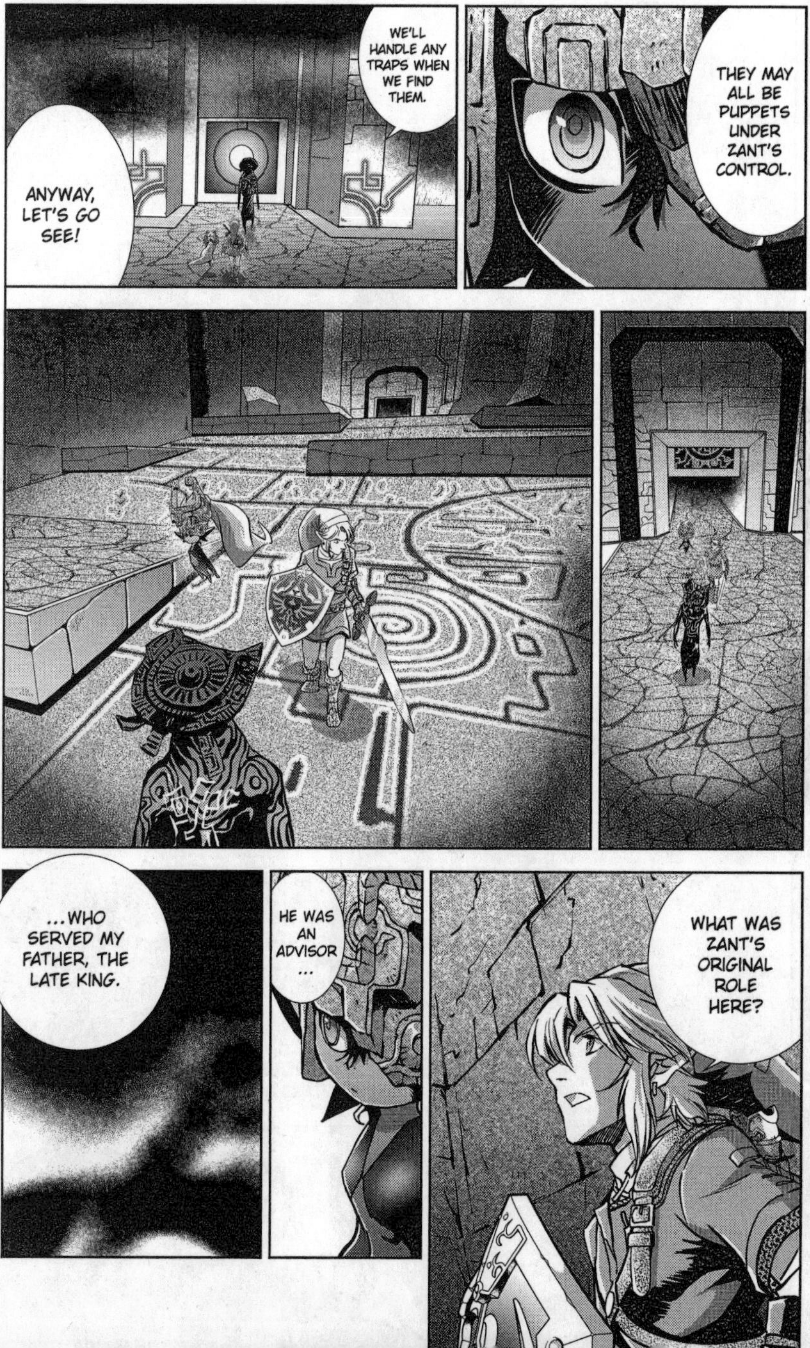
THEY MAY ALL BE PUPPETS UNDER ZANT'S CONTROL.
WE'LL HANDLE ANY TRAPS WHEN WE FIND THEM.
ANYWAY, LET'S GO SEE!
WHAT WAS ZANT'S ORIGINAL ROLE HERE?
HE WAS AN ADVISOR ...
...WHO SERVED MY FATHER, THE LATE KING.

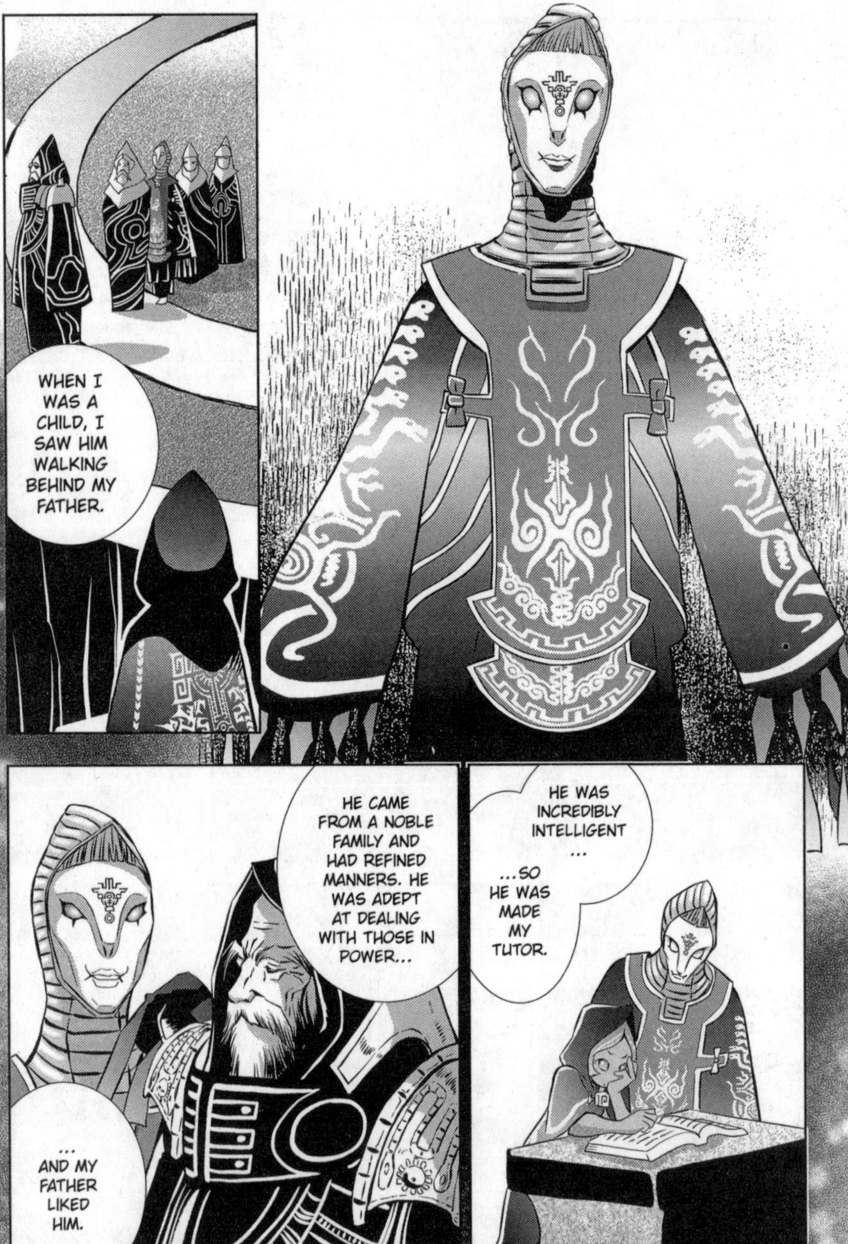
WHEN I WAS A CHILD, I SAW HIM WALKING BEHIND MY FATHER.
HE WAS INCREDIBLY INTELLIGENT ...
...SO HE WAS MADE MY TUTOR.
HE CAME FROM A NOBLE FAMILY AND HAD REFINED MANNERS. HE WAS ADEPT AT DEALING WITH THOSE IN POWER...
... AND MY FATHER LIKED HIM.

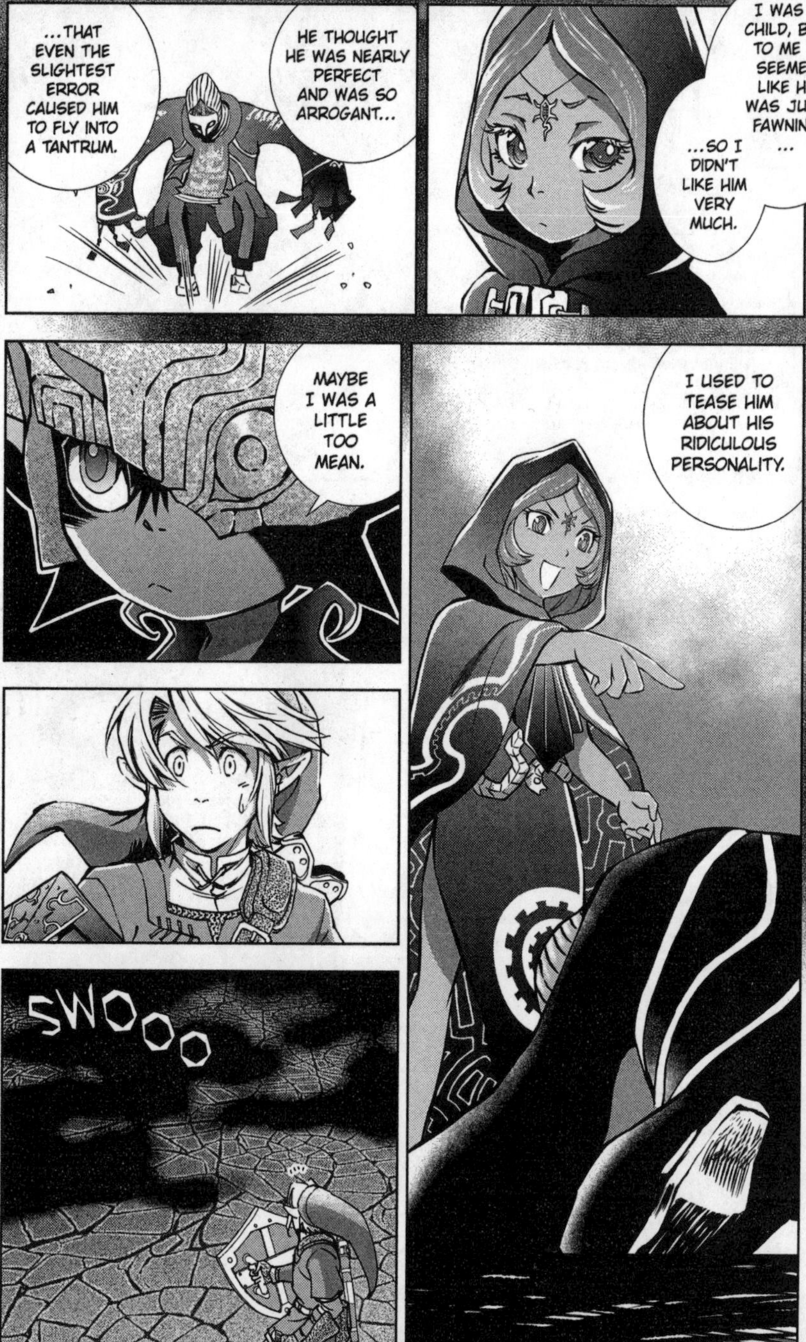
I WAS A CHILD, BL TO ME IT SEEMED LIKE HE WAS JUS FAWNING...
...SO I DIDN'T LIKE HIM VERY MUCH.
HE THOUGHT HE WAS NEARLY PERFECT AND WAS SO ARROGANT...
...THAT EVEN THE SLIGHTEST ERROR CAUSED HIM TO FLY INTO A TANTRUM.
I USED TO TEASE HIM ABOUT HIS RIDICULOUS PERSONALITY.
MAYBE I WAS A LITTLE TOO MEAN.
SWOOO

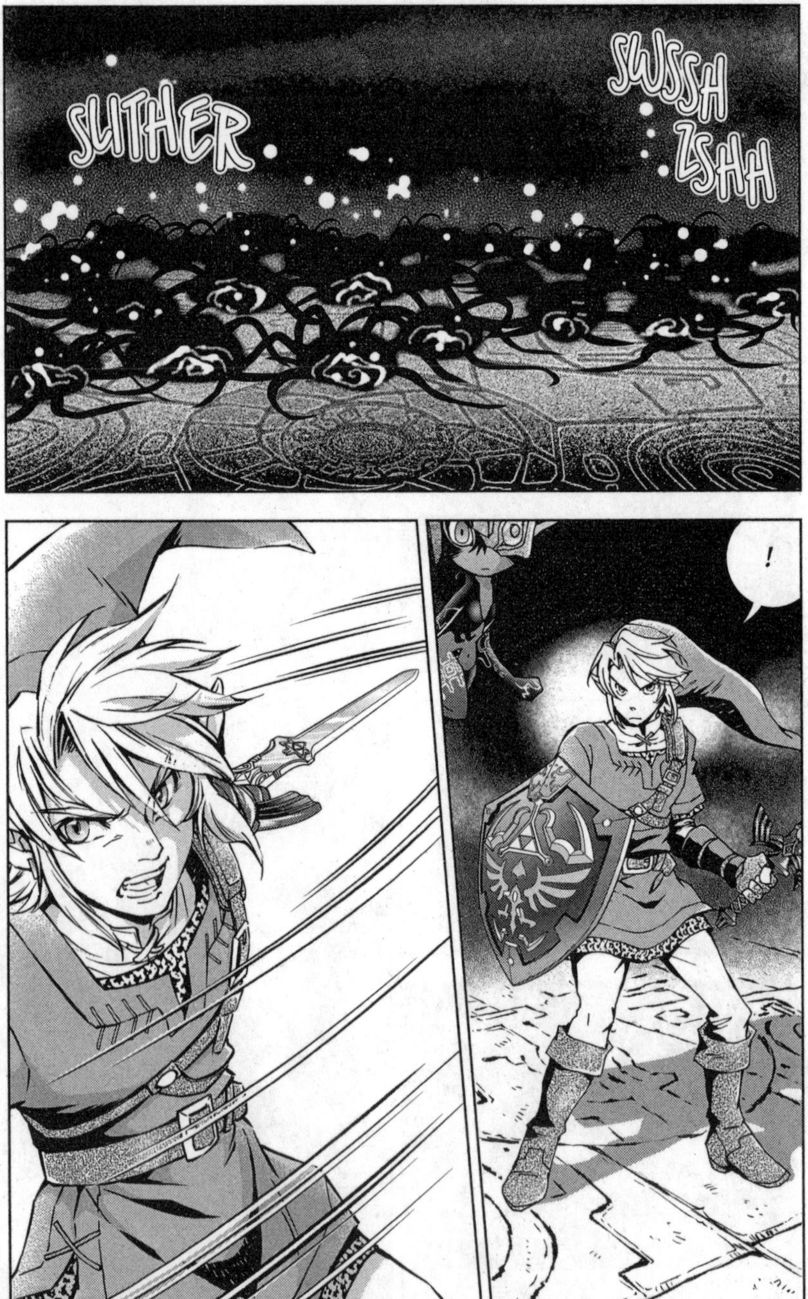
SWSSH ZSHH
SLITHER
!

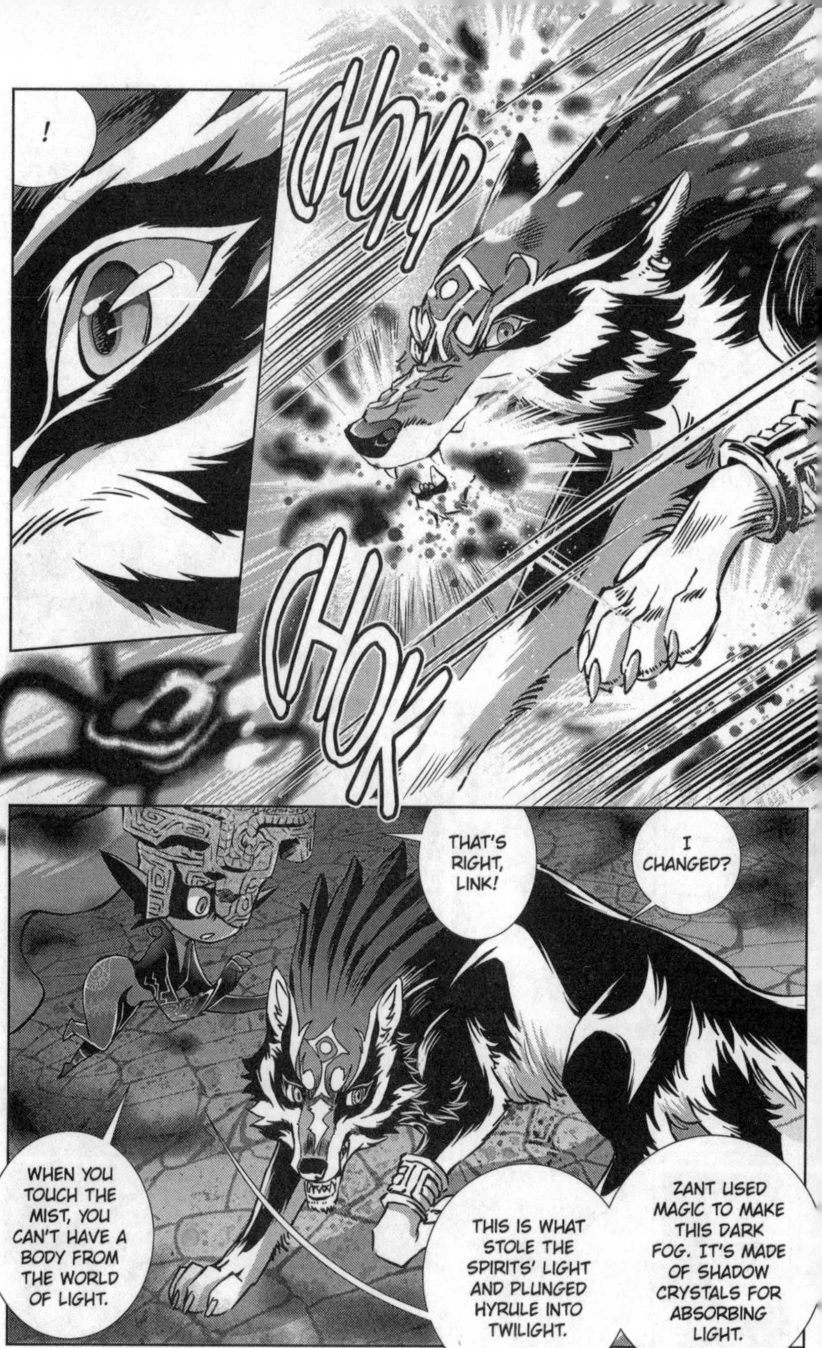
CHOMP
CHOK
!
I CHANGED?
THAT'S RIGHT, LINK!
ZANT USED MAGIC TO MAKE THIS DARK FOG. IT'S MADE OF SHADOW CRYSTALS FOR ABSORBING LIGHT.
THIS IS WHAT STOLE THE SPIRITS' LIGHT AND PLUNGED HYRULE INTO TWILIGHT.
WHEN YOU TOUCH THE MIST, YOU CAN'T HAVE A BODY FROM THE WORLD OF LIGHT.

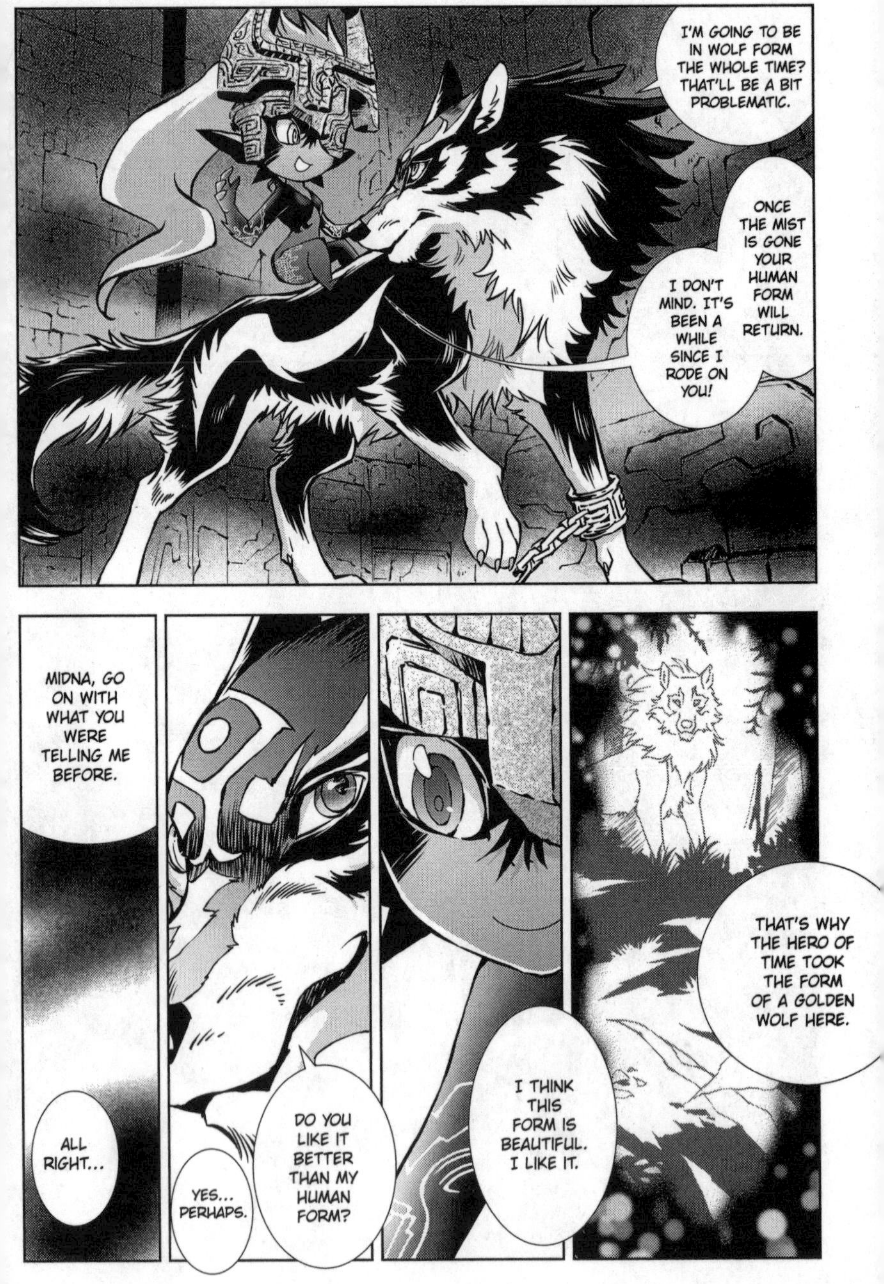
I'M GOING TO BE IN WOLF FORM THE WHOLE TIME? THAT'LL BE A BIT PROBLEMATIC.
ONCE THE MIST IS GONE YOUR HUMAN FORM WILL RETURN.
I DON'T MIND. IT'S BEEN A WHILE SINCE I RODE ON YOU!
THAT'S WHY THE HERO OF TIME TOOK THE FORM OF A GOLDEN WOLF HERE.
I THINK THIS FORM IS BEAUTIFUL. I LIKE IT.
DO YOU LIKE IT BETTER THAN MY HUMAN FORM?
YES... PERHAPS.
MIDNA, GO ON WITH WHAT YOU WERE TELLING ME BEFORE.
ALL RIGHT...

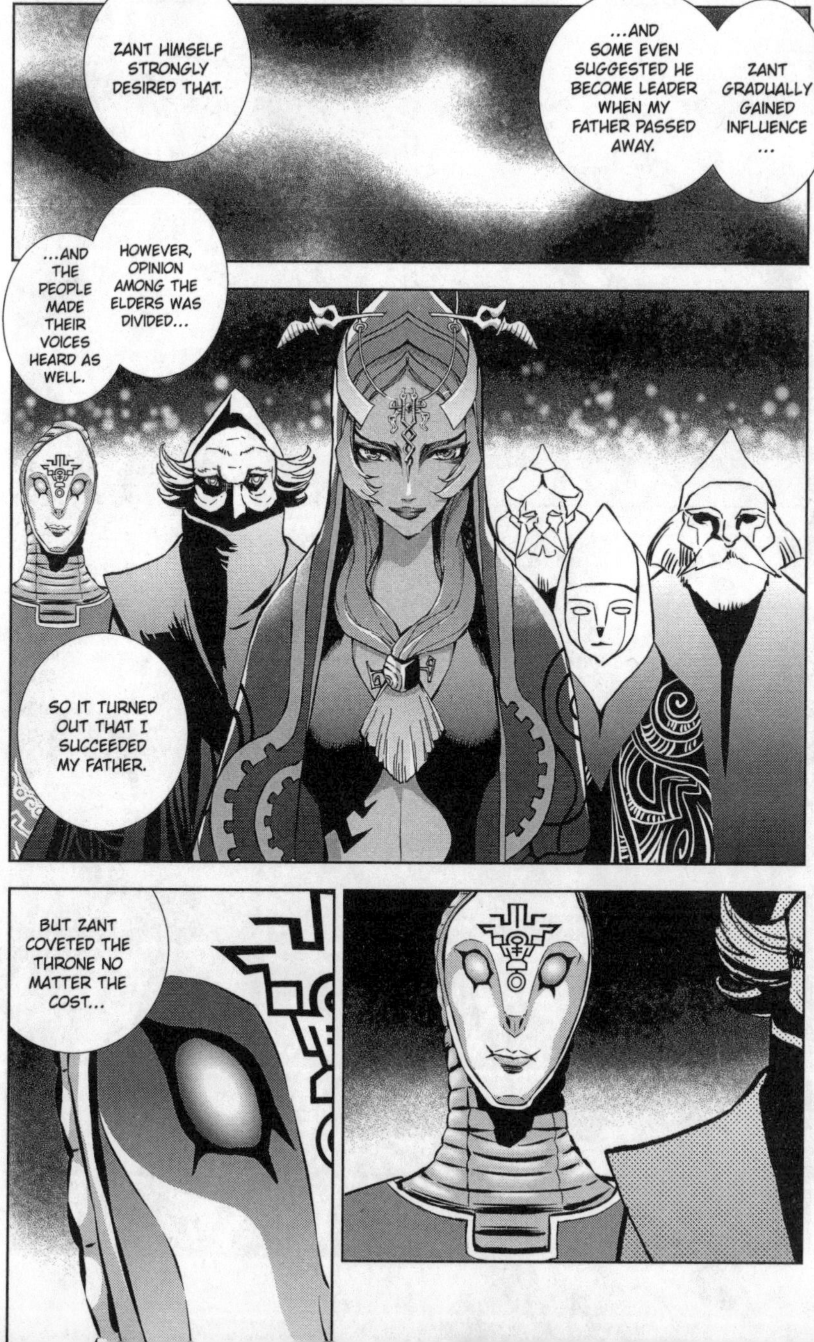
ZANT GRADUALLY GAINED INFLUENCE ...
...AND SOME EVEN SUGGESTED HE BECOME LEADER WHEN MY FATHER PASSED AWAY.
ZANT HIMSELF STRONGLY DESIRED THAT.
HOWEVER, OPINION AMONG THE ELDERS WAS DIVIDED...
...AND THE PEOPLE MADE THEIR VOICES HEARD AS WELL.
SO IT TURNED OUT THAT I SUCCEEDED MY FATHER.
BUT ZANT COVETED THE THRONE NO MATTER THE COST...

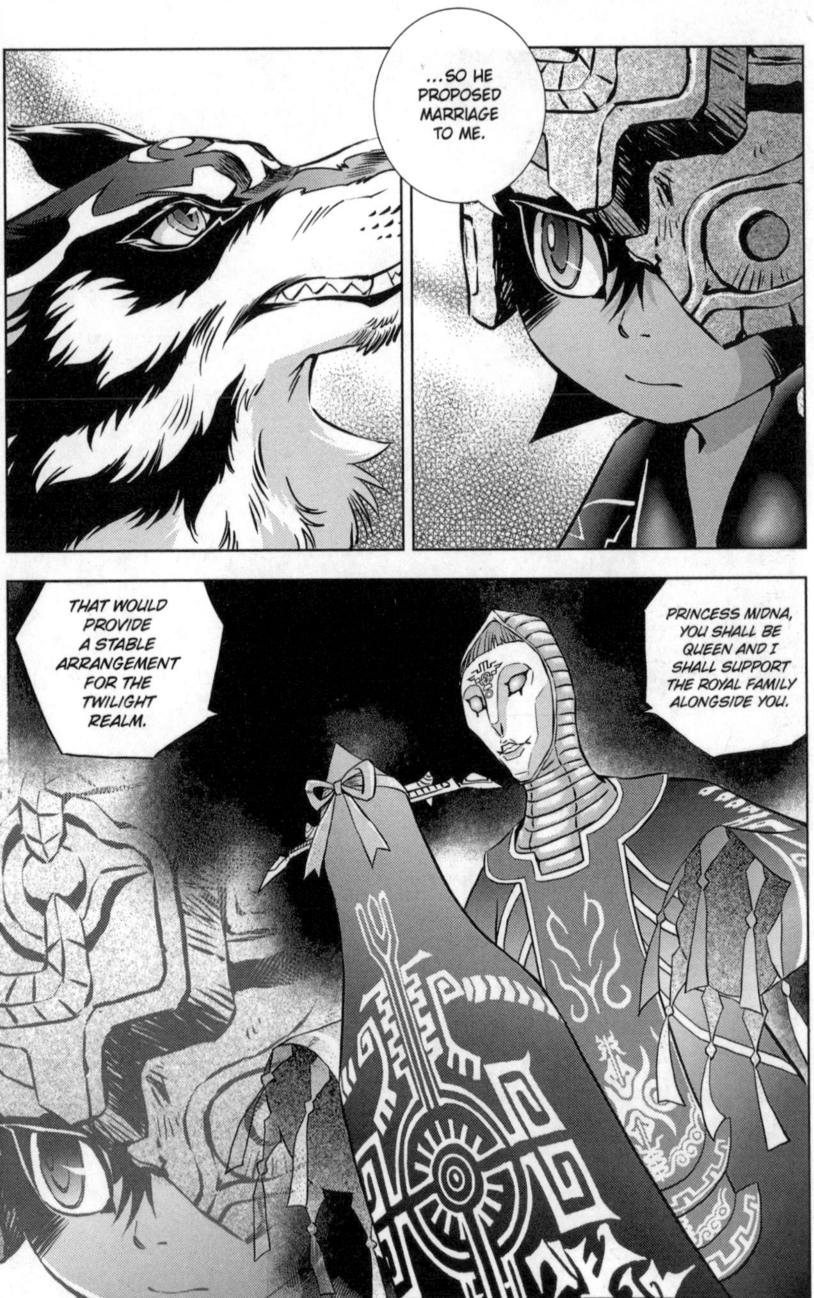
...SO HE PROPOSED MARRIAGE TO ME.
PRINCESS MIDNA, YOU SHALL BE QUEEN AND I SHALL SUPPORT THE ROYAL FAMILY ALONGSIDE YOU.
THAT WOULD PROVIDE A STABLE ARRANGEMENT FOR THE TWILIGHT REALM.

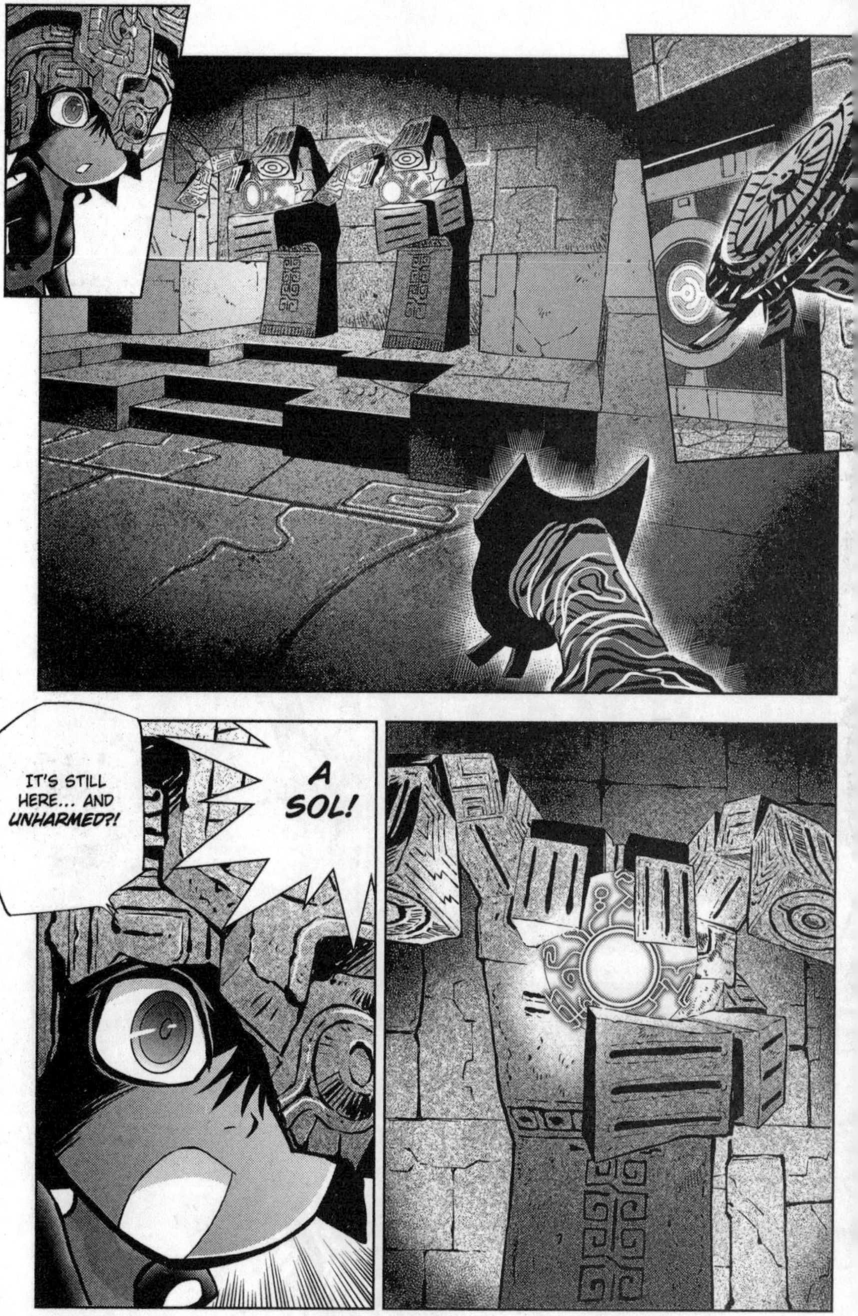
A SOL!
IT'S STILL HERE... AND UNHARMED?!

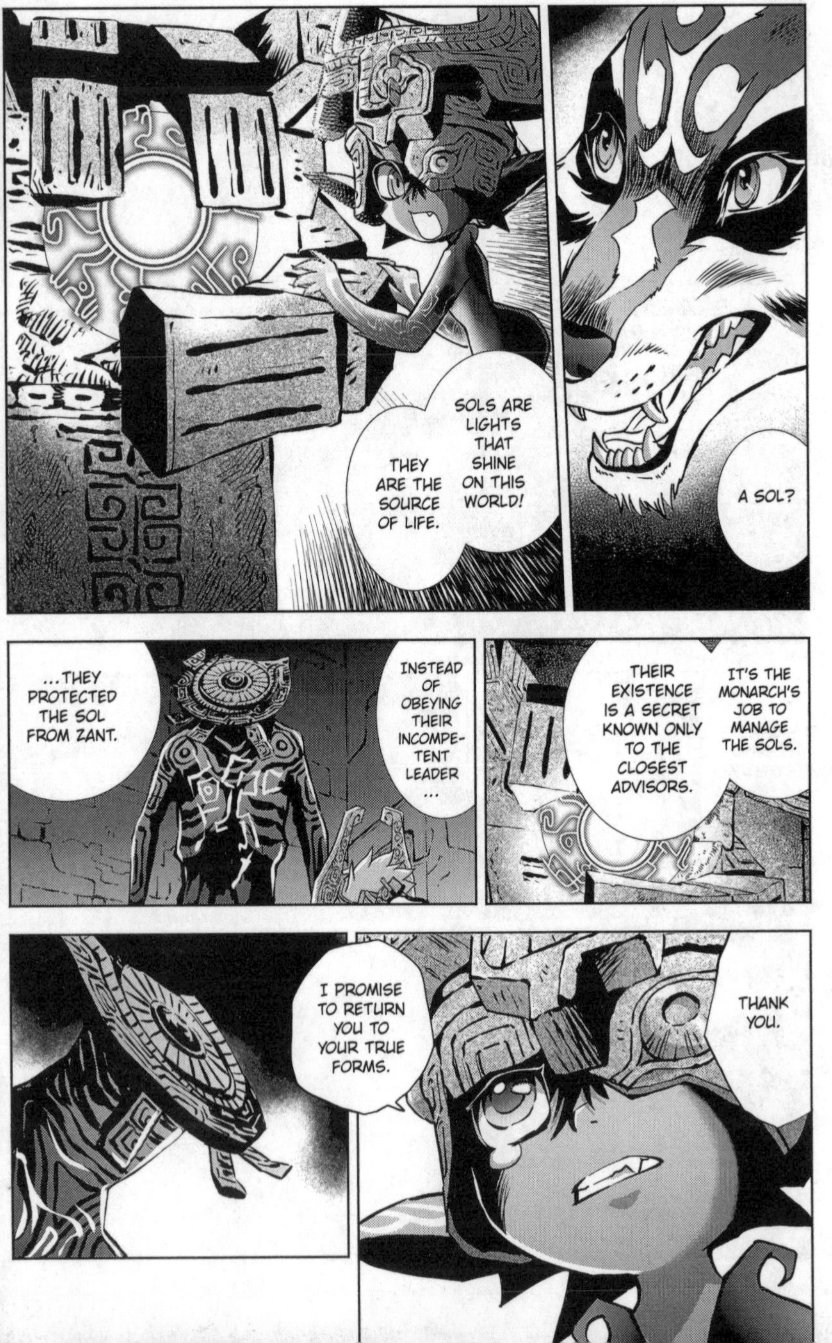
A SOL?
SOLS ARE LIGHTS THAT SHINE ON THIS WORLD! THEY ARE THE SOURCE OF LIFE.
IT'S THE MONARCH'S JOB TO MANAGE THE SOLS.
THEIR EXISTENCE IS A SECRET KNOWN ONLY TO THE CLOSEST ADVISORS.
INSTEAD OF OBEYING THEIR INCOMPETENT LEADER ...
...THEY PROTECTED THE SOL FROM ZANT.
THANK YOU.
I PROMISE TO RETURN YOU TO YOUR TRUE FORMS.

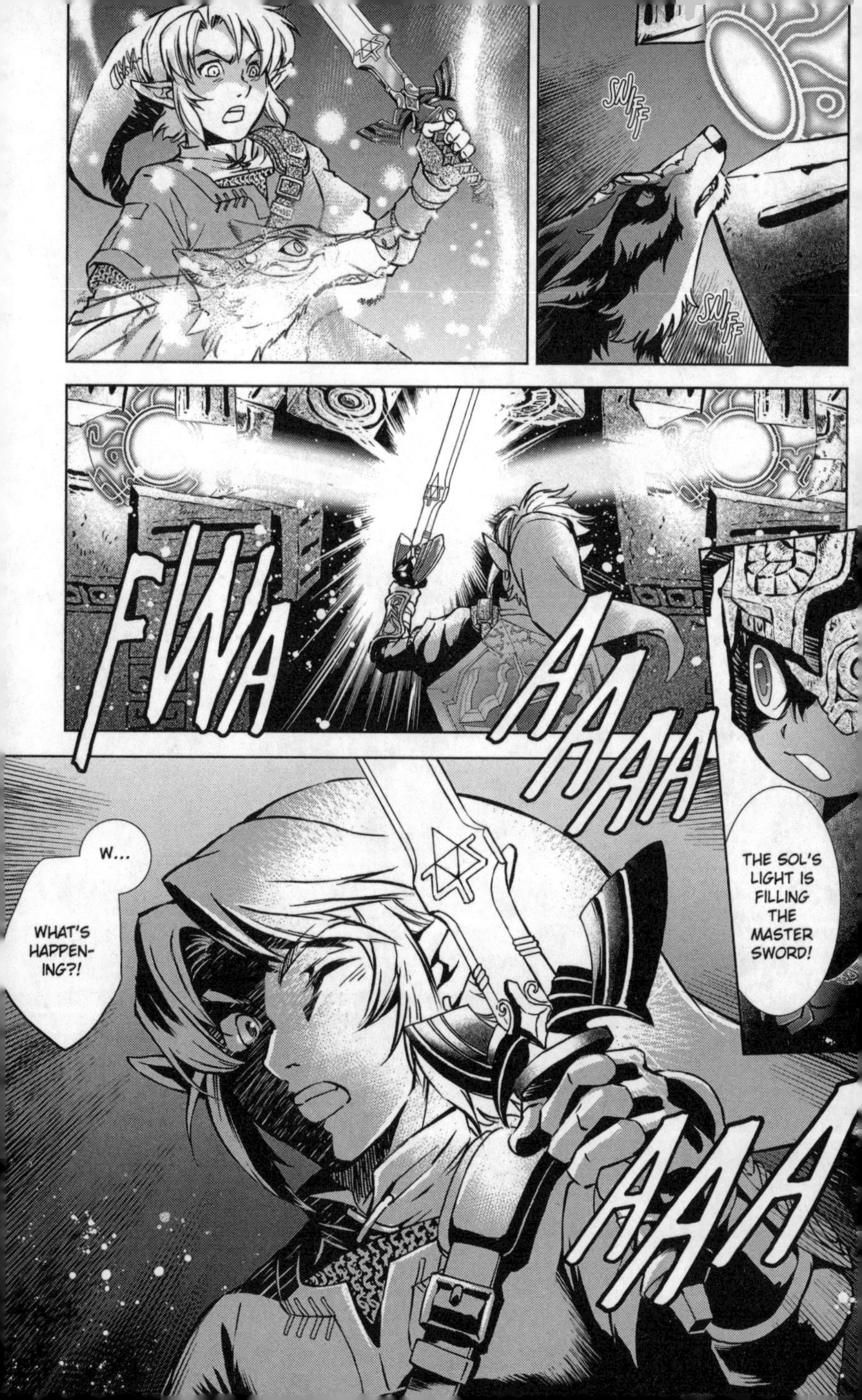
SNIFF
SNIFF
FWAAAAAA
THE SOL'S LIGHT IS FILLING THE MASTER SWORD!
W...
WHAT'S HAPPENING?!
AAAA

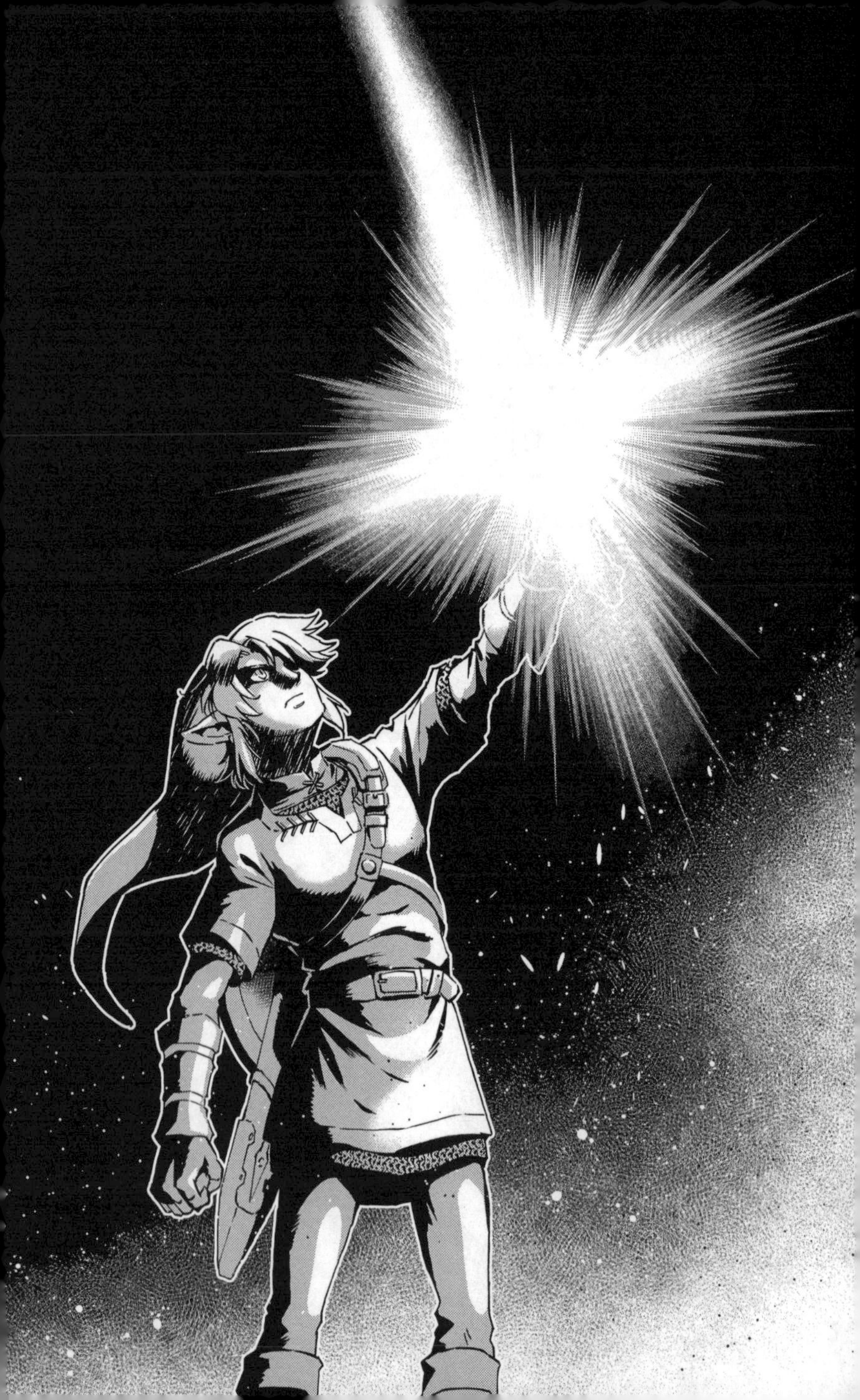

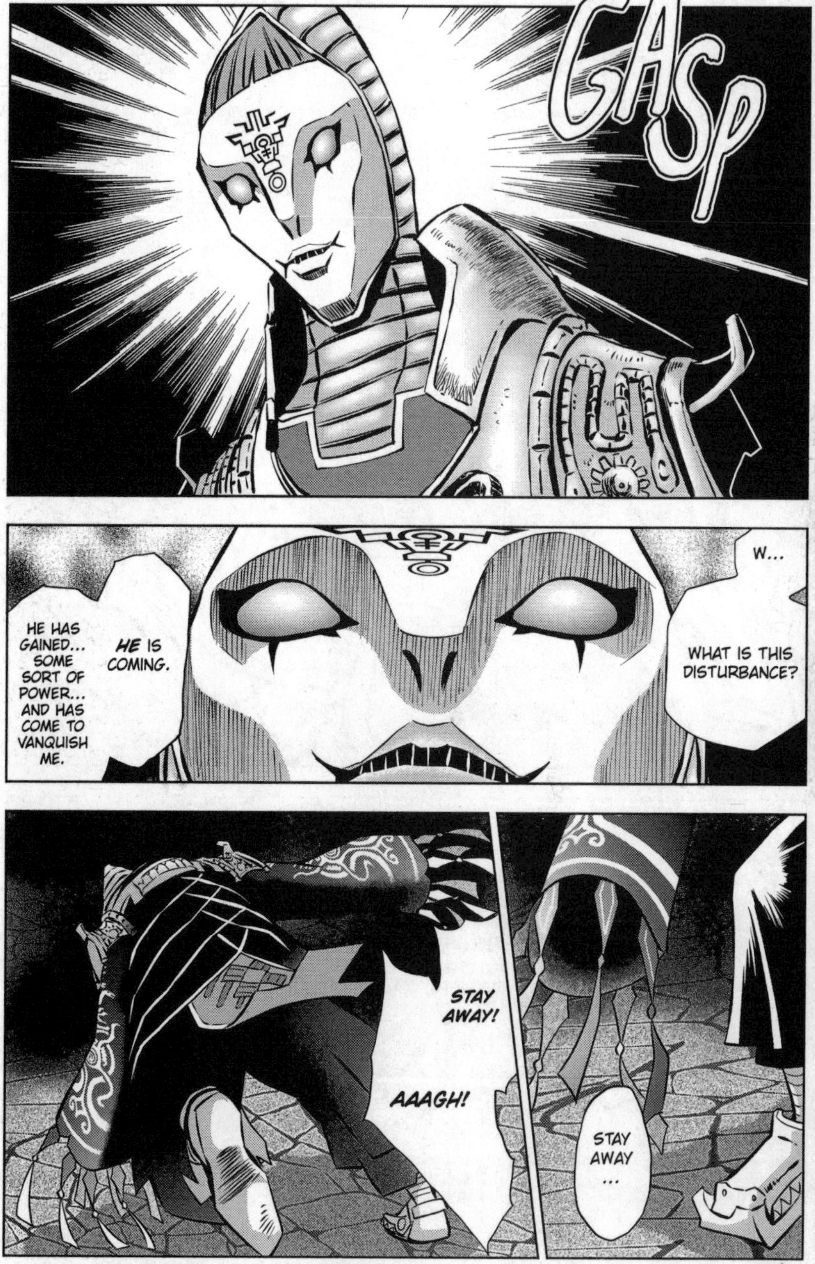
GASP
W...
WHAT IS THIS DISTURBANCE?
HE IS COMING.
HE HAS GAINED... SOME SORT OF POWER... AND HAS COME TO VANQUISH ME.
STAY AWAY ...
STAY AWAY!
AAAGH!

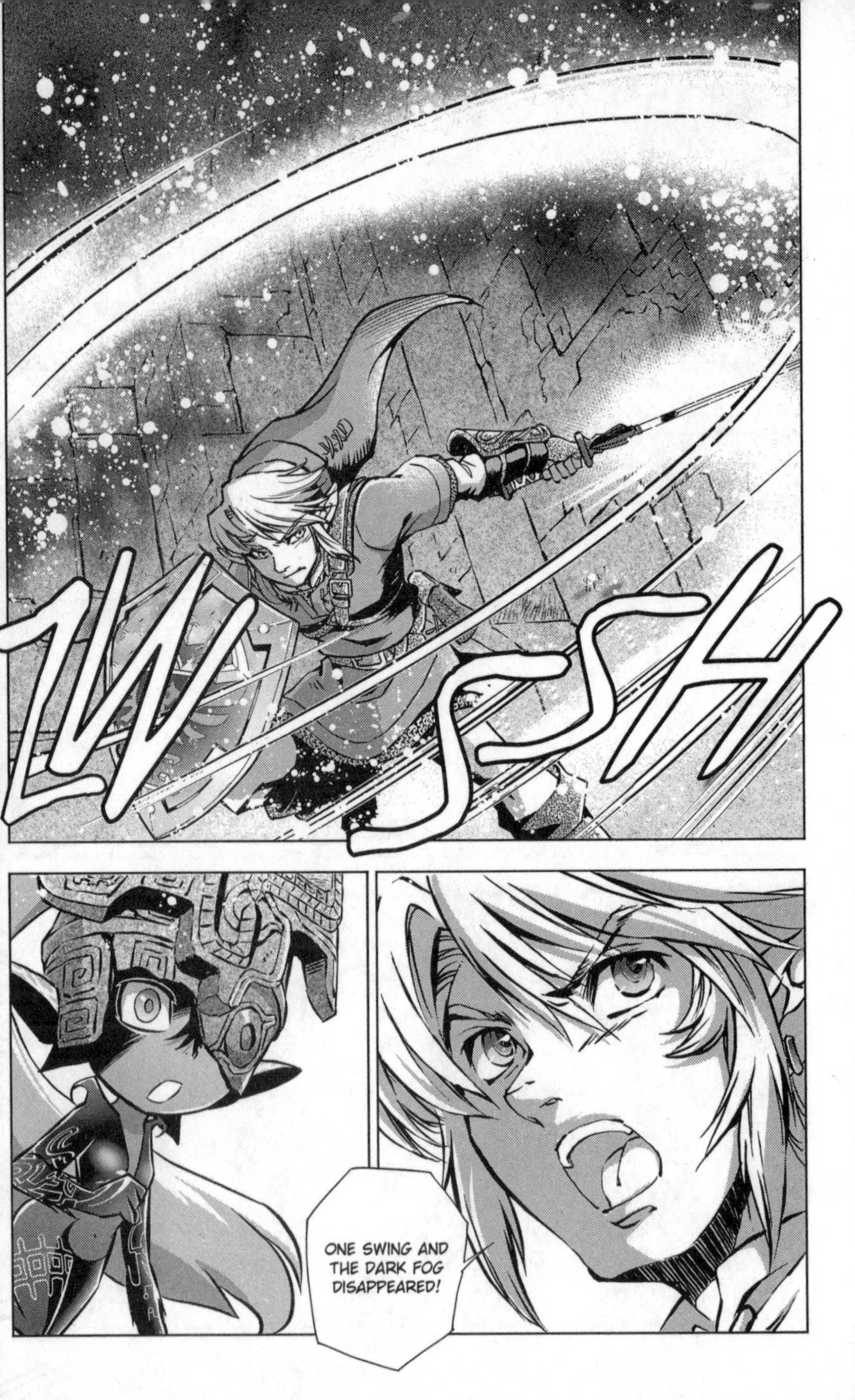
ZWSSH
ONE SWING AND THE DARK FOG DISAPPEARED!

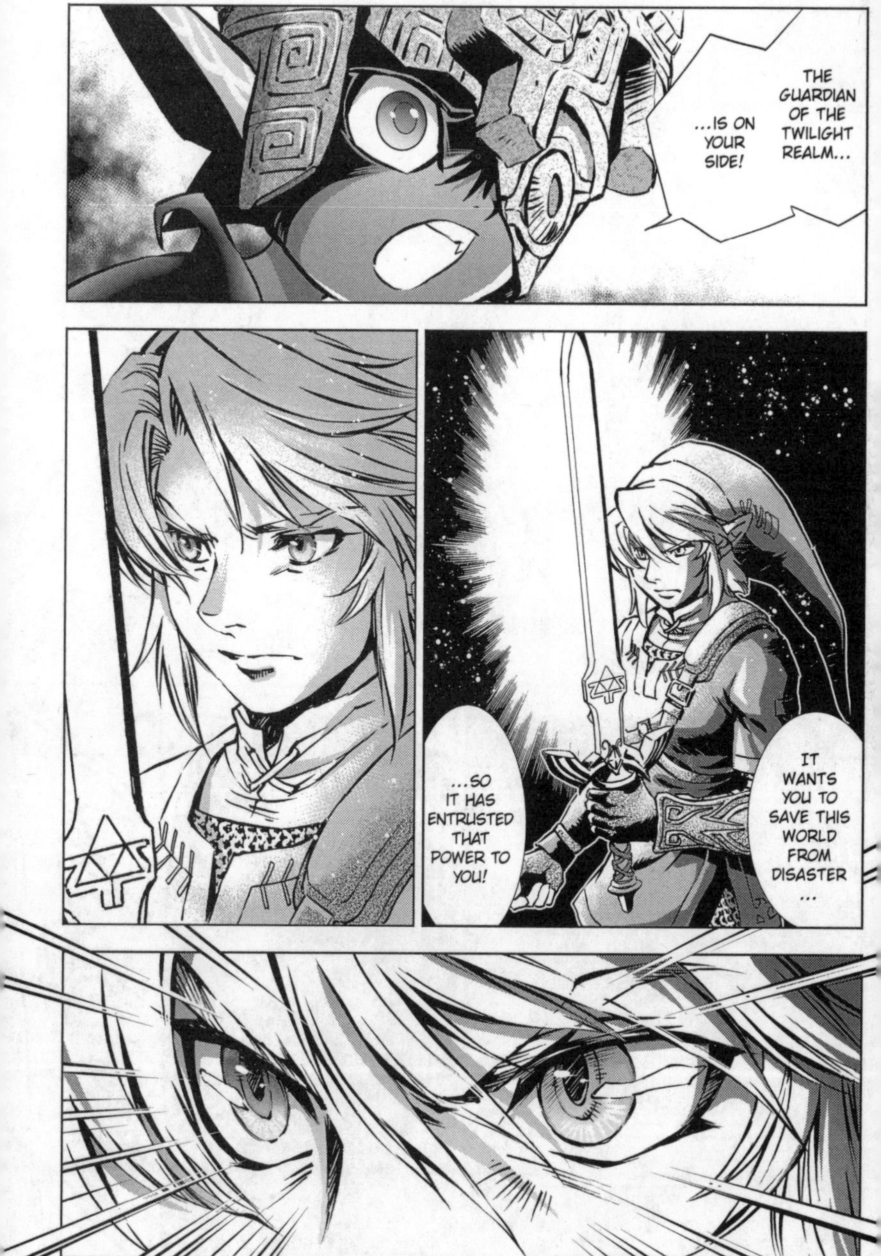
THE GUARDIAN OF THE TWILIGHT REALM...
...IS ON YOUR SIDE!
IT WANTS YOU TO SAVE THIS WORLD FROM DISASTER ...
...SO IT HAS ENTRUSTED THAT POWER TO YOU!

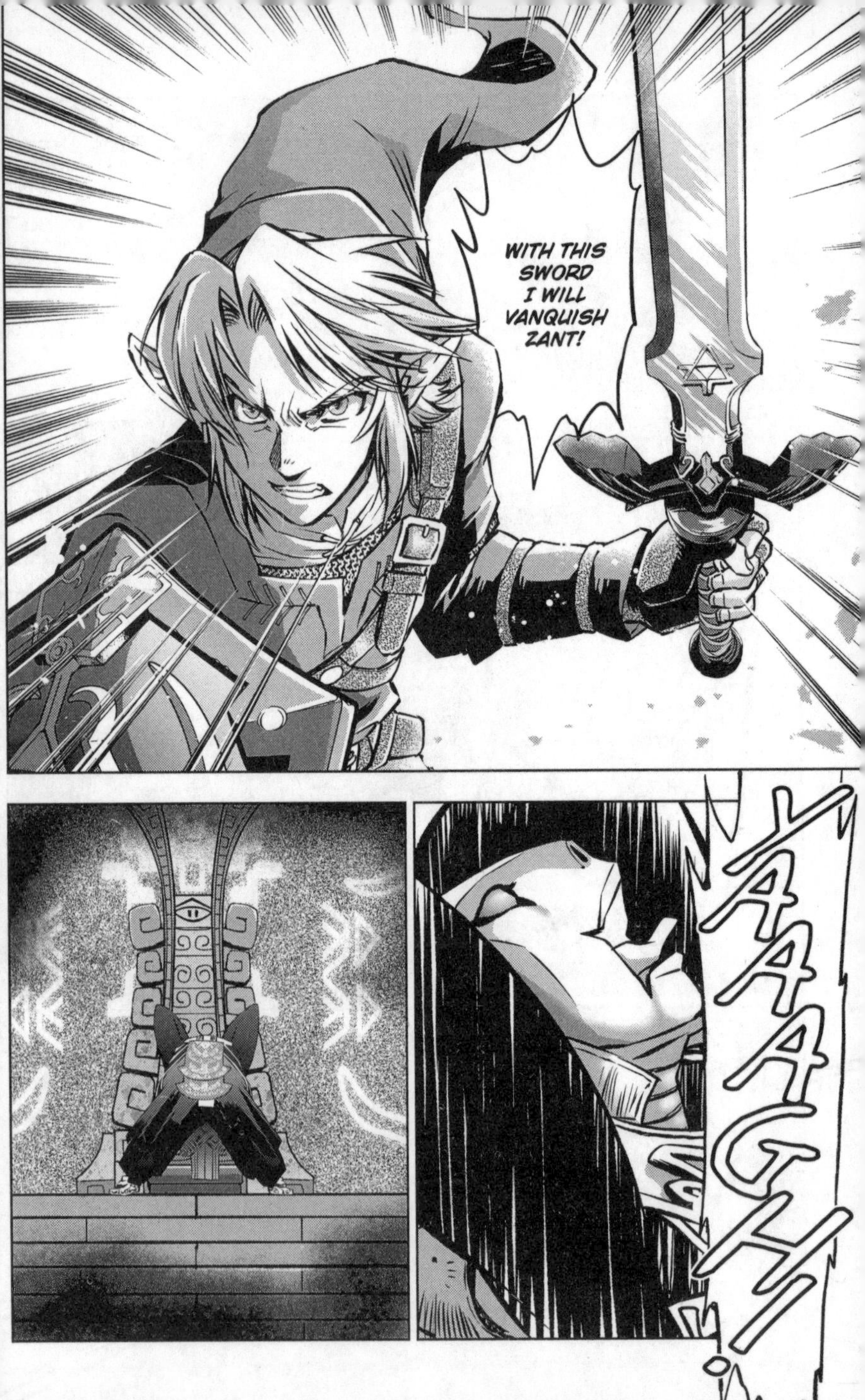
WITH THIS SWORD I WILL VANQUISH ZANT!
YAAAGH!!

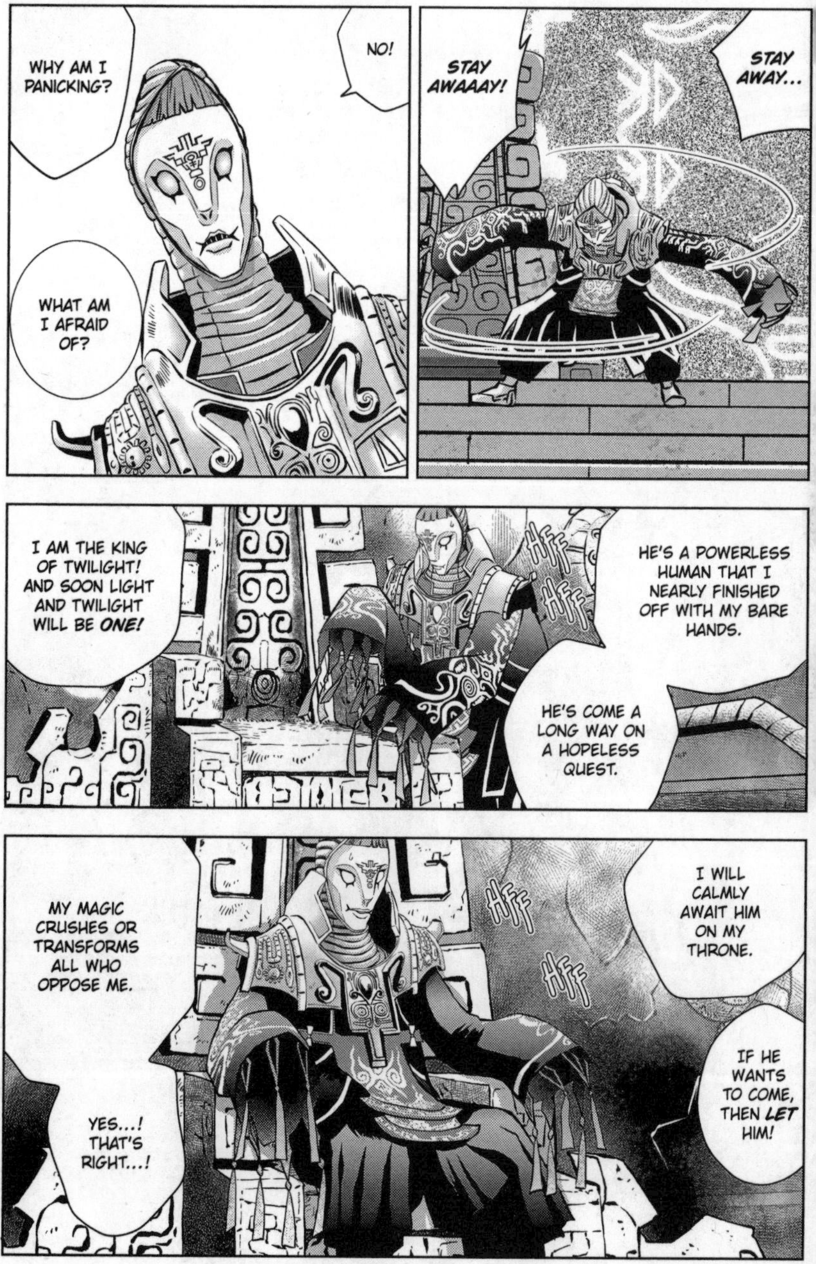
STAY AWAY...
STAY AWAAAY!
NO!
WHY AM I PANICKING?
WHAT AM I AFRAID OF?
HE'S A POWERLESS HUMAN THAT I NEARLY FINISHED OFF WITH MY BARE HANDS.
HFF HFF
HE'S COME A LONG WAY ON A HOPELESS QUEST.
I AM THE KING OF TWILIGHT! AND SOON LIGHT AND TWILIGHT WILL BE *ONE!*
I WILL CALMLY AWAIT HIM ON MY THRONE.
HFF HFF
MY MAGIC CRUSHES OR TRANSFORMS ALL WHO OPPOSE ME.
IF HE WANTS TO COME, THEN *LET* HIM!
YES...! THAT'S RIGHT...!

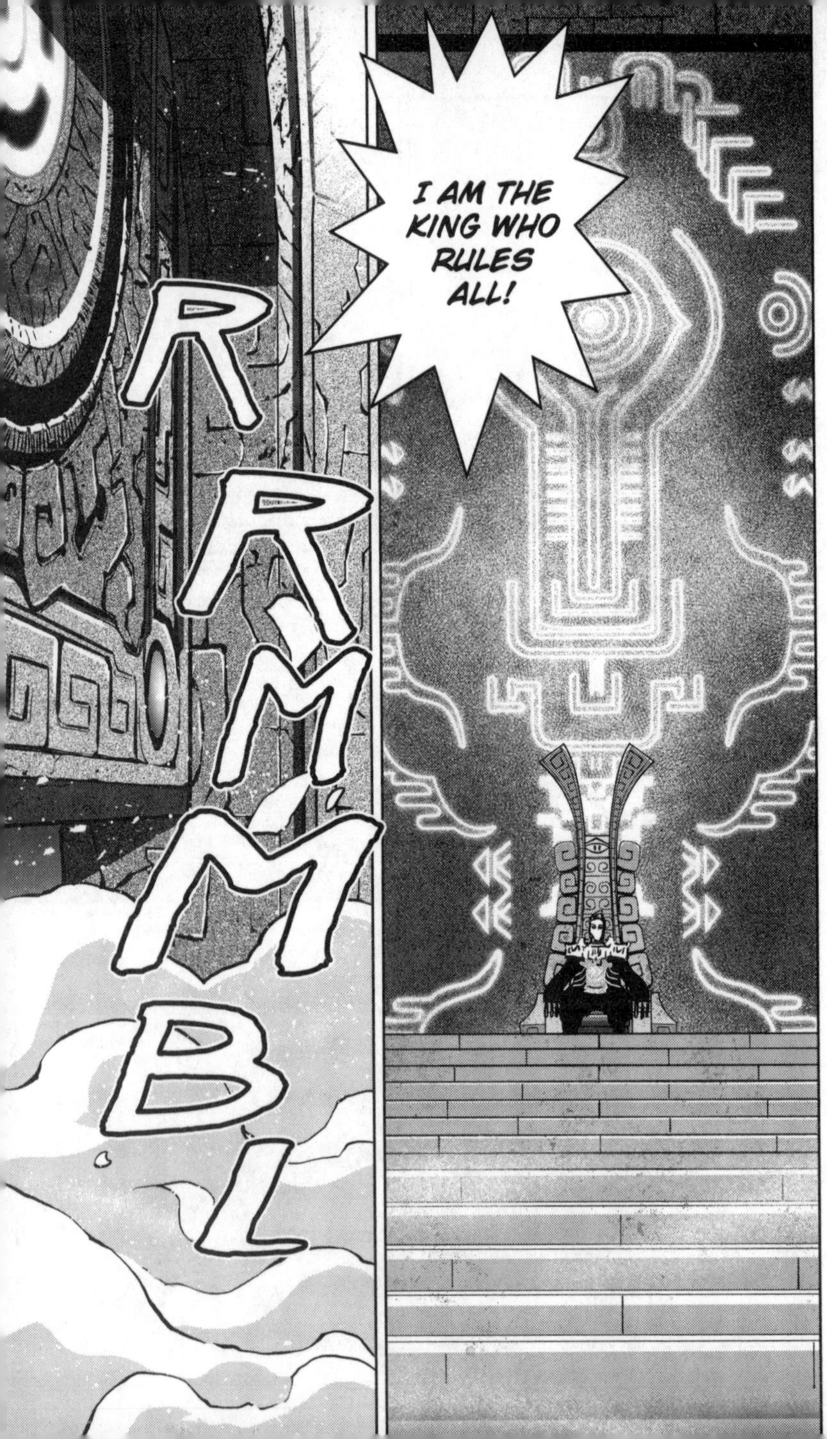
I AM THE KING WHO RULES ALL!
RRMMBL

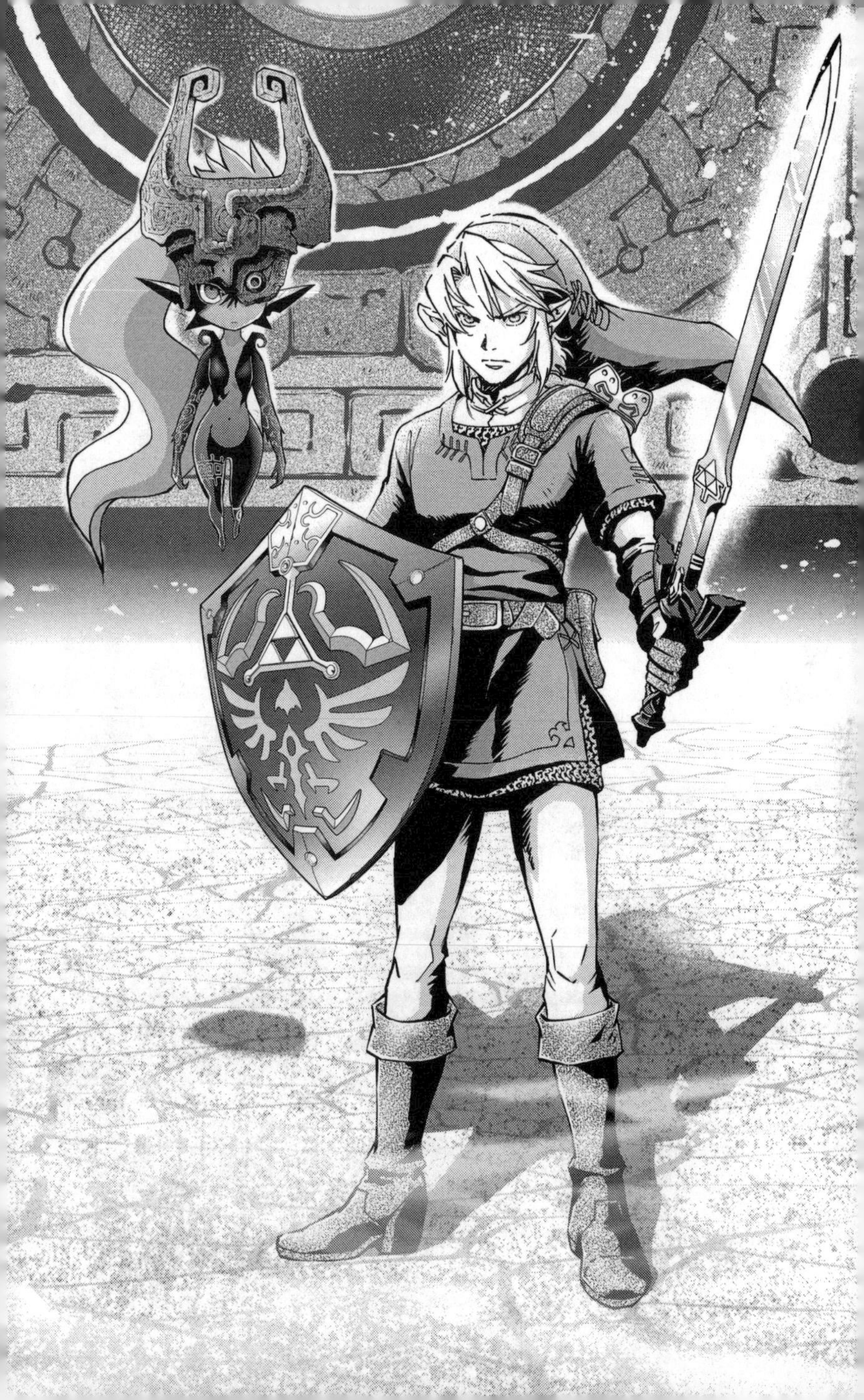

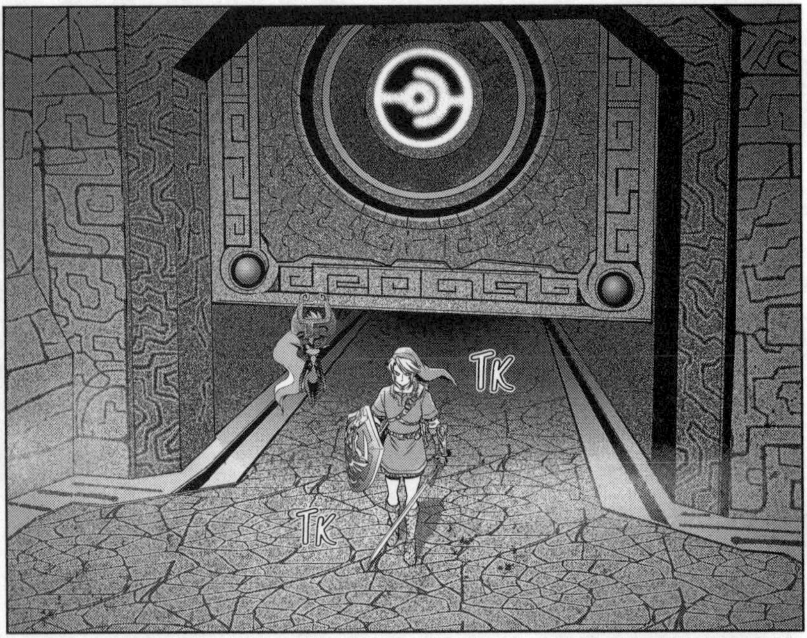
TK
TK
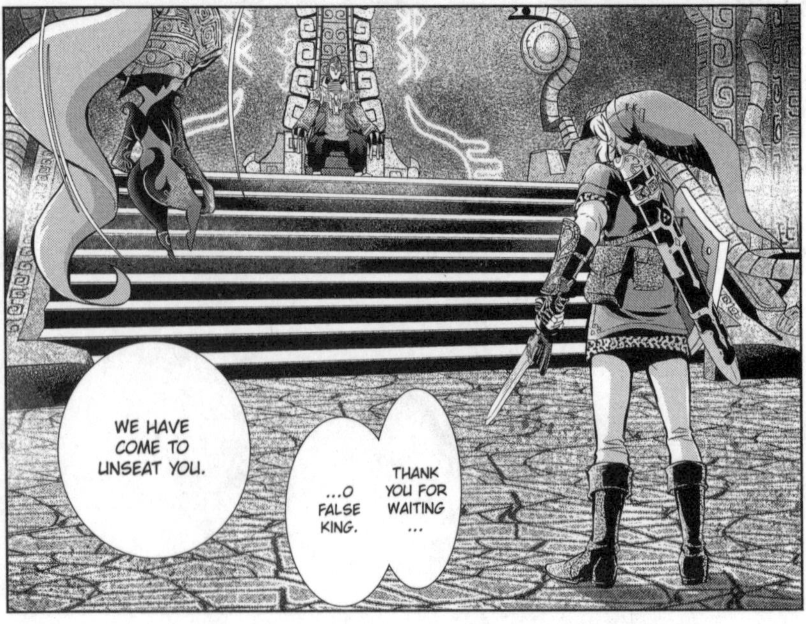
THANK YOU FOR WAITING ...
...O FALSE KING.
WE HAVE COME TO UNSEAT YOU.

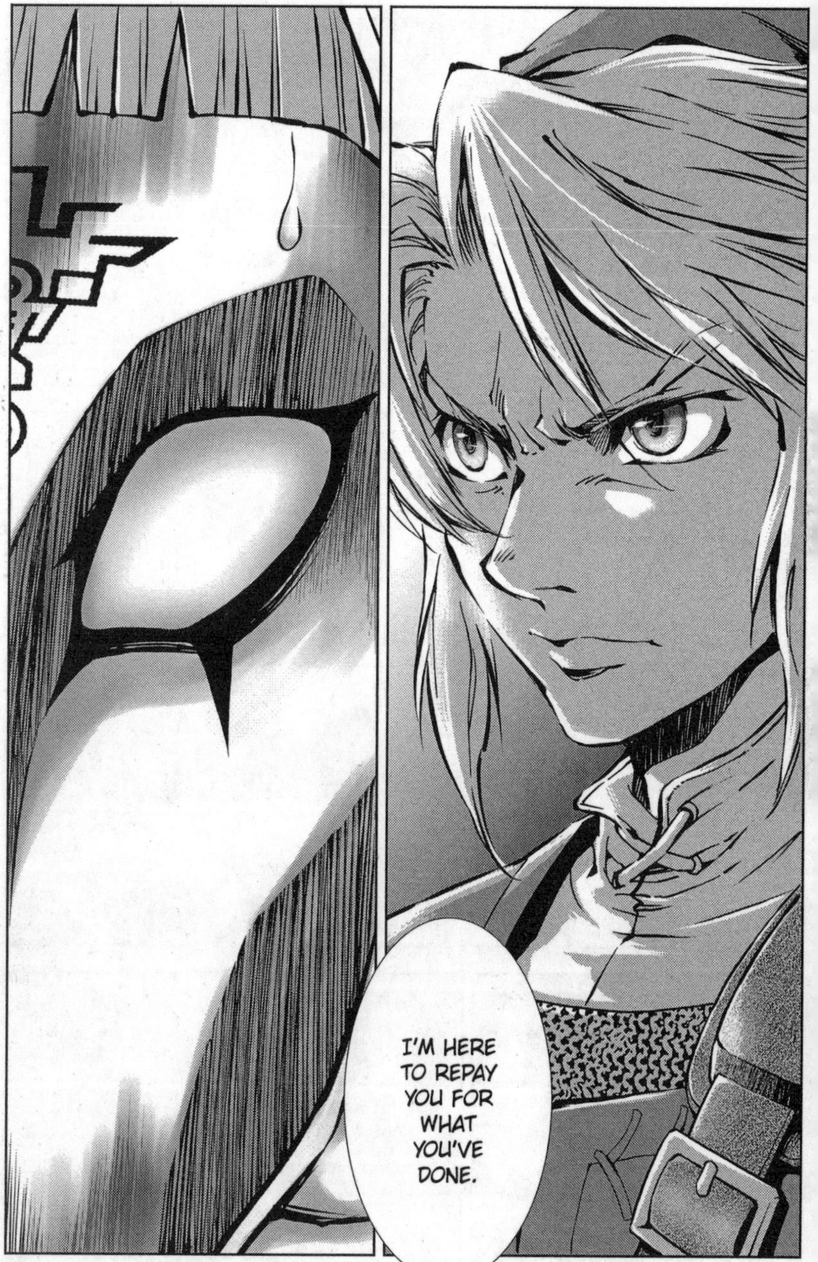
I'M HERE TO REPAY YOU FOR WHAT YOU'VE DONE.

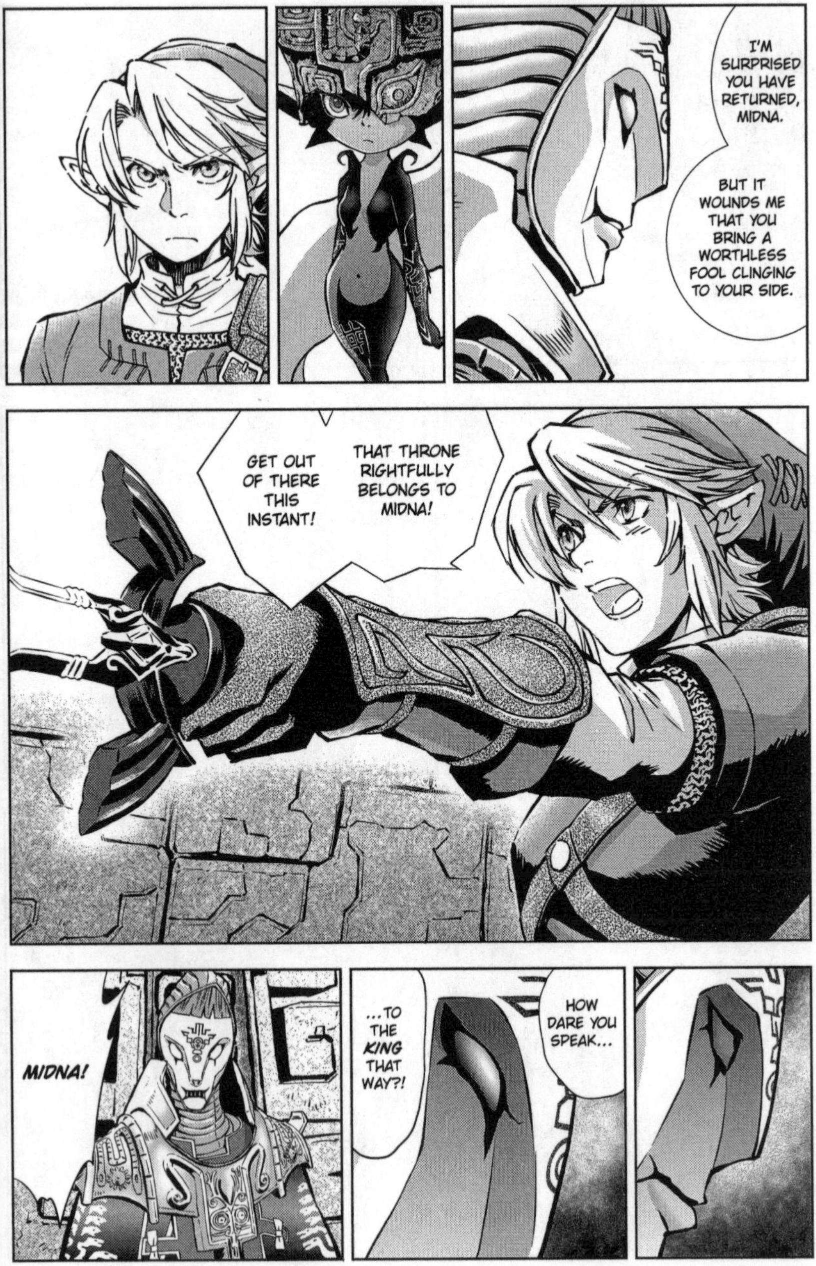
I'M SURPRISED YOU HAVE RETURNED, MIDNA.
BUT IT WOUNDS ME THAT YOU BRING A WORTHLESS FOOL CLINGING TO YOUR SIDE.
THAT THRONE RIGHTFULLY BELONGS TO MIDNA!
GET OUT OF THERE THIS INSTANT!
HOW DARE YOU SPEAK...
...TO THE *KING* THAT WAY?!
MIDNA!

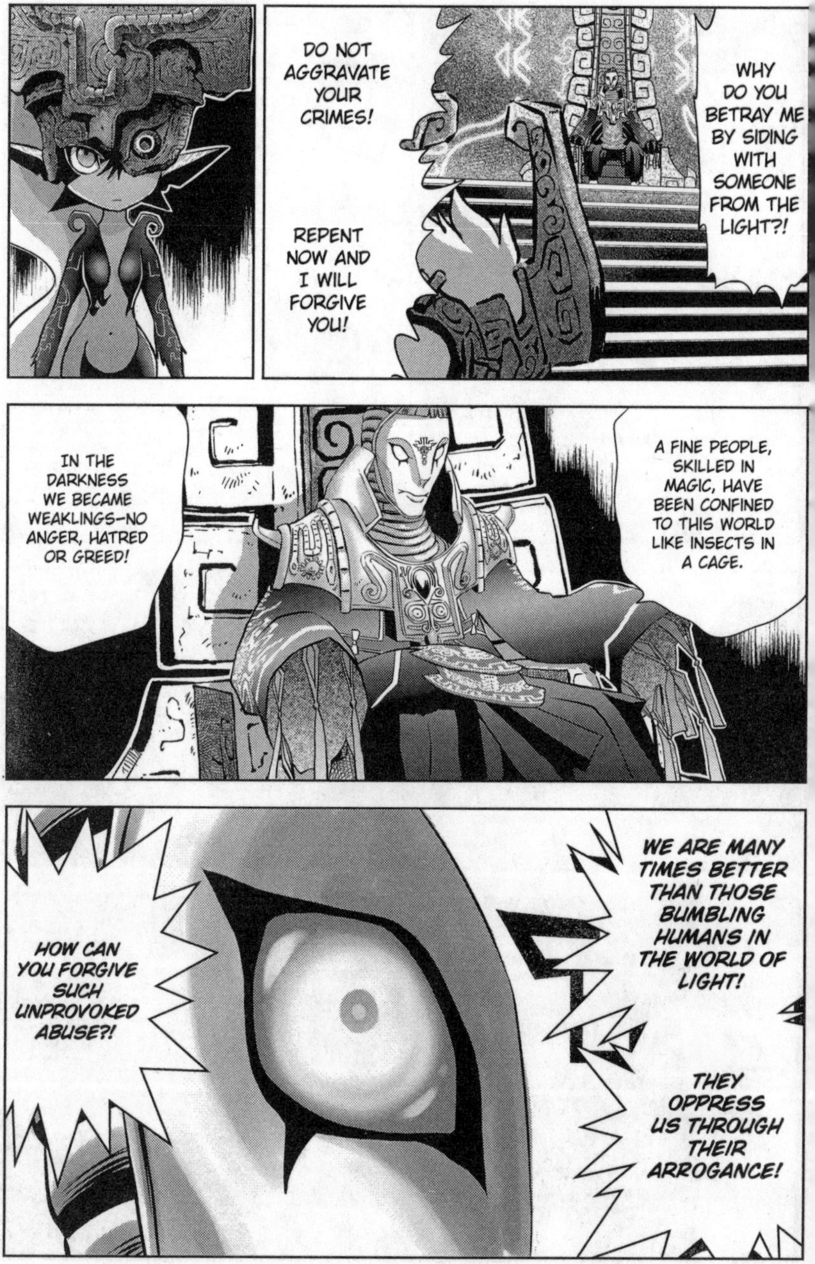
WHY DO YOU BETRAY ME BY SIDING WITH SOMEONE FROM THE LIGHT?!
DO NOT AGGRAVATE YOUR CRIMES!
REPENT NOW AND I WILL FORGIVE YOU!
A FINE PEOPLE, SKILLED IN MAGIC, HAVE BEEN CONFINED TO THIS WORLD LIKE INSECTS IN A CAGE.
IN THE DARKNESS WE BECAME WEAKLINGS—NO ANGER, HATRED OR GREED!
WE ARE MANY TIMES BETTER THAN THOSE BUMBLING HUMANS IN THE WORLD OF LIGHT!
THEY OPPRESS US THROUGH THEIR ARROGANCE!
HOW CAN YOU FORGIVE SUCH UNPROVOKED ABUSE?!

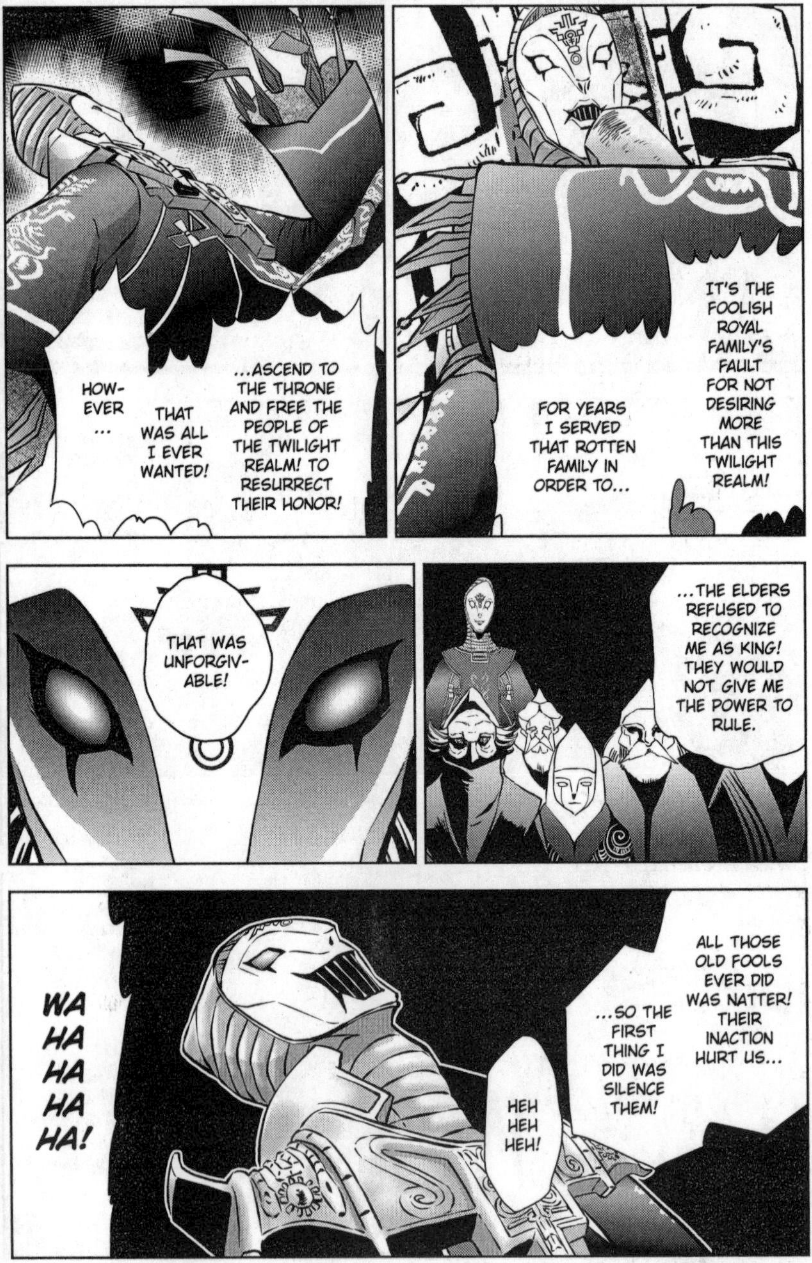
IT'S THE FOOLISH ROYAL FAMILY'S FAULT FOR NOT DESIRING MORE THAN THIS TWILIGHT REALM!
FOR YEARS I SERVED THAT ROTTEN FAMILY IN ORDER TO...
...ASCEND TO THE THRONE AND FREE THE PEOPLE OF THE TWILIGHT REALM! TO RESURRECT THEIR HONOR!
THAT WAS ALL I EVER WANTED!
HOW-EVER ...
...THE ELDERS REFUSED TO RECOGNIZE ME AS KING! THEY WOULD NOT GIVE ME THE POWER TO RULE.
THAT WAS UNFORGIV-ABLE!
ALL THOSE OLD FOOLS EVER DID WAS NATTER! THEIR INACTION HURT US...
...SO THE FIRST THING I DID WAS SILENCE THEM!
HEH HEH HEH!
WA HA HA HA HA!

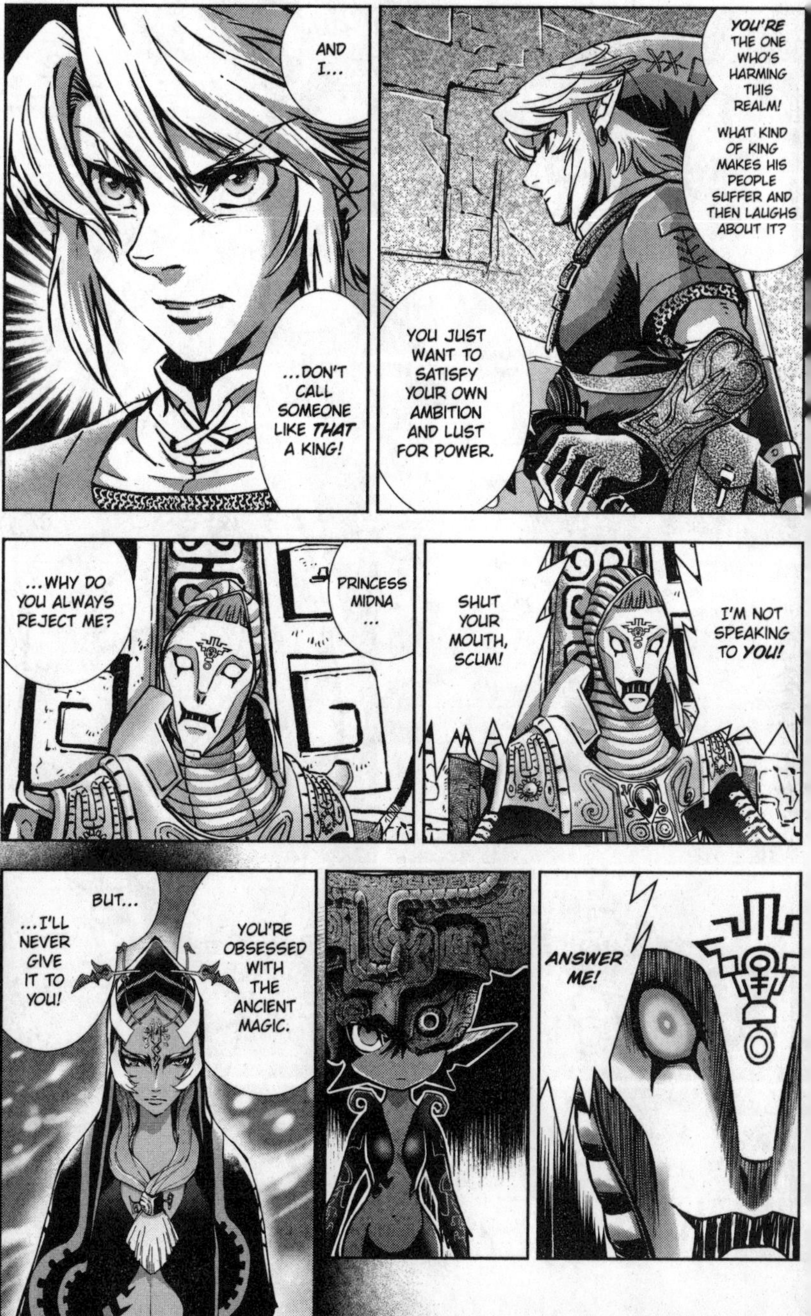
YOU'RE THE ONE WHO'S HARMING THIS REALM!
WHAT KIND OF KING MAKES HIS PEOPLE SUFFER AND THEN LAUGHS ABOUT IT?
YOU JUST WANT TO SATISFY YOUR OWN AMBITION AND LUST FOR POWER.
AND I...
...DON'T CALL SOMEONE LIKE THAT A KING!
I'M NOT SPEAKING TO YOU!
SHUT YOUR MOUTH, SCUM!
PRINCESS MIDNA ...
...WHY DO YOU ALWAYS REJECT ME?
ANSWER ME!
YOU'RE OBSESSED WITH THE ANCIENT MAGIC.
BUT...
...I'LL NEVER GIVE IT TO YOU!

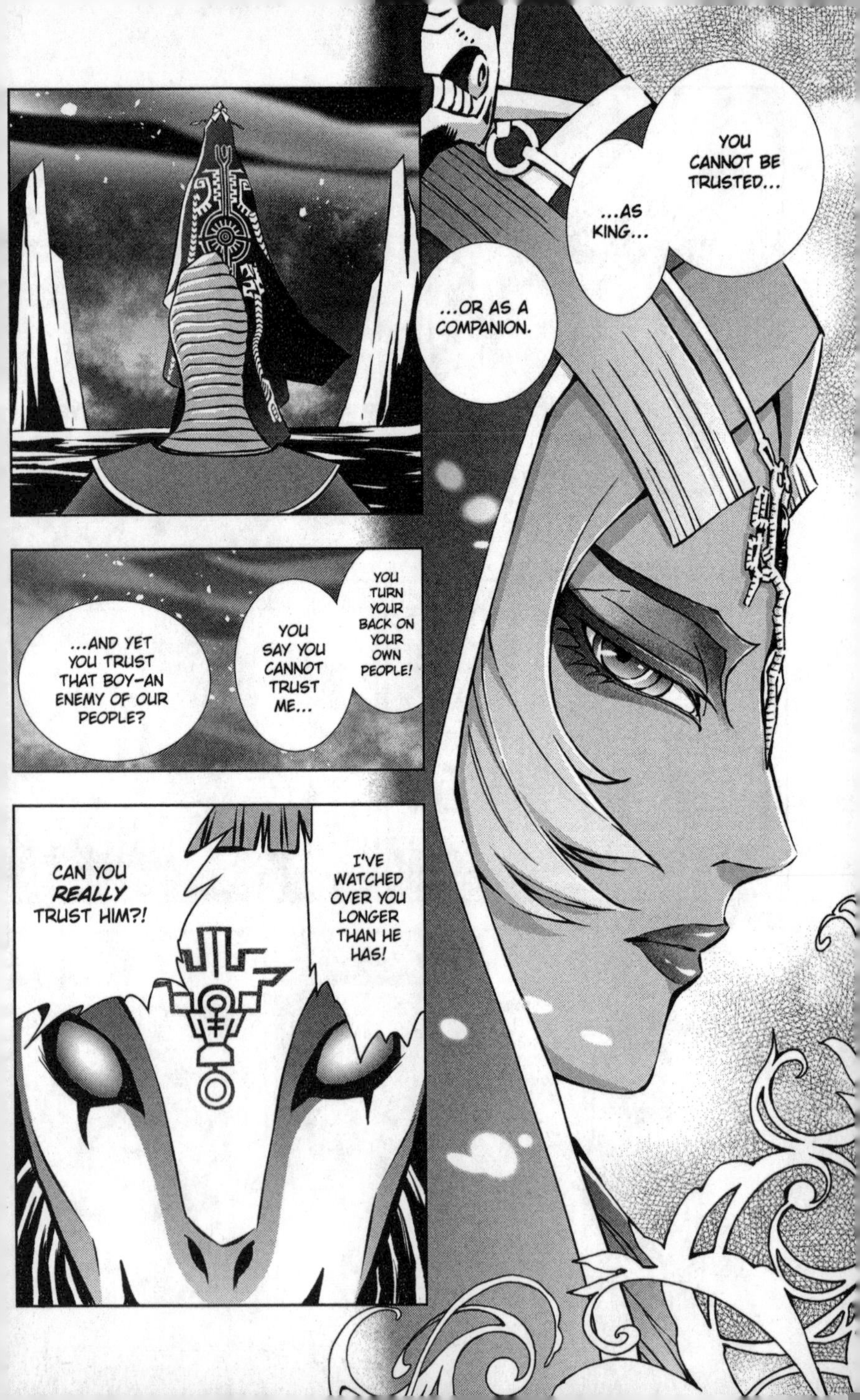

YOU CANNOT BE TRUSTED...
...AS KING...
...OR AS A COMPANION.
YOU TURN YOUR BACK ON YOUR OWN PEOPLE!
YOU SAY YOU CANNOT TRUST ME...
...AND YET YOU TRUST THAT BOY—AN ENEMY OF OUR PEOPLE?
I'VE WATCHED OVER YOU LONGER THAN HE HAS!
CAN YOU *REALLY* TRUST HIM?!

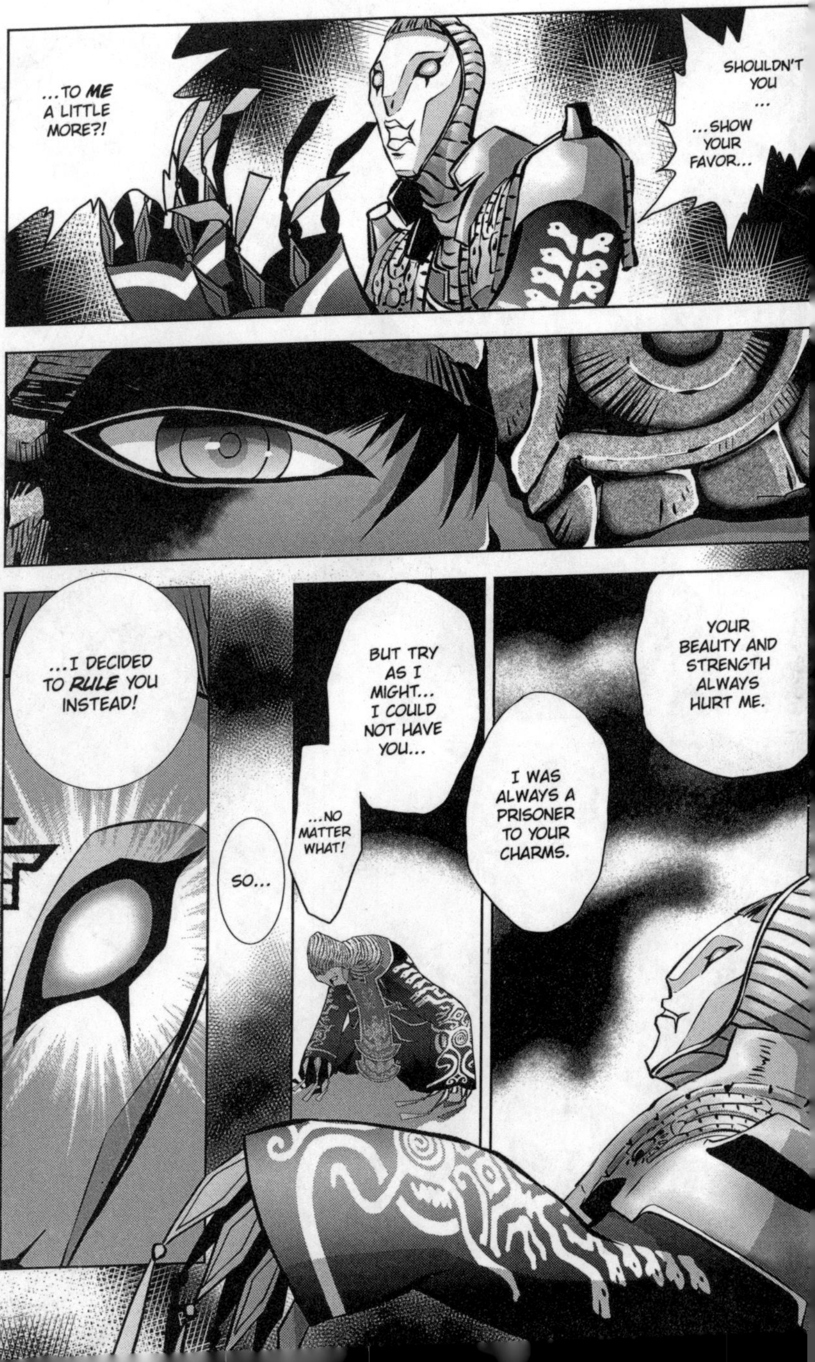
SHOULDN'T YOU ...
...SHOW YOUR FAVOR...
...TO ME A LITTLE MORE?!
YOUR BEAUTY AND STRENGTH ALWAYS HURT ME.
I WAS ALWAYS A PRISONER TO YOUR CHARMS.
BUT TRY AS I MIGHT... I COULD NOT HAVE YOU...
...NO MATTER WHAT!
SO...
...I DECIDED TO RULE YOU INSTEAD!

...AND TRANS-FORMING ME WAS AN EXPRESSION OF *LOVE*?

ARE YOU SAYING THAT CURSING ME...

ONLY BY RULING ALL...

...COULD I *HAVE* YOU!

SUCH EGO!

AND YOU WANT ME TO *ACCEPT* THAT?

I REFUSE YOU... *FOREVER!*

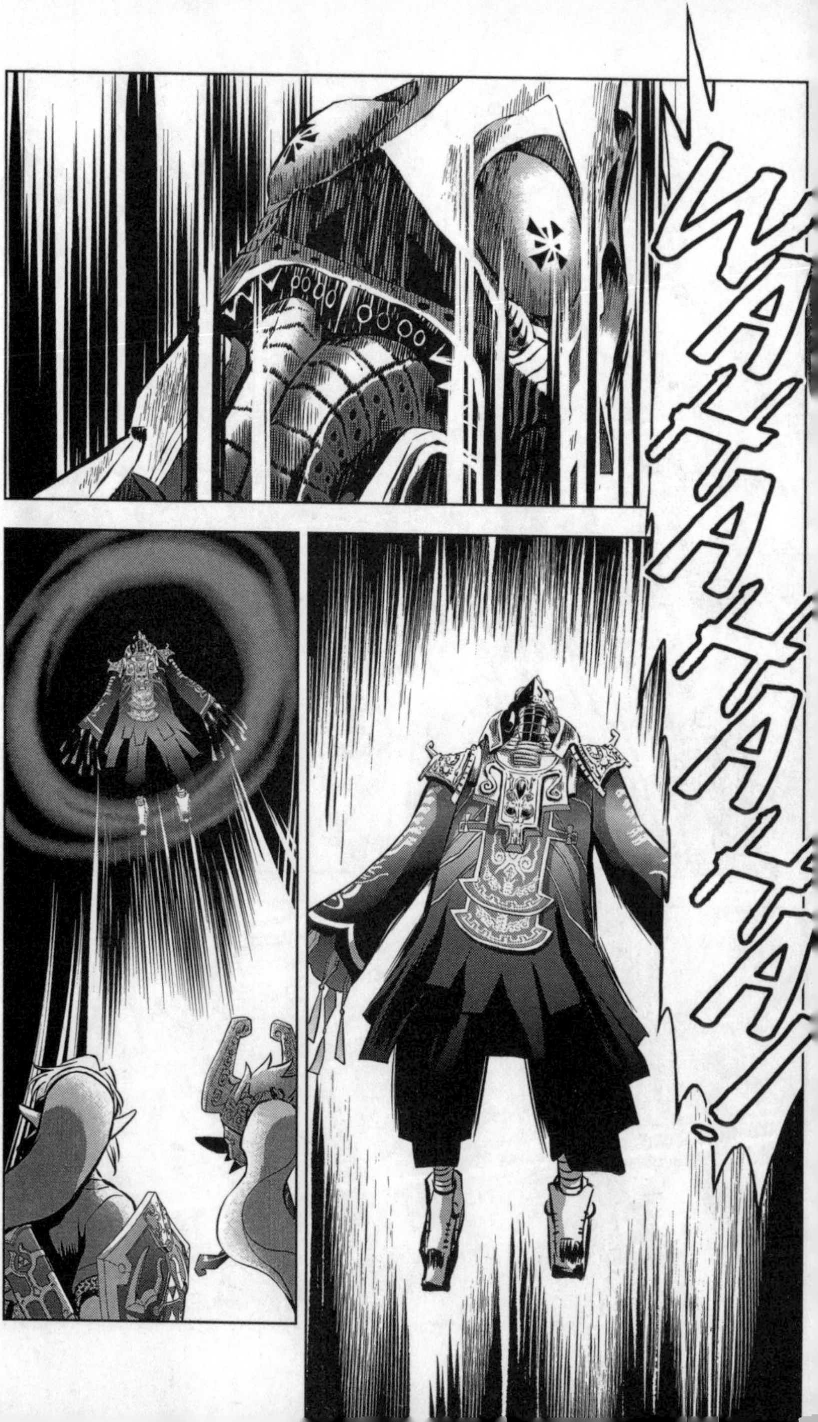
WAHAHAHAHA!

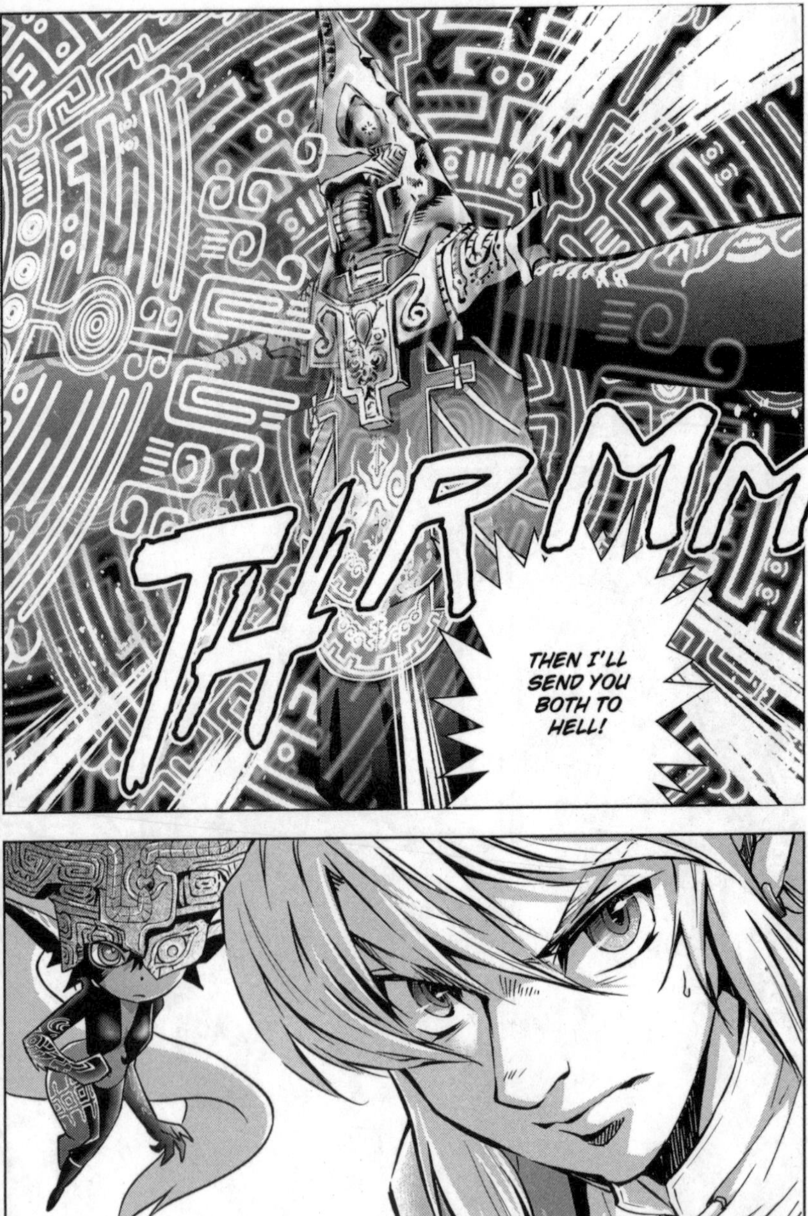
THRMM
THEN I'LL SEND YOU BOTH TO HELL!

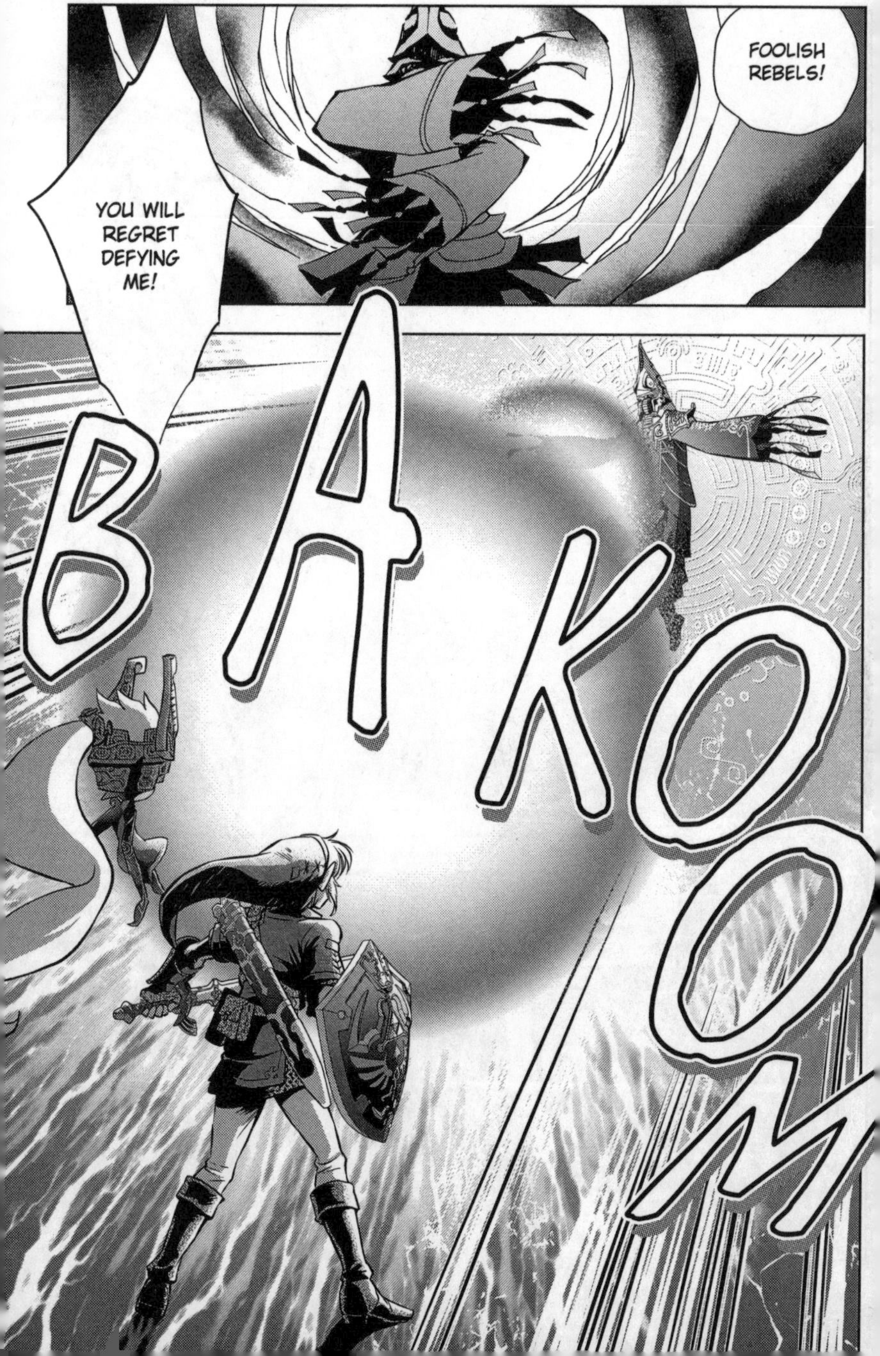
FOOLISH REBELS!
YOU WILL REGRET DEFYING ME!
BAKOOM

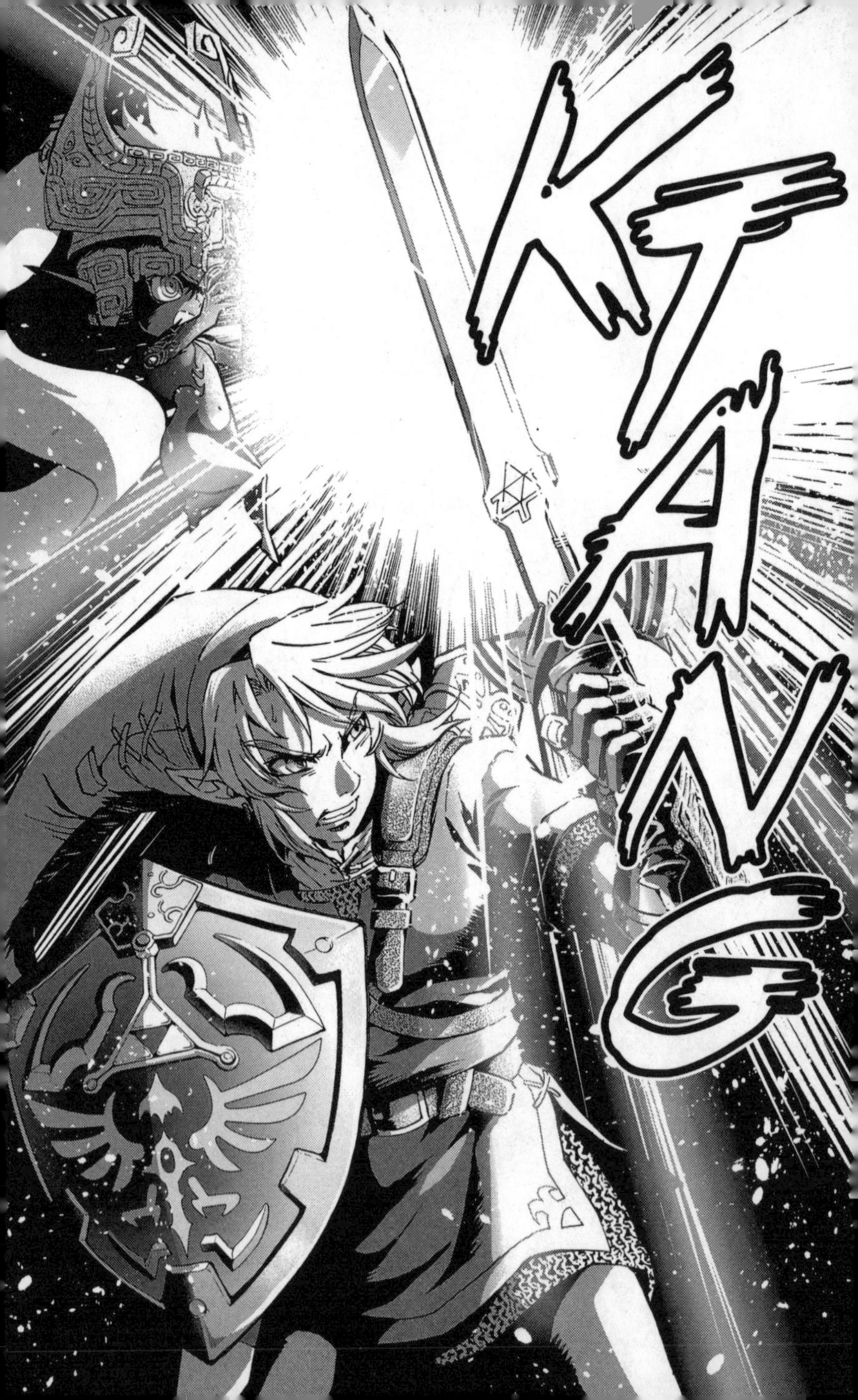
KYANG

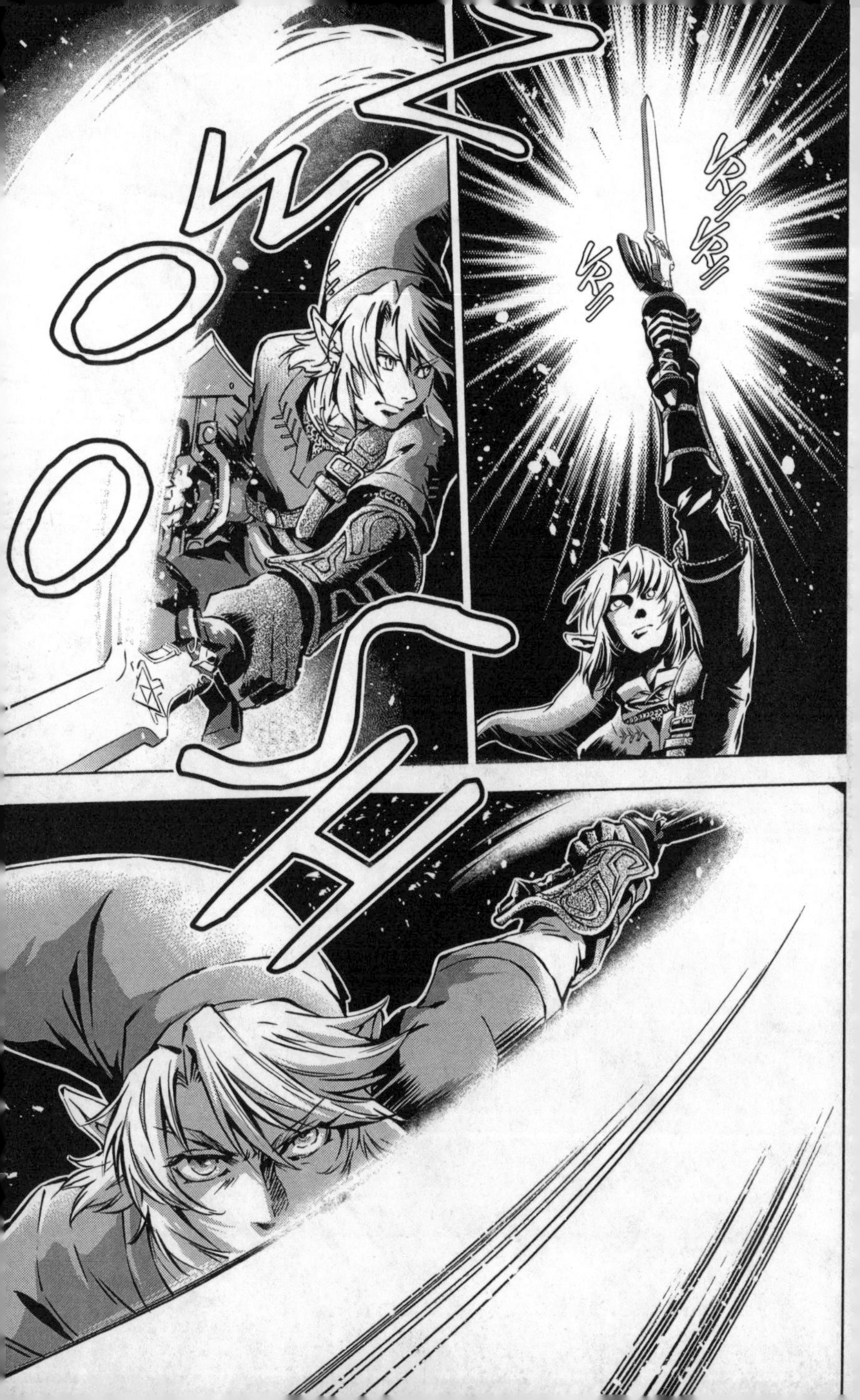
SWOOSH
VRI VRI
VRI

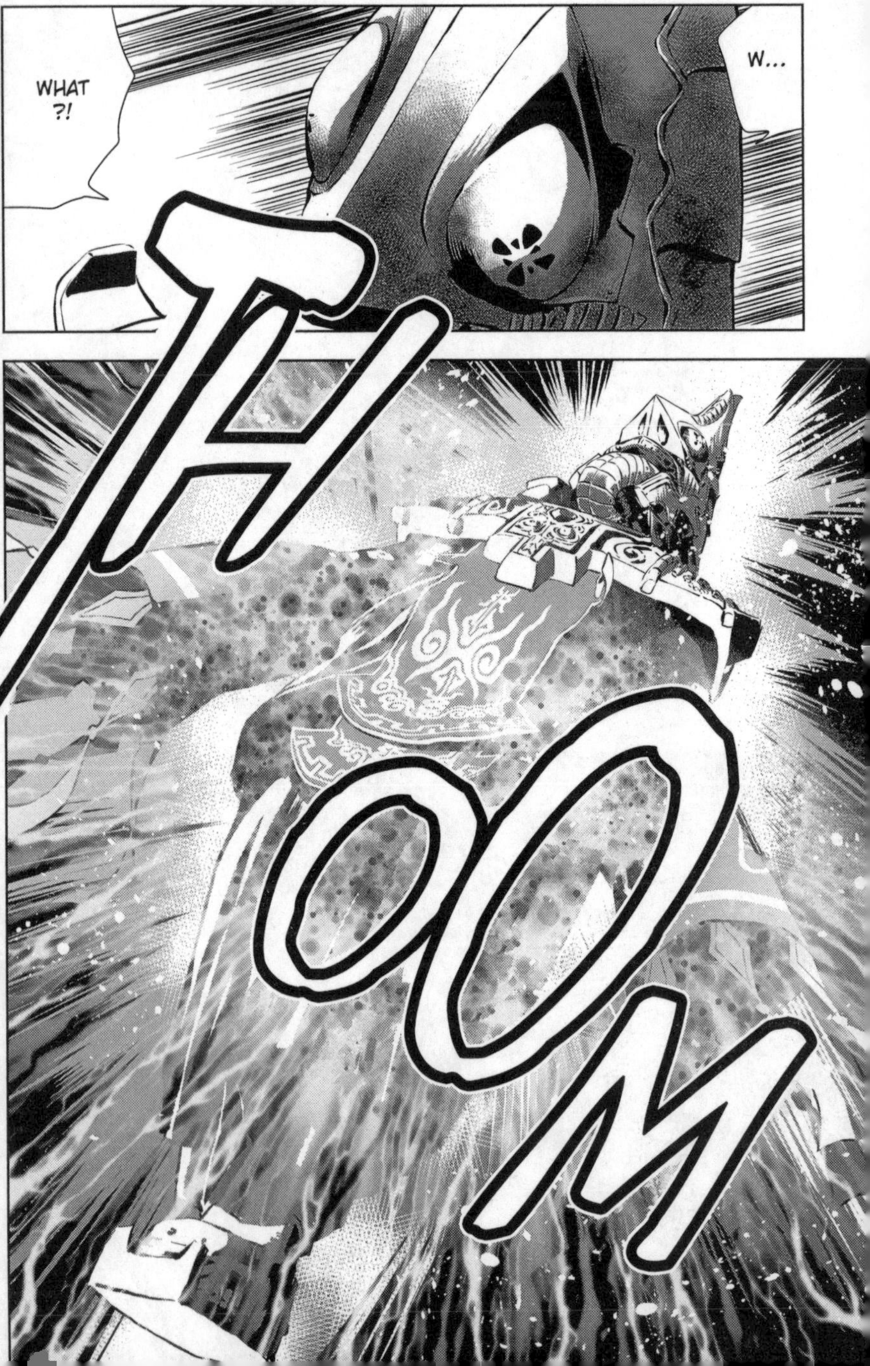
W...
WHAT ?!
HOOM

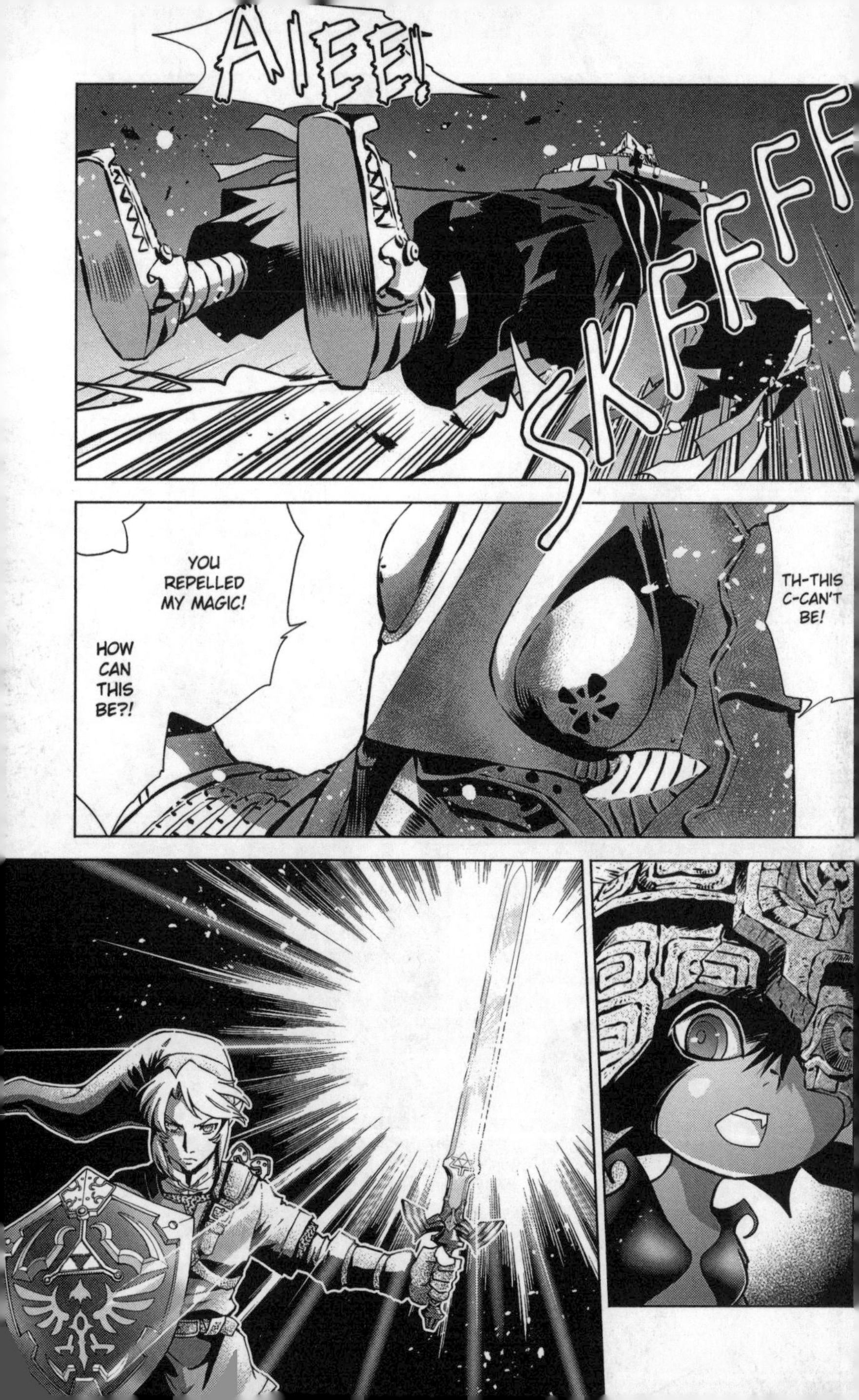
AIEEE!
SKFFFFF
TH-THIS C-CAN'T BE!
YOU REPELLED MY MAGIC!
HOW CAN THIS BE?!

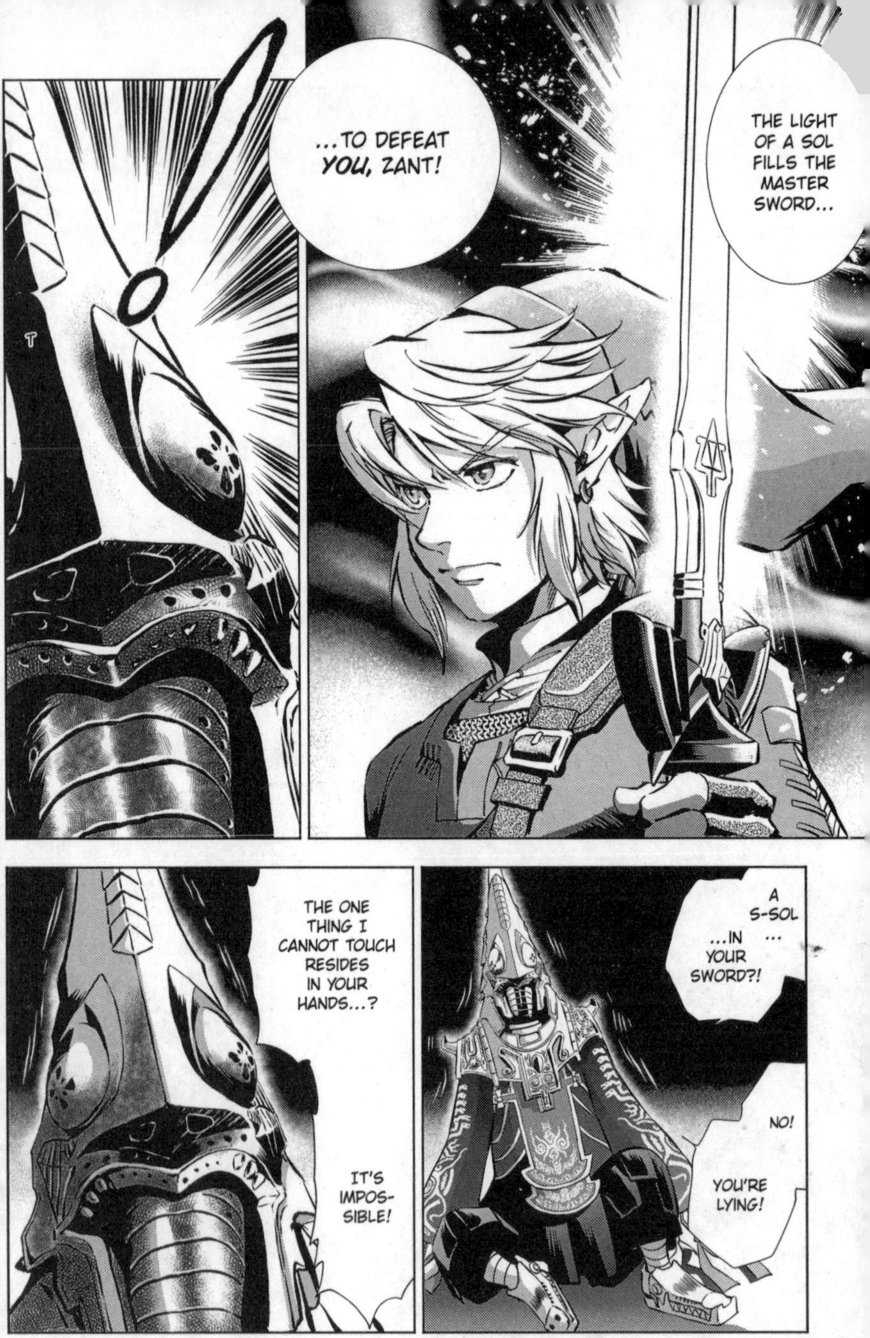
THE LIGHT OF A SOL FILLS THE MASTER SWORD...
...TO DEFEAT *YOU*, ZANT!
A S-SOL ...
...IN YOUR SWORD?!
NO!
YOU'RE LYING!
THE ONE THING I CANNOT TOUCH RESIDES IN YOUR HANDS...?
IT'S IMPOS-SIBLE!

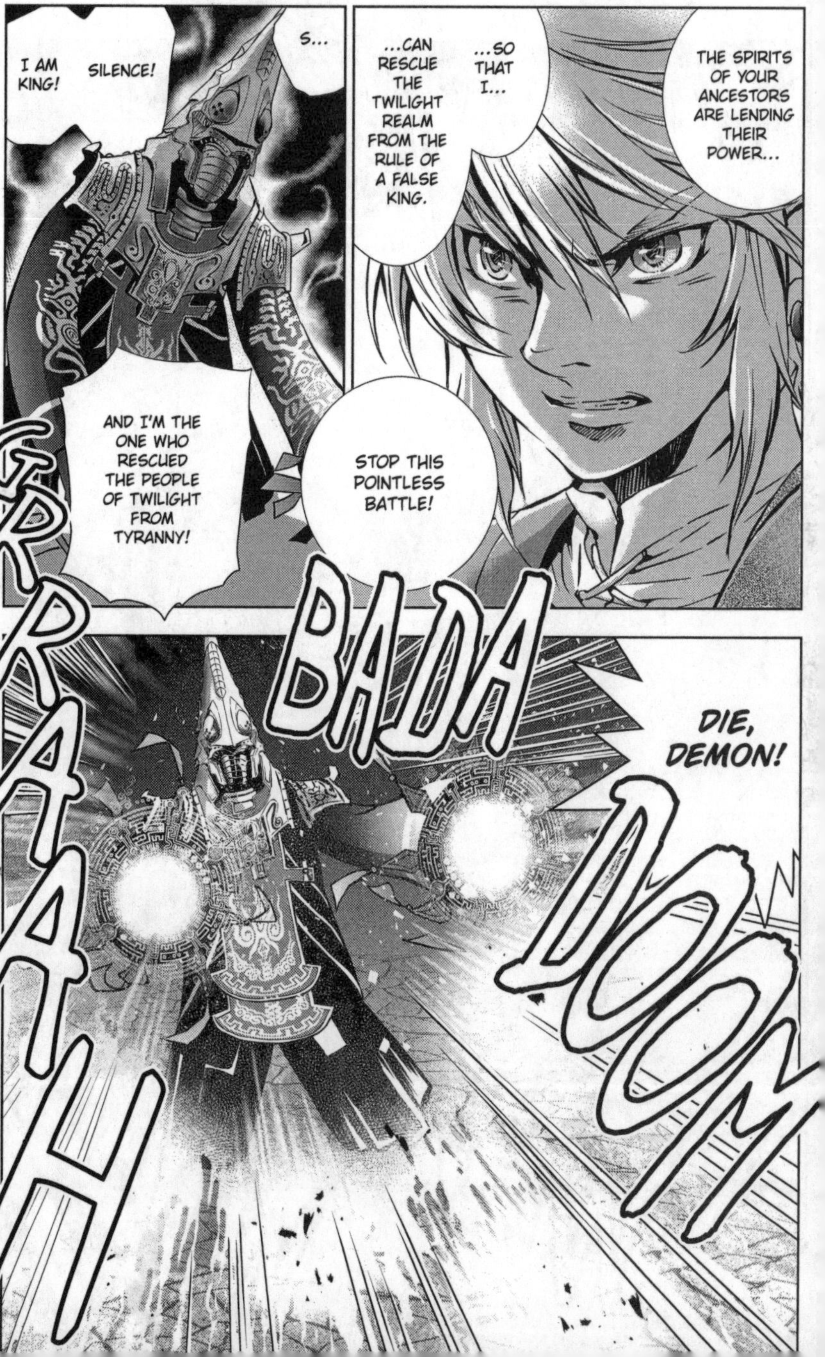
THE SPIRITS OF YOUR ANCESTORS ARE LENDING THEIR POWER...
...SO THAT I...
...CAN RESCUE THE TWILIGHT REALM FROM THE RULE OF A FALSE KING.
STOP THIS POINTLESS BATTLE!
S...
SILENCE!
I AM KING!
AND I'M THE ONE WHO RESCUED THE PEOPLE OF TWILIGHT FROM TYRANNY!
DIE, DEMON!
BADA
DOOM
GRRAAHH

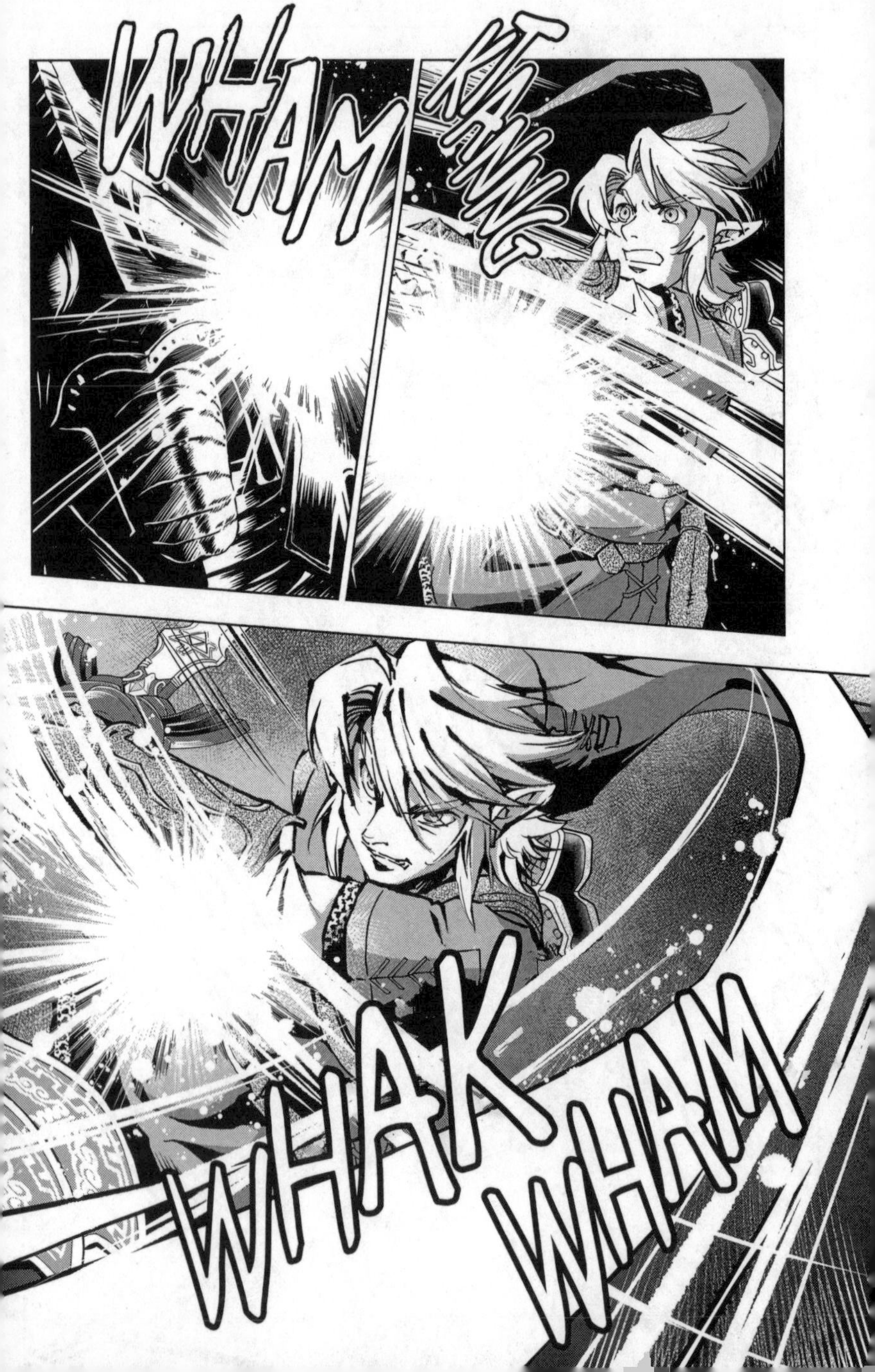
KANNNG
WHAM
WHAM
WHAK

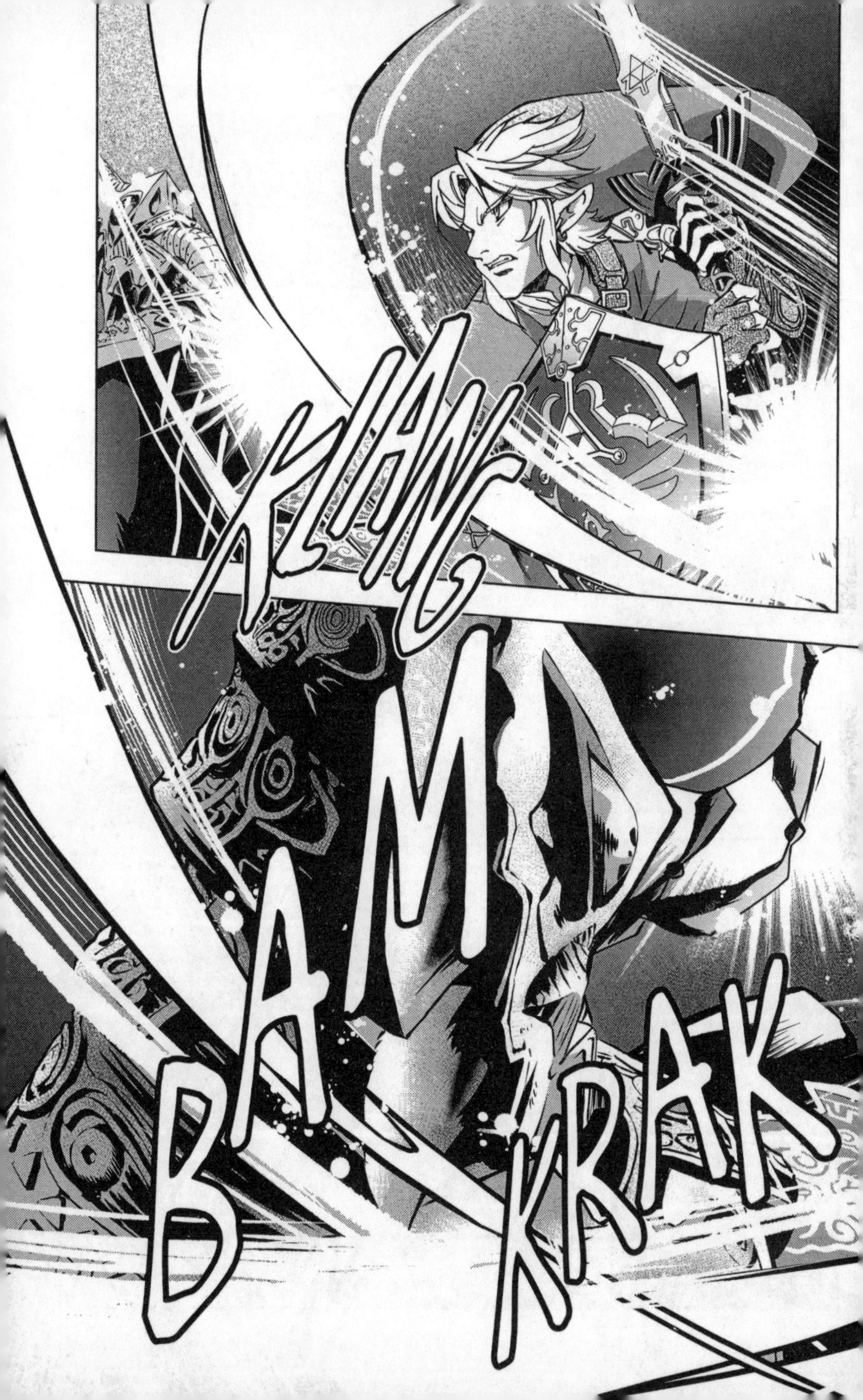
XLANG
BAM
KRAK

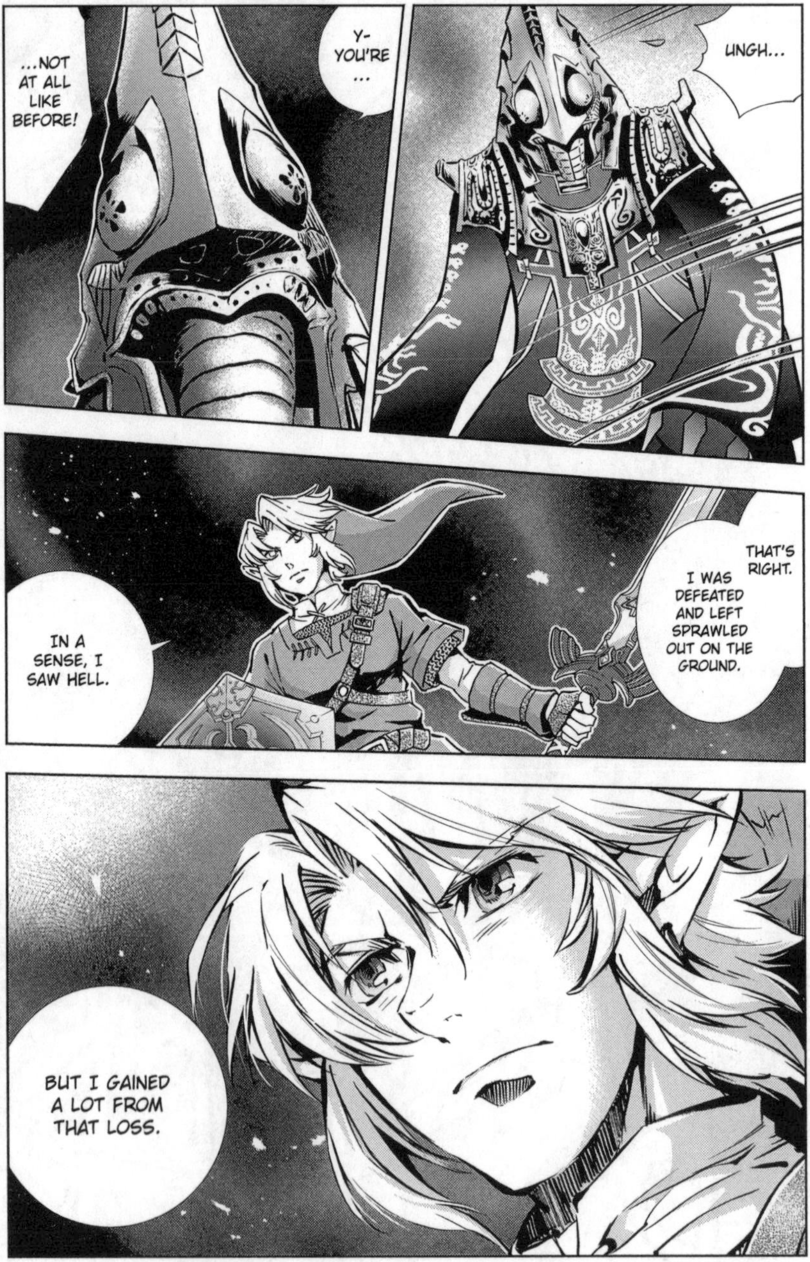
UNGH...
Y- YOU'RE ...
...NOT AT ALL LIKE BEFORE!
THAT'S RIGHT.
I WAS DEFEATED AND LEFT SPRAWLED OUT ON THE GROUND.
IN A SENSE, I SAW HELL.
BUT I GAINED A LOT FROM THAT LOSS.

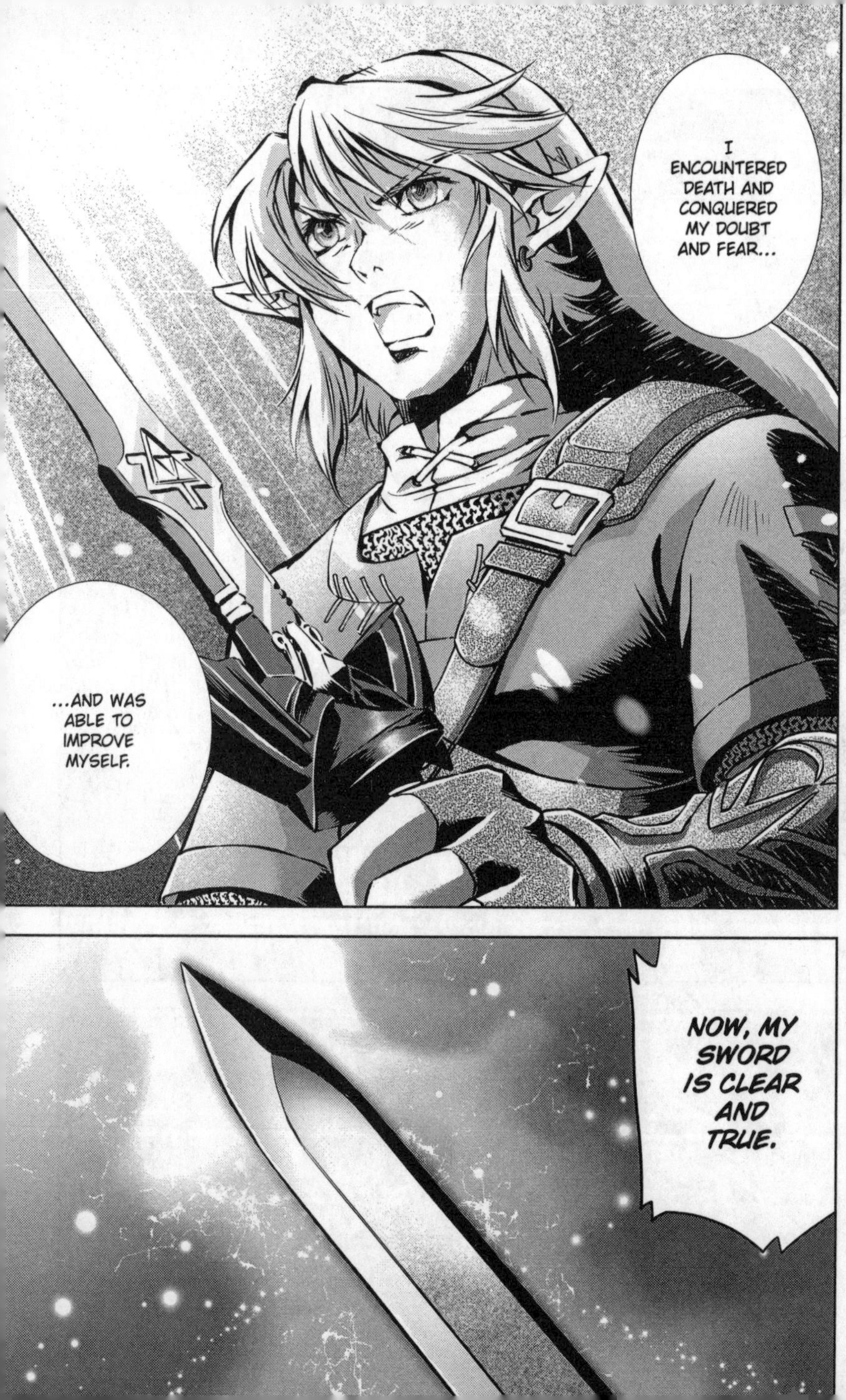
I ENCOUNTERED DEATH AND CONQUERED MY DOUBT AND FEAR...
...AND WAS ABLE TO IMPROVE MYSELF.
NOW, MY SWORD IS CLEAR AND TRUE.

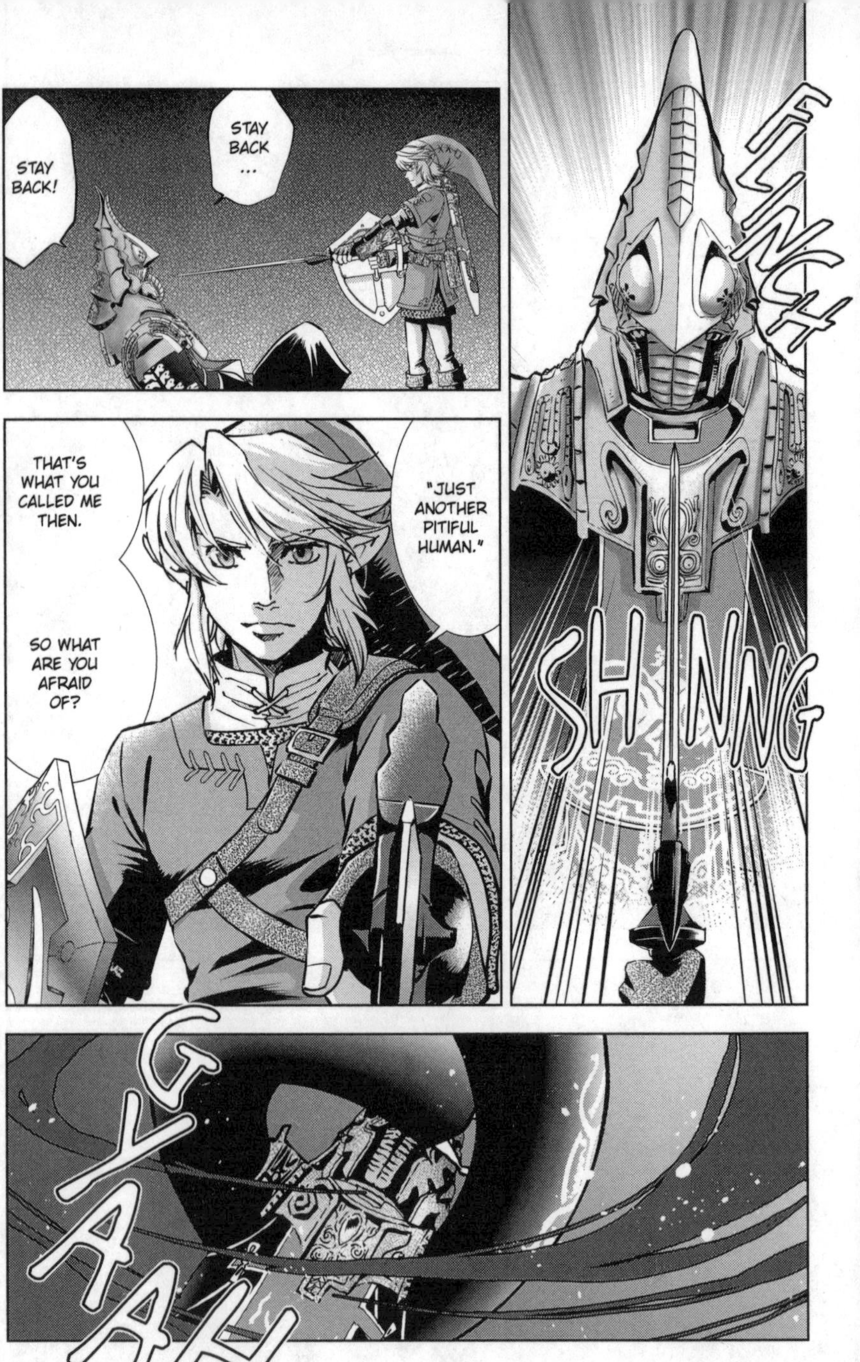
FLINCH
SHINNG
STAY BACK ...
STAY BACK!
"JUST ANOTHER PITIFUL HUMAN."
THAT'S WHAT YOU CALLED ME THEN.
SO WHAT ARE YOU AFRAID OF?
GYAAAH

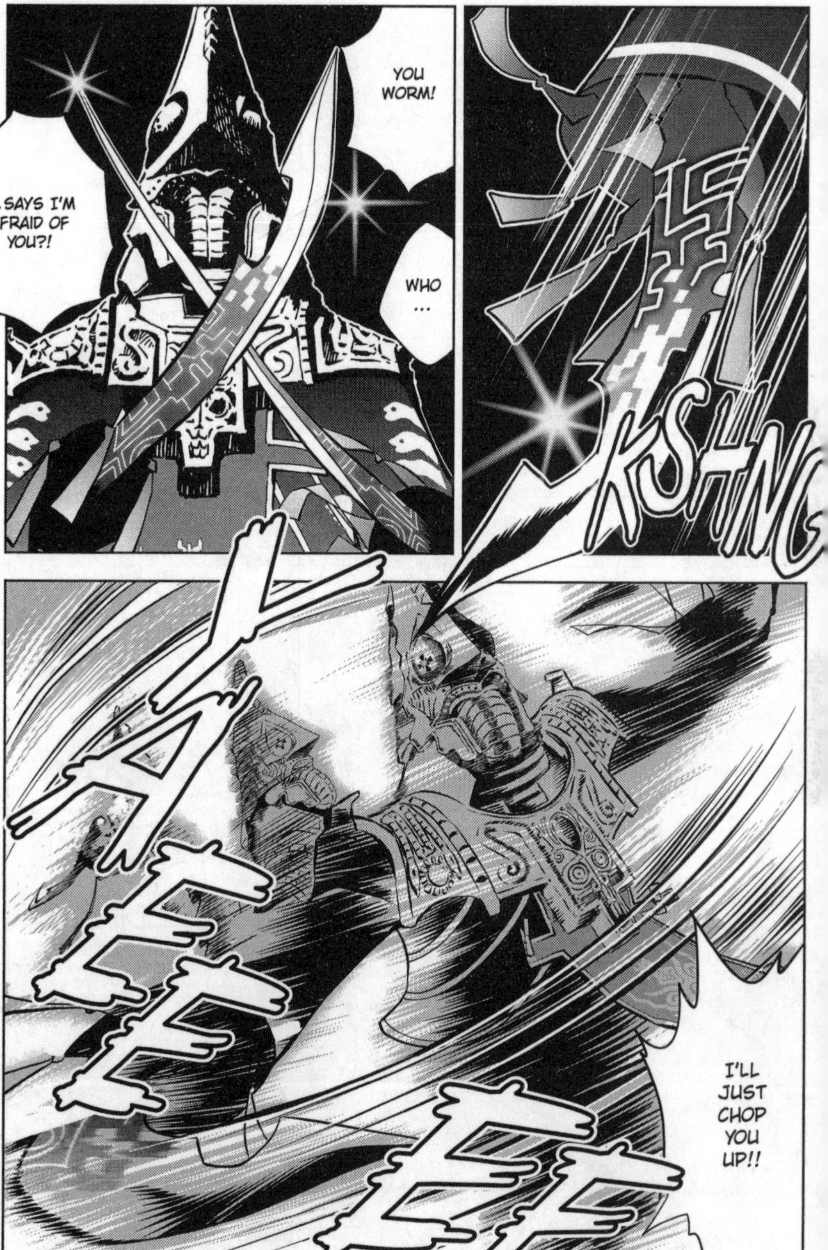
KSHING
YOU WORM!
WHO...
...SAYS I'M AFRAID OF YOU?!
I'LL JUST CHOP YOU UP!!

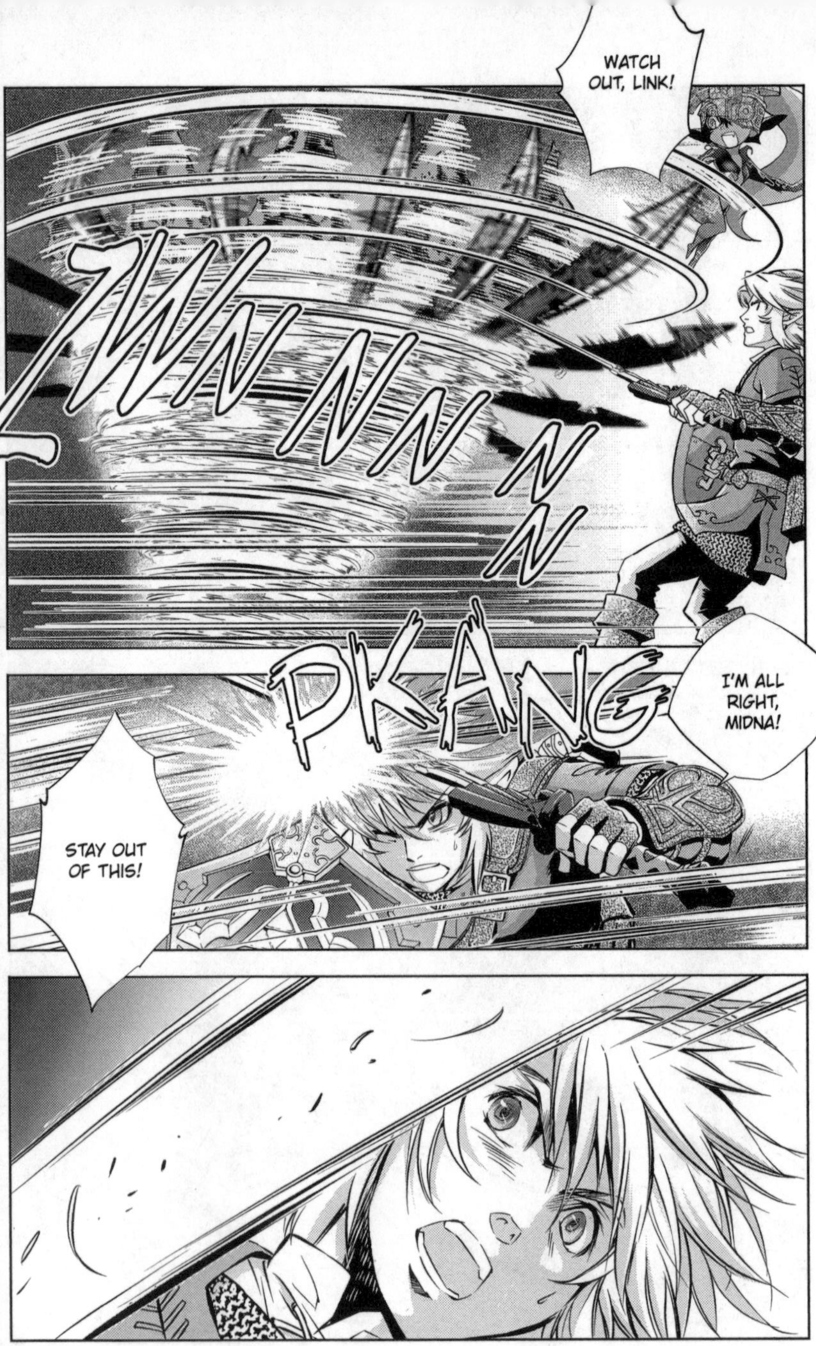
WATCH OUT, LINK!
ZWNNNNN
PKANG
I'M ALL RIGHT, MIDNA!
STAY OUT OF THIS!

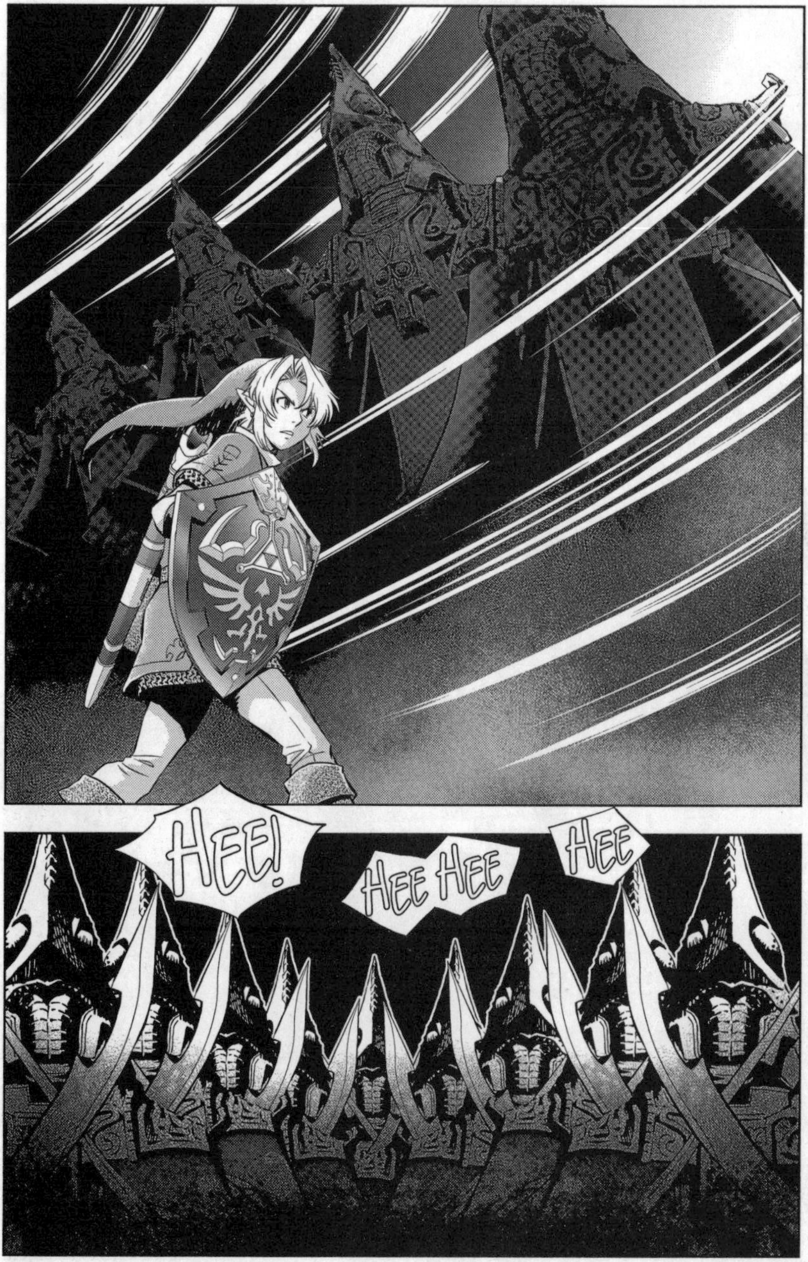
HEE
HEE HEE
HEE!

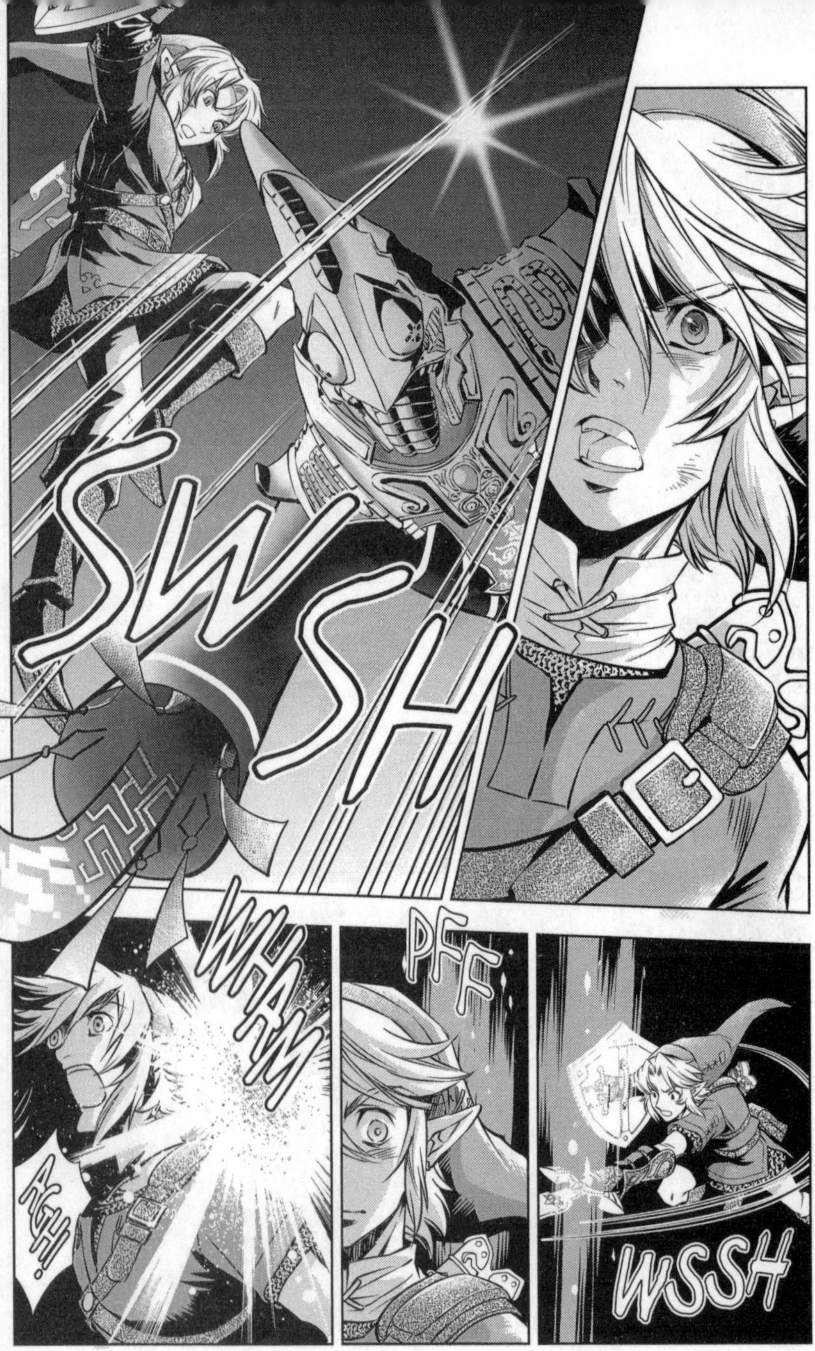
SWSH
WSSH
PFF
WHAM
AGH!

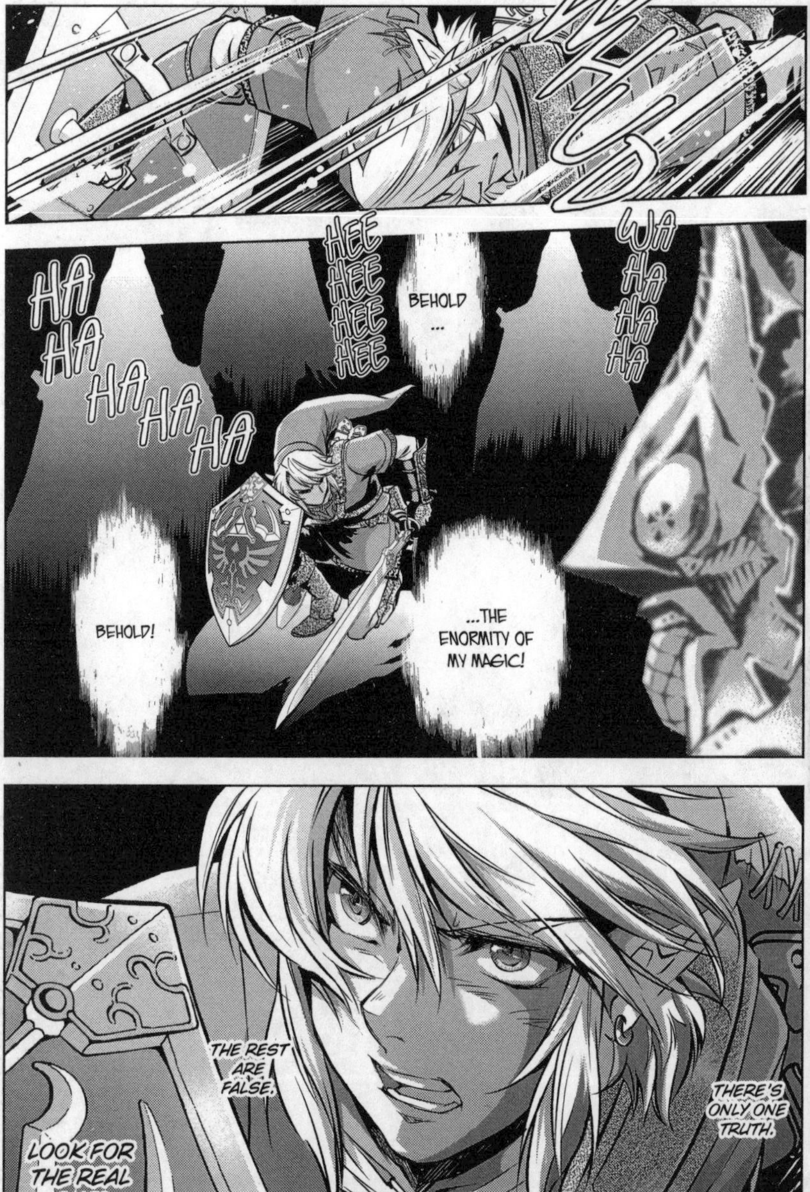
WHUD
WA HA HA HA HA
BEHOLD ...
HEE HEE HEE HEE
HA HA HA HA HA HA
...THE ENORMITY OF MY MAGIC!
BEHOLD!
THERE'S ONLY ONE TRUTH.
THE REST ARE FALSE.
LOOK FOR THE REAL ONE!

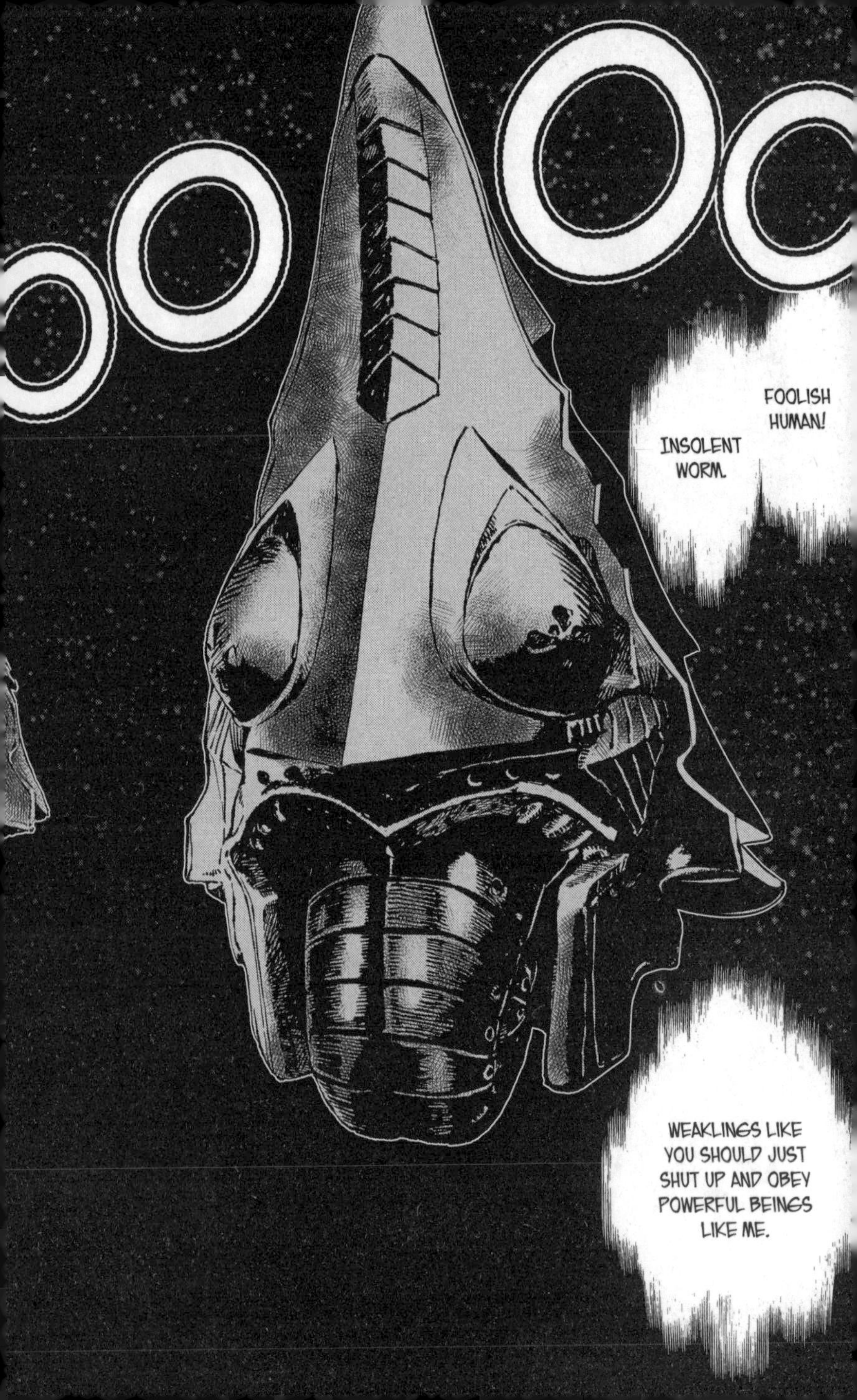
FOOLISH HUMAN!
INSOLENT WORM.
WEAKLINGS LIKE YOU SHOULD JUST SHUT UP AND OBEY POWERFUL BEINGS LIKE ME.

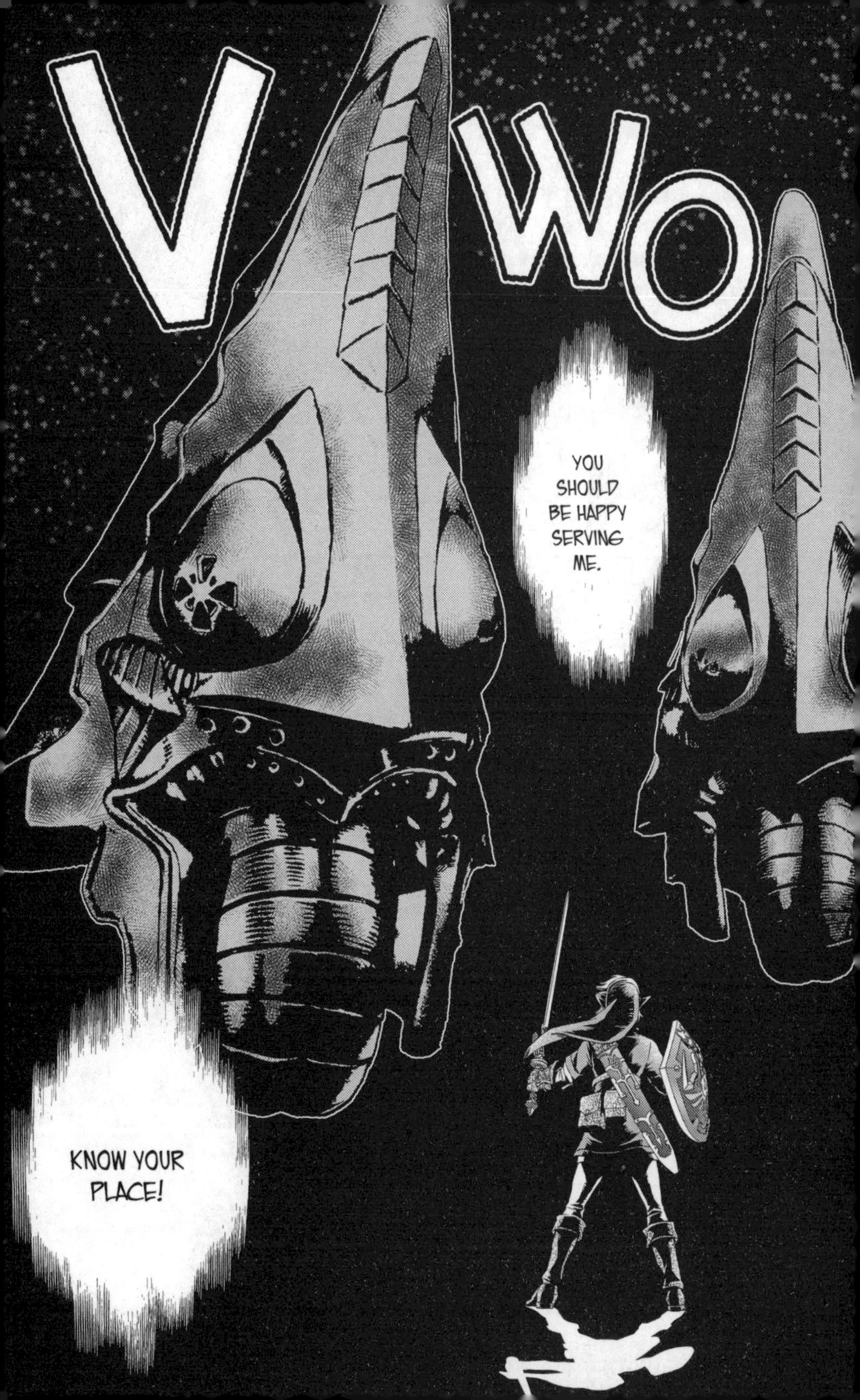
VWOO
YOU SHOULD BE HAPPY SERVING ME.
KNOW YOUR PLACE!

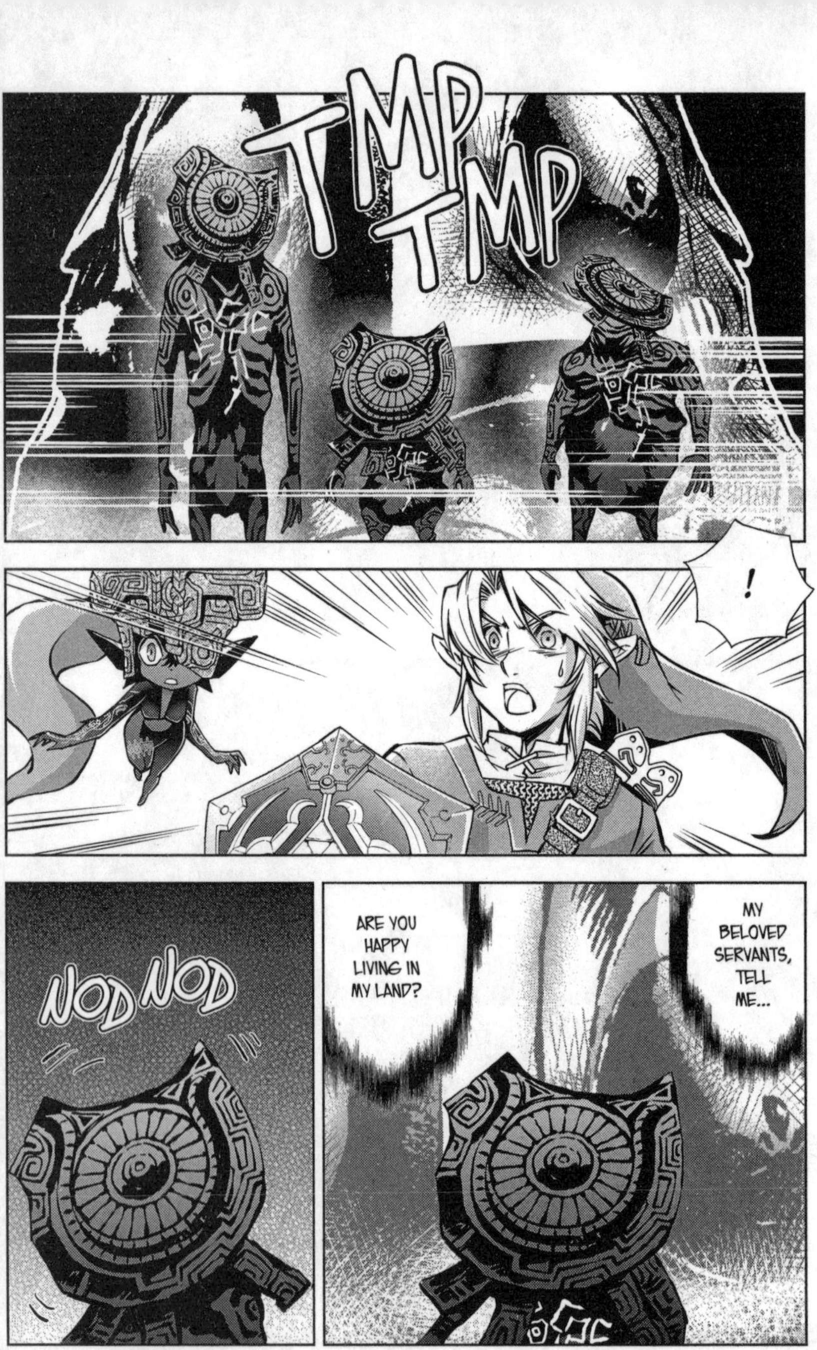
TMP TMP
!
MY BELOVED SERVANTS, TELL ME...
ARE YOU HAPPY LIVING IN MY LAND?
NOD NOD

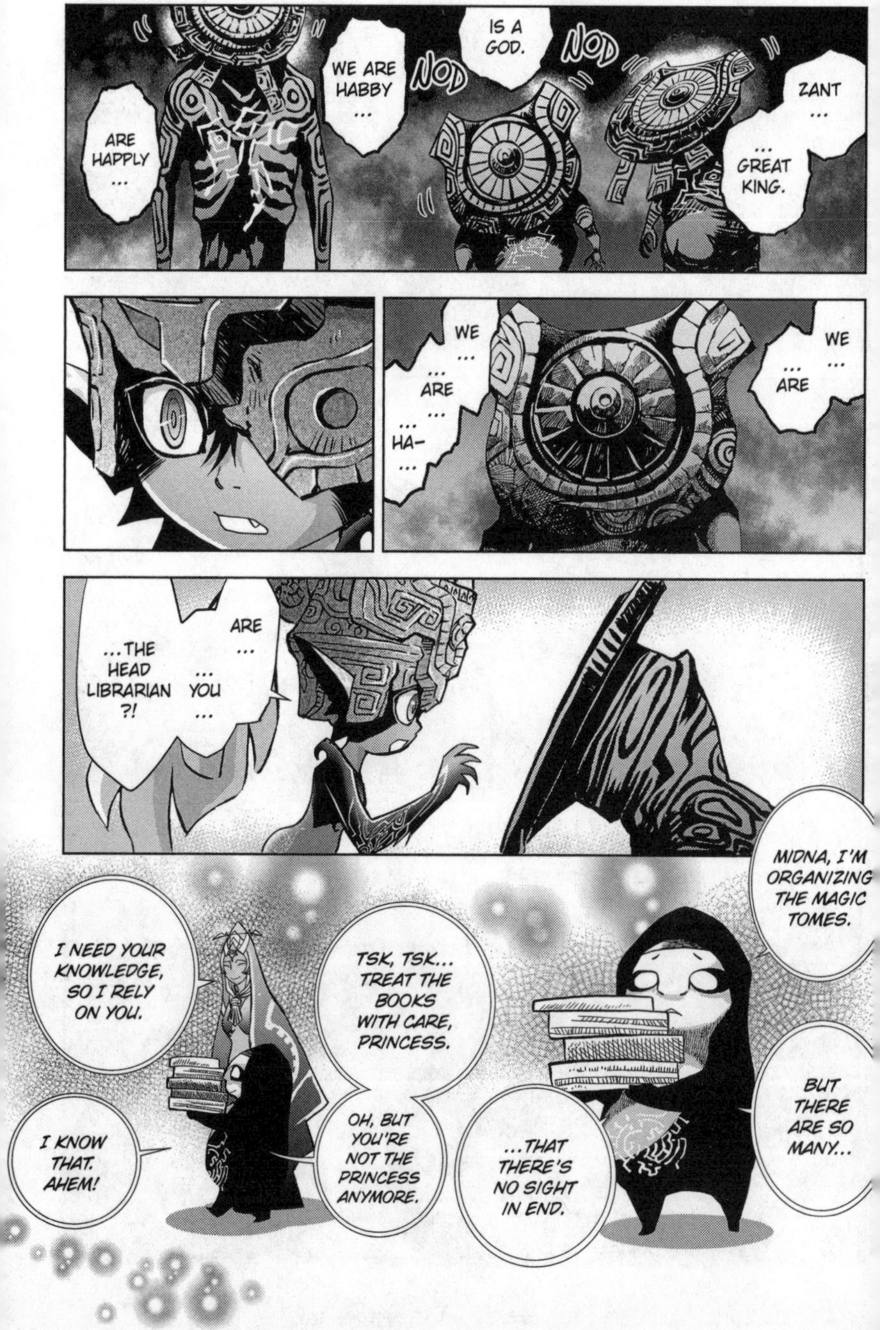
ZANT ... ... GREAT KING.
NOD
IS A GOD.
NOD
WE ARE HABBY ...
ARE HAPPLY ...
WE ... ... ARE
WE ... ... ARE ... ... HA- ...
ARE ... ... YOU ...
...THE HEAD LIBRARIAN ?!
MIDNA, I'M ORGANIZING THE MAGIC TOMES.
BUT THERE ARE SO MANY...
...THAT THERE'S NO SIGHT IN END.
TSK, TSK... TREAT THE BOOKS WITH CARE, PRINCESS.
OH, BUT YOU'RE NOT THE PRINCESS ANYMORE.
I NEED YOUR KNOWLEDGE, SO I RELY ON YOU.
I KNOW THAT. AHEM!

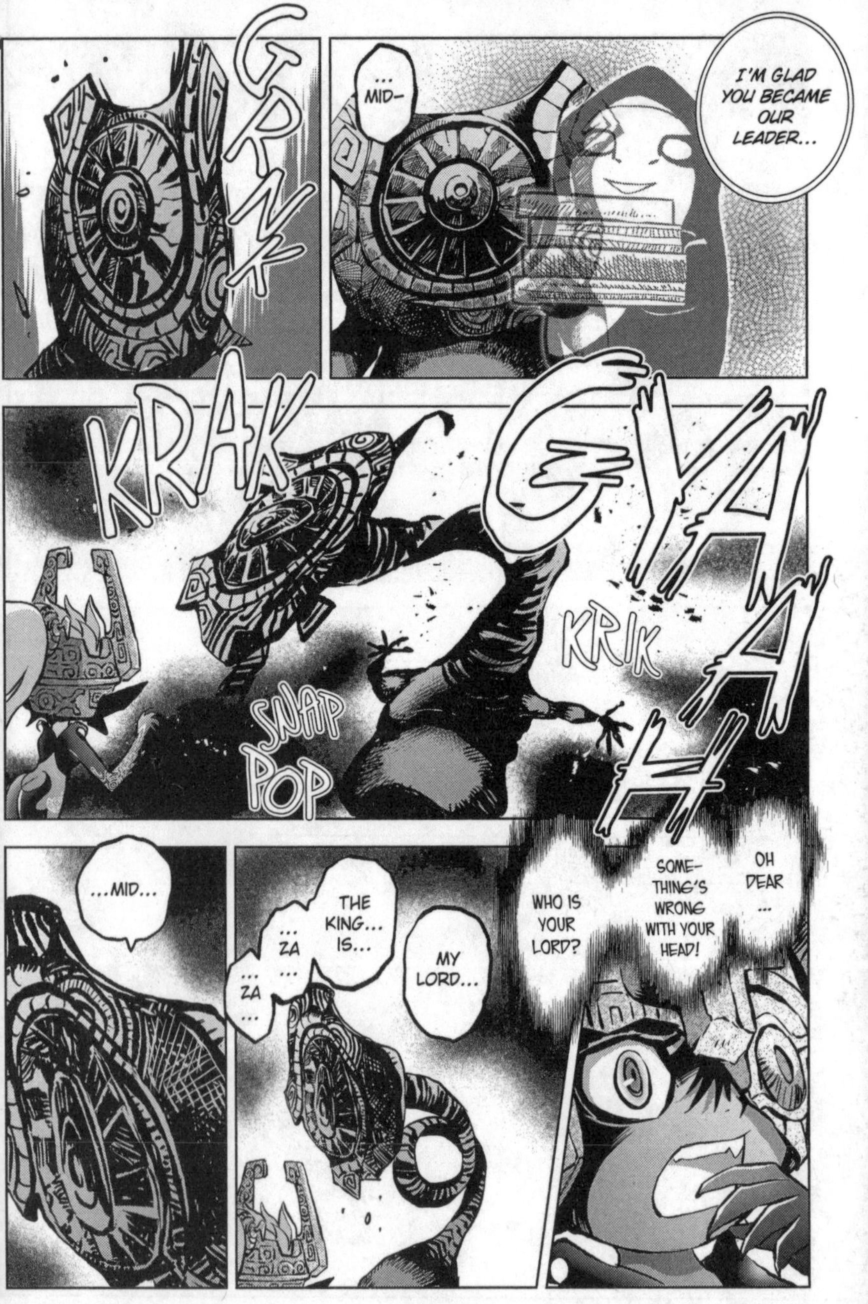
I'M GLAD YOU BECAME OUR LEADER...
... MID-
GRNK
GYAAH
KRIK
KRAK
SNAP
POP
OH DEAR ...
SOME-THING'S WRONG WITH YOUR HEAD!
WHO IS YOUR LORD?
MY LORD...
THE KING... IS...
... ZA ...
... ZA ...
...MID...

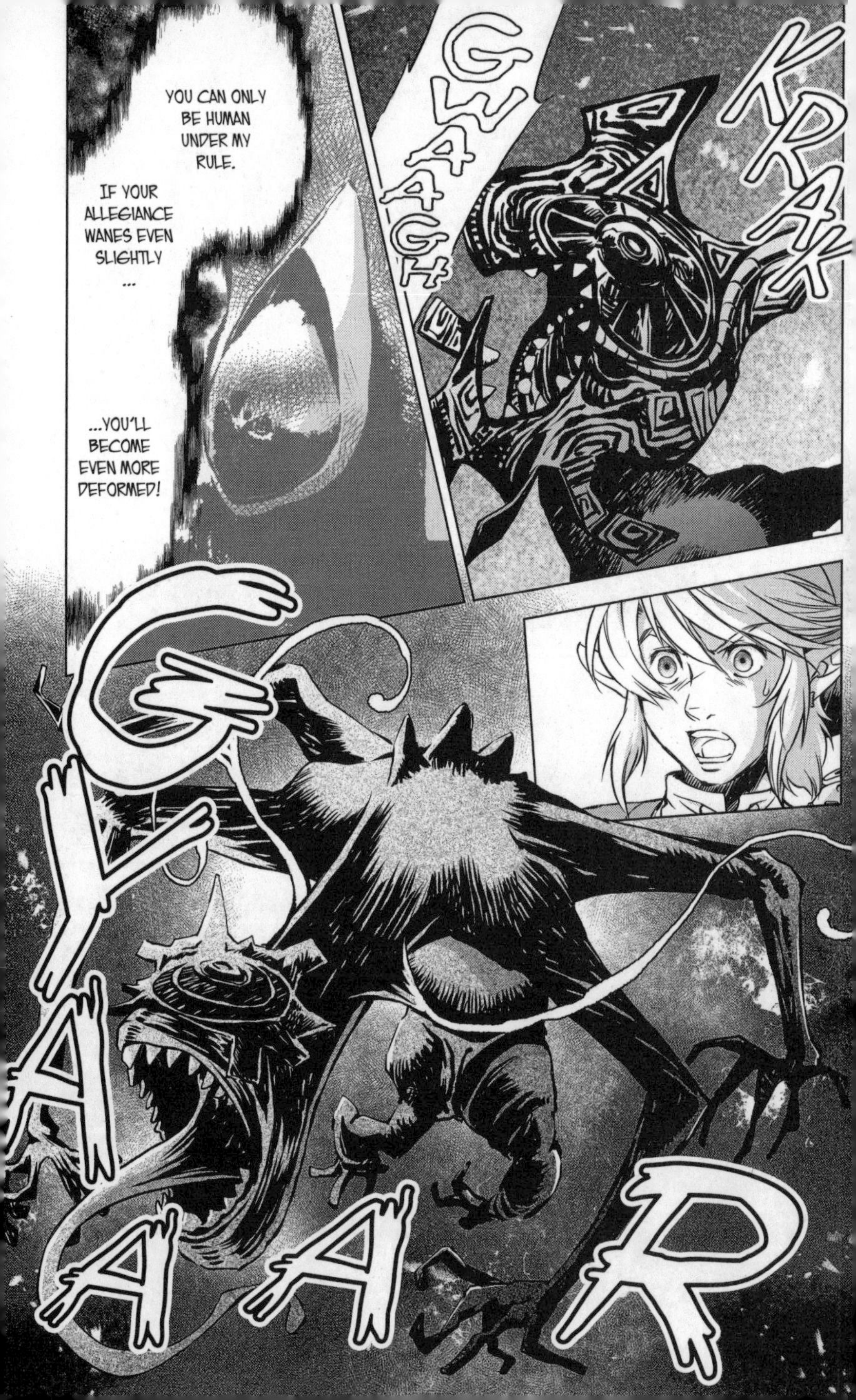
KRAK
GWAAGH
YOU CAN ONLY BE HUMAN UNDER MY RULE.
IF YOUR ALLEGIANCE WANES EVEN SLIGHTLY ...
...YOU'LL BECOME EVEN MORE DEFORMED!
GYAAAR

FORGET ME, EVERYONE! DON'T THINK!

ZANT! STOP!

STOP, PLEASE!

STOP!

I SAID DON'T THINK!

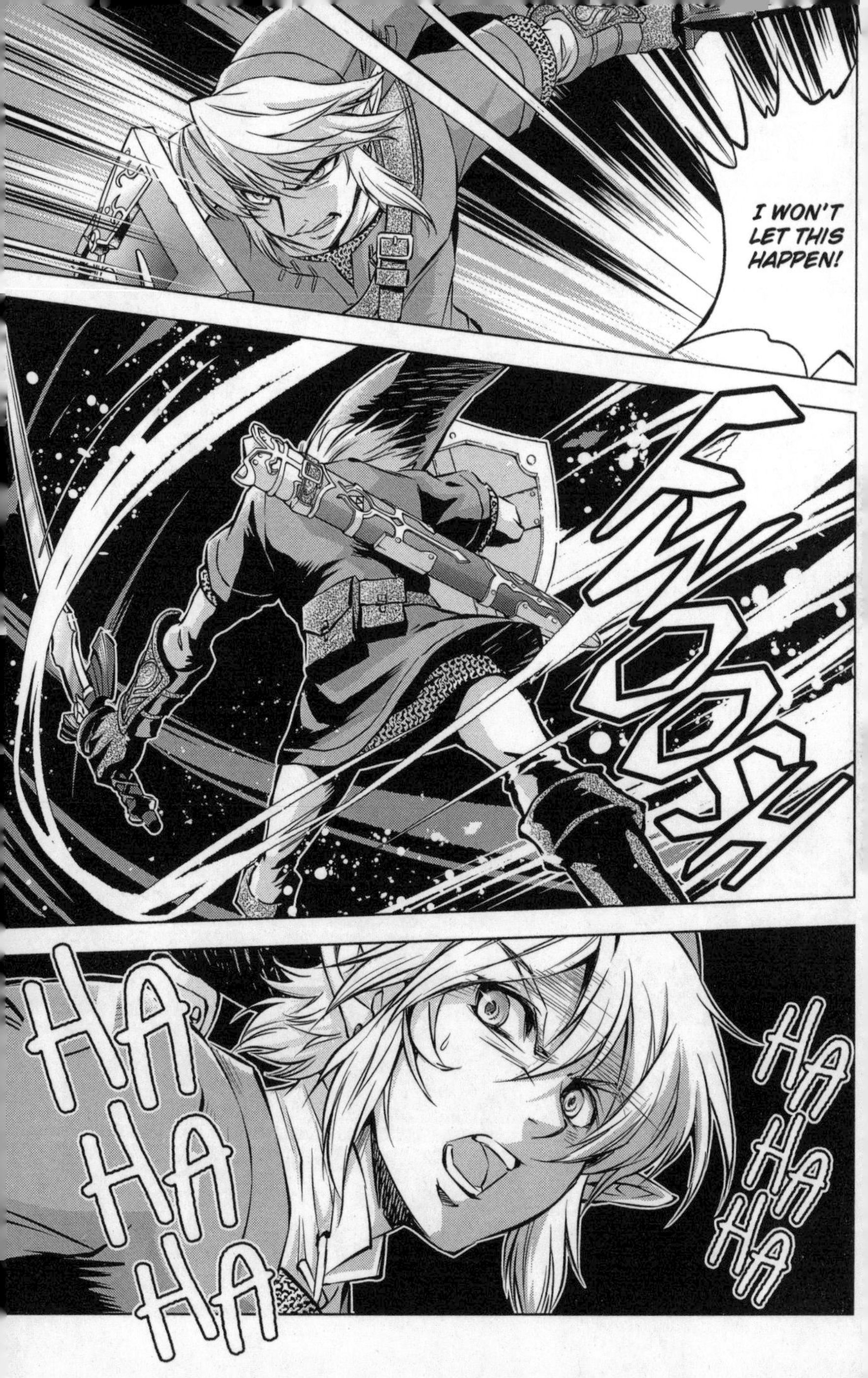
I WON'T LET THIS HAPPEN!
VWOOSH
HA HA HA HA HA
HA HA HA

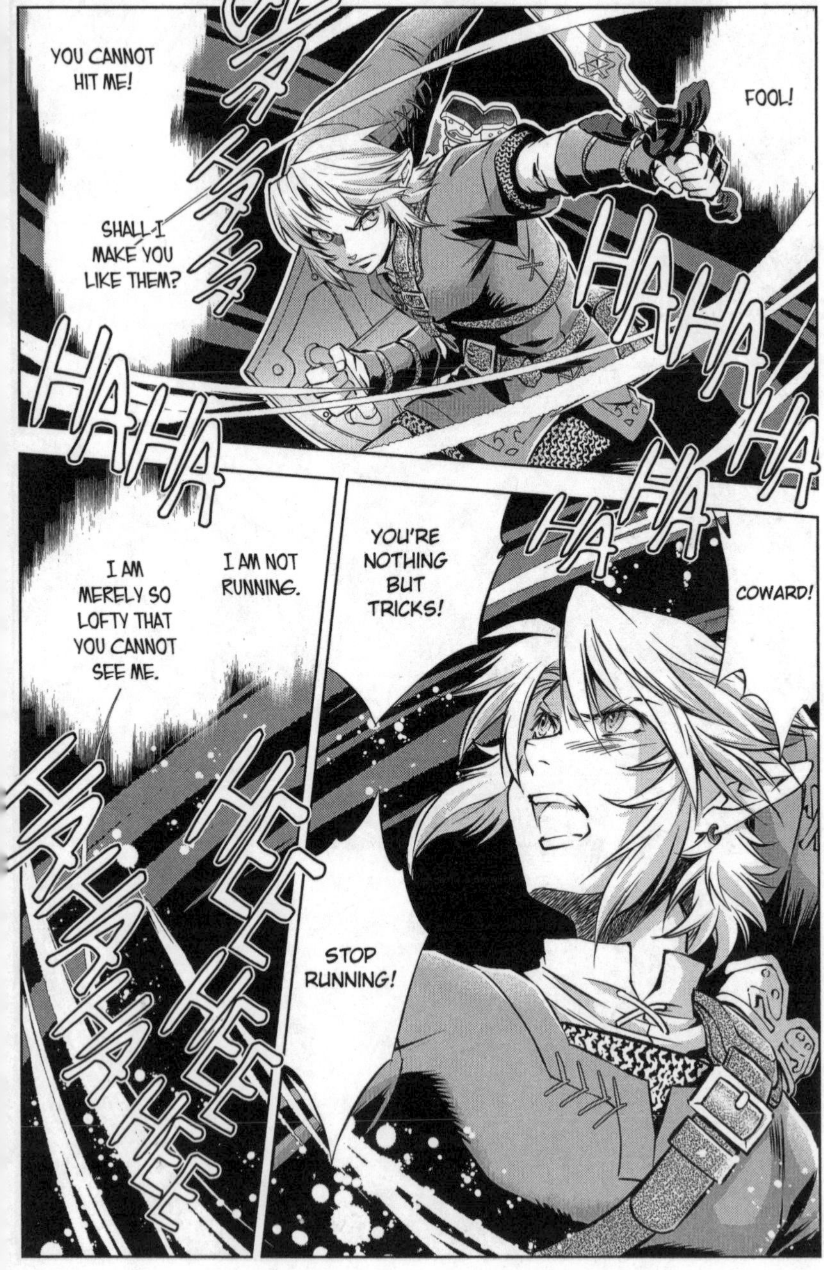
FOOL!
YOU CANNOT HIT ME!
GYAHAHAHA
SHALL I MAKE YOU LIKE THEM?
HAHAHAHA
HAHAHA
HAHAHA
COWARD!
YOU'RE NOTHING BUT TRICKS!
STOP RUNNING!
I AM NOT RUNNING.
I AM MERELY SO LOFTY THAT YOU CANNOT SEE ME.
HEE HEE HEE HEE
HAHAHAHAHA

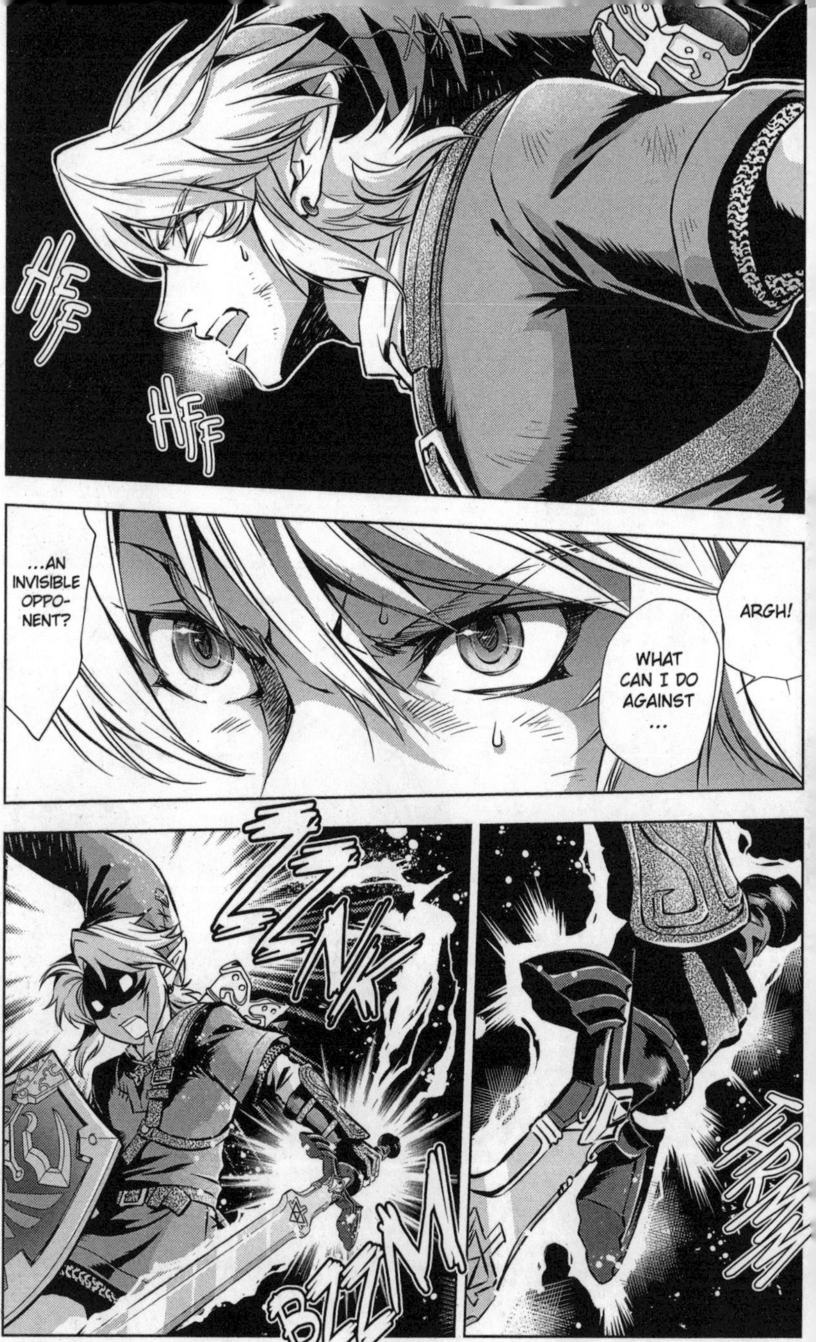
HFF
HFF
ARGH!
WHAT CAN I DO AGAINST ...
...AN INVISIBLE OPPO-NENT?

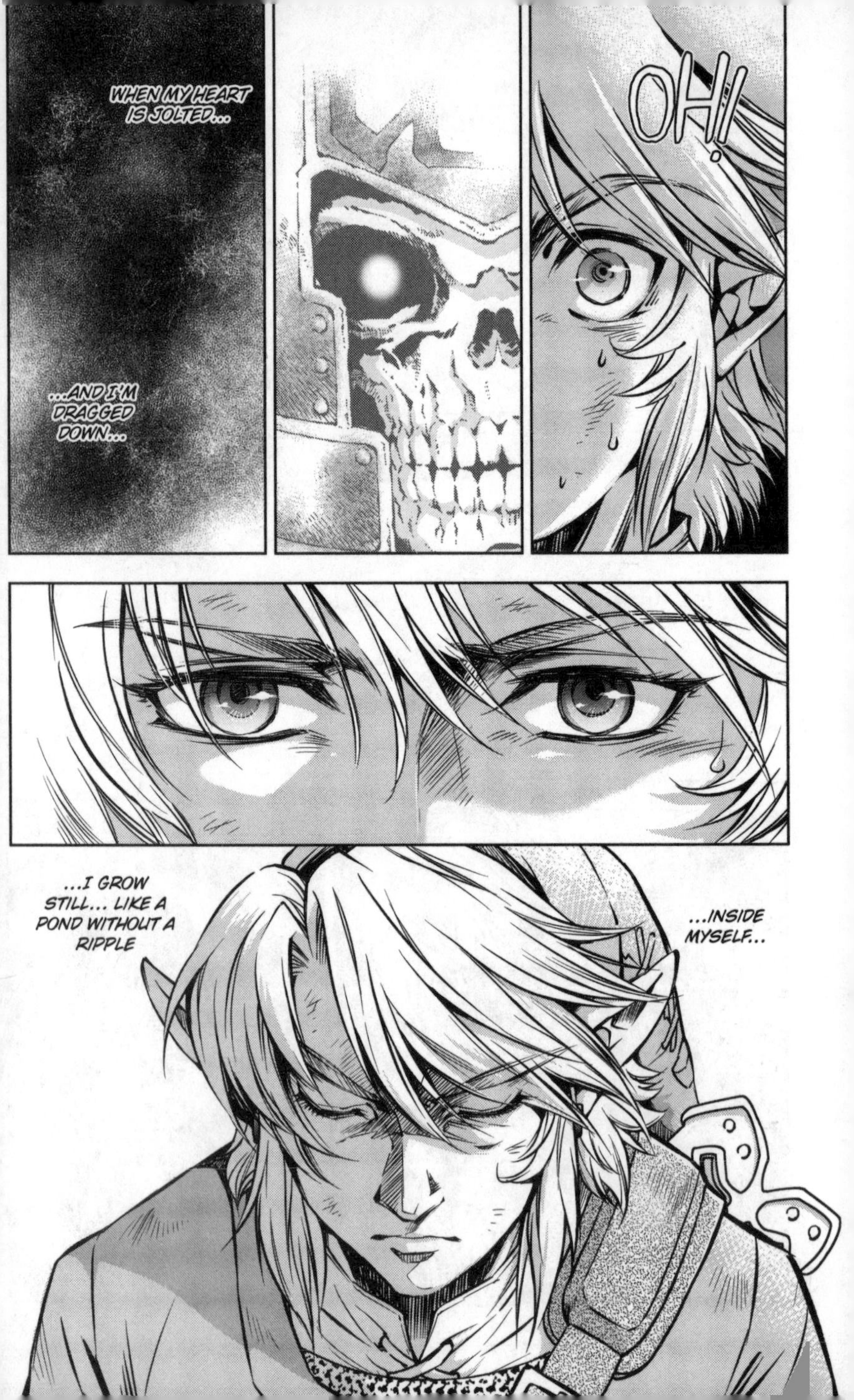
OH!
WHEN MY HEART IS JOLTED...
...AND I'M DRAGGED DOWN...
...I GROW STILL... LIKE A POND WITHOUT A RIPPLE
...INSIDE MYSELF...

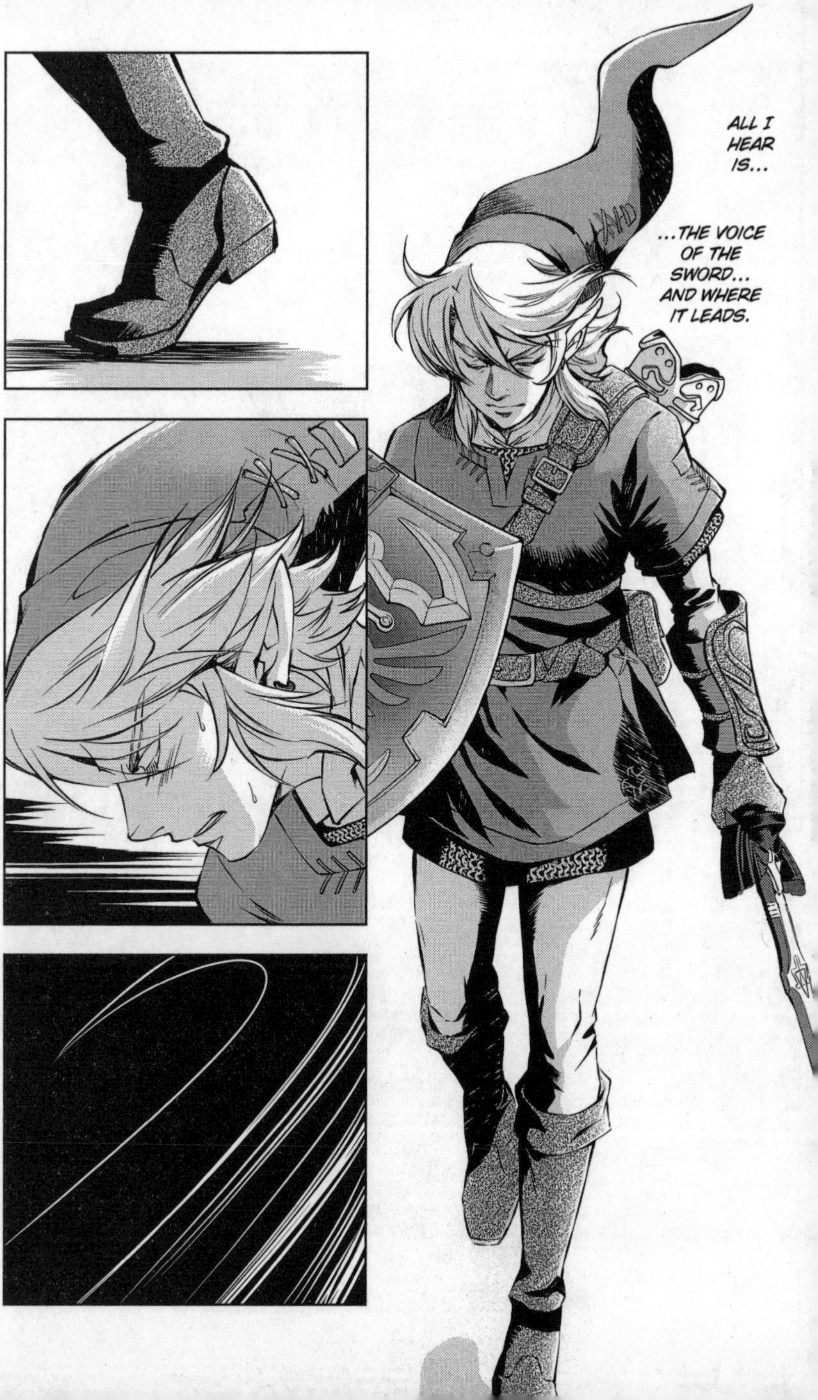
ALL I HEAR IS...
...THE VOICE OF THE SWORD... AND WHERE IT LEADS.

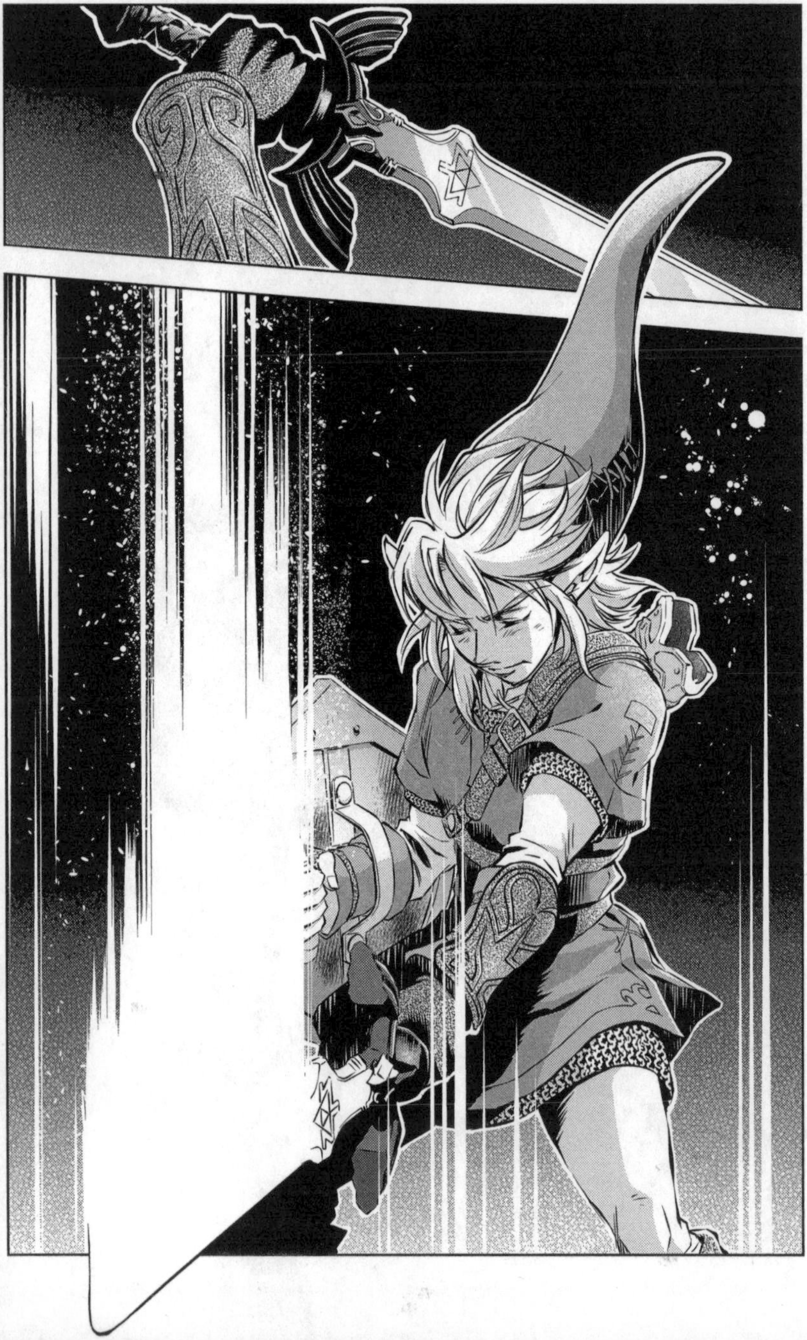

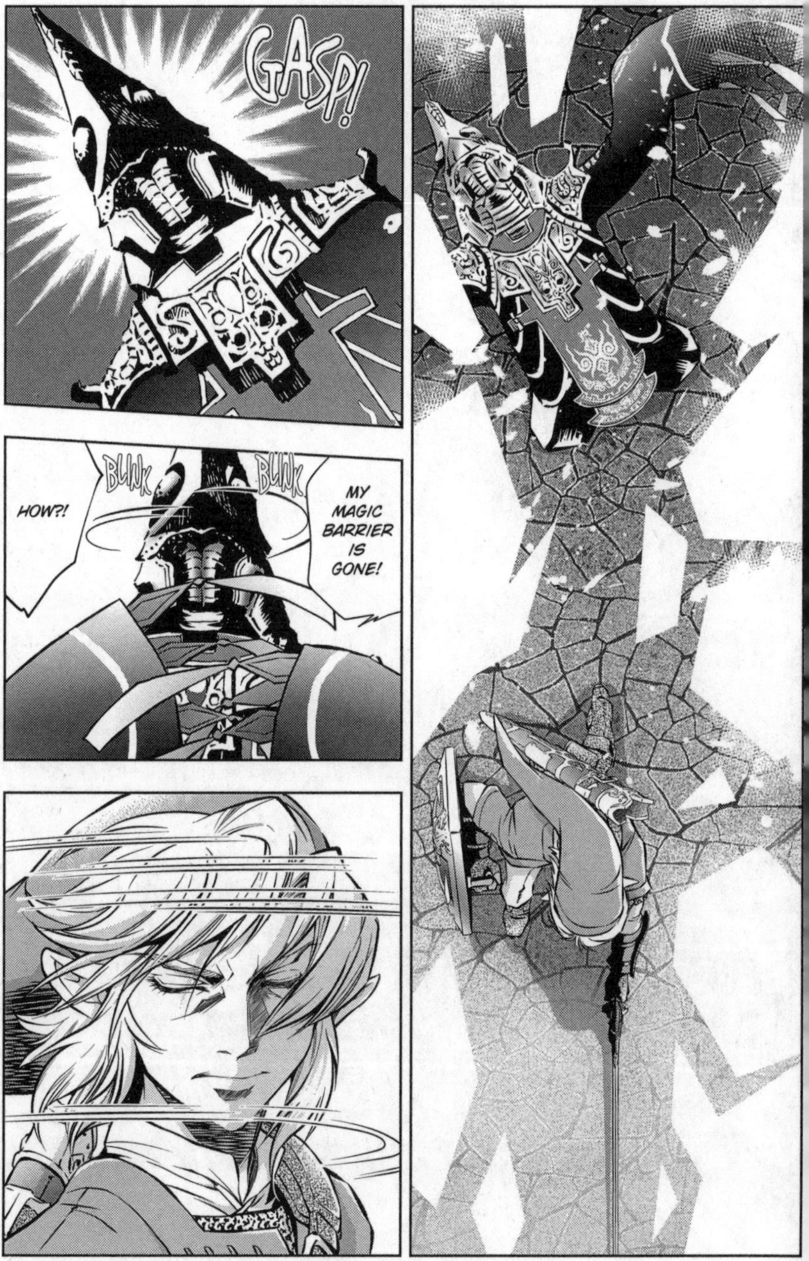
GASP!
BLINK
BLINK
MY MAGIC BARRIER IS GONE!
HOW?!

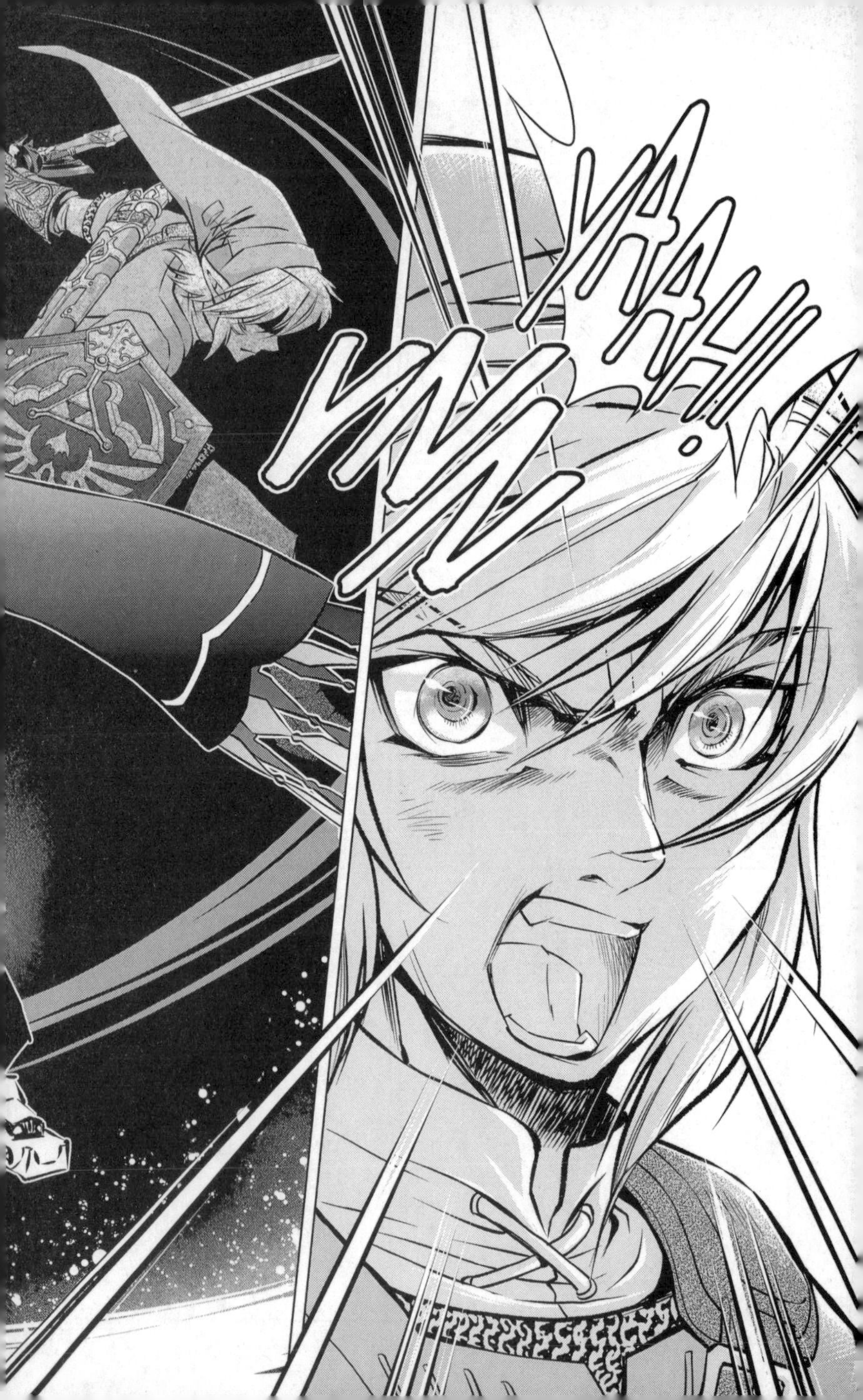
YAAH!!

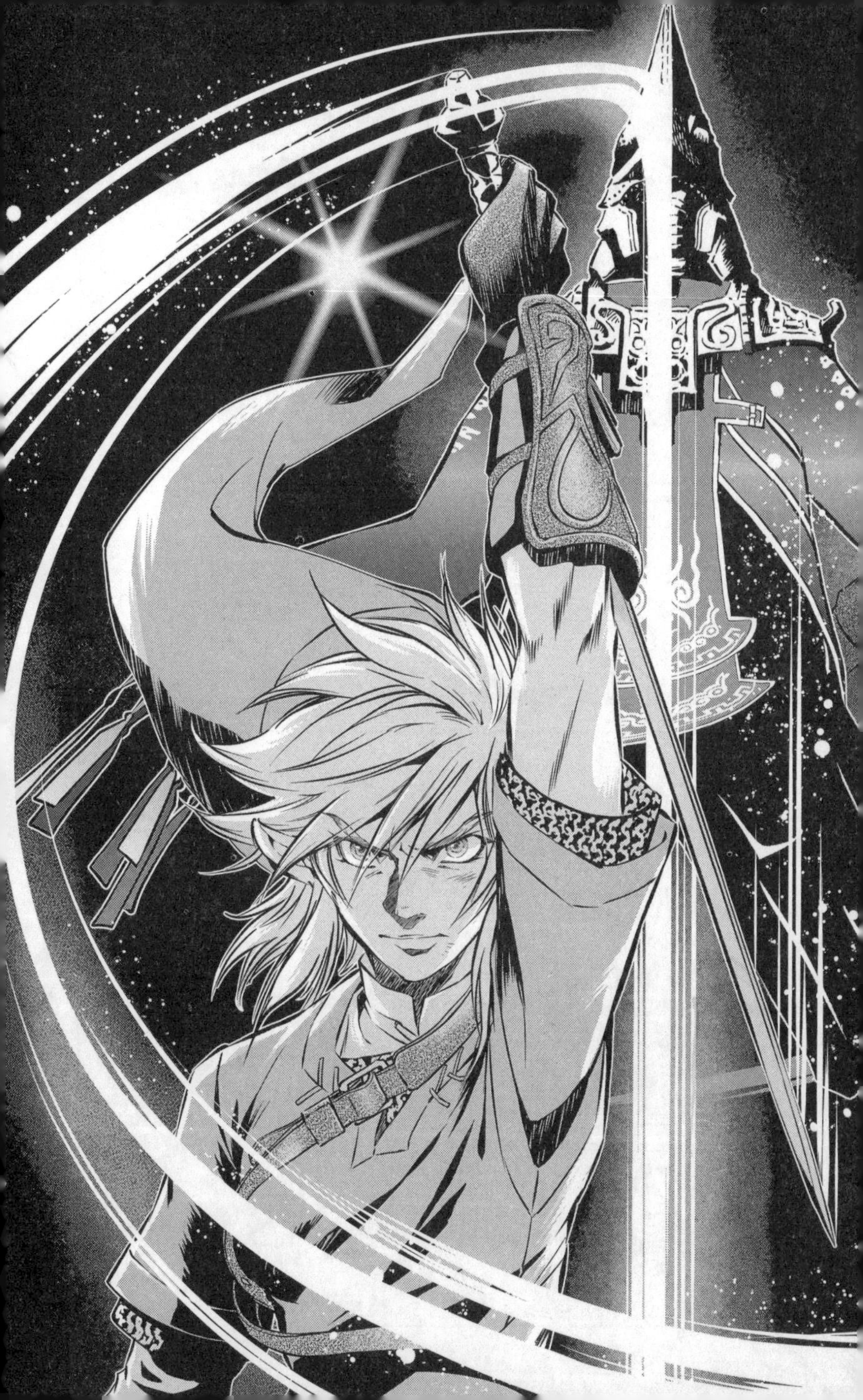

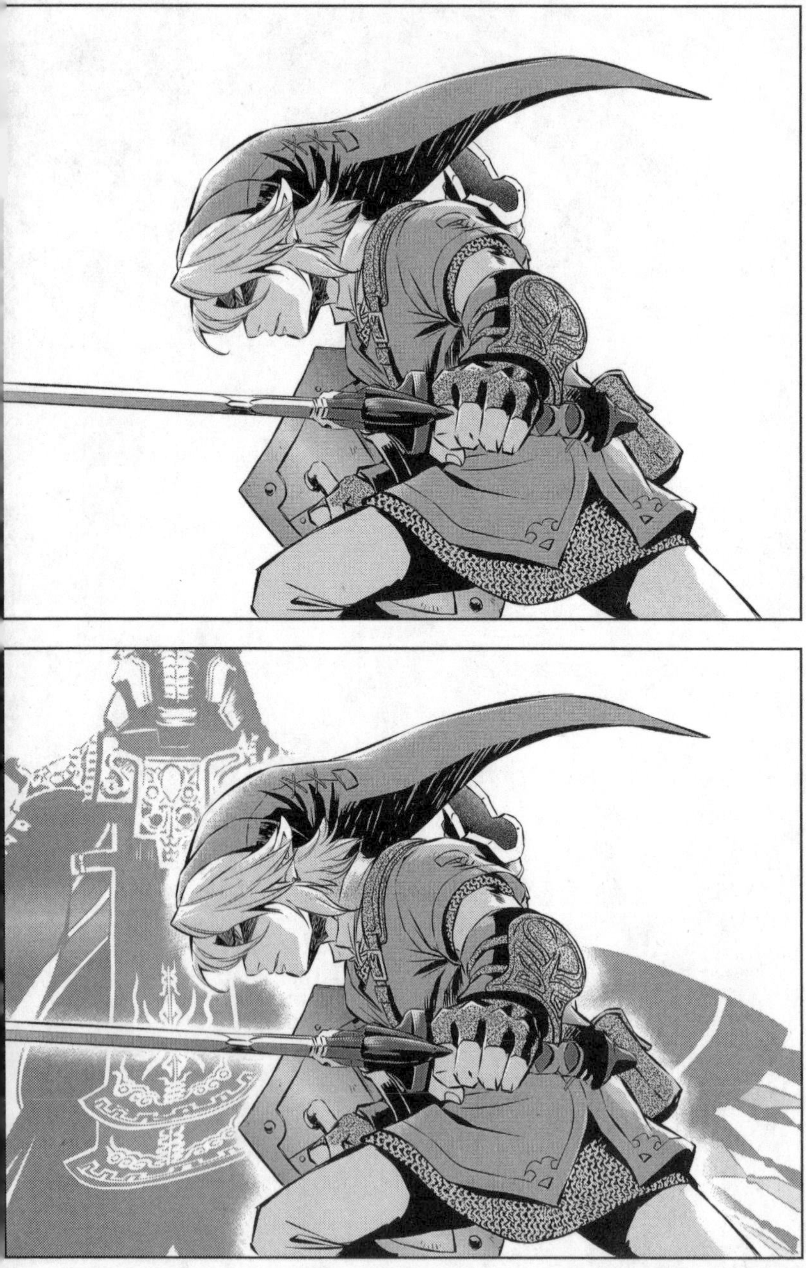

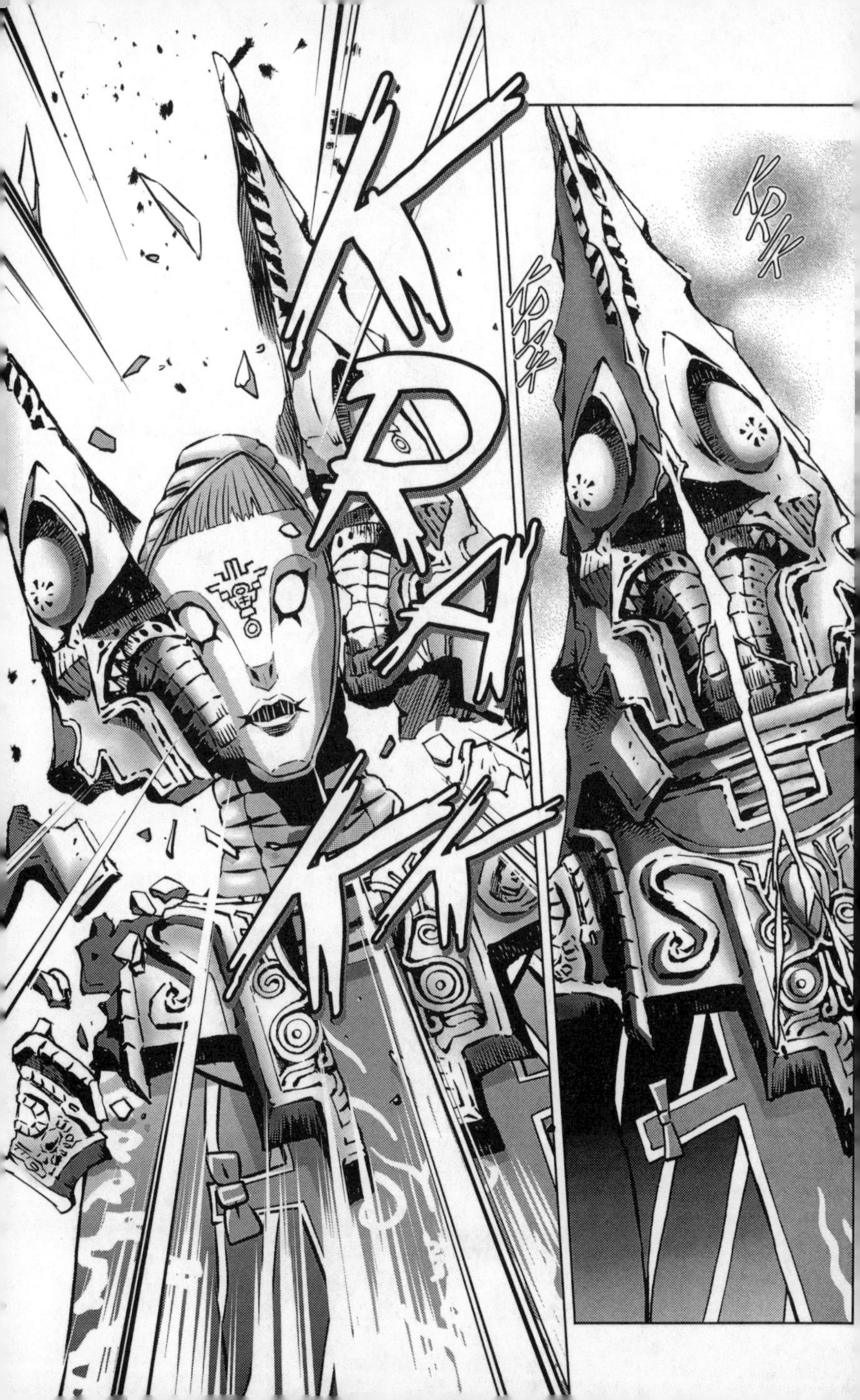
KRIK
KRAK
KRAK

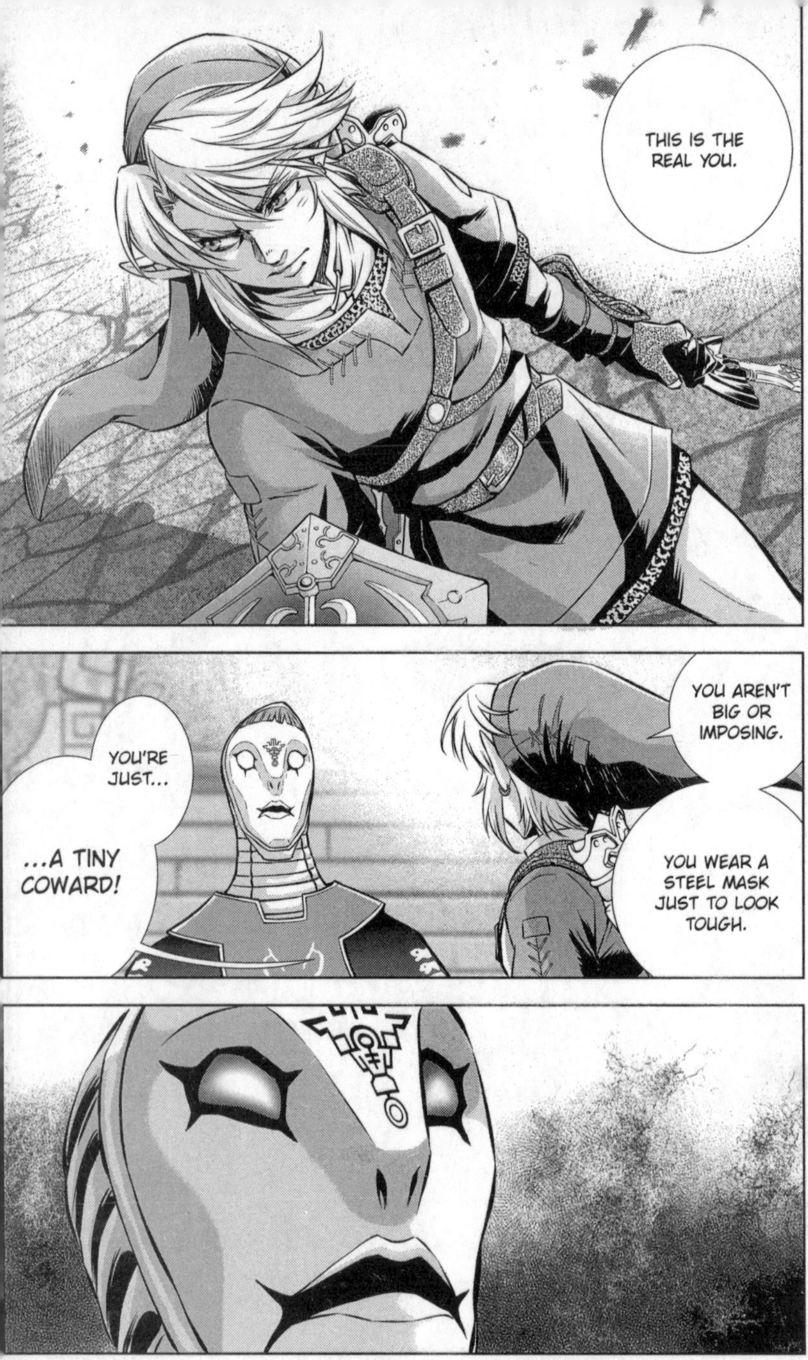
THIS IS THE REAL YOU.
YOU AREN'T BIG OR IMPOSING.
YOU WEAR A STEEL MASK JUST TO LOOK TOUGH.
YOU'RE JUST...
...A TINY COWARD!

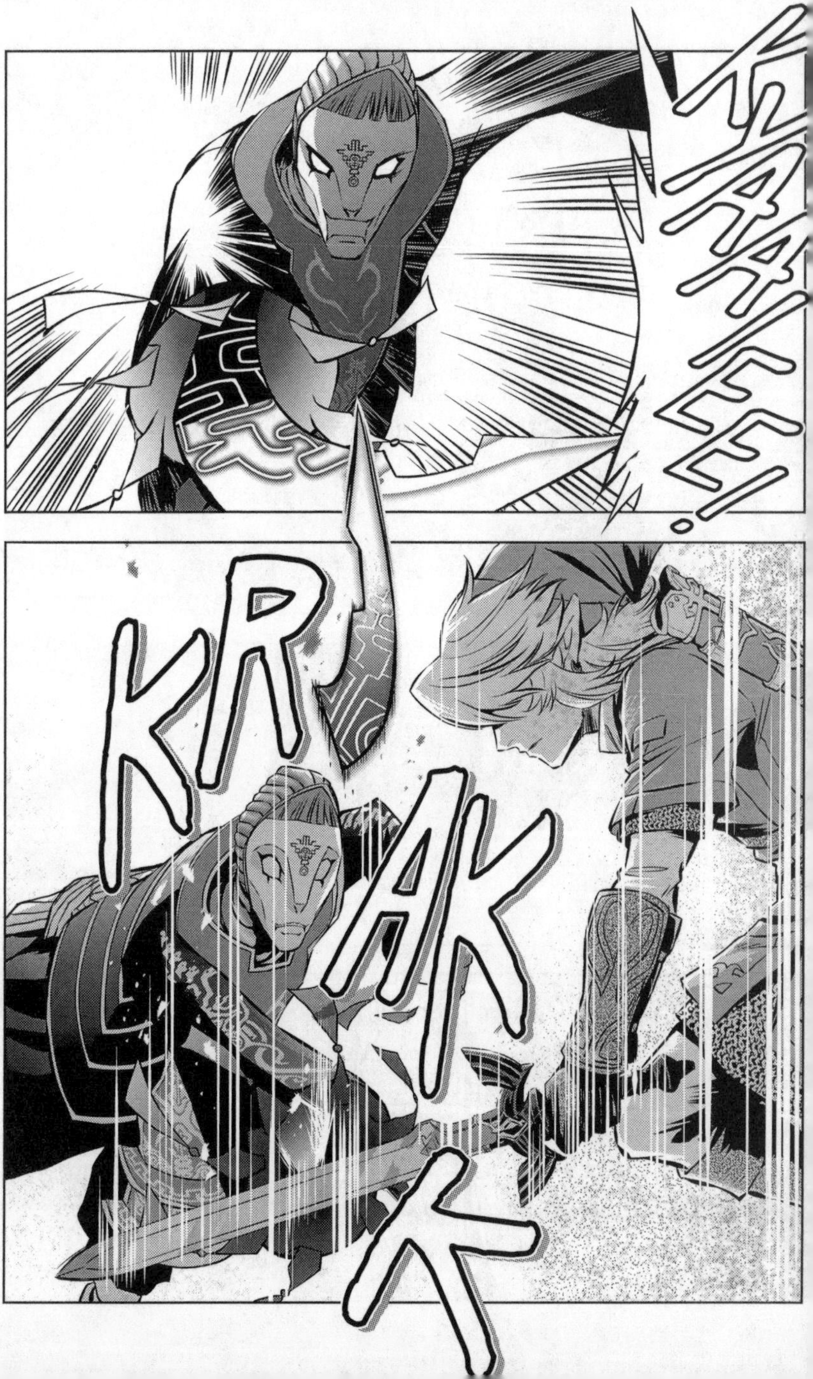
KYAAHEEE!!
KRAKK

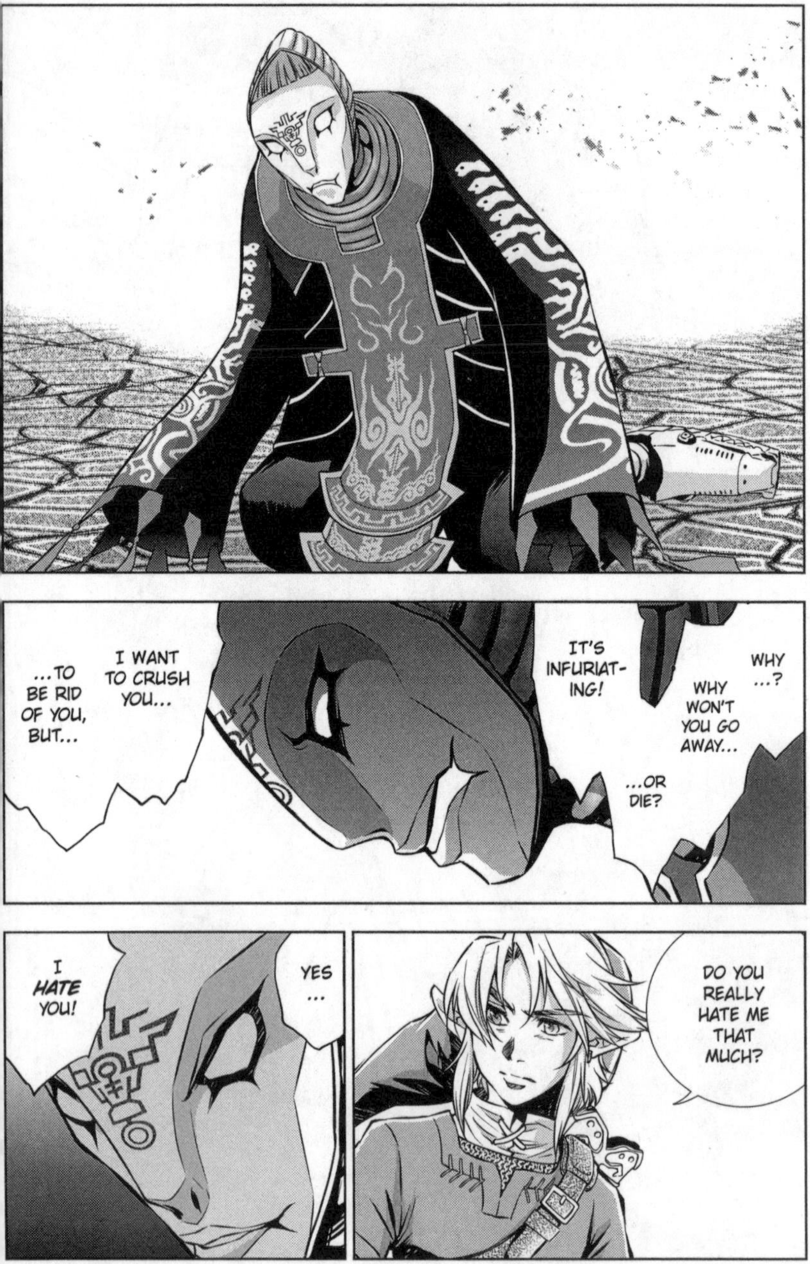
WHY ...?
WHY WON'T YOU GO AWAY...
...OR DIE?
IT'S INFURIAT-ING!
I WANT TO CRUSH YOU...
...TO BE RID OF YOU, BUT...
DO YOU REALLY HATE ME THAT MUCH?
YES ...
I *HATE* YOU!

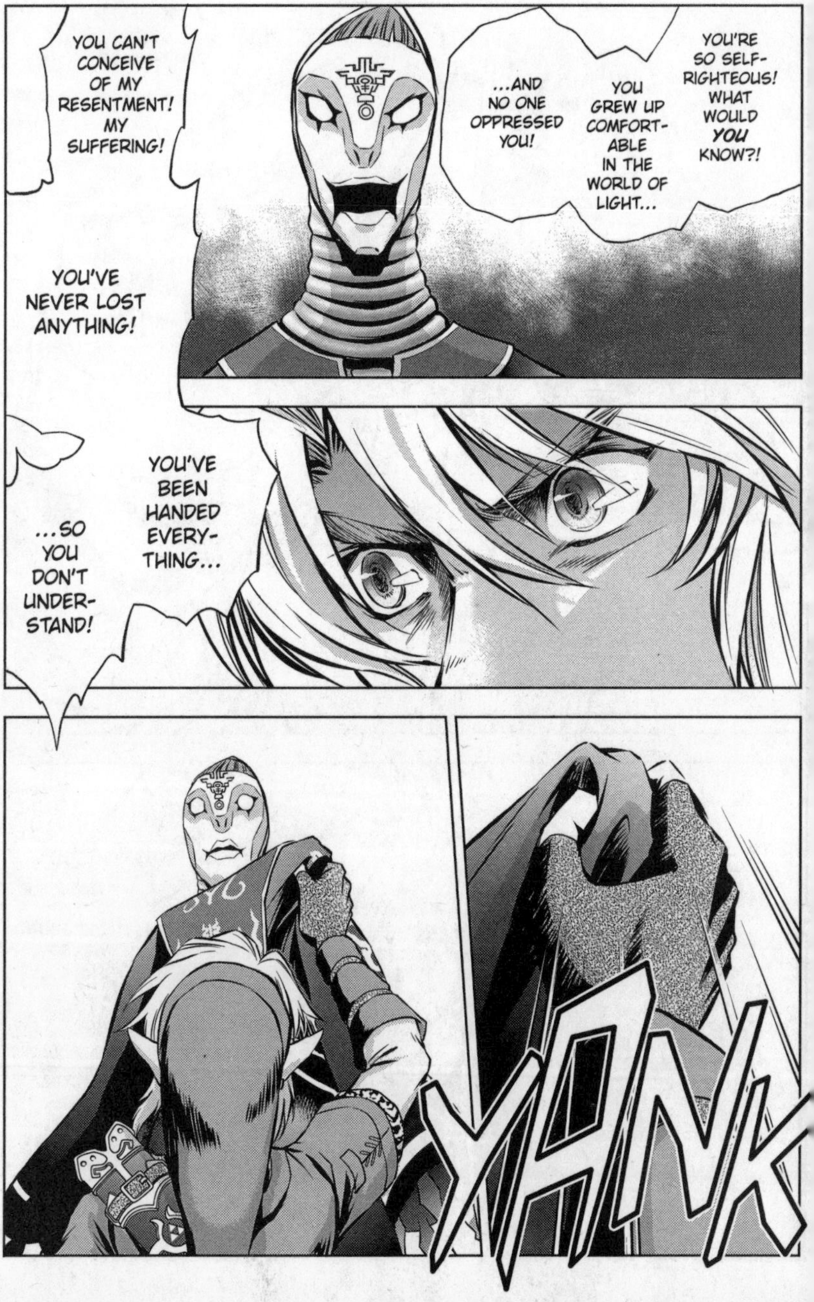
YOU'RE SO SELF-RIGHTEOUS! WHAT WOULD *YOU* KNOW?!
YOU GREW UP COMFORTABLE IN THE WORLD OF LIGHT...
...AND NO ONE OPPRESSED YOU!
YOU CAN'T CONCEIVE OF MY RESENTMENT! MY SUFFERING!
YOU'VE NEVER LOST ANYTHING!
YOU'VE BEEN HANDED EVERYTHING...
...SO YOU DON'T UNDERSTAND!
YANK

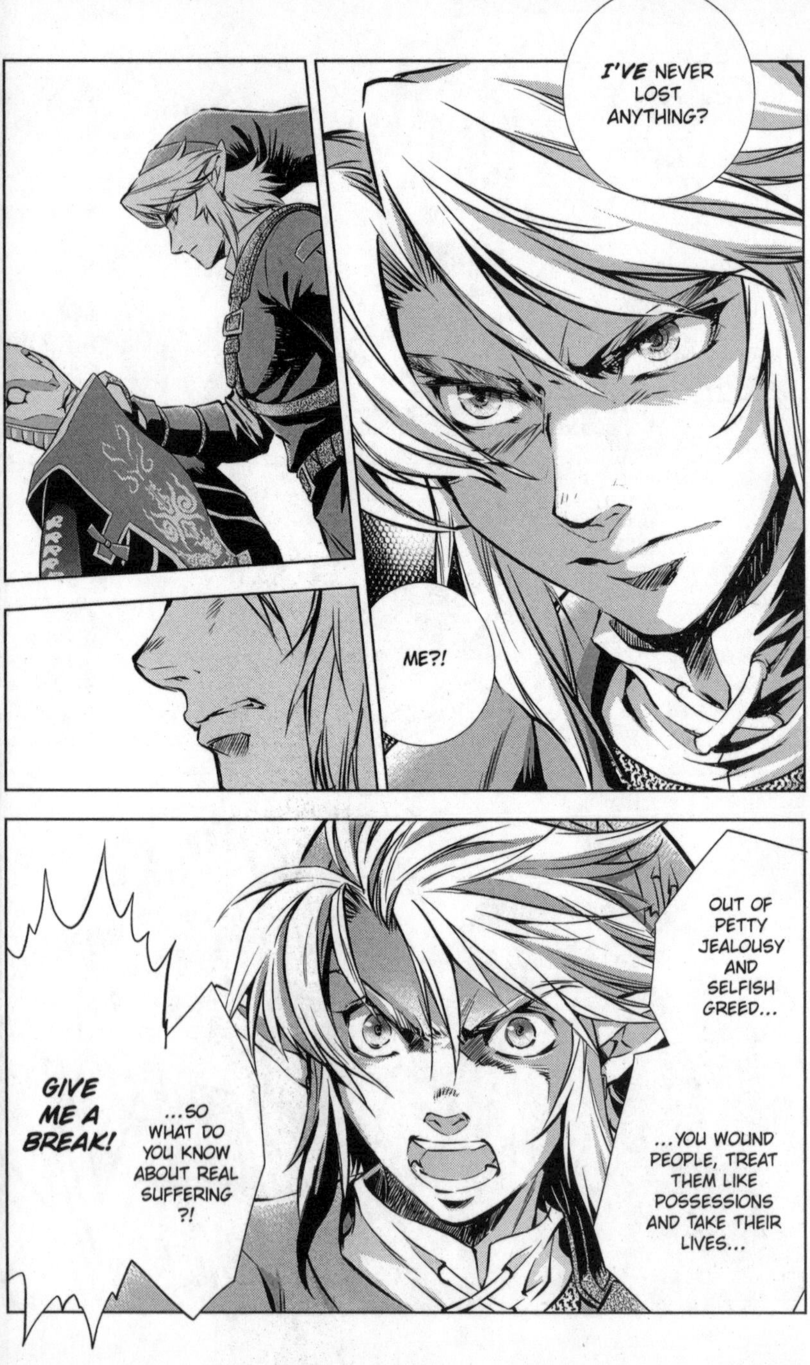
I'VE NEVER LOST ANYTHING?
ME?!
OUT OF PETTY JEALOUSY AND SELFISH GREED...
...YOU WOUND PEOPLE, TREAT THEM LIKE POSSESSIONS AND TAKE THEIR LIVES...
...SO WHAT DO YOU KNOW ABOUT REAL SUFFERING?!
GIVE ME A BREAK!

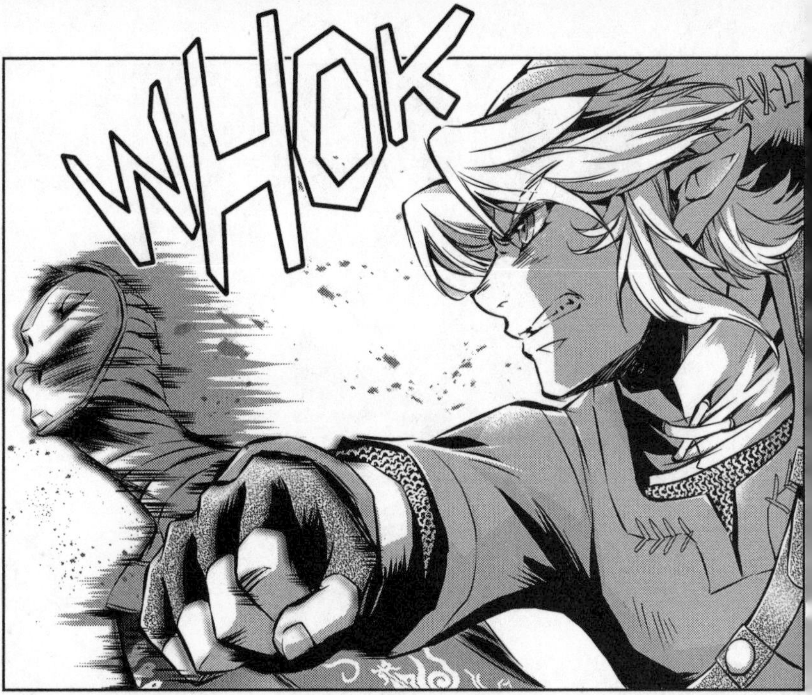
WHOK

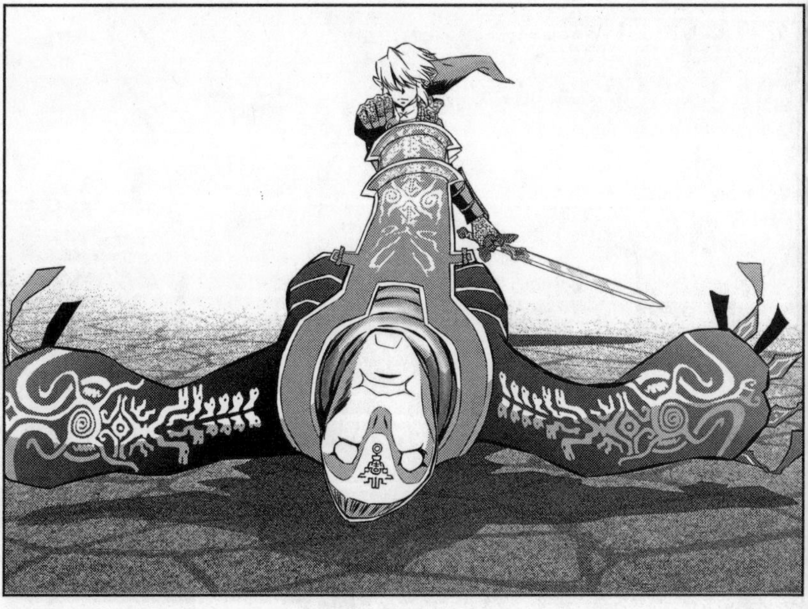

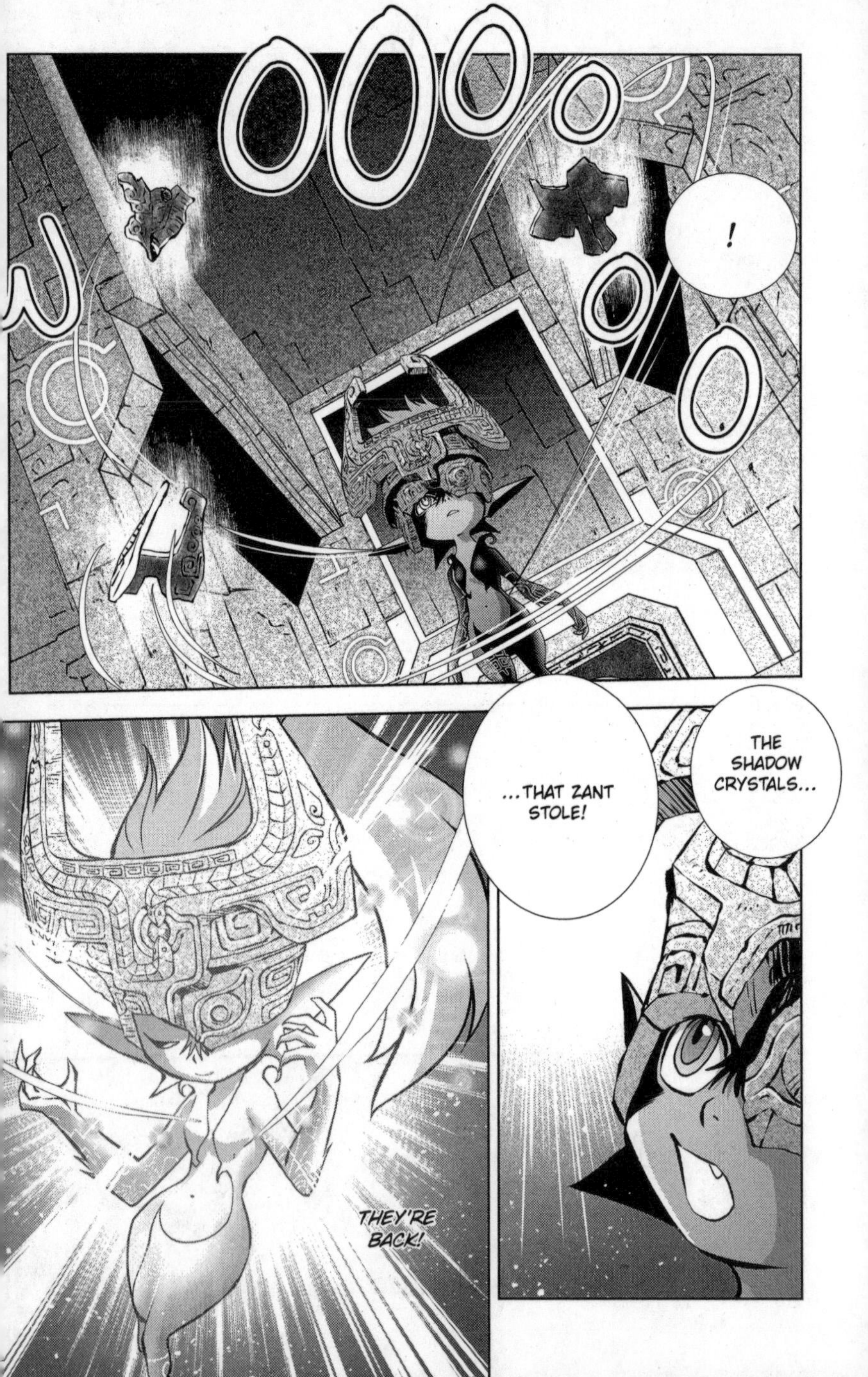
!
THE SHADOW CRYSTALS...
...THAT ZANT STOLE!
THEY'RE BACK!

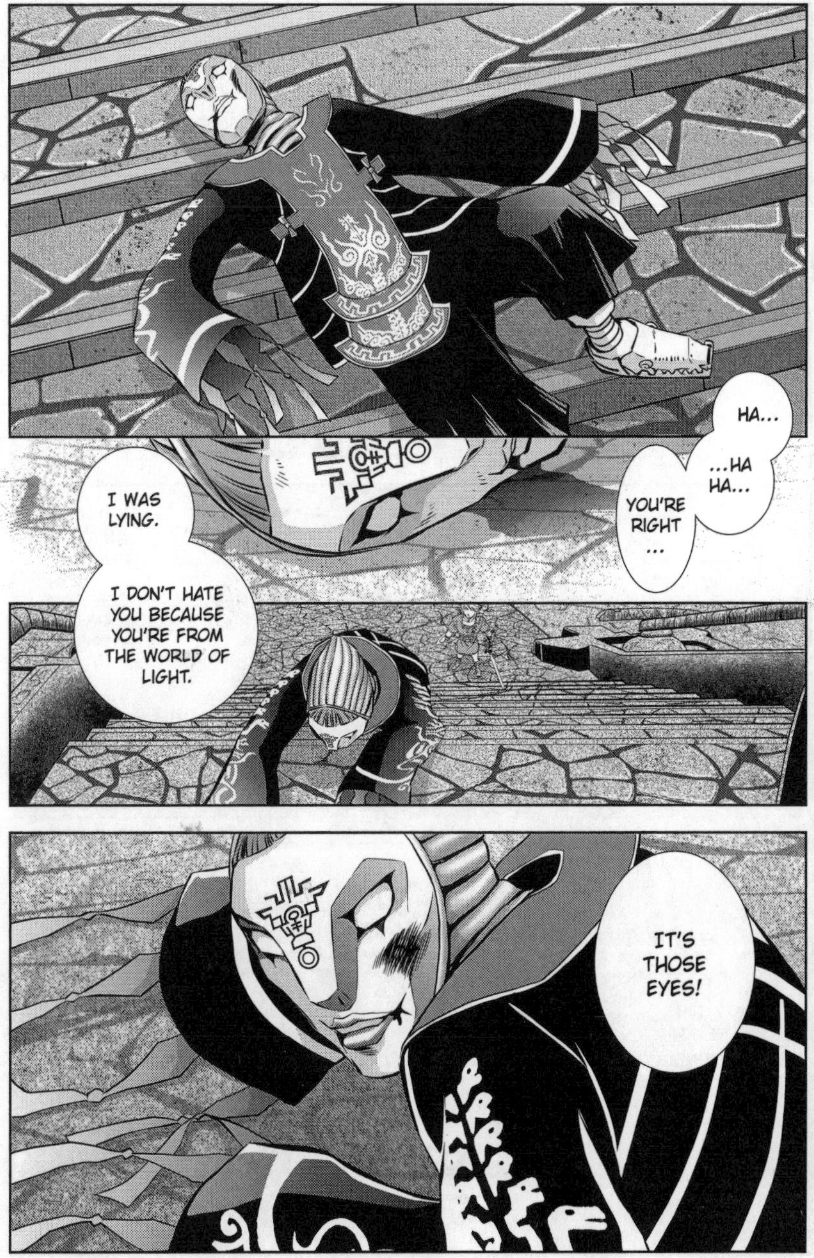
HA...
...HA HA...
YOU'RE RIGHT ...
I WAS LYING.
I DON'T HATE YOU BECAUSE YOU'RE FROM THE WORLD OF LIGHT.
IT'S THOSE EYES!

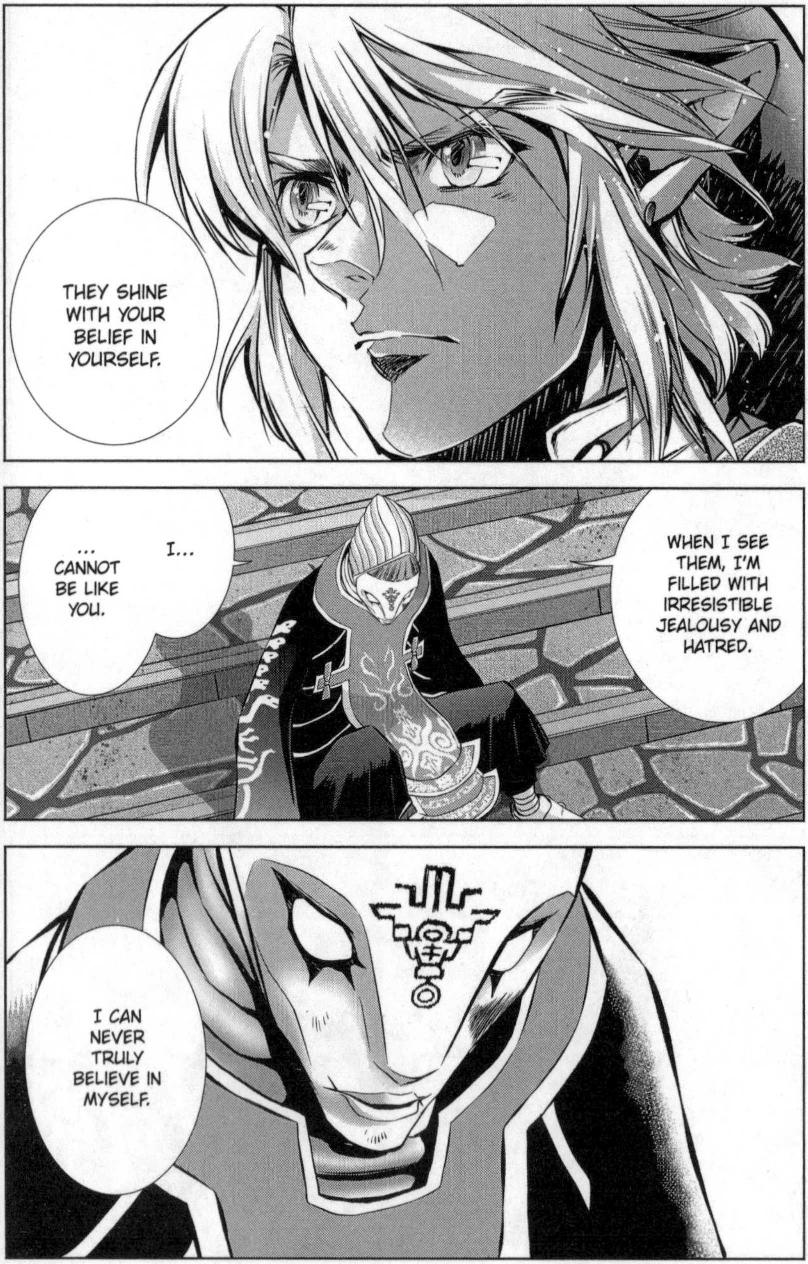
THEY SHINE WITH YOUR BELIEF IN YOURSELF.
WHEN I SEE THEM, I'M FILLED WITH IRRESISTIBLE JEALOUSY AND HATRED.
I...
... CANNOT BE LIKE YOU.
I CAN NEVER TRULY BELIEVE IN MYSELF.

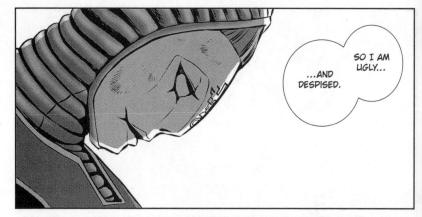

SO I AM UGLY...

...AND DESPISED.

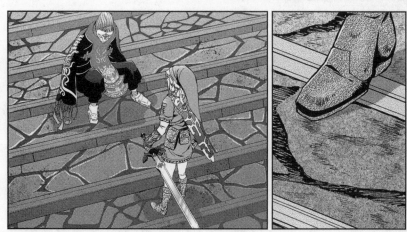

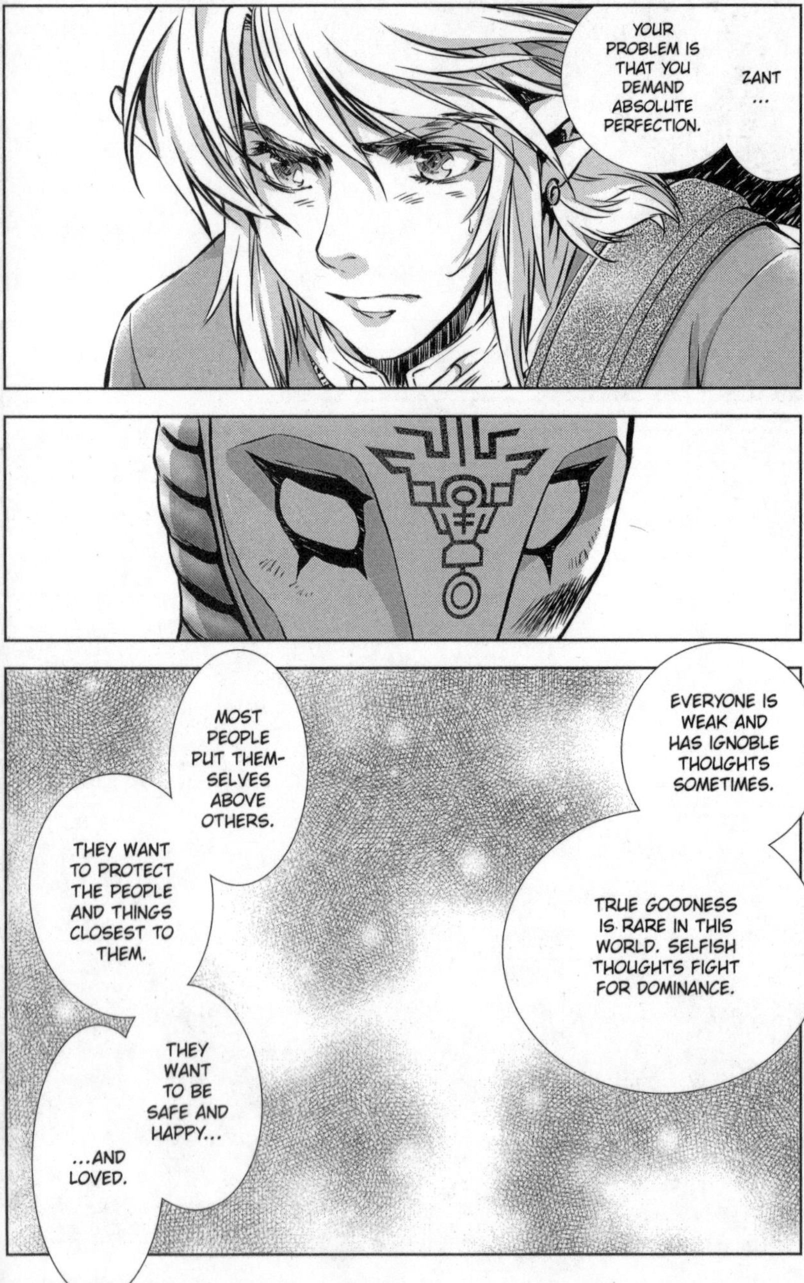
ZANT ...
YOUR PROBLEM IS THAT YOU DEMAND ABSOLUTE PERFECTION.
EVERYONE IS WEAK AND HAS IGNOBLE THOUGHTS SOMETIMES.
TRUE GOODNESS IS RARE IN THIS WORLD. SELFISH THOUGHTS FIGHT FOR DOMINANCE.
MOST PEOPLE PUT THEM-SELVES ABOVE OTHERS.
THEY WANT TO PROTECT THE PEOPLE AND THINGS CLOSEST TO THEM.
THEY WANT TO BE SAFE AND HAPPY...
...AND LOVED.

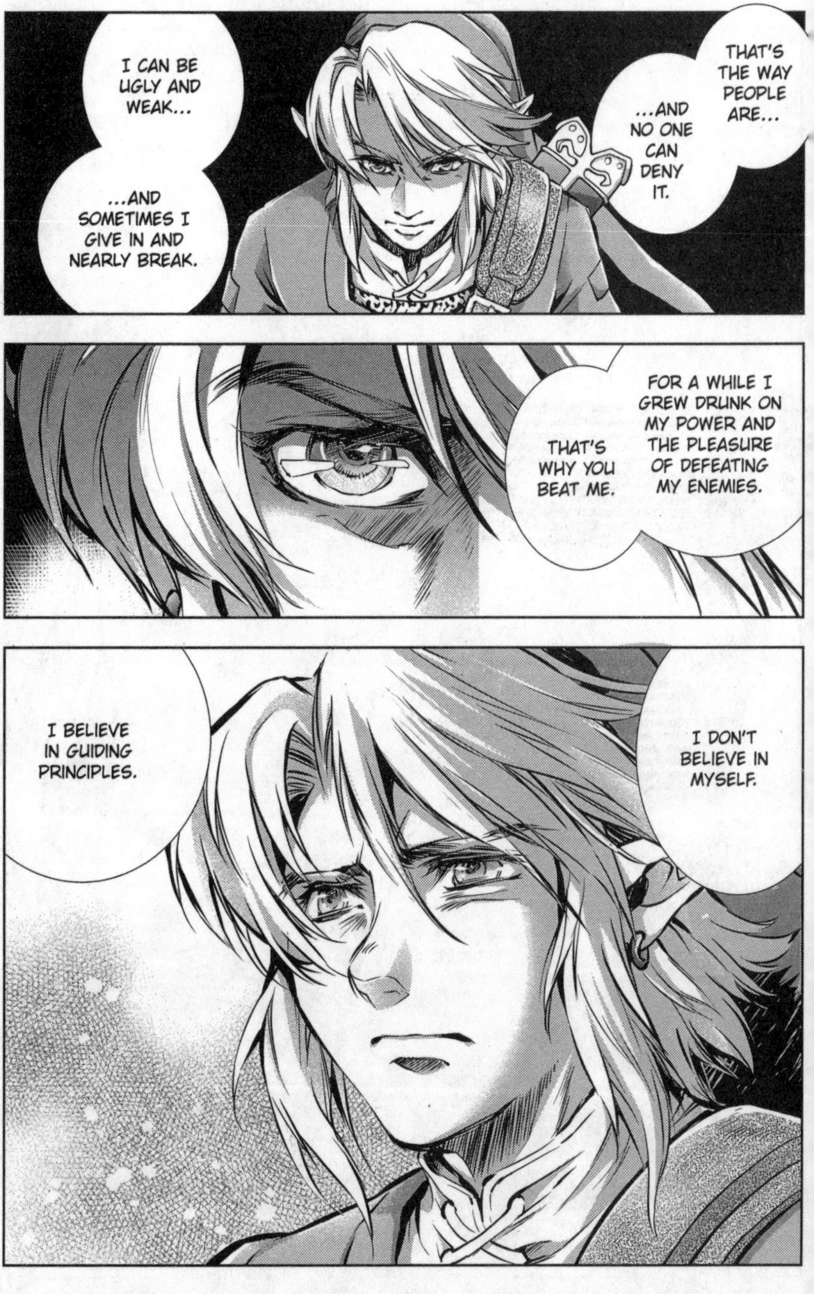
THAT'S THE WAY PEOPLE ARE...
...AND NO ONE CAN DENY IT.
I CAN BE UGLY AND WEAK...
...AND SOMETIMES I GIVE IN AND NEARLY BREAK.
FOR A WHILE I GREW DRUNK ON MY POWER AND THE PLEASURE OF DEFEATING MY ENEMIES.
THAT'S WHY YOU BEAT ME.
I DON'T BELIEVE IN MYSELF.
I BELIEVE IN GUIDING PRINCIPLES.

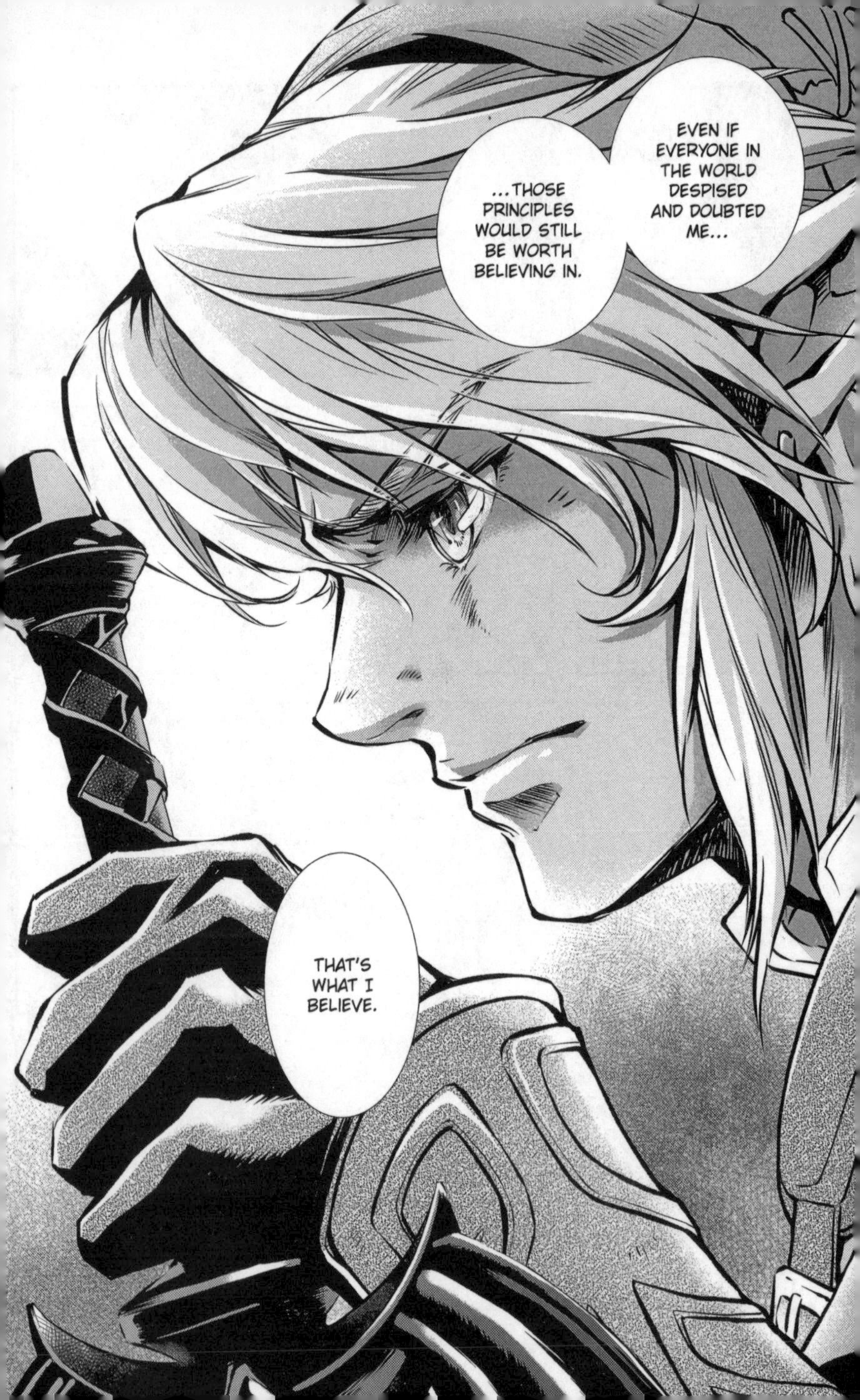
EVEN IF EVERYONE IN THE WORLD DESPISED AND DOUBTED ME...
...THOSE PRINCIPLES WOULD STILL BE WORTH BELIEVING IN.
THAT'S WHAT I BELIEVE.

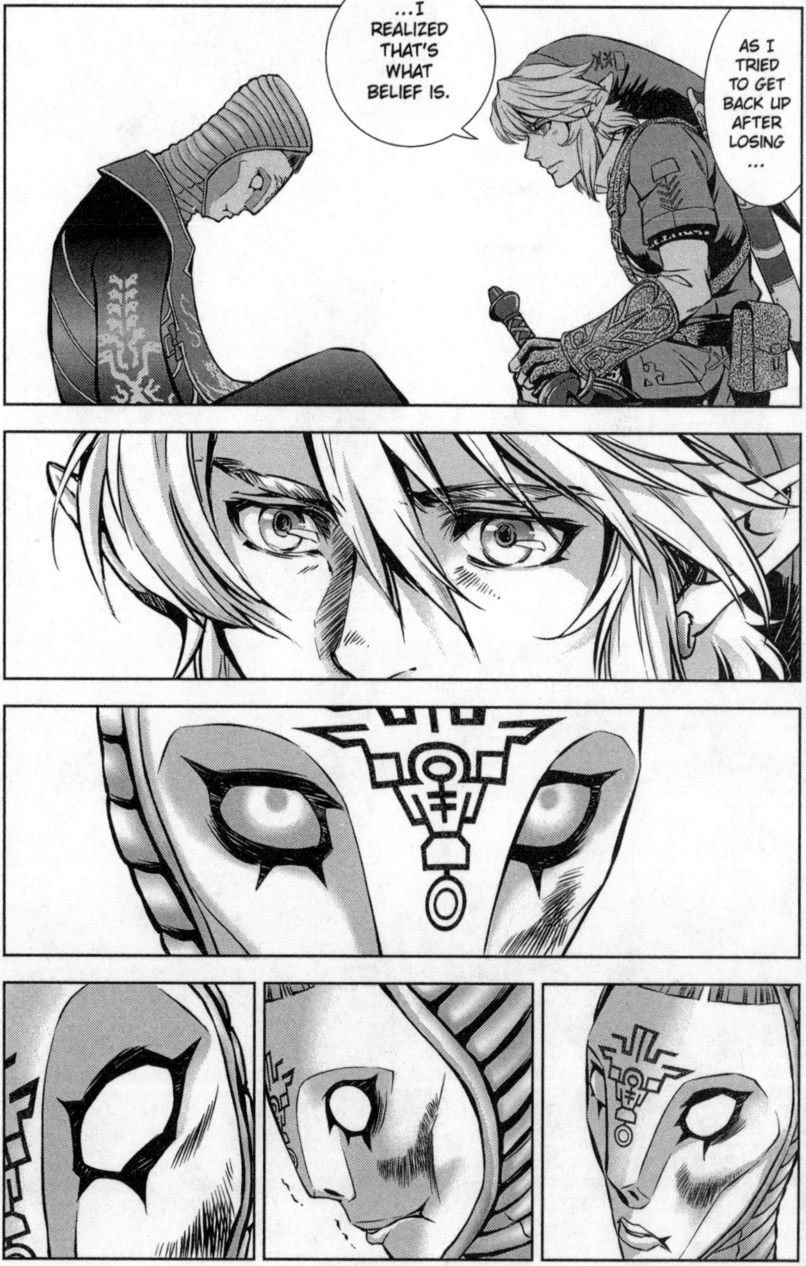
AS I TRIED TO GET BACK UP AFTER LOSING ...
...I REALIZED THAT'S WHAT BELIEF IS.

YOU'RE TRYING TO STEAL MY THRONE THROUGH TRICKERY...

...BUT I WON'T FALL FOR IT!

THE ROYAL THRONE BELONGS TO ME!

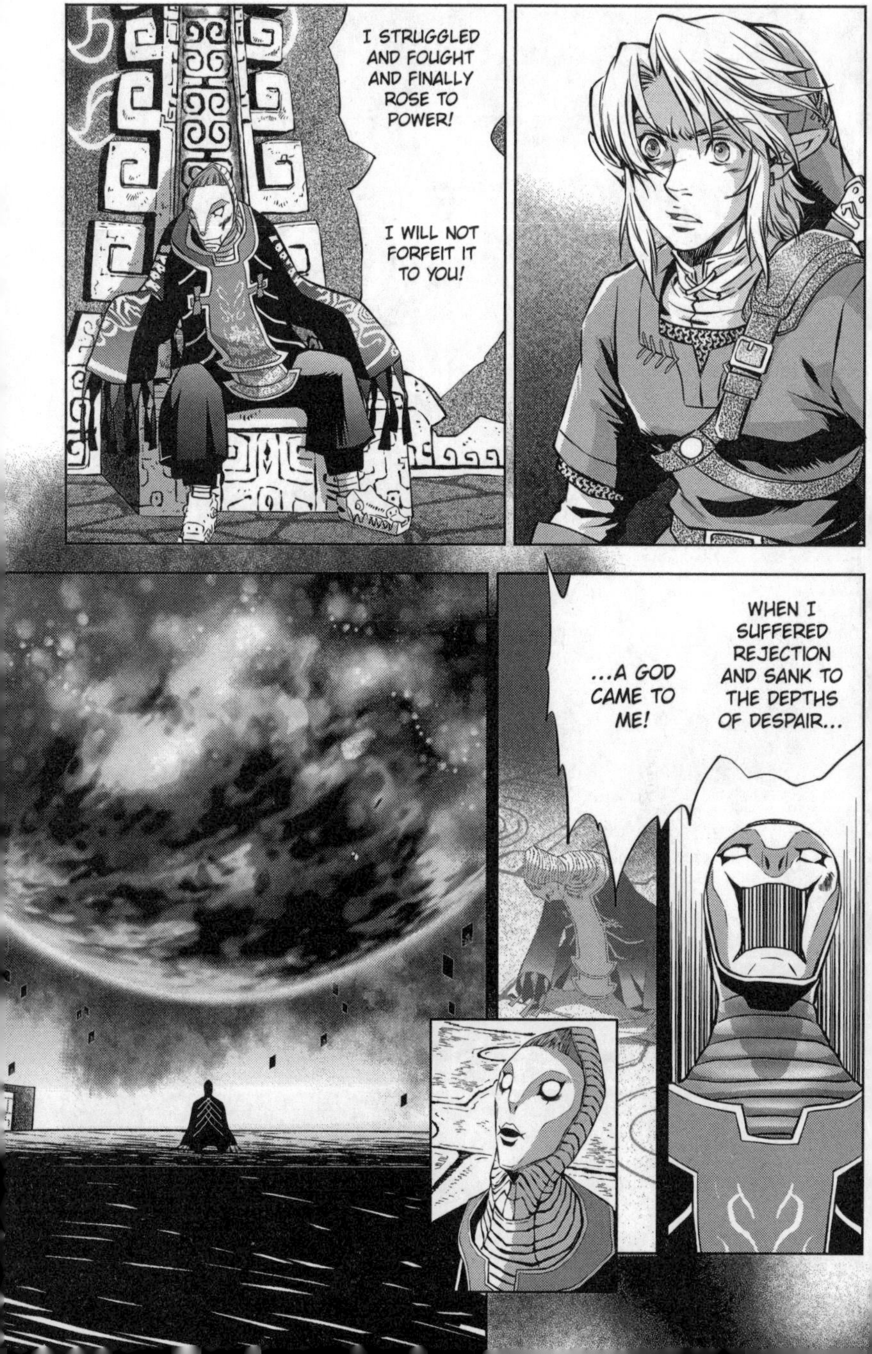
I STRUGGLED AND FOUGHT AND FINALLY ROSE TO POWER!
I WILL NOT FORFEIT IT TO YOU!
WHEN I SUFFERED REJECTION AND SANK TO THE DEPTHS OF DESPAIR...
...A GOD CAME TO ME!

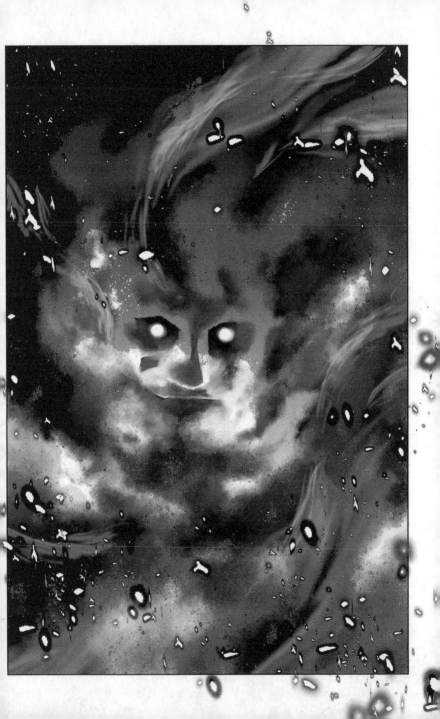

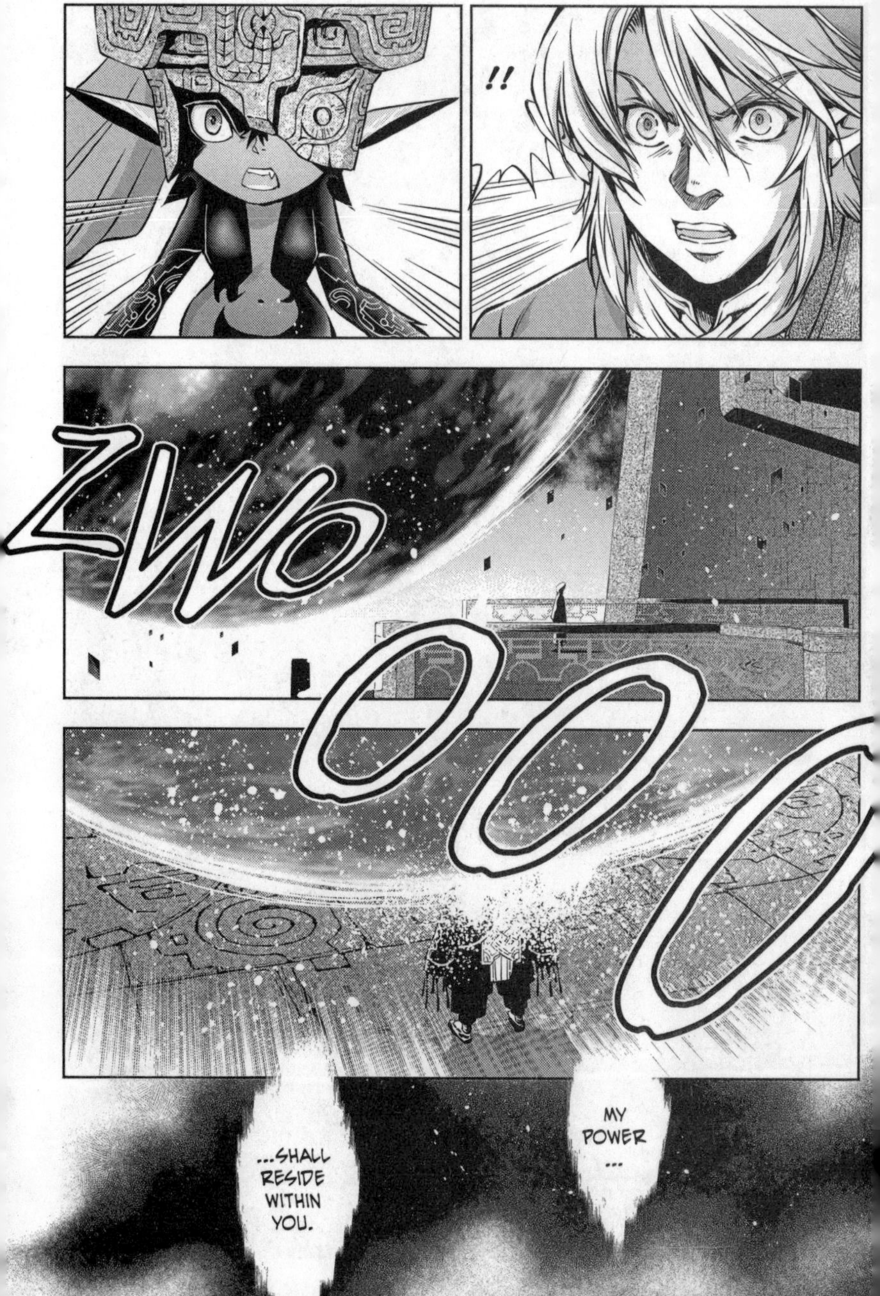
!!
ZWOOOO
MY POWER ...
...SHALL RESIDE WITHIN YOU.

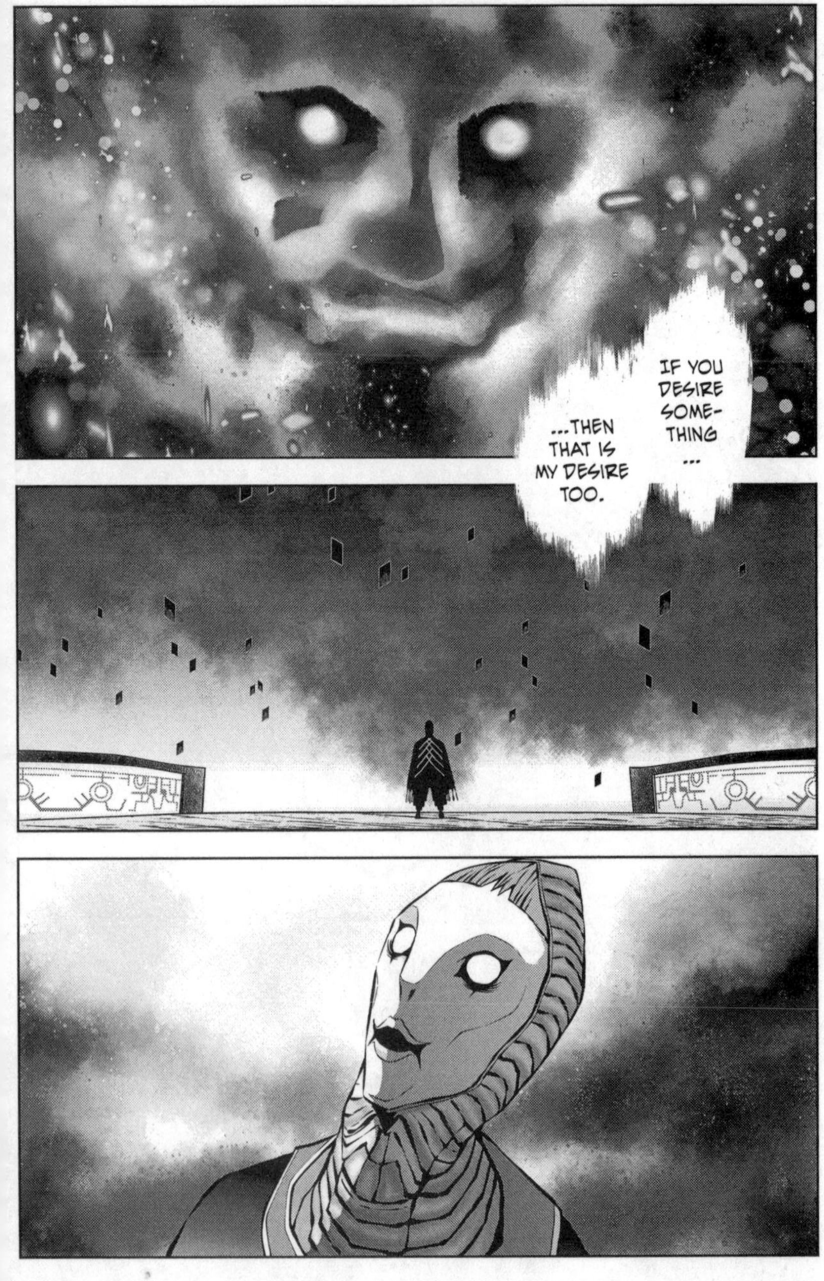
IF YOU DESIRE SOME-THING...
...THEN THAT IS MY DESIRE TOO.

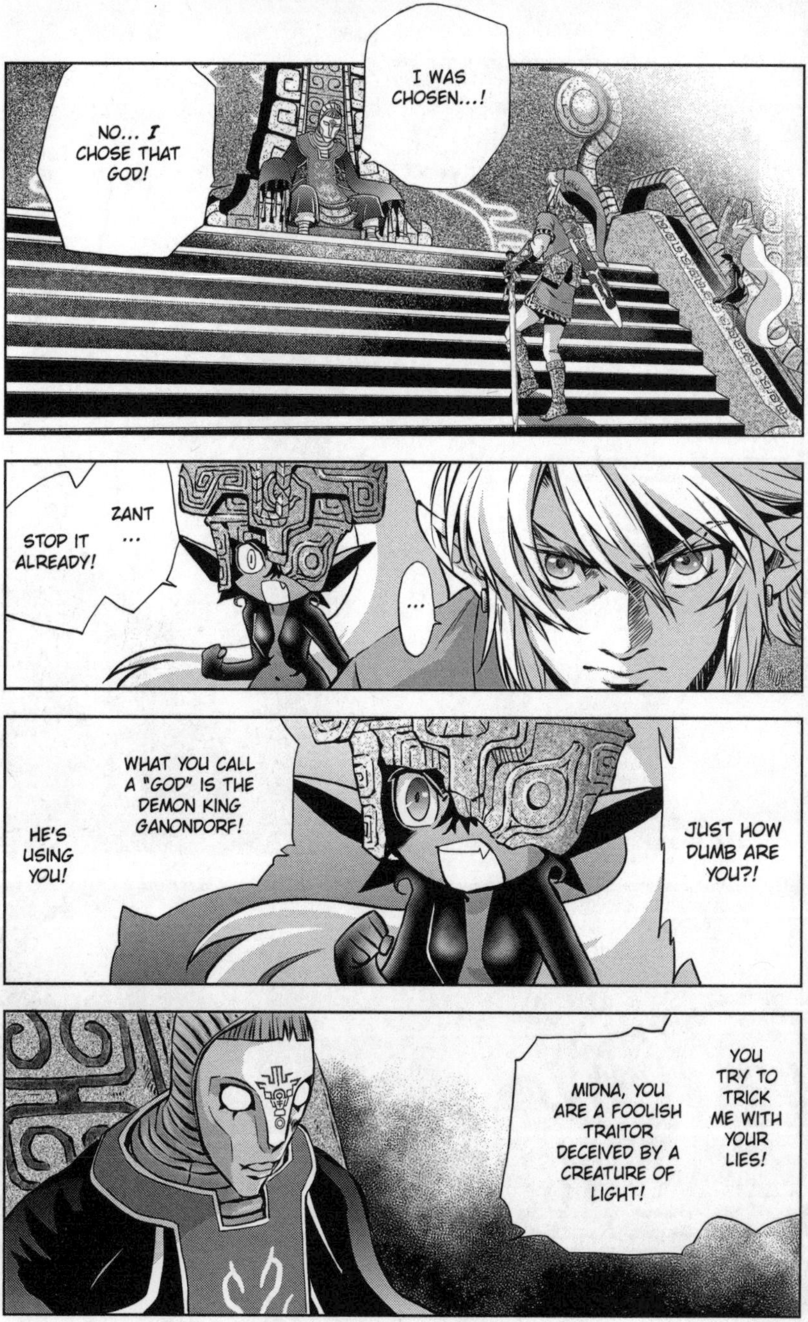
I WAS CHOSEN...!
NO... I CHOSE THAT GOD!
...
ZANT ...
STOP IT ALREADY!
JUST HOW DUMB ARE YOU?!
WHAT YOU CALL A "GOD" IS THE DEMON KING GANONDORF!
HE'S USING YOU!
YOU TRY TO TRICK ME WITH YOUR LIES!
MIDNA, YOU ARE A FOOLISH TRAITOR DECEIVED BY A CREATURE OF LIGHT!

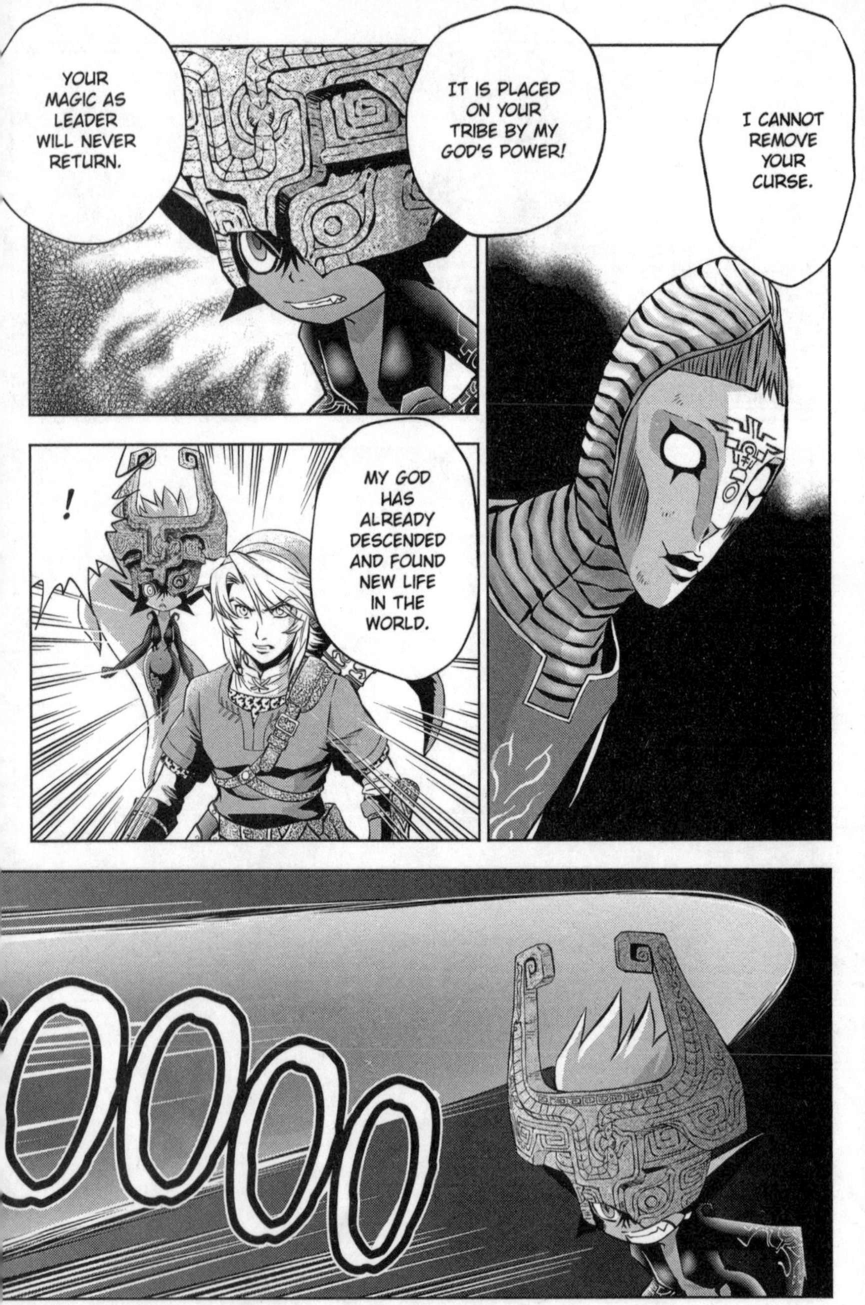
I CANNOT REMOVE YOUR CURSE.
IT IS PLACED ON YOUR TRIBE BY MY GOD'S POWER!
YOUR MAGIC AS LEADER WILL NEVER RETURN.
MY GOD HAS ALREADY DESCENDED AND FOUND NEW LIFE IN THE WORLD.
!
OOOOO

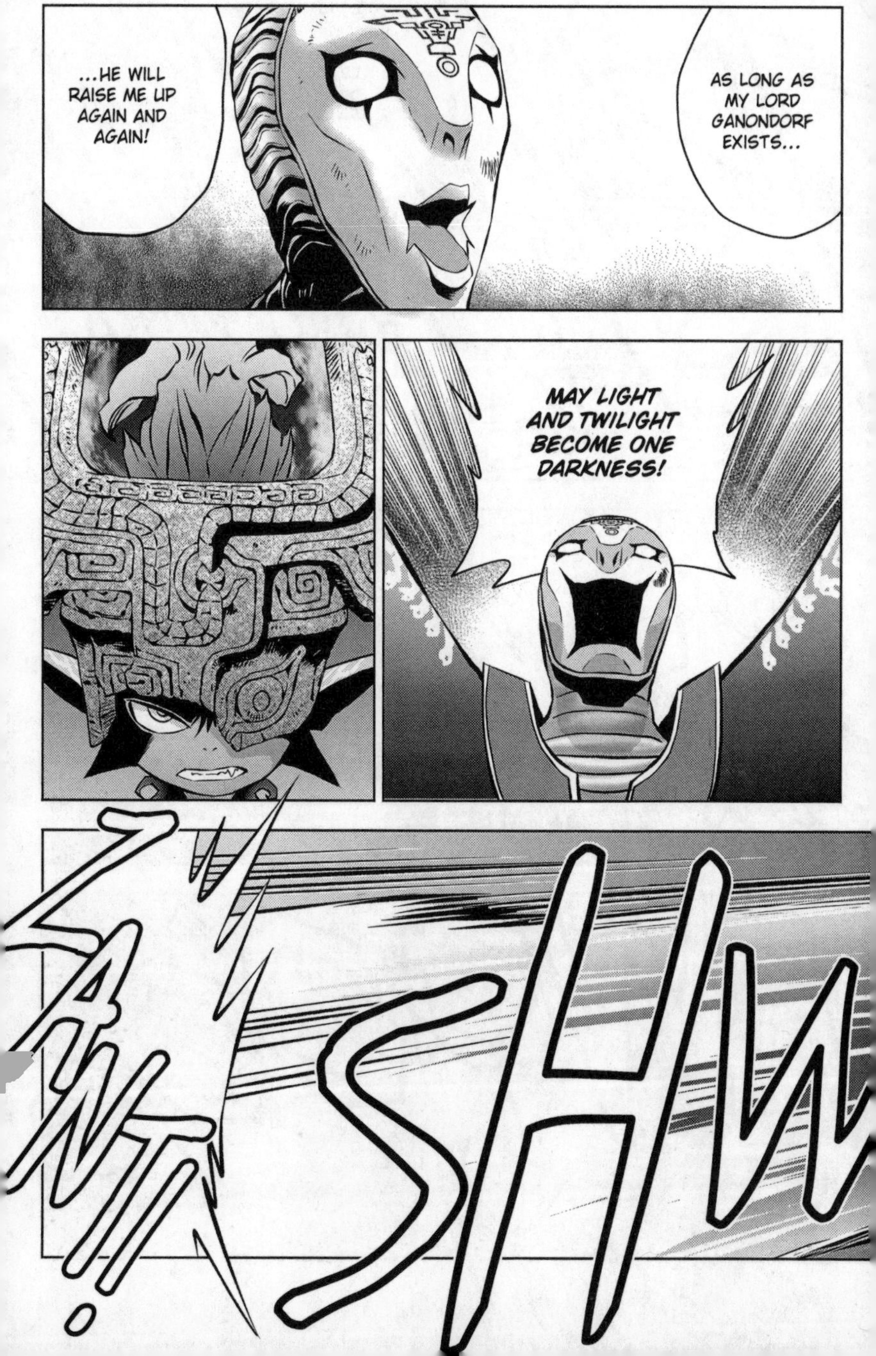
AS LONG AS MY LORD GANONDORF EXISTS...
...HE WILL RAISE ME UP AGAIN AND AGAIN!
MAY LIGHT AND TWILIGHT BECOME ONE DARKNESS!
SHU
ZANT!!

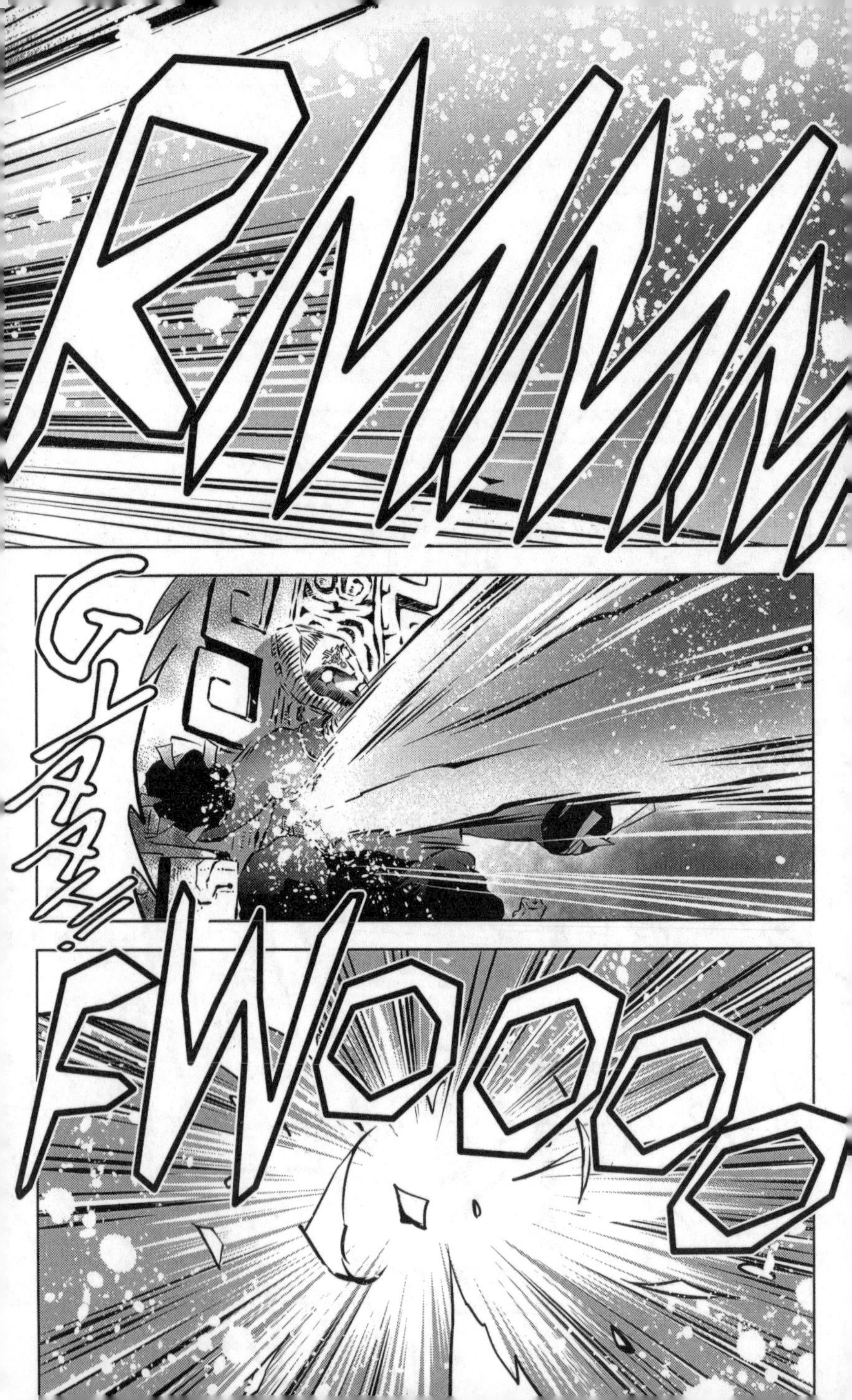
GYAAH!!
FWOOOO

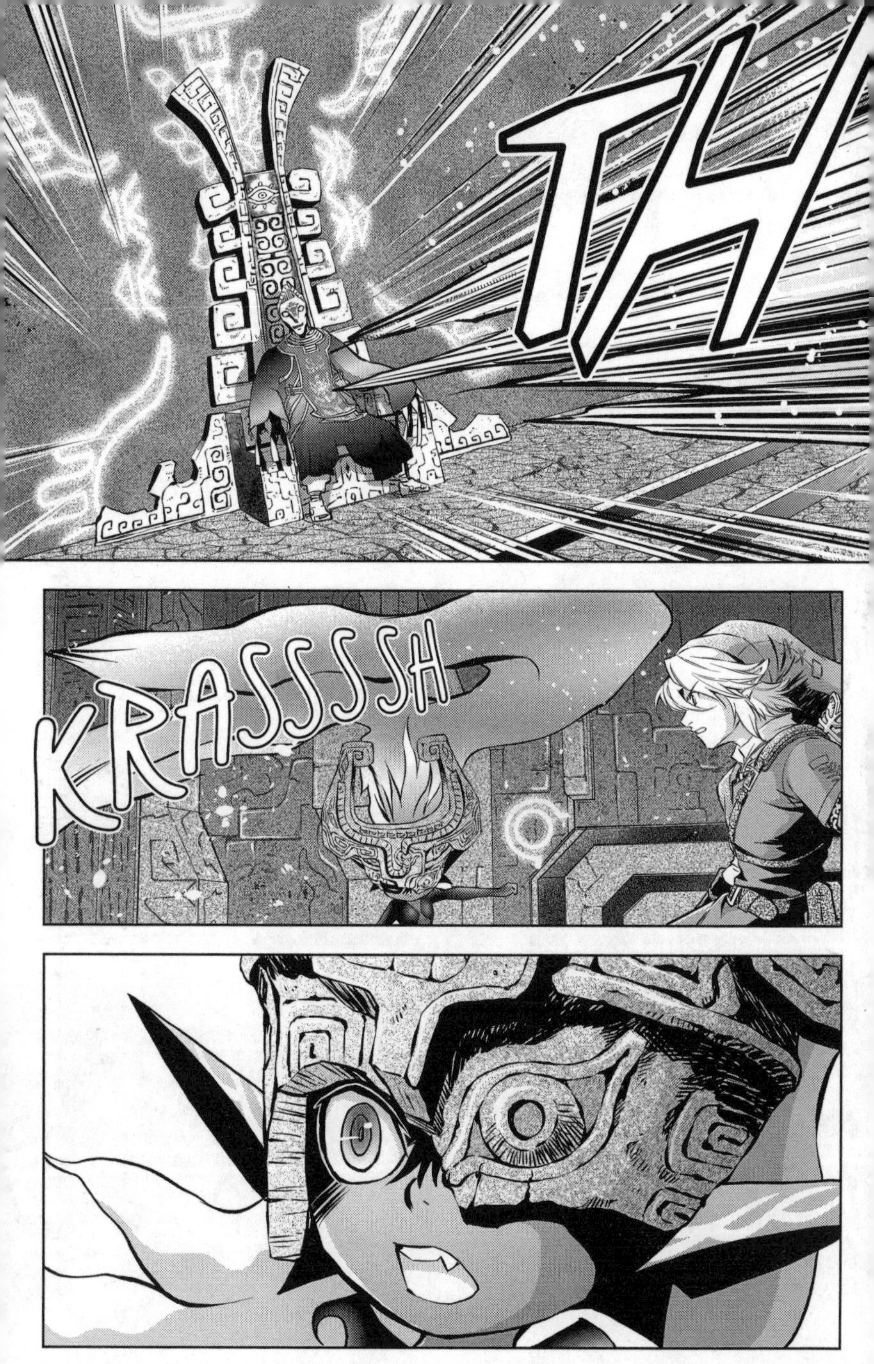
TH
KRASSSSH

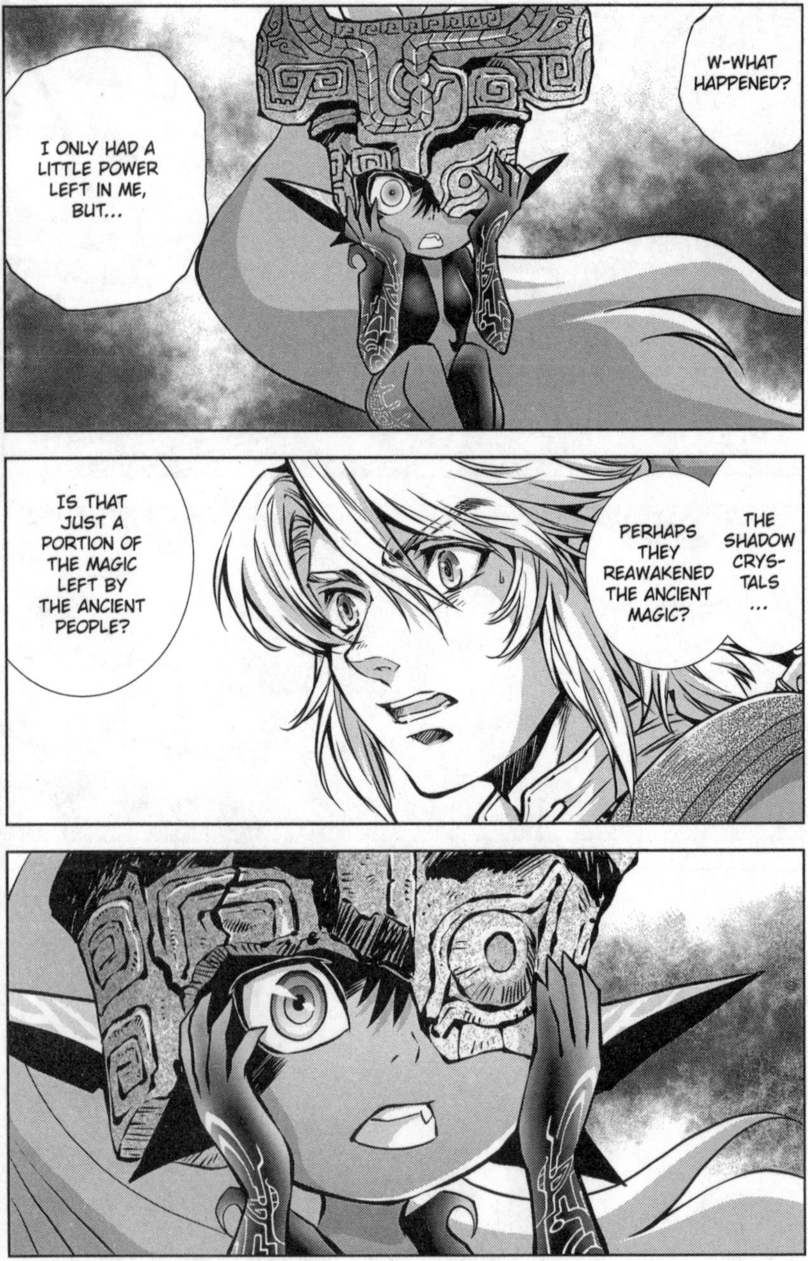
W-WHAT HAPPENED?
I ONLY HAD A LITTLE POWER LEFT IN ME, BUT...
THE SHADOW CRYS-TALS ...
PERHAPS THEY REAWAKENED THE ANCIENT MAGIC?
IS THAT JUST A PORTION OF THE MAGIC LEFT BY THE ANCIENT PEOPLE?

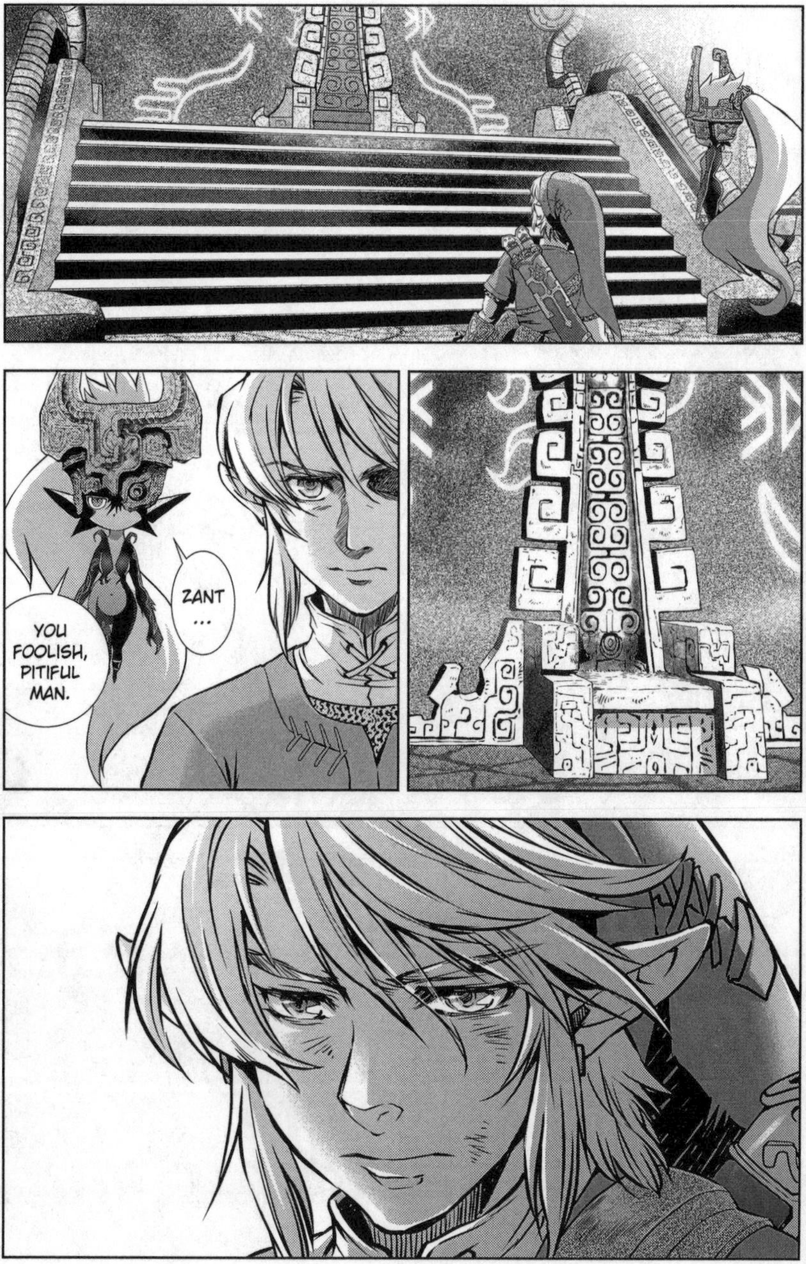
ZANT ...
YOU FOOLISH, PITIFUL MAN.

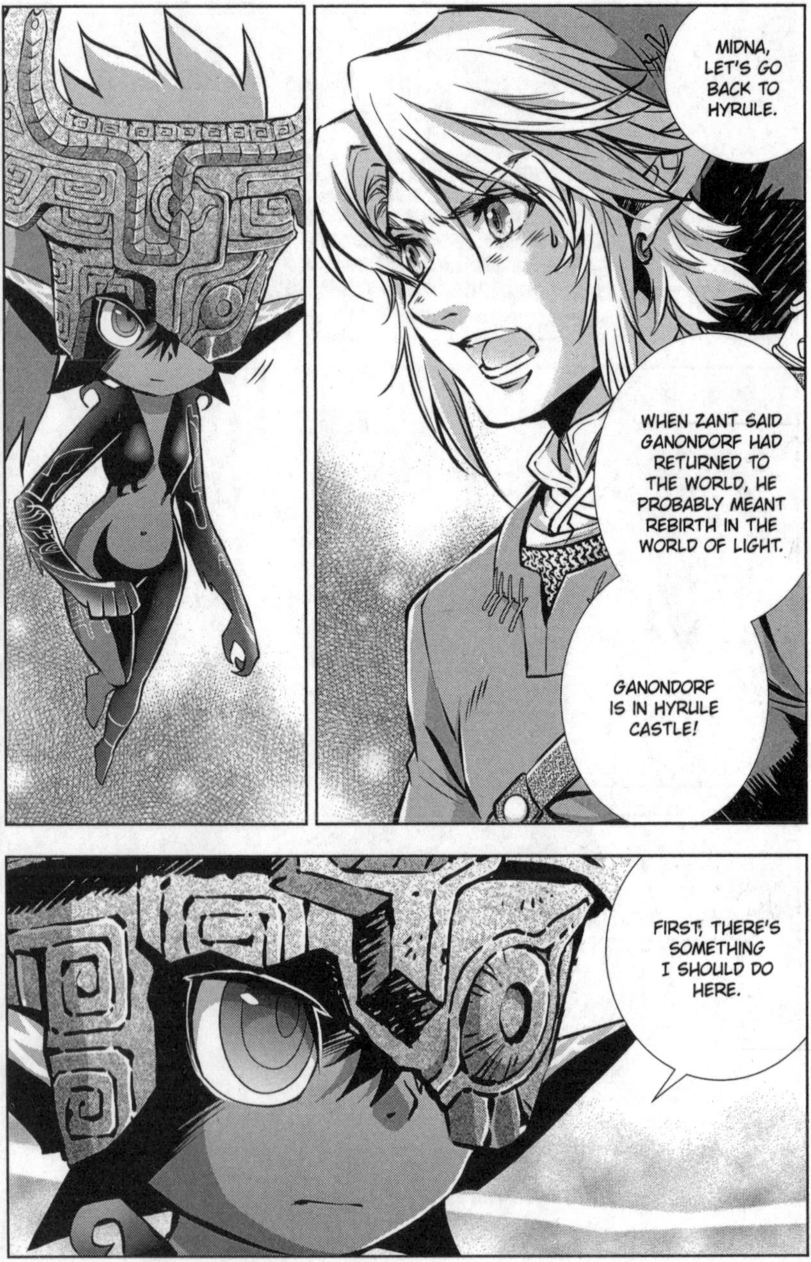
MIDNA, LET'S GO BACK TO HYRULE.
WHEN ZANT SAID GANONDORF HAD RETURNED TO THE WORLD, HE PROBABLY MEANT REBIRTH IN THE WORLD OF LIGHT.
GANONDORF IS IN HYRULE CASTLE!
FIRST, THERE'S SOMETHING I SHOULD DO HERE.

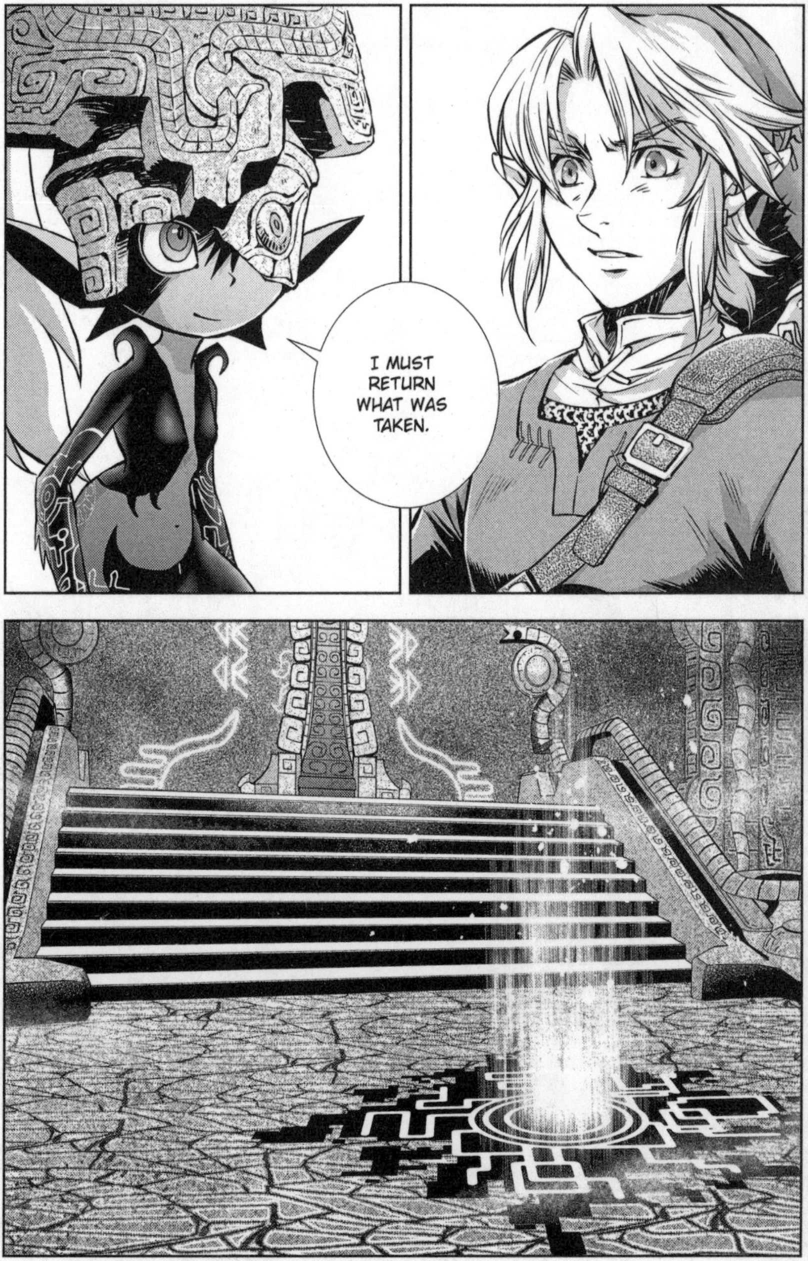
I MUST RETURN WHAT WAS TAKEN.

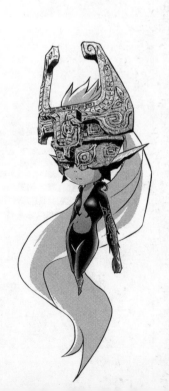

#48. DIFFERENCE

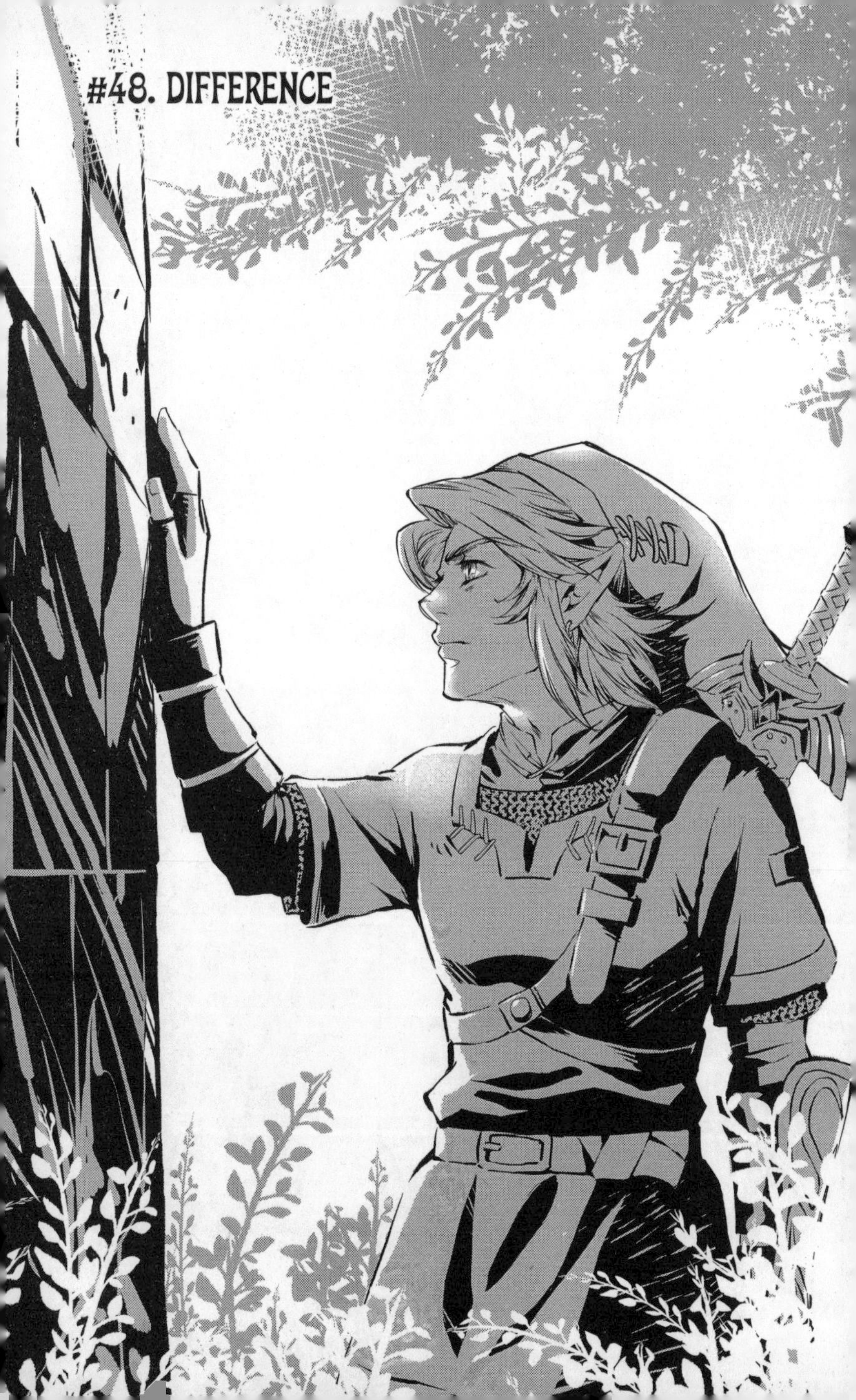

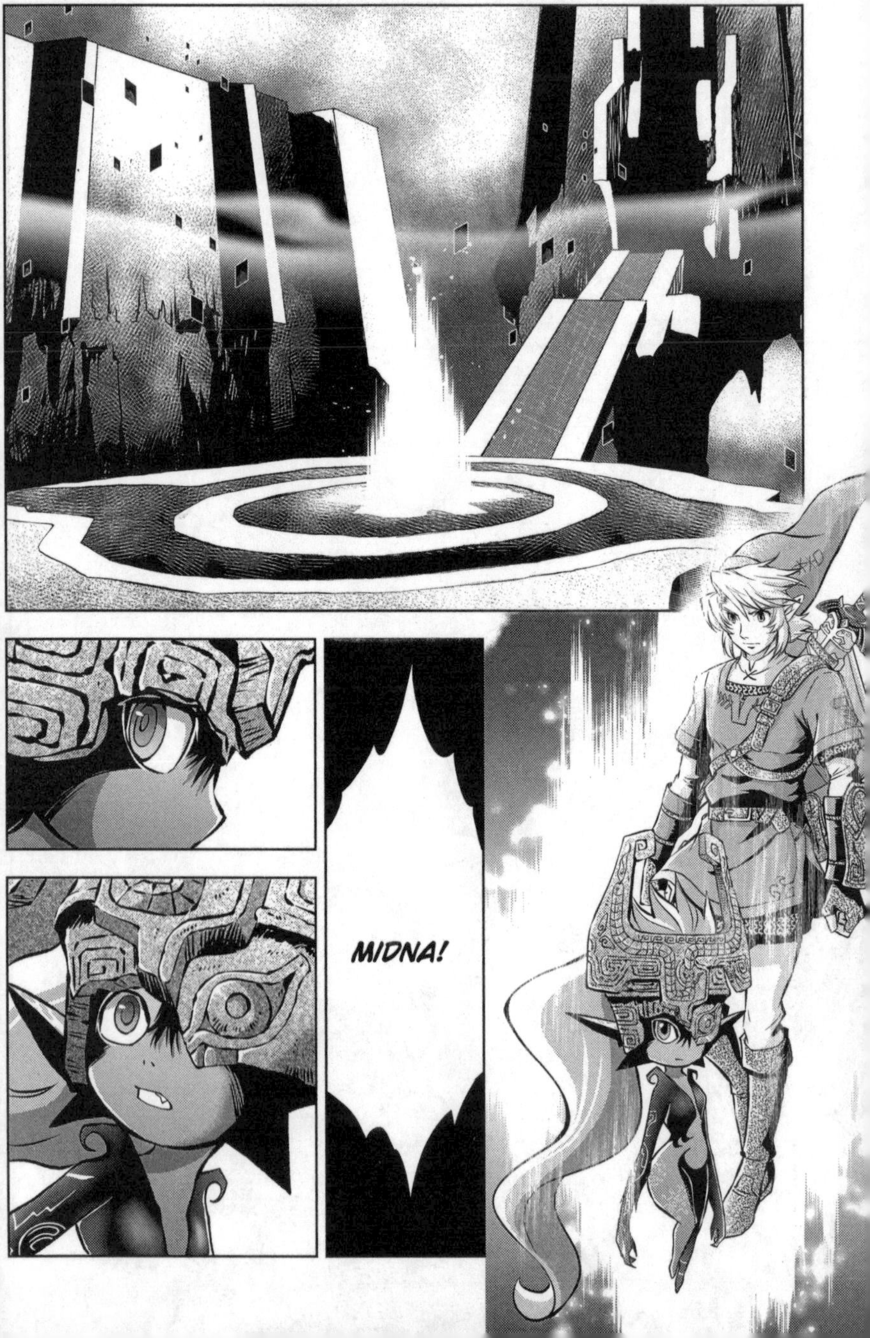
MIDNA!

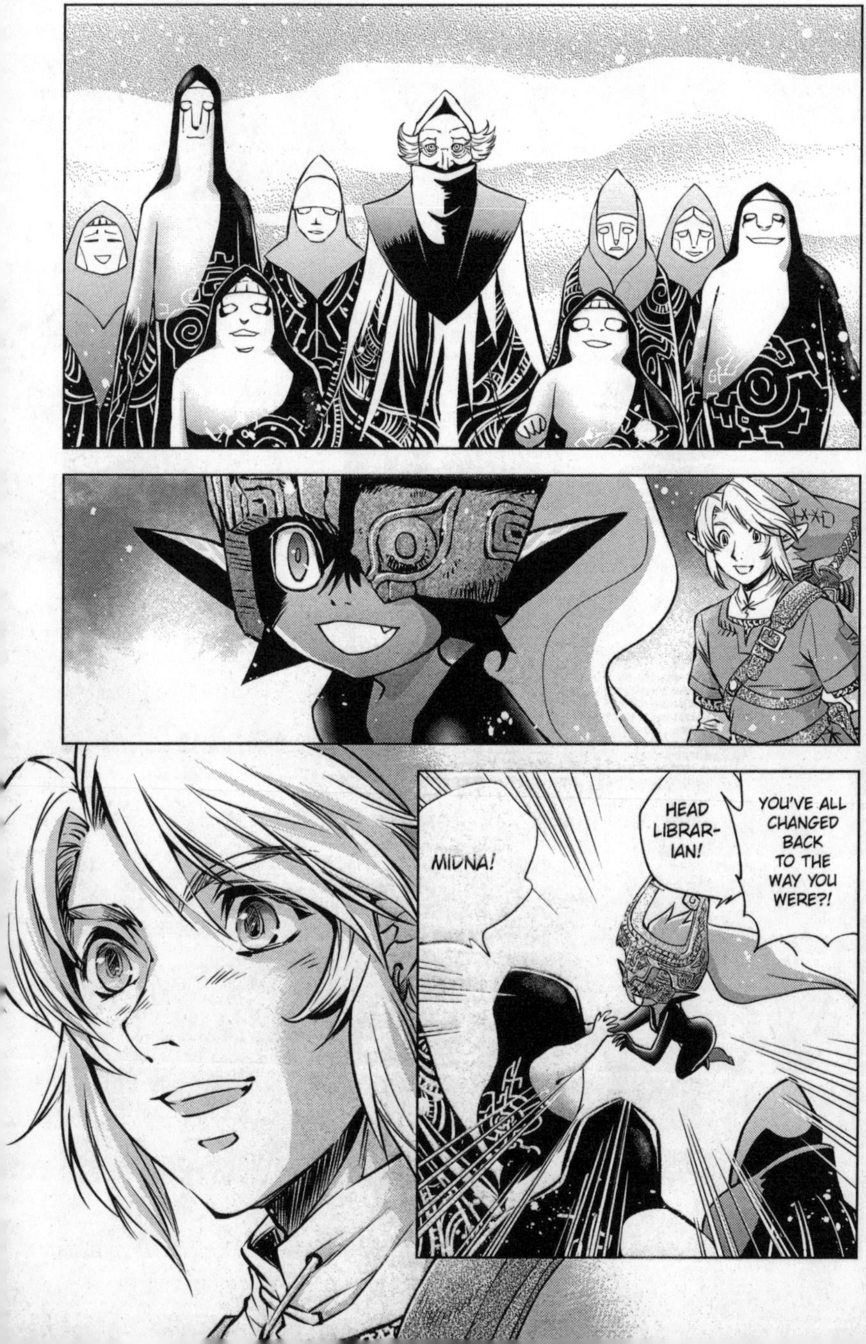
YOU'VE ALL CHANGED BACK TO THE WAY YOU WERE?!
HEAD LIBRARIAN!
MIDNA!

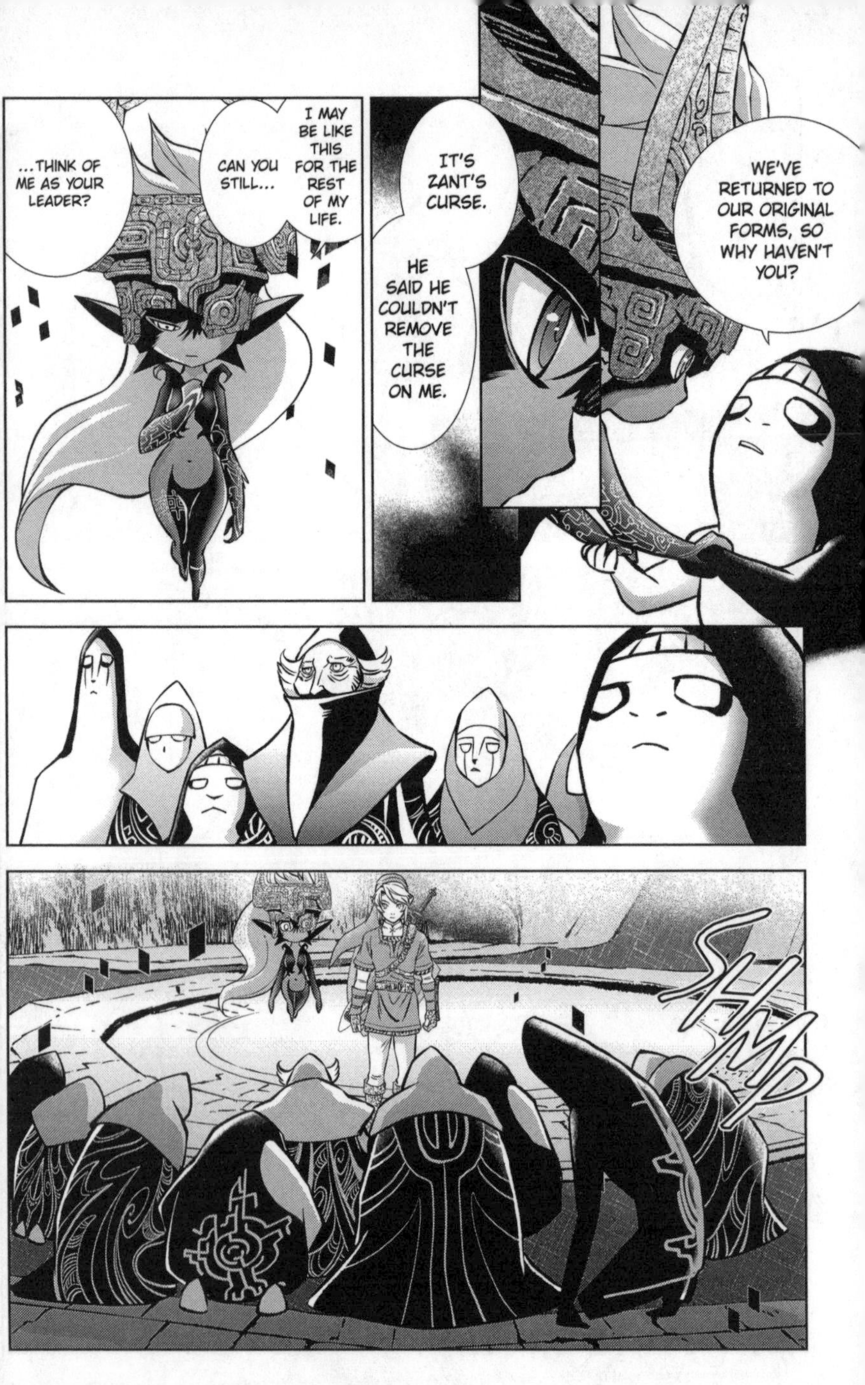
WE'VE RETURNED TO OUR ORIGINAL FORMS, SO WHY HAVEN'T YOU?
IT'S ZANT'S CURSE.
HE SAID HE COULDN'T REMOVE THE CURSE ON ME.
I MAY BE LIKE THIS FOR THE REST OF MY LIFE.
CAN YOU STILL...
...THINK OF ME AS YOUR LEADER?
SHMP

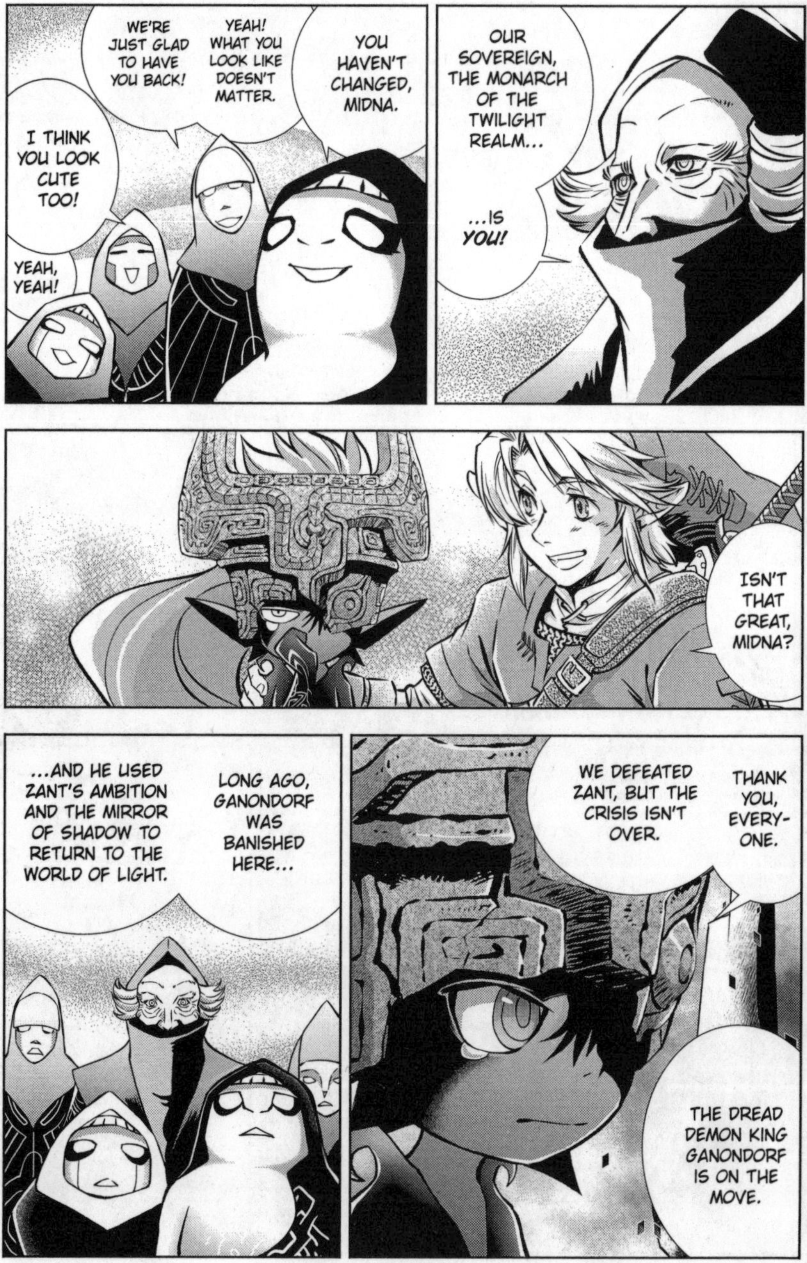
OUR SOVEREIGN, THE MONARCH OF THE TWILIGHT REALM...
...IS *YOU!*
YOU HAVEN'T CHANGED, MIDNA.
YEAH! WHAT YOU LOOK LIKE DOESN'T MATTER.
WE'RE JUST GLAD TO HAVE YOU BACK!
I THINK YOU LOOK CUTE TOO!
YEAH, YEAH!
ISN'T THAT GREAT, MIDNA?
THANK YOU, EVERY-ONE.
WE DEFEATED ZANT, BUT THE CRISIS ISN'T OVER.
THE DREAD DEMON KING GANONDORF IS ON THE MOVE.
LONG AGO, GANONDORF WAS BANISHED HERE...
...AND HE USED ZANT'S AMBITION AND THE MIRROR OF SHADOW TO RETURN TO THE WORLD OF LIGHT.

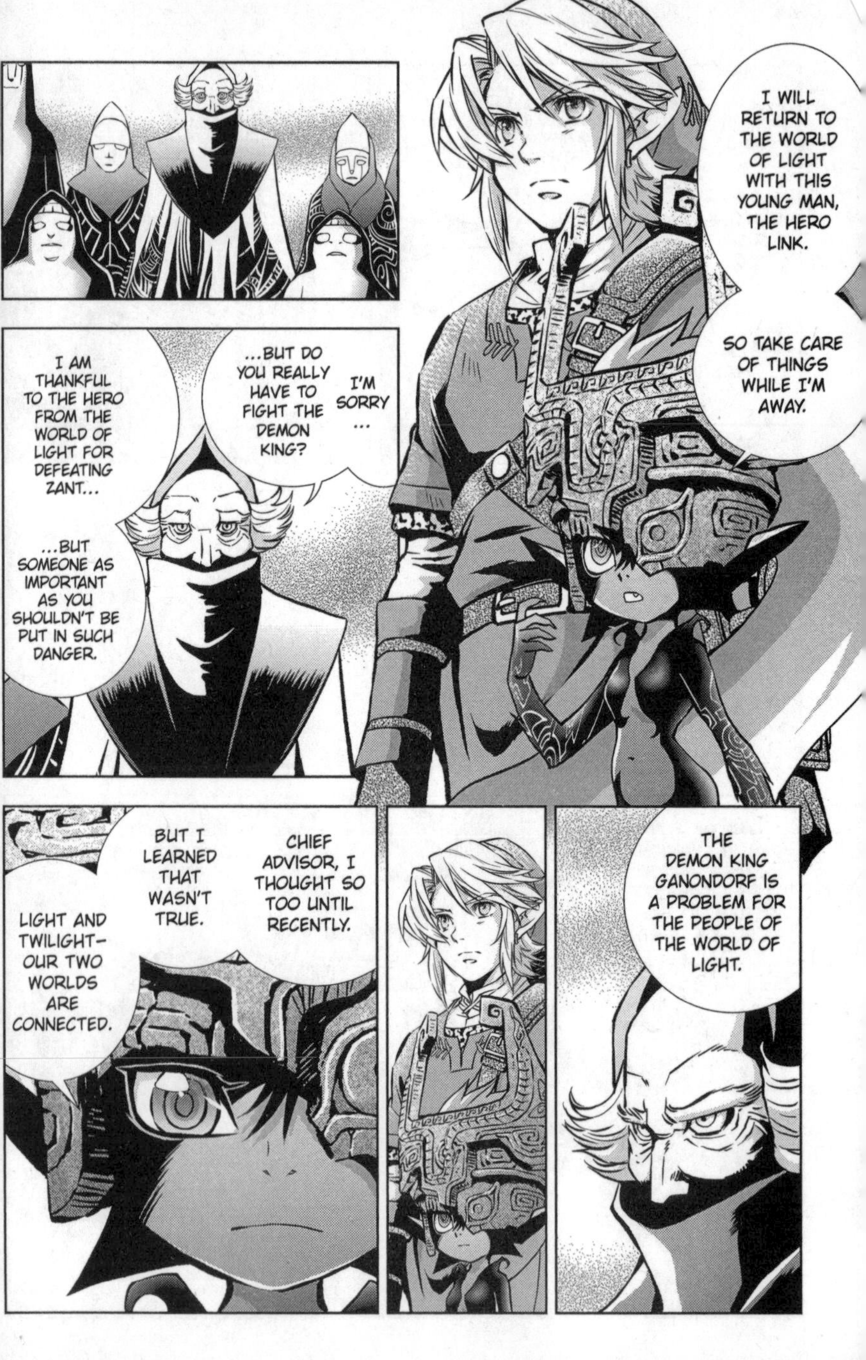
I WILL RETURN TO THE WORLD OF LIGHT WITH THIS YOUNG MAN, THE HERO LINK.
SO TAKE CARE OF THINGS WHILE I'M AWAY.
I'M SORRY ...
...BUT DO YOU REALLY HAVE TO FIGHT THE DEMON KING?
I AM THANKFUL TO THE HERO FROM THE WORLD OF LIGHT FOR DEFEATING ZANT...
...BUT SOMEONE AS IMPORTANT AS YOU SHOULDN'T BE PUT IN SUCH DANGER.
THE DEMON KING GANONDORF IS A PROBLEM FOR THE PEOPLE OF THE WORLD OF LIGHT.
CHIEF ADVISOR, I THOUGHT SO TOO UNTIL RECENTLY.
BUT I LEARNED THAT WASN'T TRUE.
LIGHT AND TWILIGHT— OUR TWO WORLDS ARE CONNECTED.

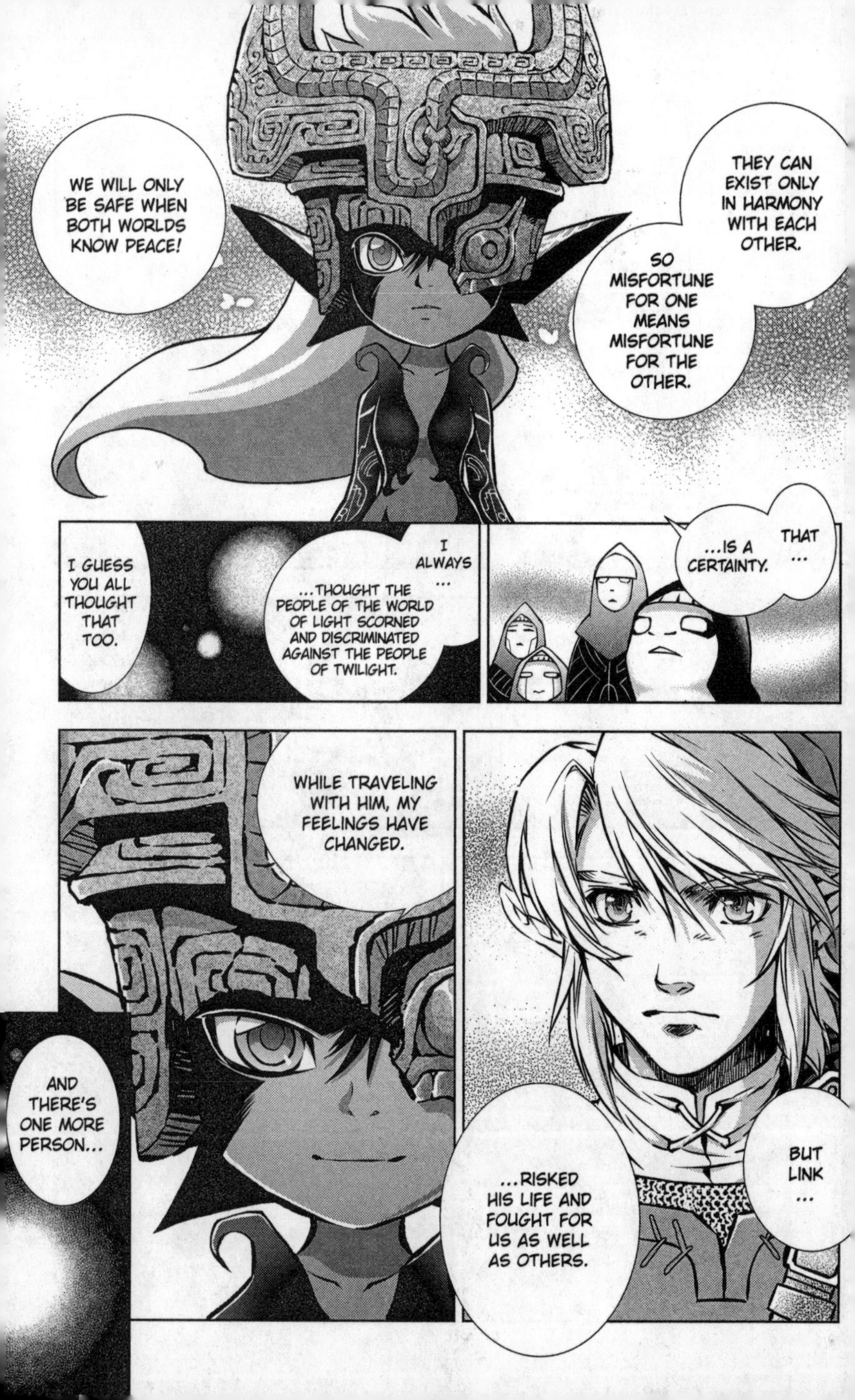
THEY CAN EXIST ONLY IN HARMONY WITH EACH OTHER.
SO MISFORTUNE FOR ONE MEANS MISFORTUNE FOR THE OTHER.
WE WILL ONLY BE SAFE WHEN BOTH WORLDS KNOW PEACE!
THAT ...
...IS A CERTAINTY.
I ALWAYS ...
...THOUGHT THE PEOPLE OF THE WORLD OF LIGHT SCORNED AND DISCRIMINATED AGAINST THE PEOPLE OF TWILIGHT.
I GUESS YOU ALL THOUGHT THAT TOO.
BUT LINK ...
...RISKED HIS LIFE AND FOUGHT FOR US AS WELL AS OTHERS.
WHILE TRAVELING WITH HIM, MY FEELINGS HAVE CHANGED.
AND THERE'S ONE MORE PERSON...

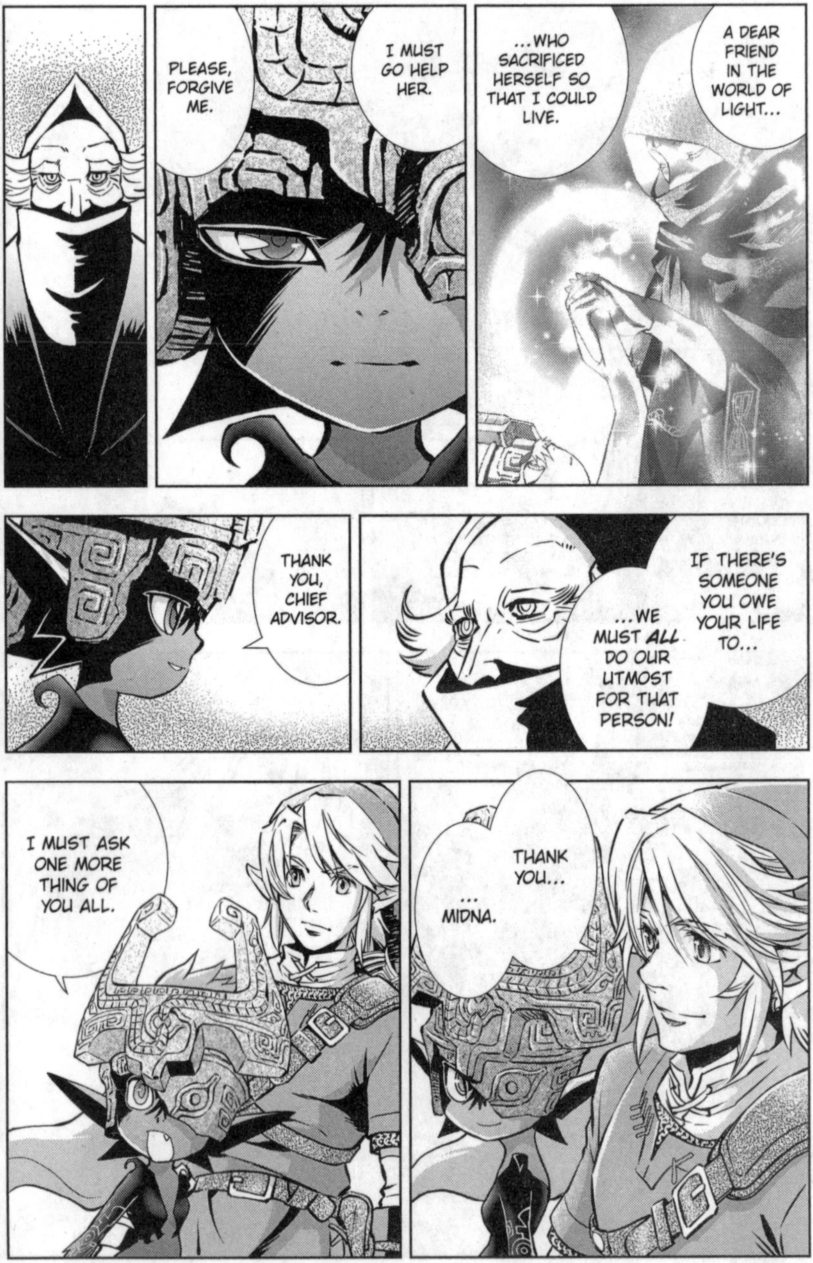
A DEAR FRIEND IN THE WORLD OF LIGHT...
...WHO SACRIFICED HERSELF SO THAT I COULD LIVE.
I MUST GO HELP HER.
PLEASE, FORGIVE ME.
IF THERE'S SOMEONE YOU OWE YOUR LIFE TO...
...WE MUST **ALL** DO OUR UTMOST FOR THAT PERSON!
THANK YOU, CHIEF ADVISOR.
THANK YOU... ... MIDNA.
I MUST ASK ONE MORE THING OF YOU ALL.

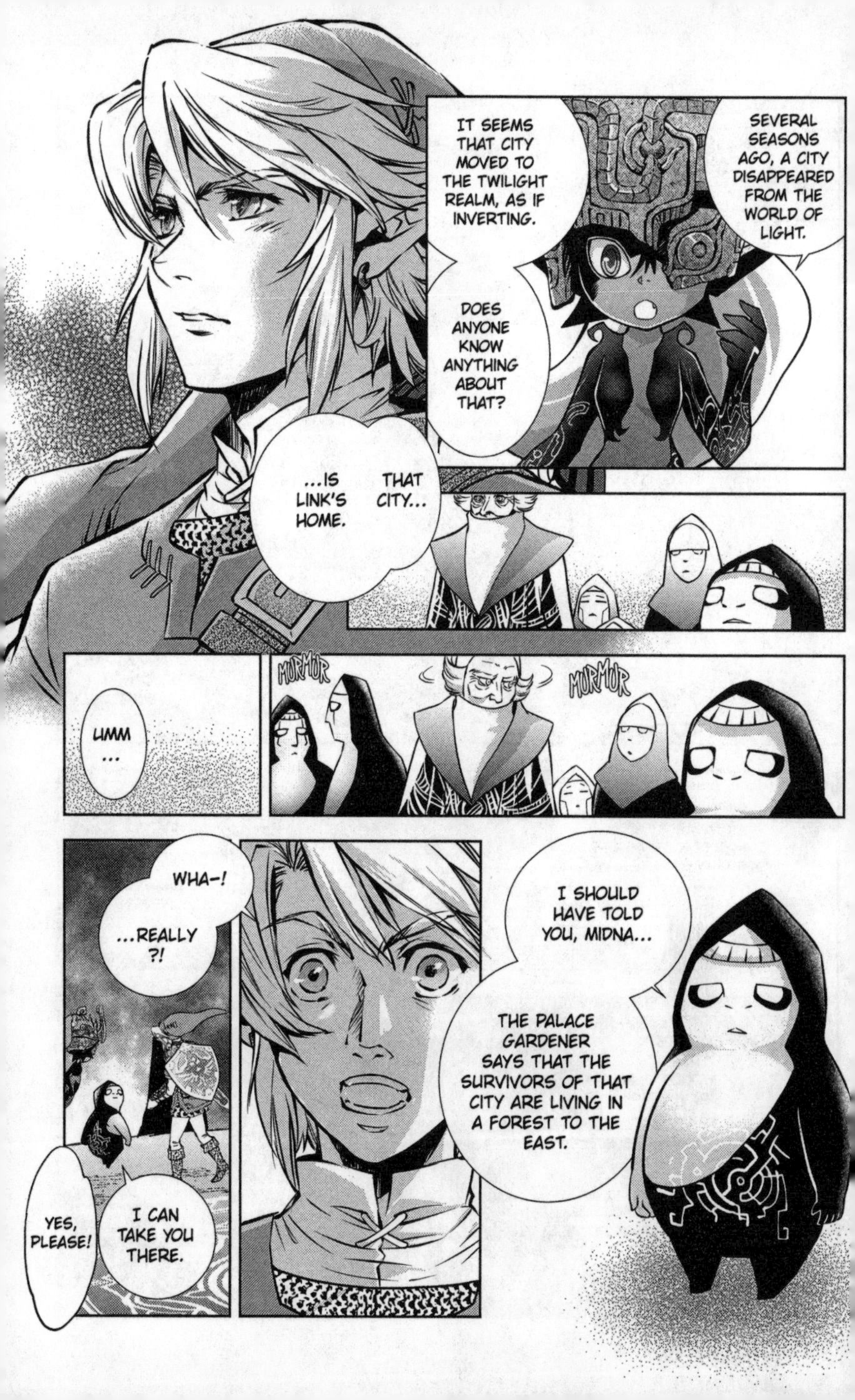
SEVERAL SEASONS AGO, A CITY DISAPPEARED FROM THE WORLD OF LIGHT.
IT SEEMS THAT CITY MOVED TO THE TWILIGHT REALM, AS IF INVERTING.
DOES ANYONE KNOW ANYTHING ABOUT THAT?
THAT CITY... ...IS LINK'S HOME.
MURMUR
MURMUR
UMM ...
I SHOULD HAVE TOLD YOU, MIDNA...
THE PALACE GARDENER SAYS THAT THE SURVIVORS OF THAT CITY ARE LIVING IN A FOREST TO THE EAST.
WHA-!
...REALLY ?!
I CAN TAKE YOU THERE.
YES, PLEASE!

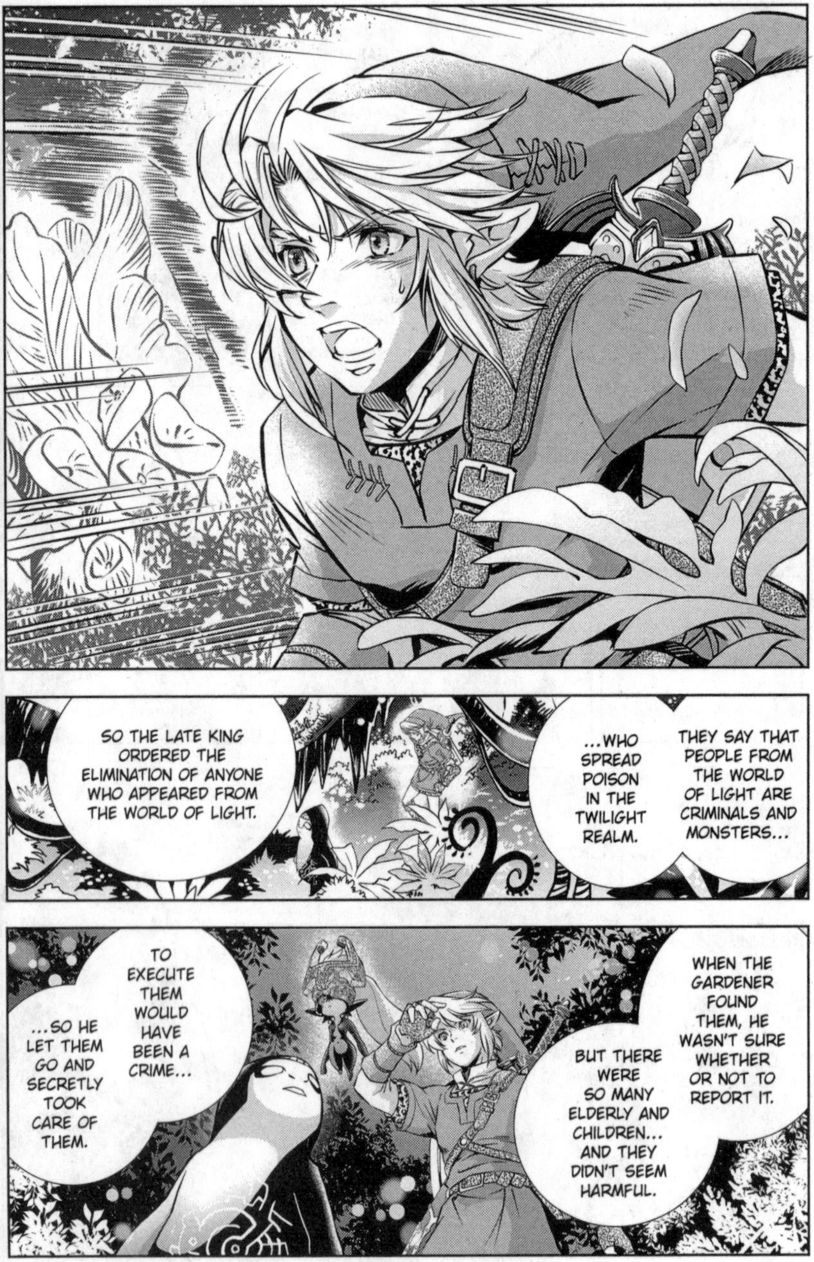
THEY SAY THAT PEOPLE FROM THE WORLD OF LIGHT ARE CRIMINALS AND MONSTERS...
...WHO SPREAD POISON IN THE TWILIGHT REALM.
SO THE LATE KING ORDERED THE ELIMINATION OF ANYONE WHO APPEARED FROM THE WORLD OF LIGHT.
WHEN THE GARDENER FOUND THEM, HE WASN'T SURE WHETHER OR NOT TO REPORT IT.
BUT THERE WERE SO MANY ELDERLY AND CHILDREN... AND THEY DIDN'T SEEM HARMFUL.
TO EXECUTE THEM WOULD HAVE BEEN A CRIME...
...SO HE LET THEM GO AND SECRETLY TOOK CARE OF THEM.

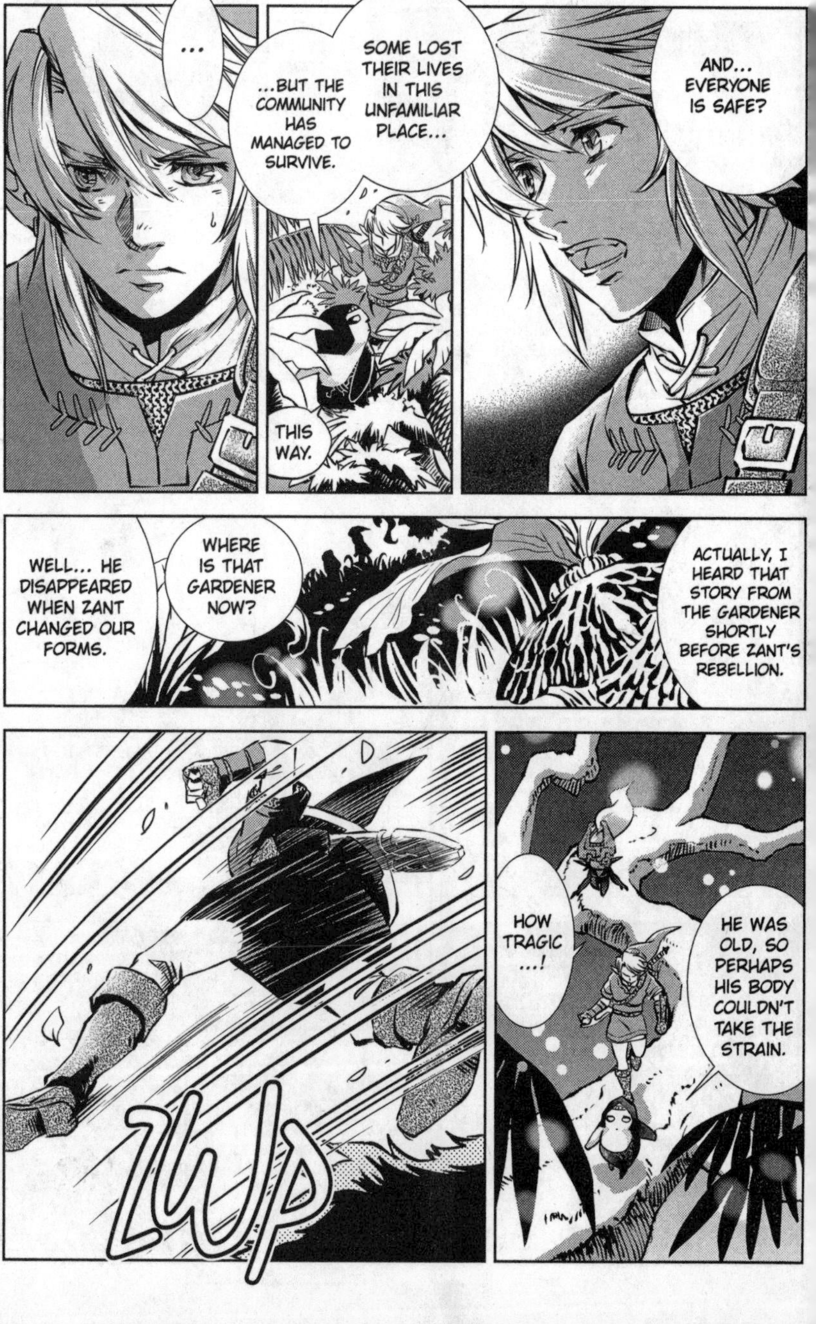
AND... EVERYONE IS SAFE?
SOME LOST THEIR LIVES IN THIS UNFAMILIAR PLACE...
...BUT THE COMMUNITY HAS MANAGED TO SURVIVE.
THIS WAY.
...
ACTUALLY, I HEARD THAT STORY FROM THE GARDENER SHORTLY BEFORE ZANT'S REBELLION.
WHERE IS THAT GARDENER NOW?
WELL... HE DISAPPEARED WHEN ZANT CHANGED OUR FORMS.
HE WAS OLD, SO PERHAPS HIS BODY COULDN'T TAKE THE STRAIN.
HOW TRAGIC ...!
ZUP

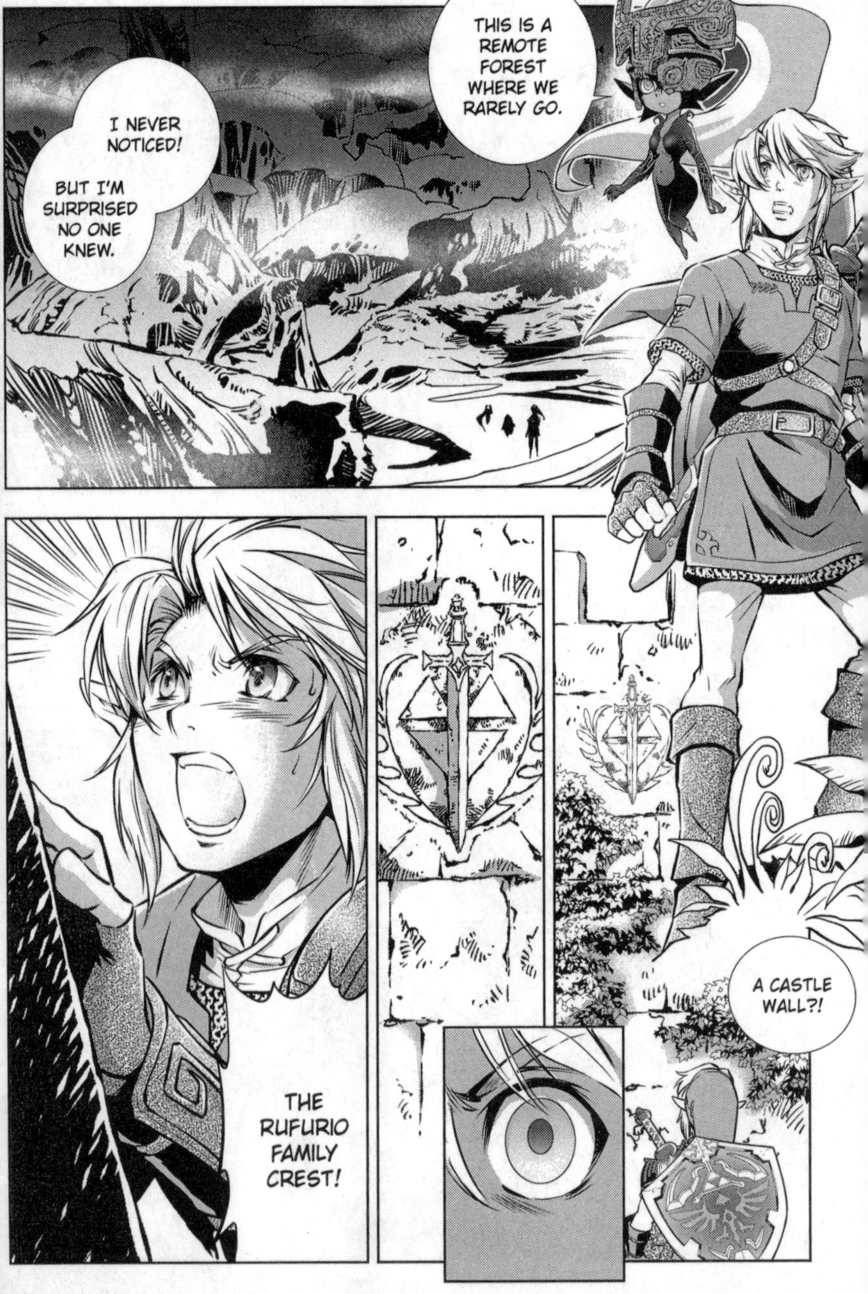
THIS IS A REMOTE FOREST WHERE WE RARELY GO.
I NEVER NOTICED!
BUT I'M SURPRISED NO ONE KNEW.
A CASTLE WALL?!
THE RUFURIO FAMILY CREST!

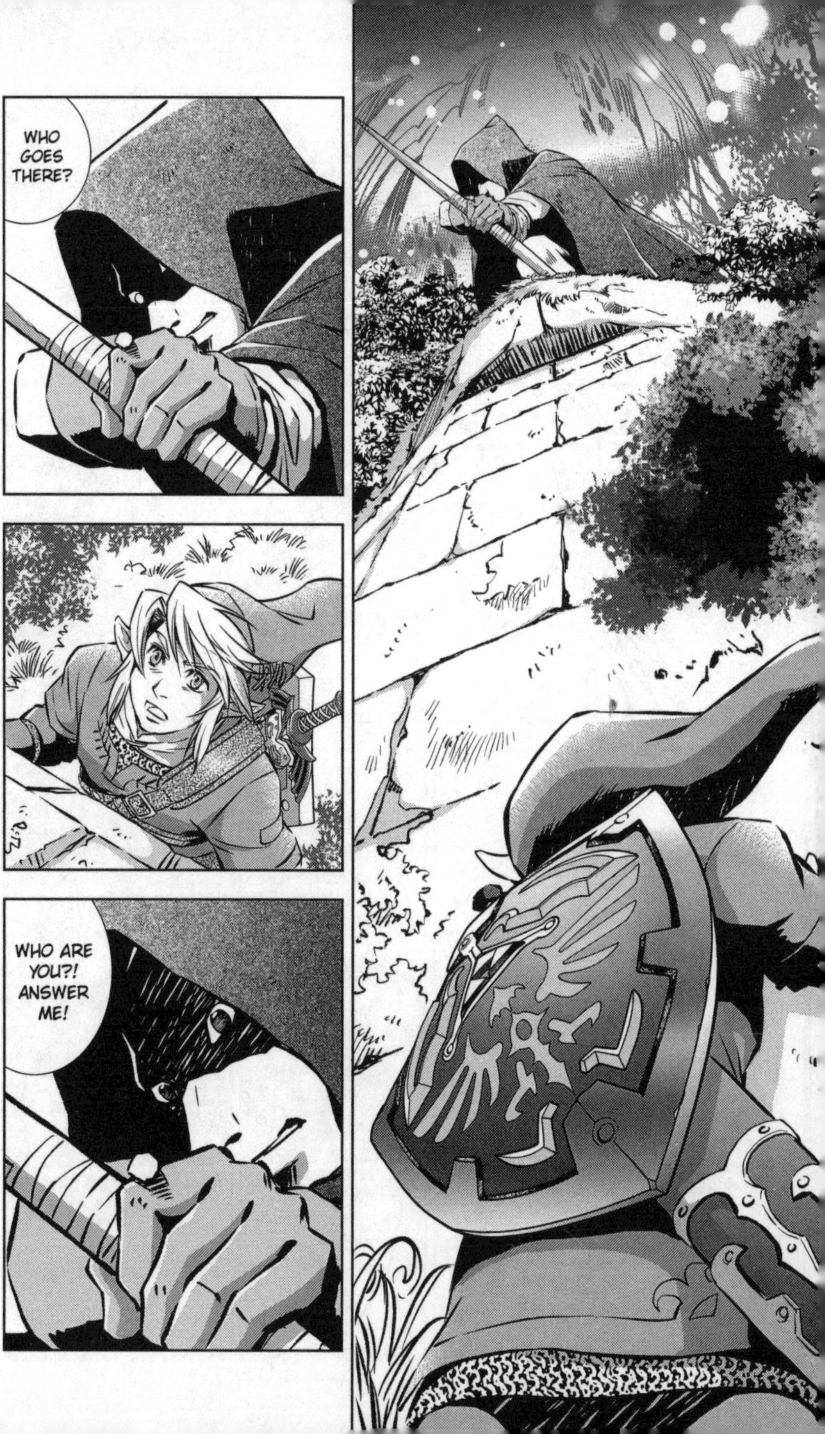
WHO GOES THERE?
WHO ARE YOU?! ANSWER ME!

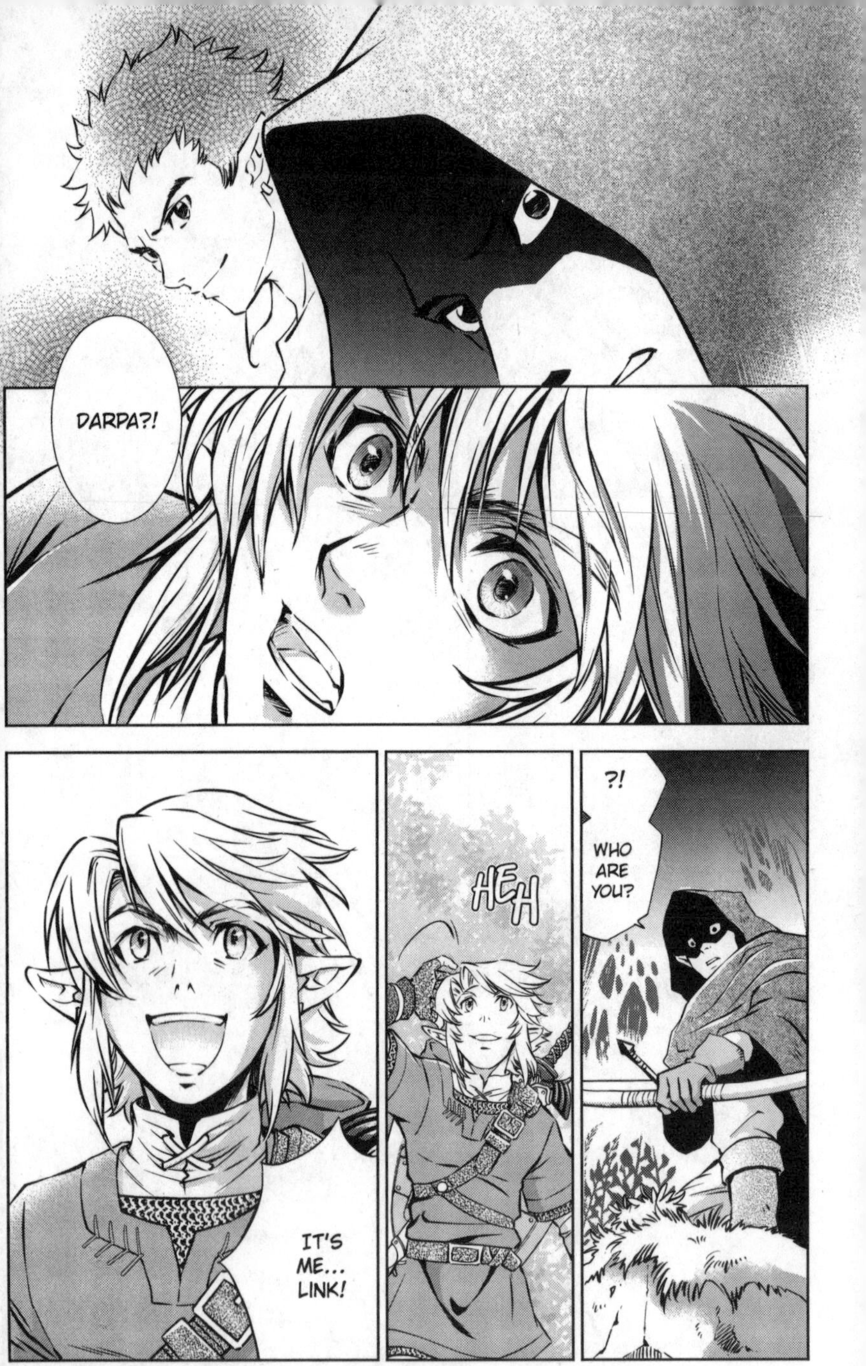
DARPA?!
?!
WHO ARE YOU?
HEH
IT'S ME... LINK!

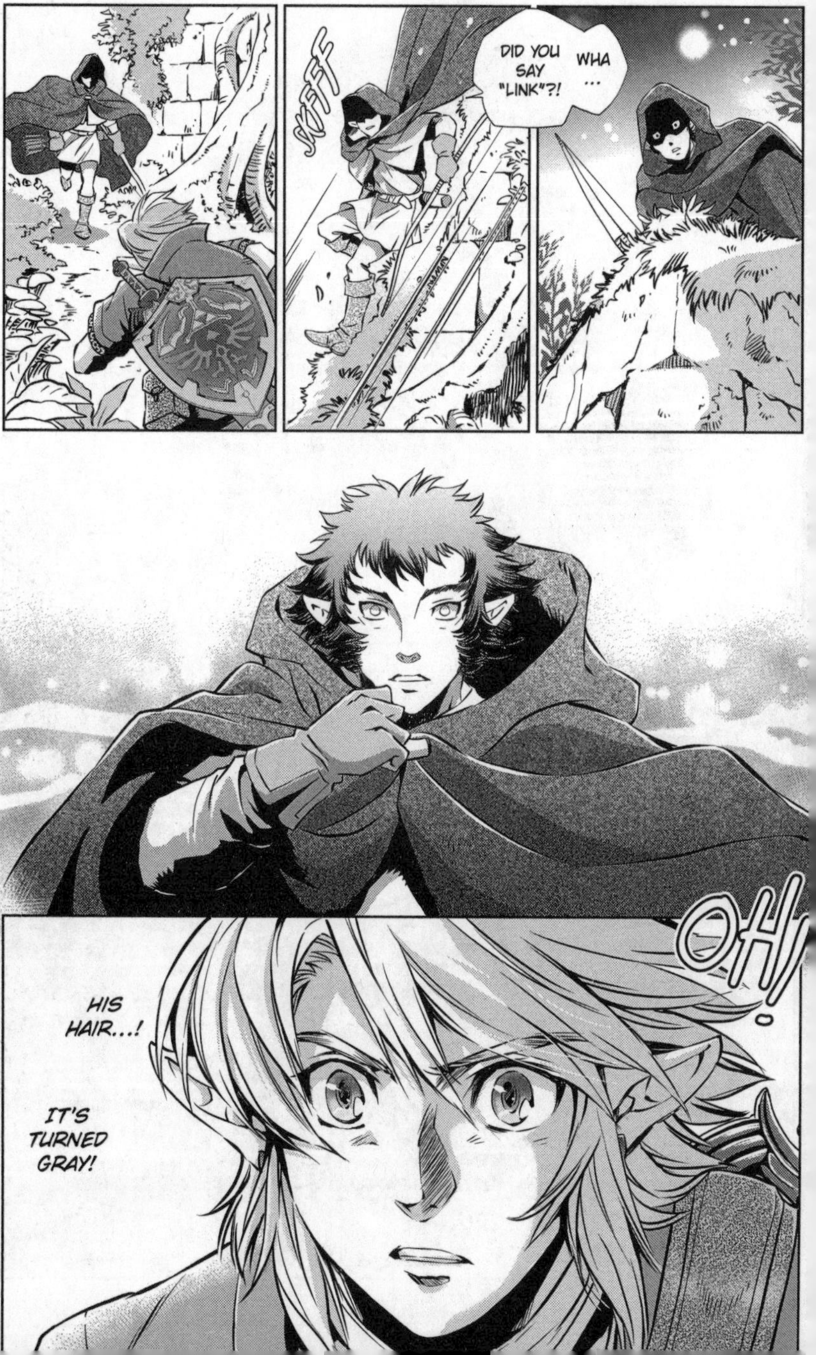
WHA ...
DID YOU SAY "LINK"?!
OH!
HIS HAIR...!
IT'S TURNED GRAY!

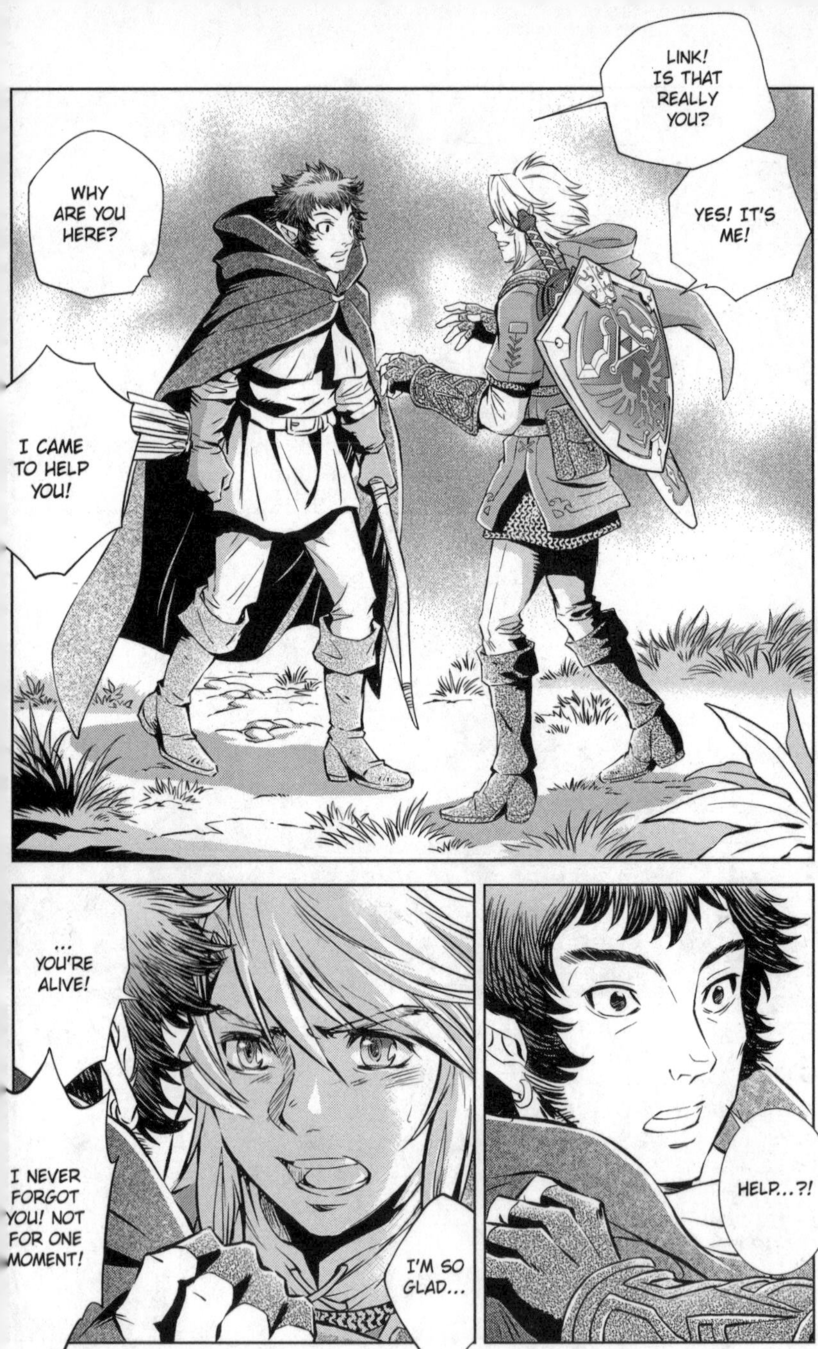
LINK! IS THAT REALLY YOU?
YES! IT'S ME!
WHY ARE YOU HERE?
I CAME TO HELP YOU!
HELP...?!
... YOU'RE ALIVE!
I'M SO GLAD...
I NEVER FORGOT YOU! NOT FOR ONE MOMENT!

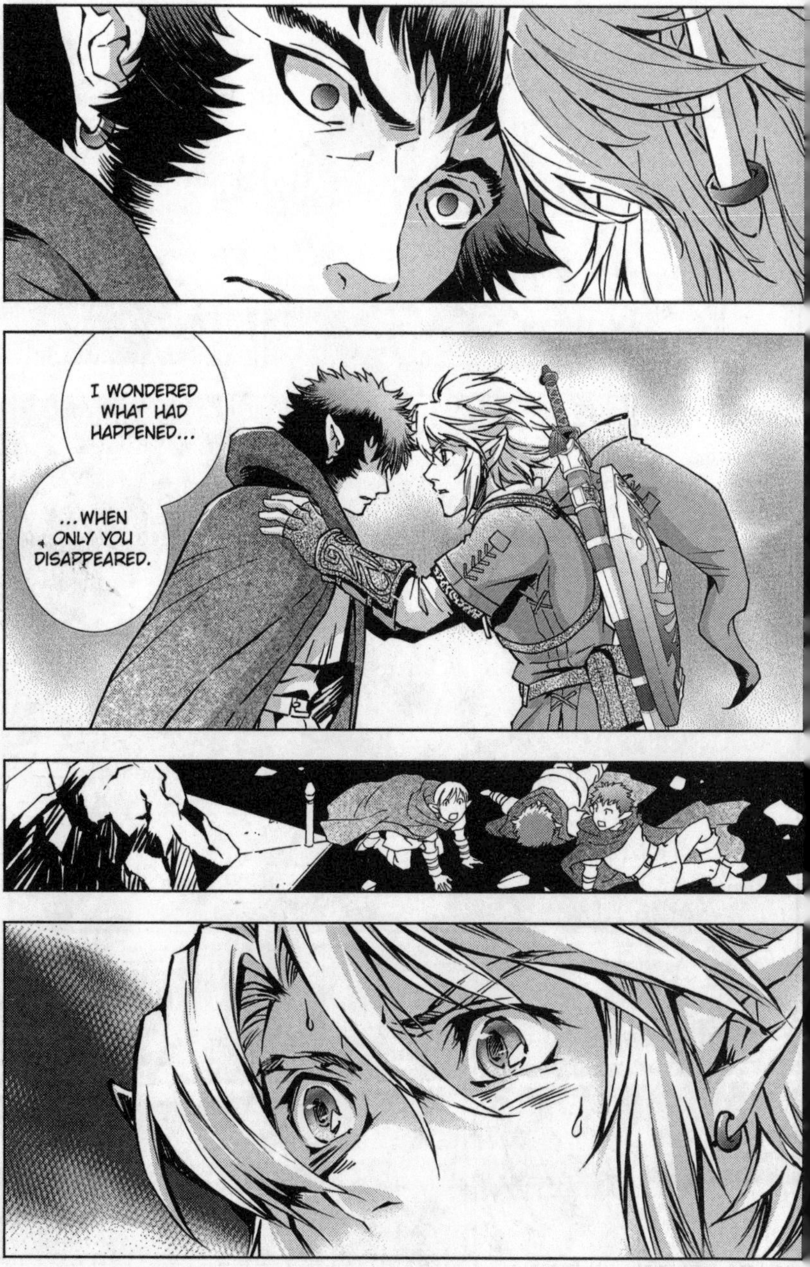
I WONDERED WHAT HAD HAPPENED...
...WHEN ONLY YOU DISAPPEARED.

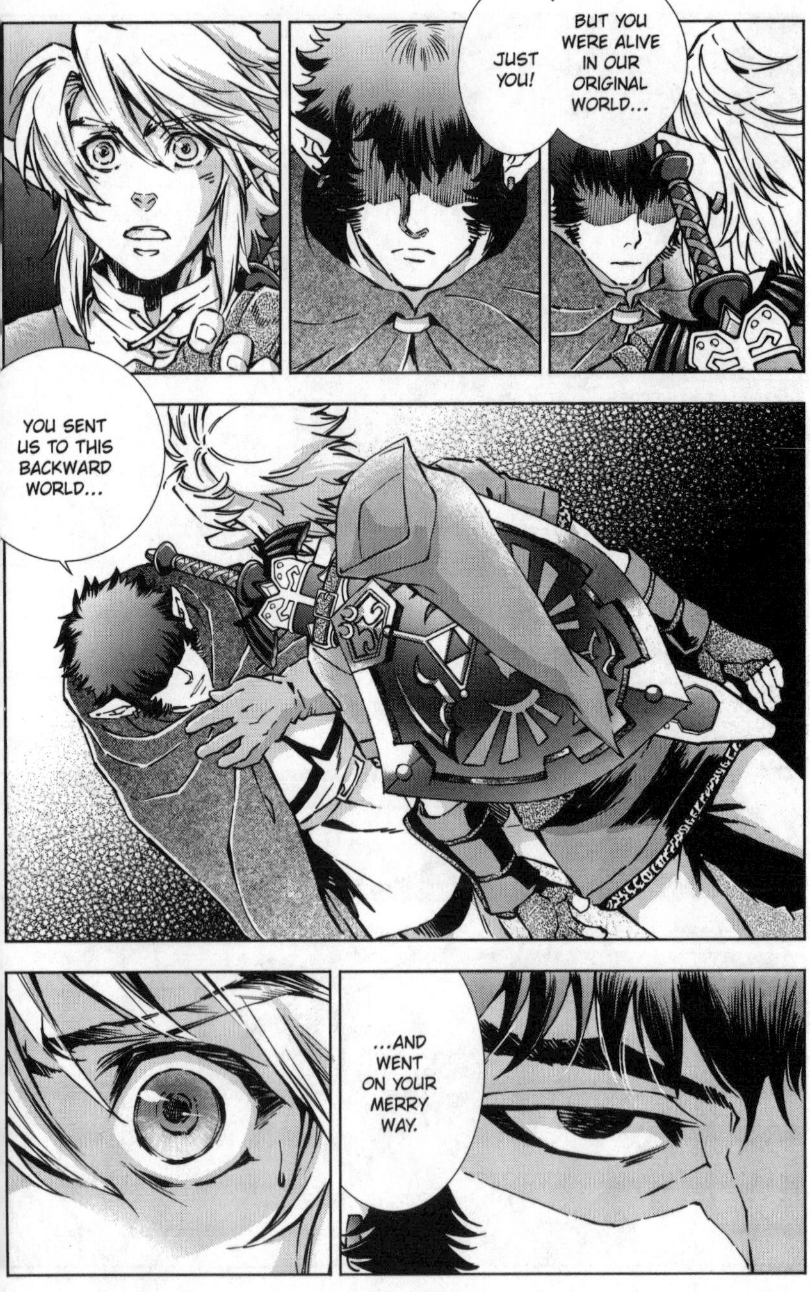
BUT YOU WERE ALIVE IN OUR ORIGINAL WORLD...
JUST YOU!
YOU SENT US TO THIS BACKWARD WORLD...
...AND WENT ON YOUR MERRY WAY.

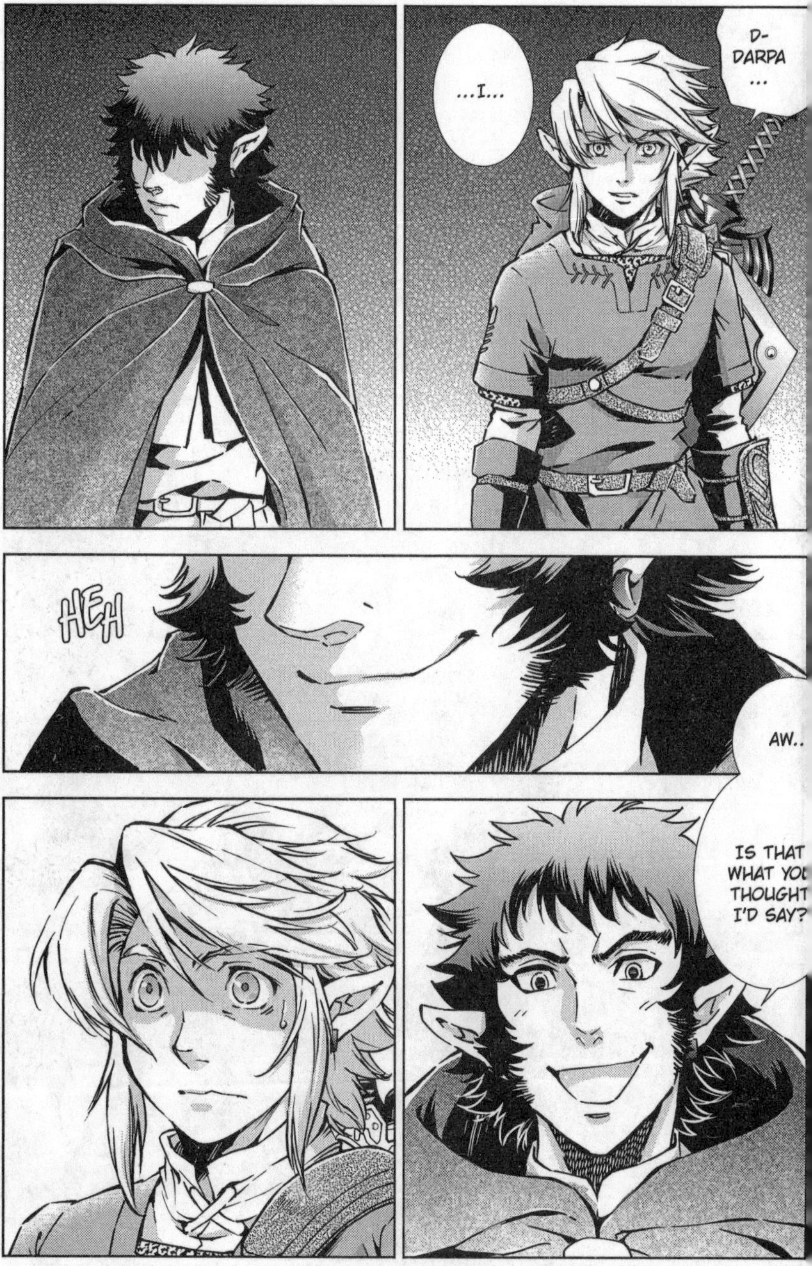
D-DARPA...
...I...
HEH
AW..
IS THAT WHAT YOU THOUGHT I'D SAY?

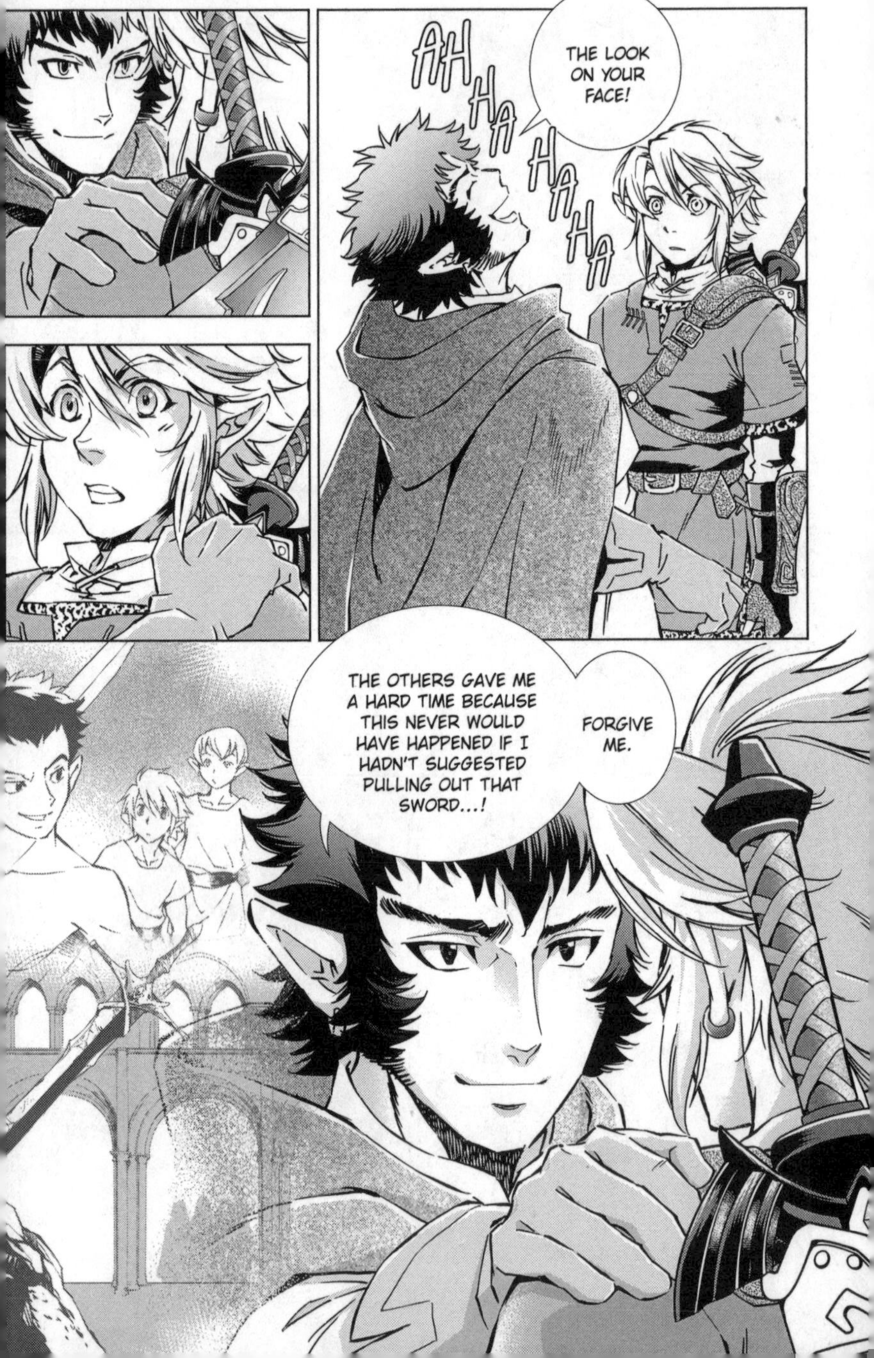
AH HA HA HA HA
THE LOOK ON YOUR FACE!
FORGIVE ME.
THE OTHERS GAVE ME A HARD TIME BECAUSE THIS NEVER WOULD HAVE HAPPENED IF I HADN'T SUGGESTED PULLING OUT THAT SWORD...!

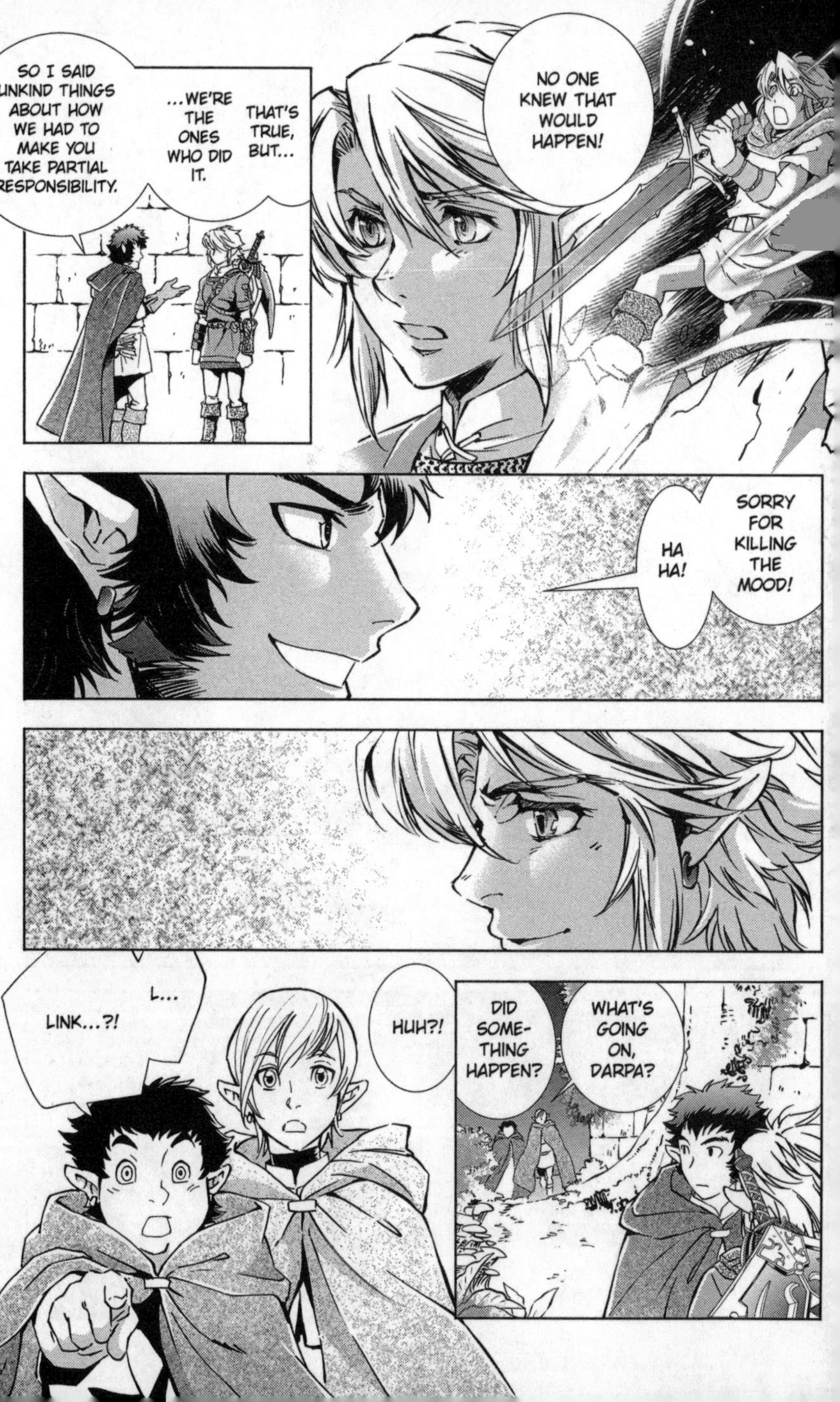
NO ONE KNEW THAT WOULD HAPPEN!
THAT'S TRUE, BUT...
...WE'RE THE ONES WHO DID IT.
SO I SAID UNKIND THINGS ABOUT HOW WE HAD TO MAKE YOU TAKE PARTIAL RESPONSIBILITY.
SORRY FOR KILLING THE MOOD!
HA HA!
WHAT'S GOING ON, DARPA?
DID SOMETHING HAPPEN?
HUH?!
L...
LINK...?!

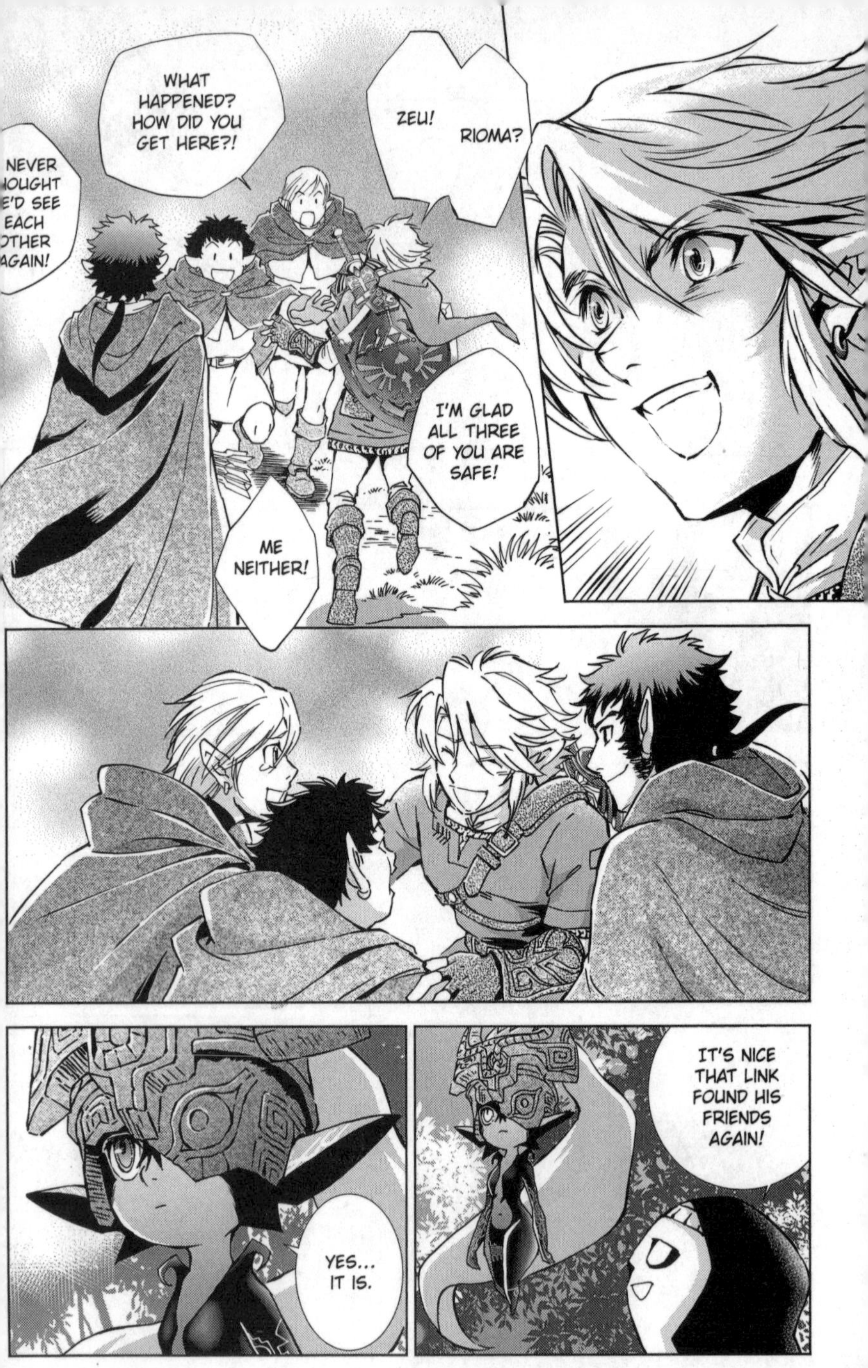

ZEU! RIOMA?
WHAT HAPPENED? HOW DID YOU GET HERE?!
I'M GLAD ALL THREE OF YOU ARE SAFE!
NEVER HOUGHT E'D SEE EACH OTHER AGAIN!
ME NEITHER!
IT'S NICE THAT LINK FOUND HIS FRIENDS AGAIN!
YES... IT IS.

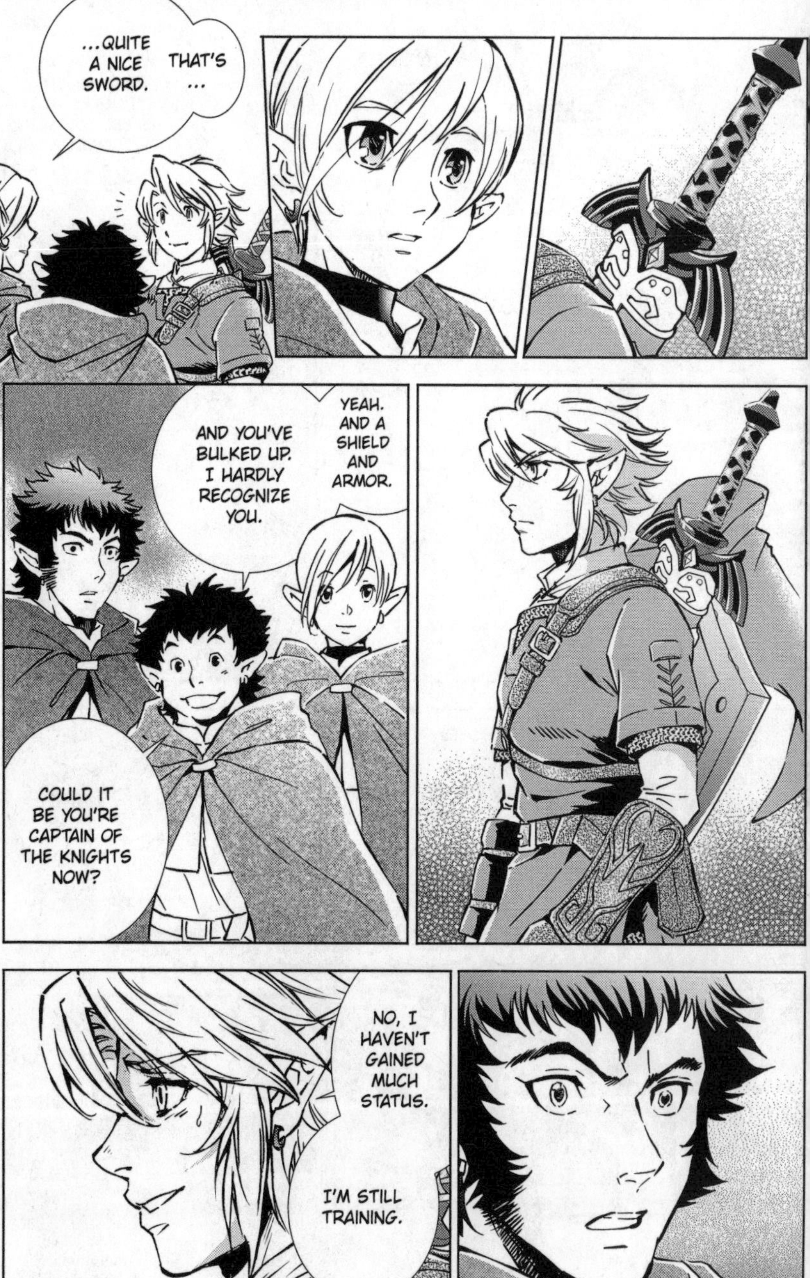
THAT'S ...
...QUITE A NICE SWORD.
YEAH. AND A SHIELD AND ARMOR.
AND YOU'VE BULKED UP. I HARDLY RECOGNIZE YOU.
COULD IT BE YOU'RE CAPTAIN OF THE KNIGHTS NOW?
NO, I HAVEN'T GAINED MUCH STATUS.
I'M STILL TRAINING.

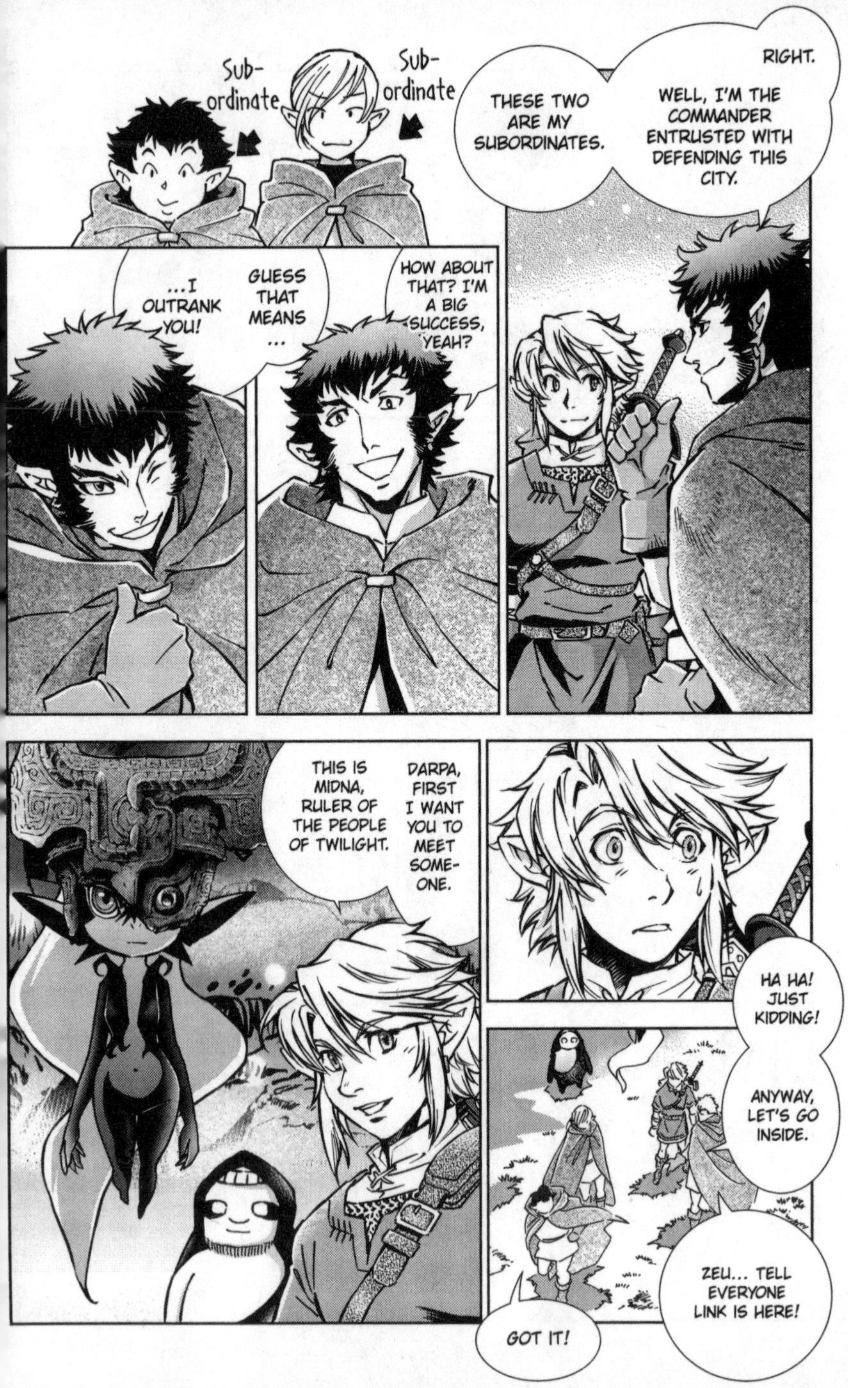
RIGHT.
WELL, I'M THE COMMANDER ENTRUSTED WITH DEFENDING THIS CITY.
THESE TWO ARE MY SUBORDINATES.
Sub-ordinate
Sub-ordinate
HOW ABOUT THAT? I'M A BIG SUCCESS, YEAH?
GUESS THAT MEANS ...
...I OUTRANK YOU!
HA HA! JUST KIDDING!
ANYWAY, LET'S GO INSIDE.
ZEU... TELL EVERYONE LINK IS HERE!
GOT IT!
DARPA, FIRST I WANT YOU TO MEET SOME-ONE.
THIS IS MIDNA, RULER OF THE PEOPLE OF TWILIGHT.

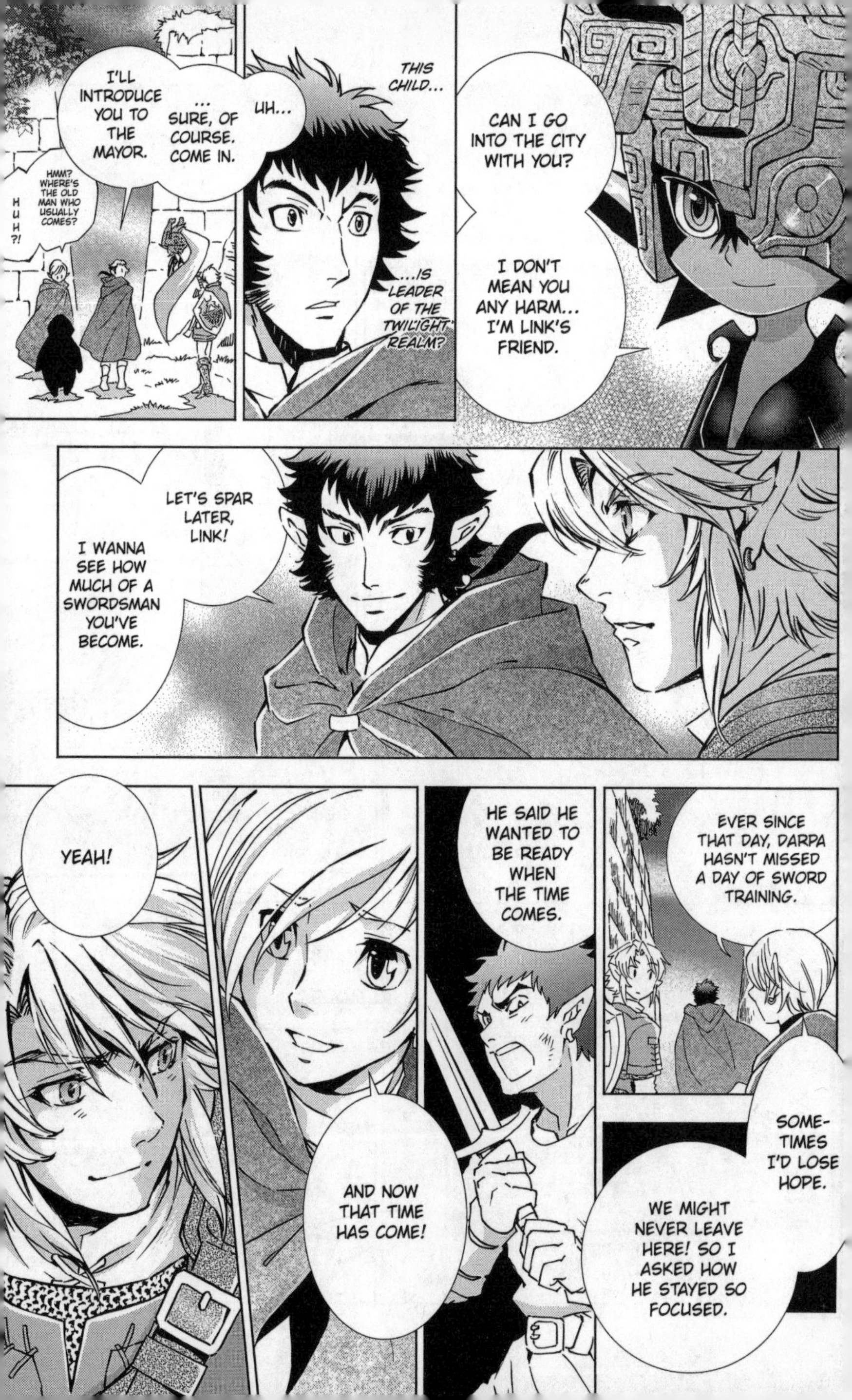
CAN I GO INTO THE CITY WITH YOU?
I DON'T MEAN YOU ANY HARM... I'M LINK'S FRIEND.
THIS CHILD...
...IS LEADER OF THE TWILIGHT REALM?
UH...
... SURE, OF COURSE. COME IN.
I'LL INTRODUCE YOU TO THE MAYOR.
HMM? WHERE'S THE OLD MAN WHO USUALLY COMES?
HUH?!
LET'S SPAR LATER, LINK!
I WANNA SEE HOW MUCH OF A SWORDSMAN YOU'VE BECOME.
EVER SINCE THAT DAY, DARPA HASN'T MISSED A DAY OF SWORD TRAINING.
SOME-TIMES I'D LOSE HOPE.
WE MIGHT NEVER LEAVE HERE! SO I ASKED HOW HE STAYED SO FOCUSED.
HE SAID HE WANTED TO BE READY WHEN THE TIME COMES.
AND NOW THAT TIME HAS COME!
YEAH!

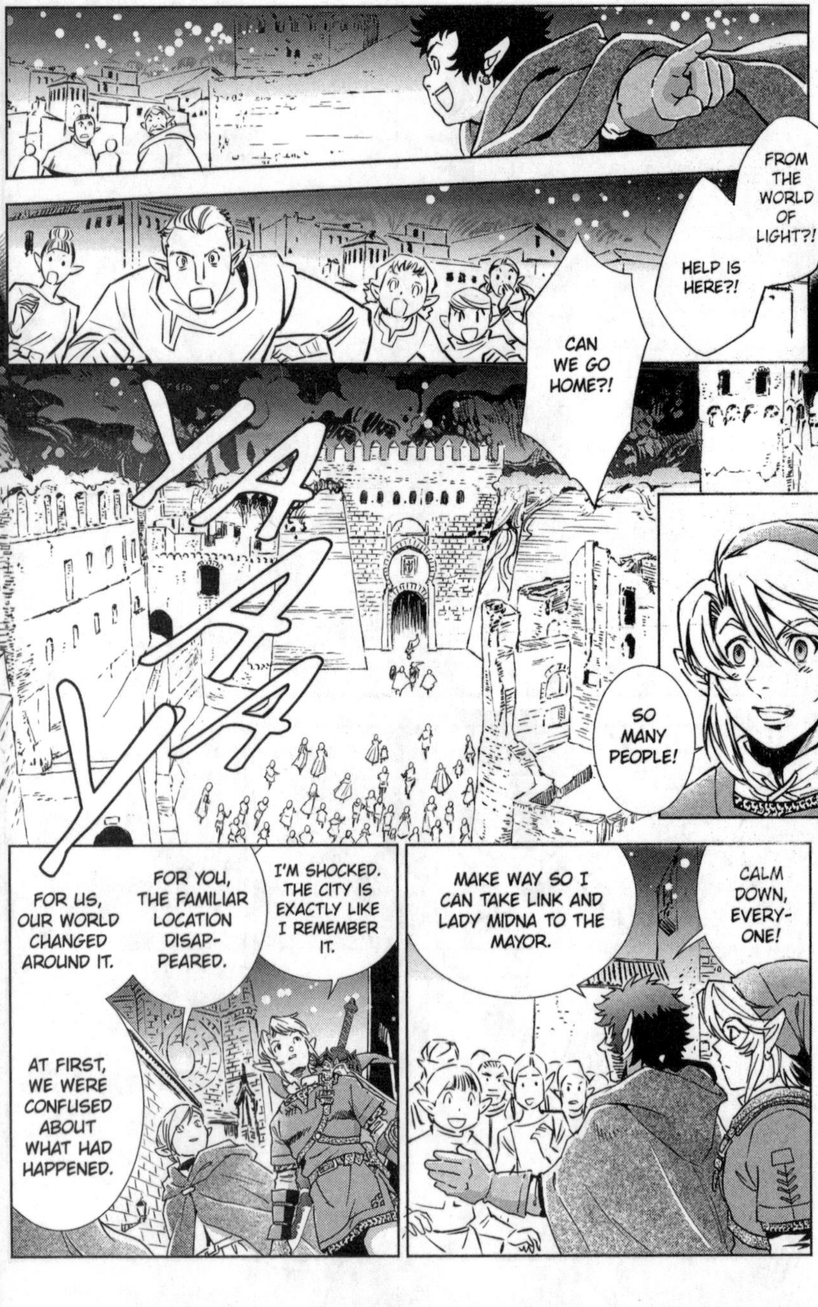
FROM THE WORLD OF LIGHT?!
HELP IS HERE?!
CAN WE GO HOME?!
YAAAA
SO MANY PEOPLE!
CALM DOWN, EVERY-ONE!
MAKE WAY SO I CAN TAKE LINK AND LADY MIDNA TO THE MAYOR.
I'M SHOCKED. THE CITY IS EXACTLY LIKE I REMEMBER IT.
FOR YOU, THE FAMILIAR LOCATION DISAP-PEARED.
FOR US, OUR WORLD CHANGED AROUND IT.
AT FIRST, WE WERE CONFUSED ABOUT WHAT HAD HAPPENED.

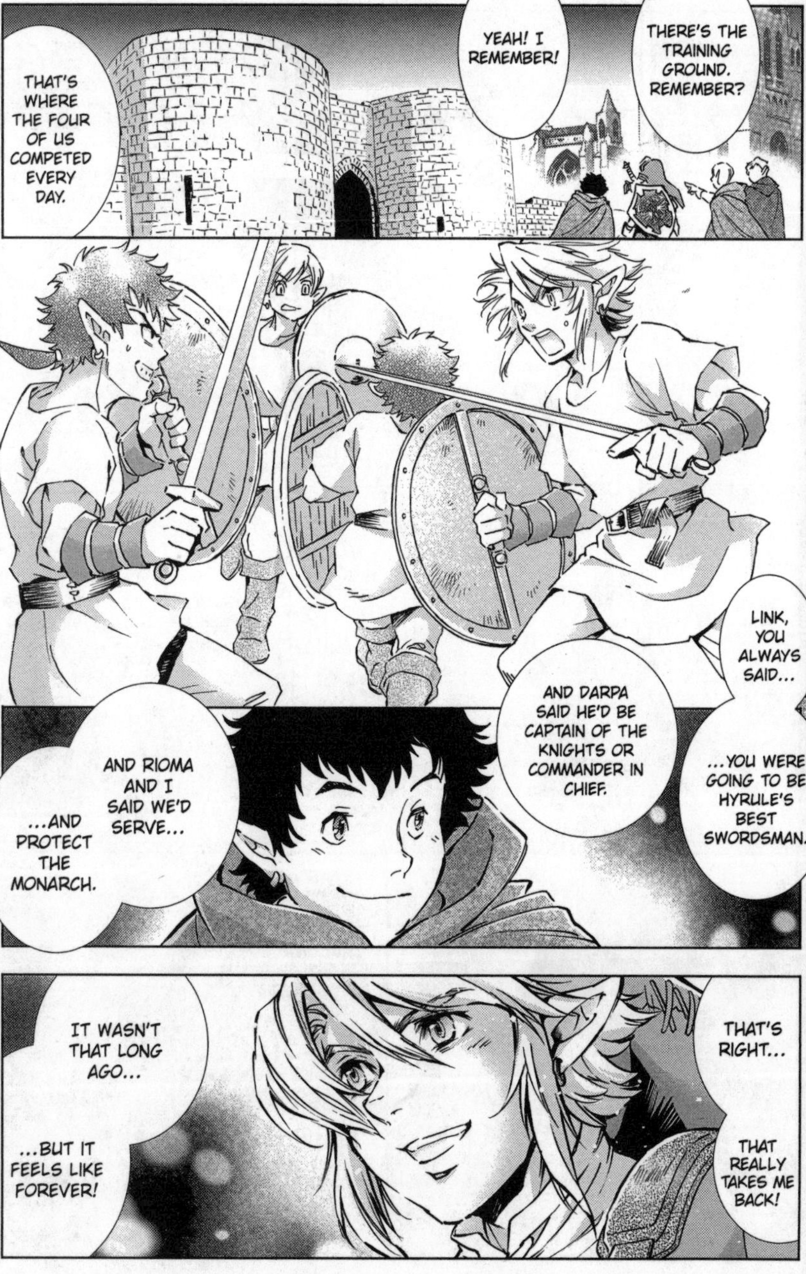
THERE'S THE TRAINING GROUND. REMEMBER?
YEAH! I REMEMBER!
THAT'S WHERE THE FOUR OF US COMPETED EVERY DAY.
LINK, YOU ALWAYS SAID...
...YOU WERE GOING TO BE HYRULE'S BEST SWORDSMAN.
AND DARPA SAID HE'D BE CAPTAIN OF THE KNIGHTS OR COMMANDER IN CHIEF.
AND RIOMA AND I SAID WE'D SERVE...
...AND PROTECT THE MONARCH.
THAT'S RIGHT...
THAT REALLY TAKES ME BACK!
IT WASN'T THAT LONG AGO...
...BUT IT FEELS LIKE FOREVER!

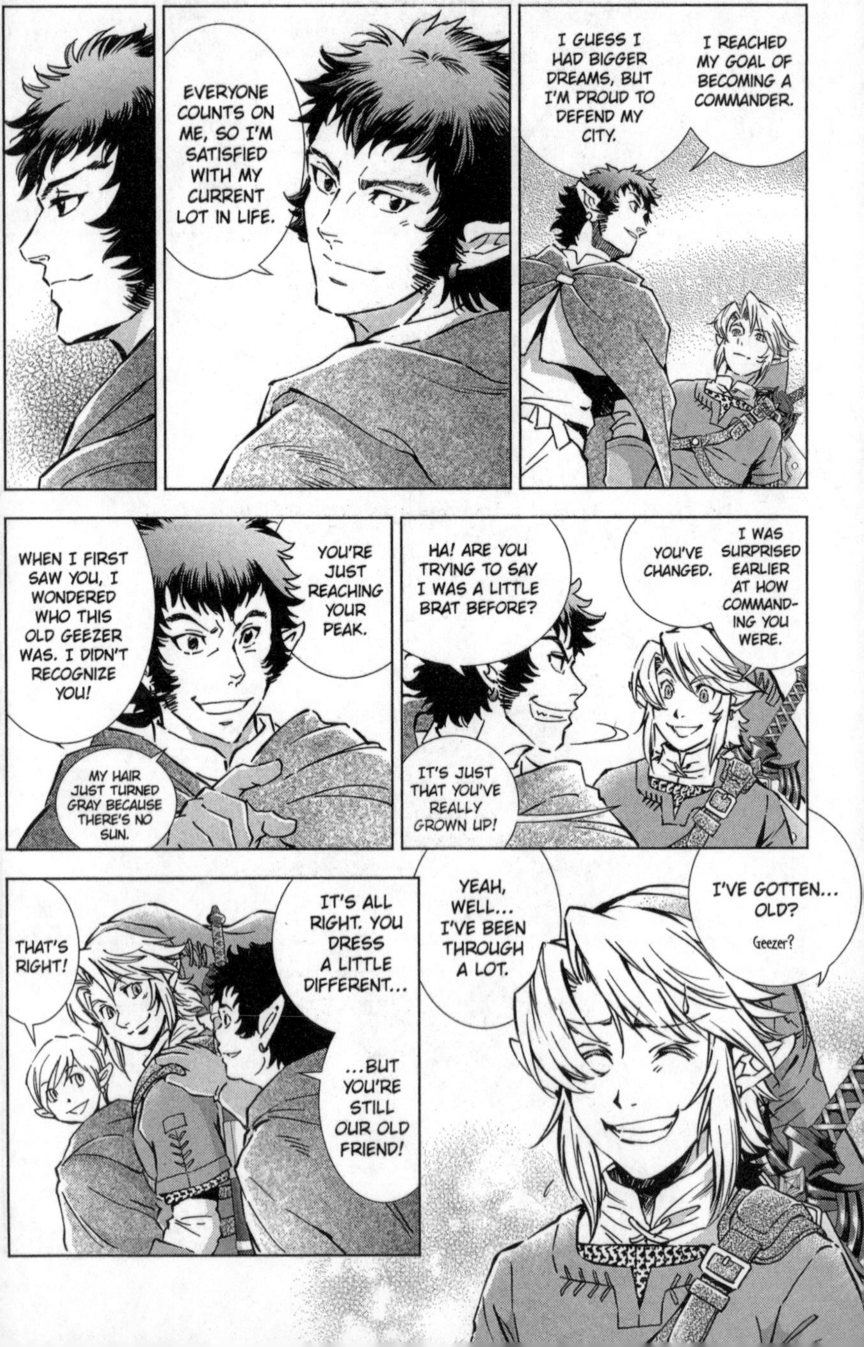
I REACHED MY GOAL OF BECOMING A COMMANDER.
I GUESS I HAD BIGGER DREAMS, BUT I'M PROUD TO DEFEND MY CITY.
EVERYONE COUNTS ON ME, SO I'M SATISFIED WITH MY CURRENT LOT IN LIFE.
I WAS SURPRISED EARLIER AT HOW COMMAND-ING YOU WERE.
YOU'VE CHANGED.
HA! ARE YOU TRYING TO SAY I WAS A LITTLE BRAT BEFORE?
IT'S JUST THAT YOU'VE REALLY GROWN UP!
YOU'RE JUST REACHING YOUR PEAK.
WHEN I FIRST SAW YOU, I WONDERED WHO THIS OLD GEEZER WAS. I DIDN'T RECOGNIZE YOU!
MY HAIR JUST TURNED GRAY BECAUSE THERE'S NO SUN.
I'VE GOTTEN... OLD?
Geezer?
YEAH, WELL... I'VE BEEN THROUGH A LOT.
IT'S ALL RIGHT. YOU DRESS A LITTLE DIFFERENT...
...BUT YOU'RE STILL OUR OLD FRIEND!
THAT'S RIGHT!

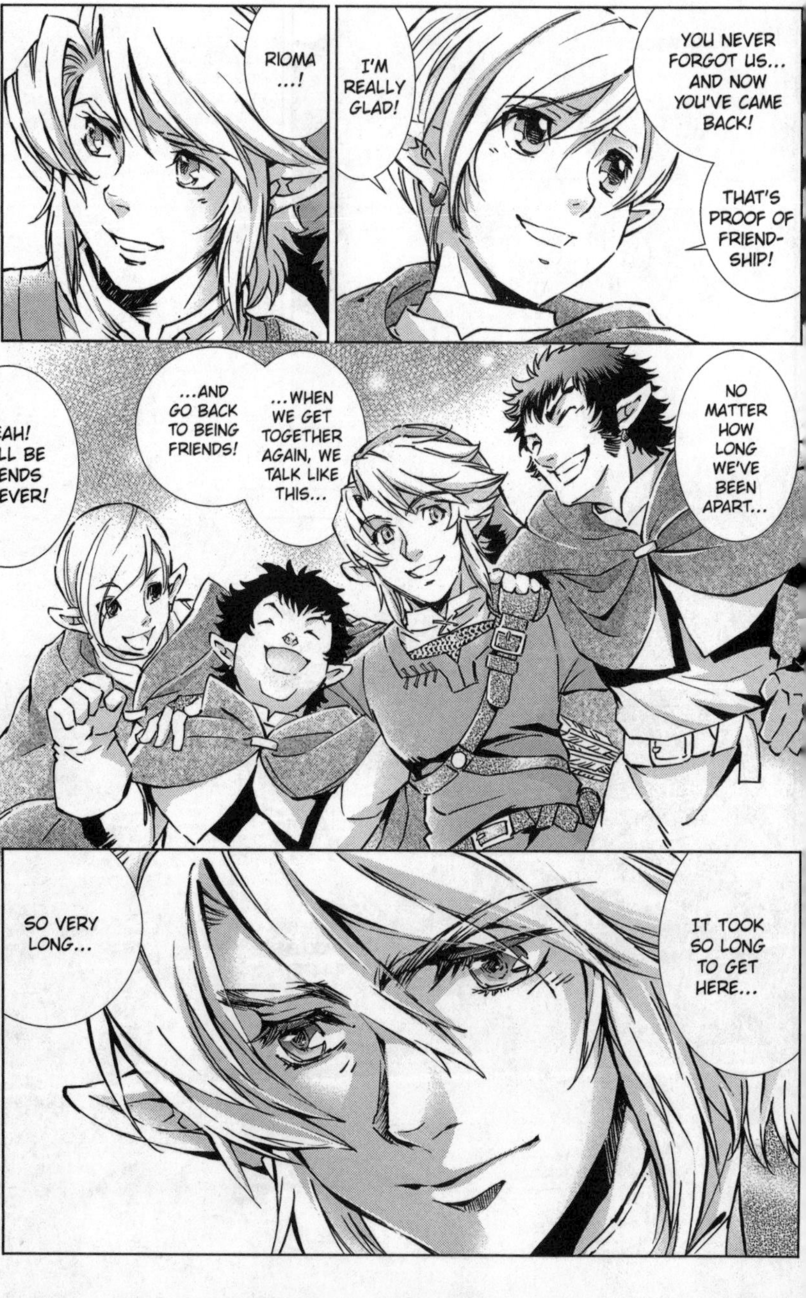
YOU NEVER FORGOT US... AND NOW YOU'VE CAME BACK!
THAT'S PROOF OF FRIEND-SHIP!
I'M REALLY GLAD!
RIOMA ...!
NO MATTER HOW LONG WE'VE BEEN APART...
...WHEN WE GET TOGETHER AGAIN, WE TALK LIKE THIS...
...AND GO BACK TO BEING FRIENDS!
YEAH! WE'LL BE FRIENDS FOREVER!
IT TOOK SO LONG TO GET HERE...
SO VERY LONG...

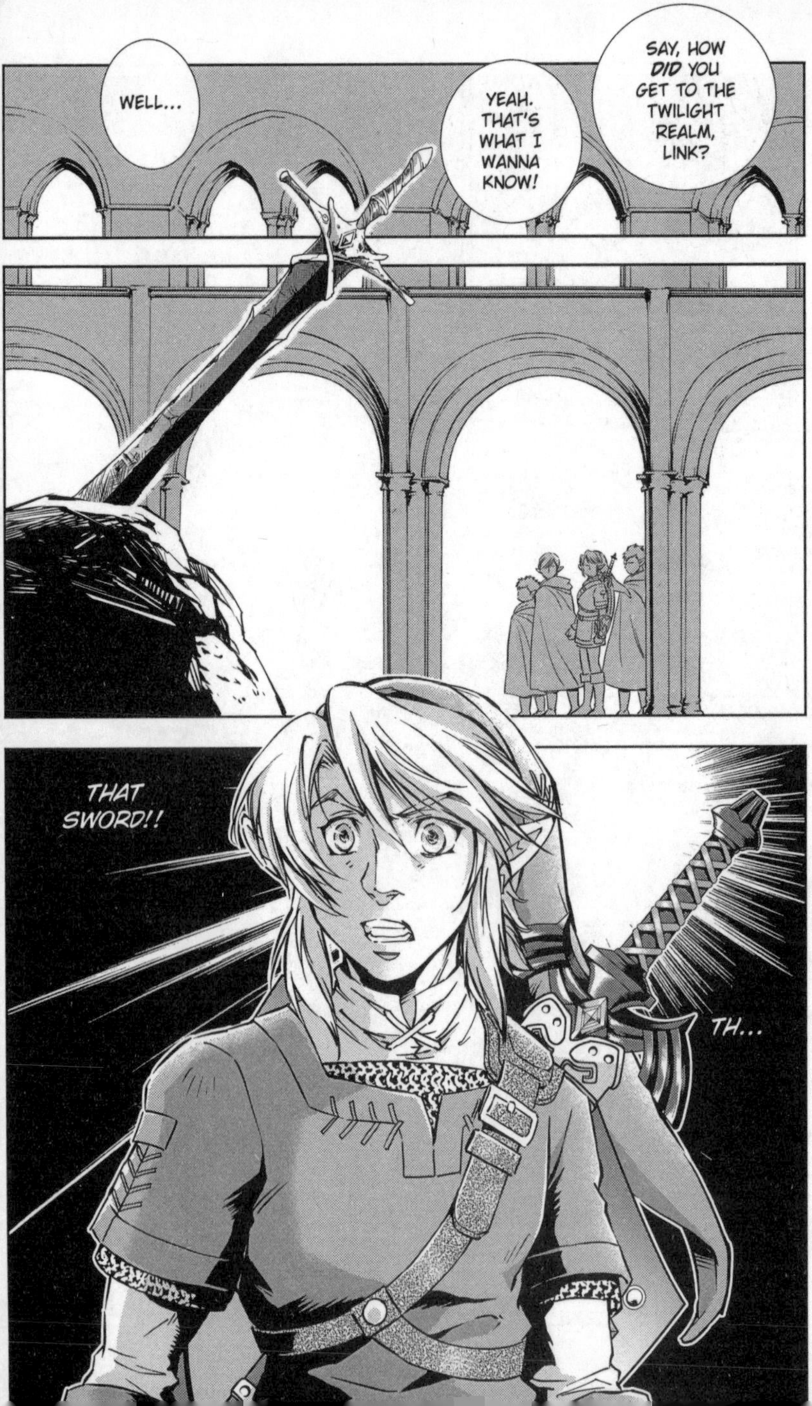
SAY, HOW *DID* YOU GET TO THE TWILIGHT REALM, LINK?
YEAH. THAT'S WHAT I WANNA KNOW!
WELL...
TH...
THAT SWORD!!

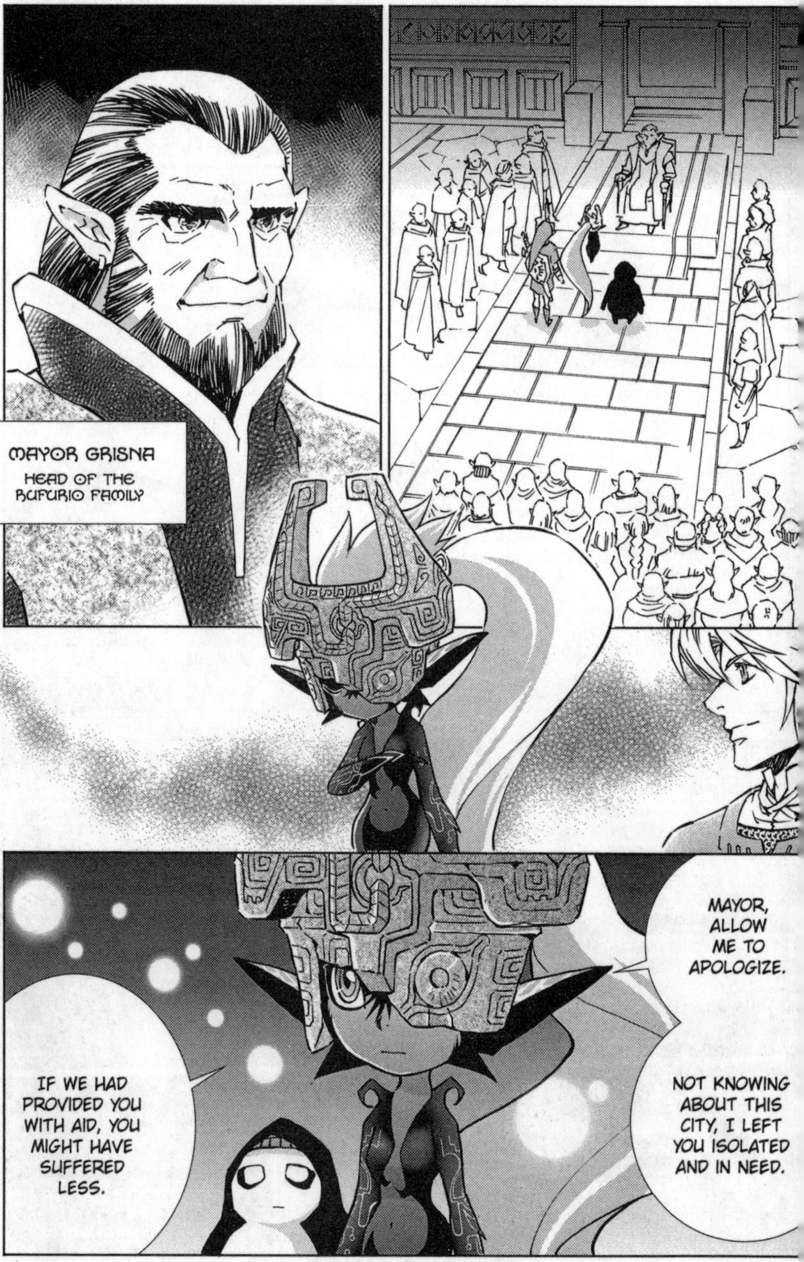
MAYOR GRISNA
HEAD OF THE BUFURIO FAMILY
MAYOR, ALLOW ME TO APOLOGIZE.
NOT KNOWING ABOUT THIS CITY, I LEFT YOU ISOLATED AND IN NEED.
IF WE HAD PROVIDED YOU WITH AID, YOU MIGHT HAVE SUFFERED LESS.

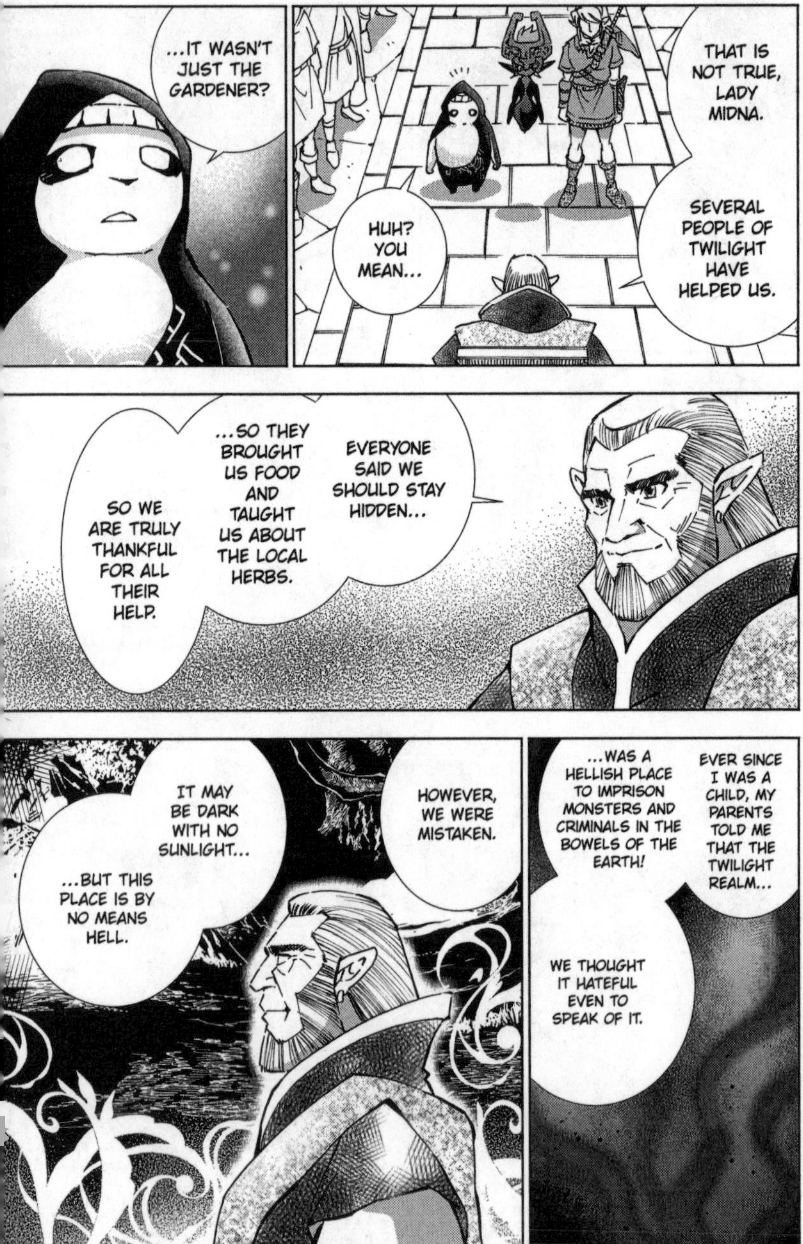
THAT IS NOT TRUE, LADY MIDNA.
SEVERAL PEOPLE OF TWILIGHT HAVE HELPED US.
HUH? YOU MEAN...
...IT WASN'T JUST THE GARDENER?
EVERYONE SAID WE SHOULD STAY HIDDEN...
...SO THEY BROUGHT US FOOD AND TAUGHT US ABOUT THE LOCAL HERBS.
SO WE ARE TRULY THANKFUL FOR ALL THEIR HELP.
EVER SINCE I WAS A CHILD, MY PARENTS TOLD ME THAT THE TWILIGHT REALM...
...WAS A HELLISH PLACE TO IMPRISON MONSTERS AND CRIMINALS IN THE BOWELS OF THE EARTH!
WE THOUGHT IT HATEFUL EVEN TO SPEAK OF IT.
HOWEVER, WE WERE MISTAKEN.
IT MAY BE DARK WITH NO SUNLIGHT...
...BUT THIS PLACE IS BY NO MEANS HELL.

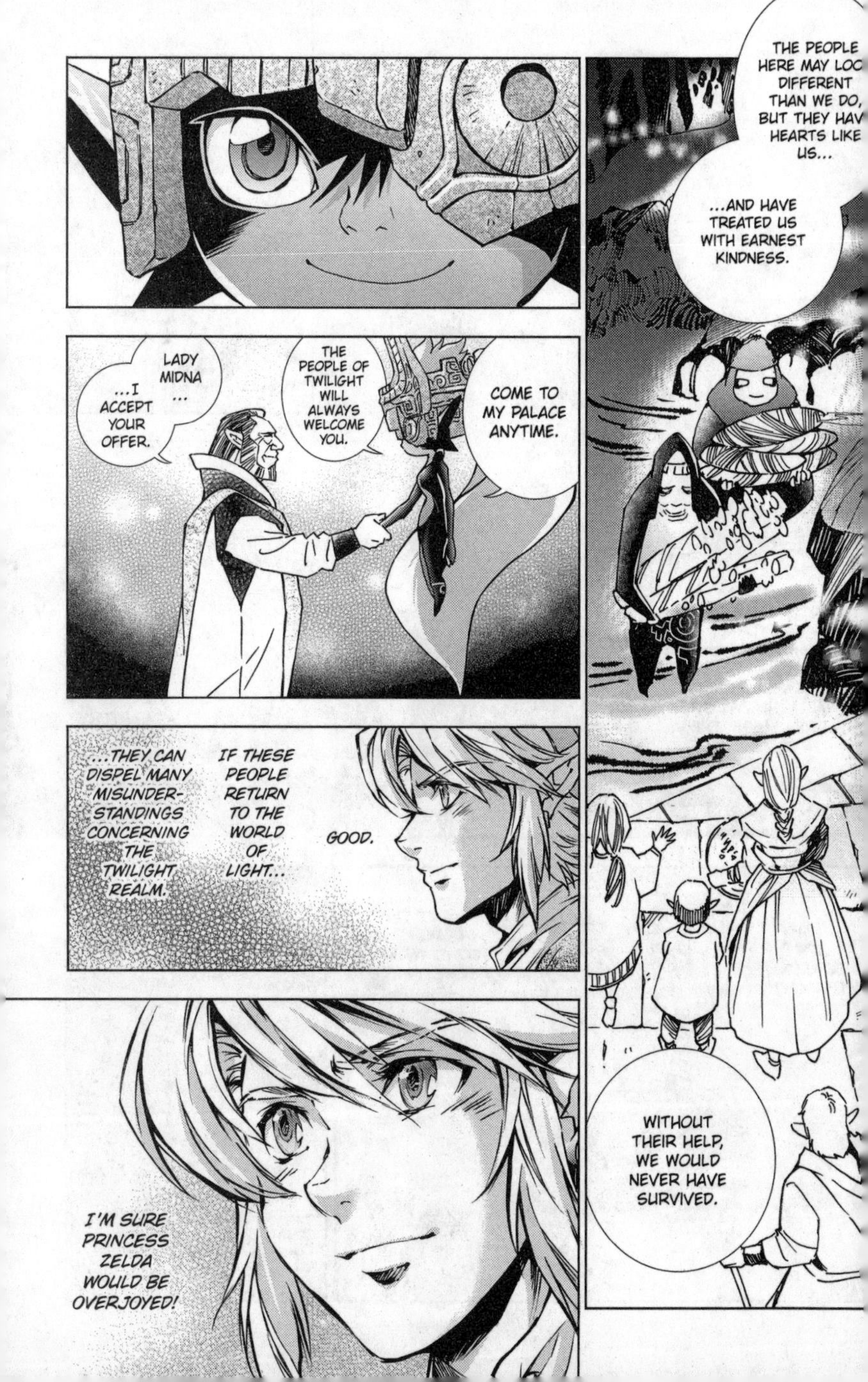
THE PEOPLE HERE MAY LOC DIFFERENT THAN WE DO, BUT THEY HAV HEARTS LIKE US...
...AND HAVE TREATED US WITH EARNEST KINDNESS.
WITHOUT THEIR HELP, WE WOULD NEVER HAVE SURVIVED.
COME TO MY PALACE ANYTIME.
THE PEOPLE OF TWILIGHT WILL ALWAYS WELCOME YOU.
LADY MIDNA ...
...I ACCEPT YOUR OFFER.
GOOD.
IF THESE PEOPLE RETURN TO THE WORLD OF LIGHT...
...THEY CAN DISPEL MANY MISUNDER-STANDINGS CONCERNING THE TWILIGHT REALM.
I'M SURE PRINCESS ZELDA WOULD BE OVERJOYED!

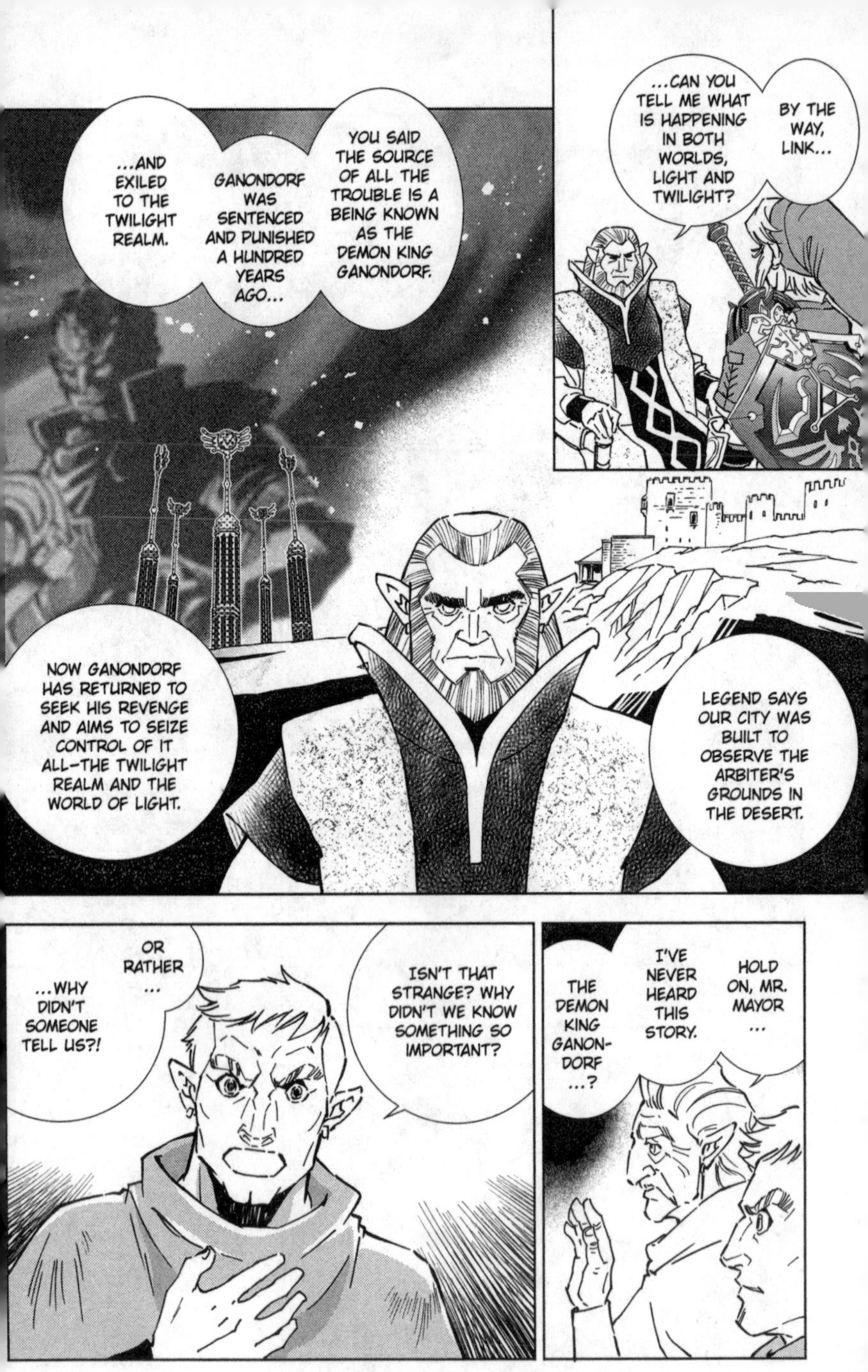
BY THE WAY, LINK...
...CAN YOU TELL ME WHAT IS HAPPENING IN BOTH WORLDS, LIGHT AND TWILIGHT?
YOU SAID THE SOURCE OF ALL THE TROUBLE IS A BEING KNOWN AS THE DEMON KING GANONDORF.
GANONDORF WAS SENTENCED AND PUNISHED A HUNDRED YEARS AGO...
...AND EXILED TO THE TWILIGHT REALM.
LEGEND SAYS OUR CITY WAS BUILT TO OBSERVE THE ARBITER'S GROUNDS IN THE DESERT.
NOW GANONDORF HAS RETURNED TO SEEK HIS REVENGE AND AIMS TO SEIZE CONTROL OF IT ALL—THE TWILIGHT REALM AND THE WORLD OF LIGHT.
HOLD ON, MR. MAYOR...
I'VE NEVER HEARD THIS STORY.
THE DEMON KING GANON-DORF...?
ISN'T THAT STRANGE? WHY DIDN'T WE KNOW SOMETHING SO IMPORTANT?
OR RATHER...
...WHY DIDN'T SOMEONE TELL US?!

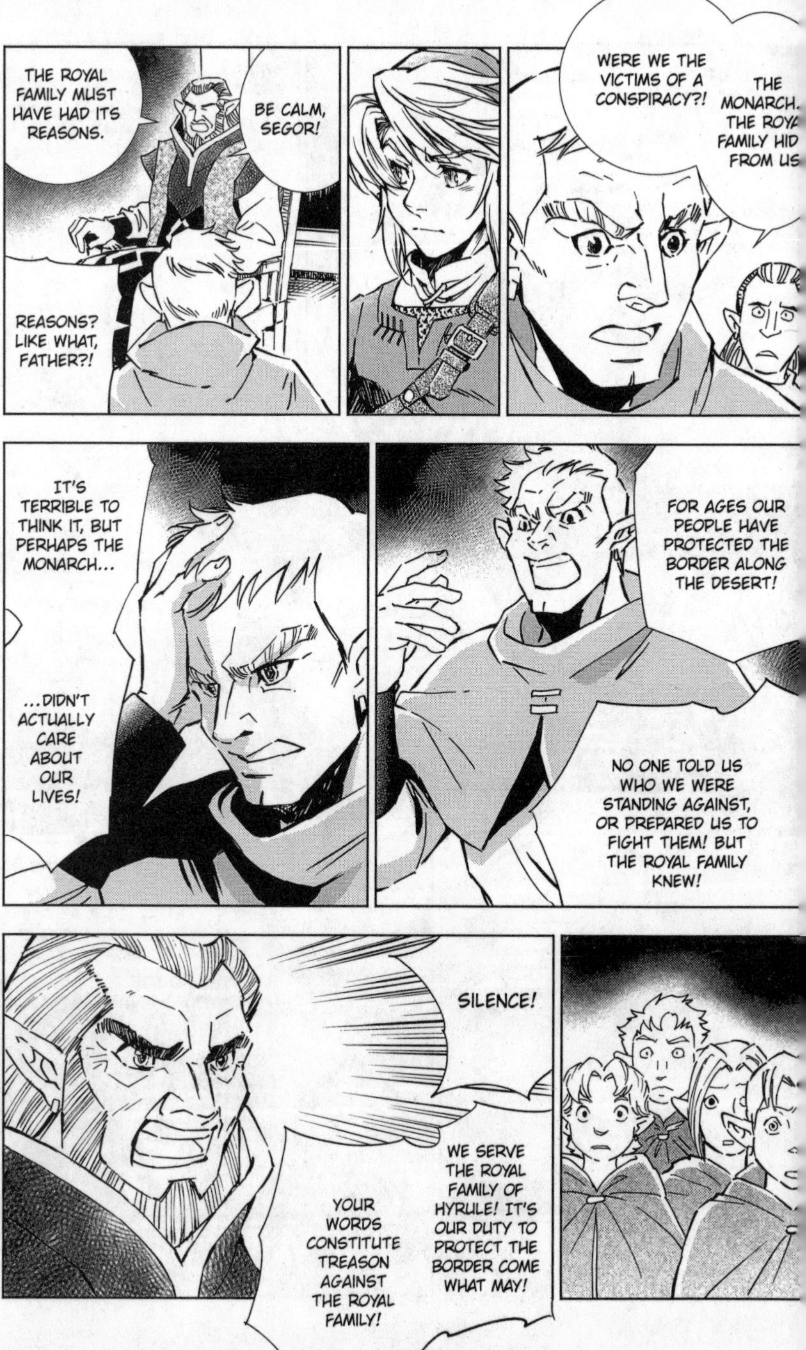
WERE WE THE VICTIMS OF A CONSPIRACY?!
THE MONARCH... THE ROYAL FAMILY HID FROM US
BE CALM, SEGOR!
THE ROYAL FAMILY MUST HAVE HAD ITS REASONS.
REASONS? LIKE WHAT, FATHER?!
FOR AGES OUR PEOPLE HAVE PROTECTED THE BORDER ALONG THE DESERT!
NO ONE TOLD US WHO WE WERE STANDING AGAINST, OR PREPARED US TO FIGHT THEM! BUT THE ROYAL FAMILY KNEW!
IT'S TERRIBLE TO THINK IT, BUT PERHAPS THE MONARCH...
...DIDN'T ACTUALLY CARE ABOUT OUR LIVES!
SILENCE!
WE SERVE THE ROYAL FAMILY OF HYRULE! IT'S OUR DUTY TO PROTECT THE BORDER COME WHAT MAY!
YOUR WORDS CONSTITUTE TREASON AGAINST THE ROYAL FAMILY!

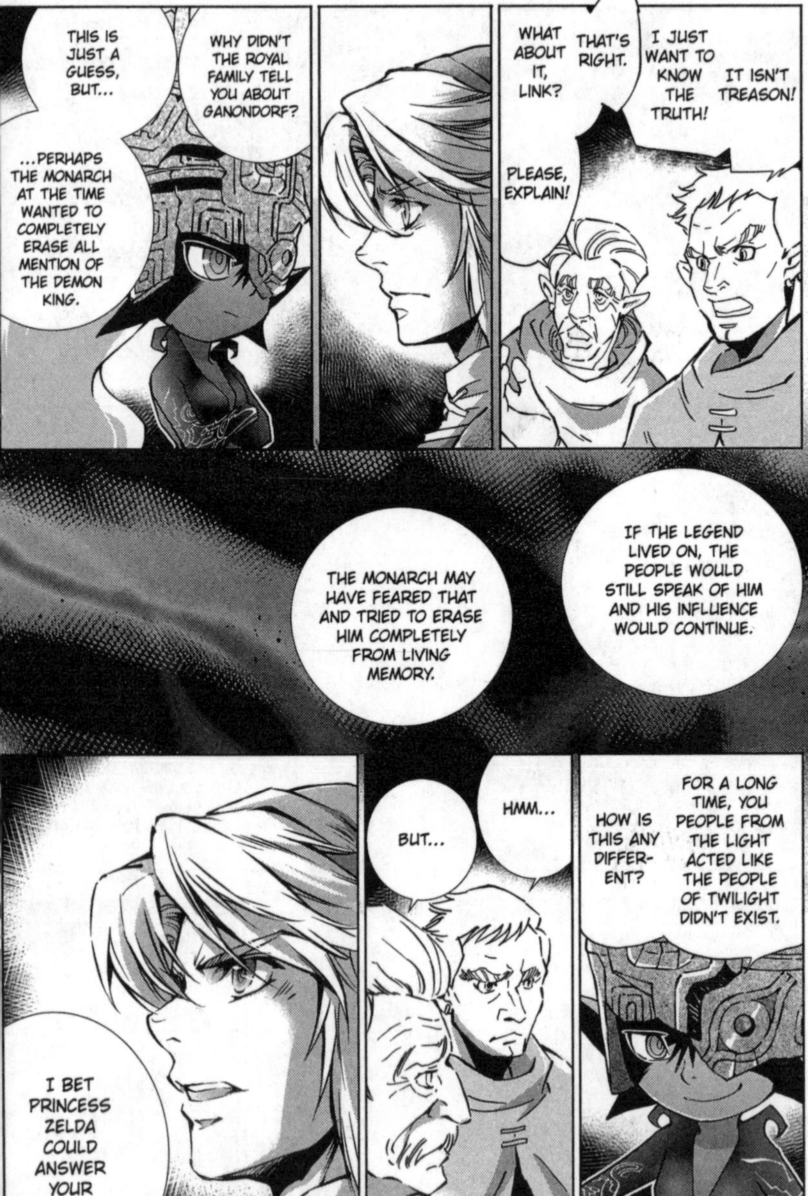
IT ISN'T TREASON!
I JUST WANT TO KNOW THE TRUTH!
THAT'S RIGHT.
WHAT ABOUT IT, LINK?
PLEASE, EXPLAIN!
WHY DIDN'T THE ROYAL FAMILY TELL YOU ABOUT GANONDORF?
THIS IS JUST A GUESS, BUT...
...PERHAPS THE MONARCH AT THE TIME WANTED TO COMPLETELY ERASE ALL MENTION OF THE DEMON KING.
IF THE LEGEND LIVED ON, THE PEOPLE WOULD STILL SPEAK OF HIM AND HIS INFLUENCE WOULD CONTINUE.
THE MONARCH MAY HAVE FEARED THAT AND TRIED TO ERASE HIM COMPLETELY FROM LIVING MEMORY.
FOR A LONG TIME, YOU PEOPLE FROM THE LIGHT ACTED LIKE THE PEOPLE OF TWILIGHT DIDN'T EXIST.
HOW IS THIS ANY DIFFER-ENT?
HMM...
BUT...
I BET PRINCESS ZELDA COULD ANSWER YOUR QUESTIONS.

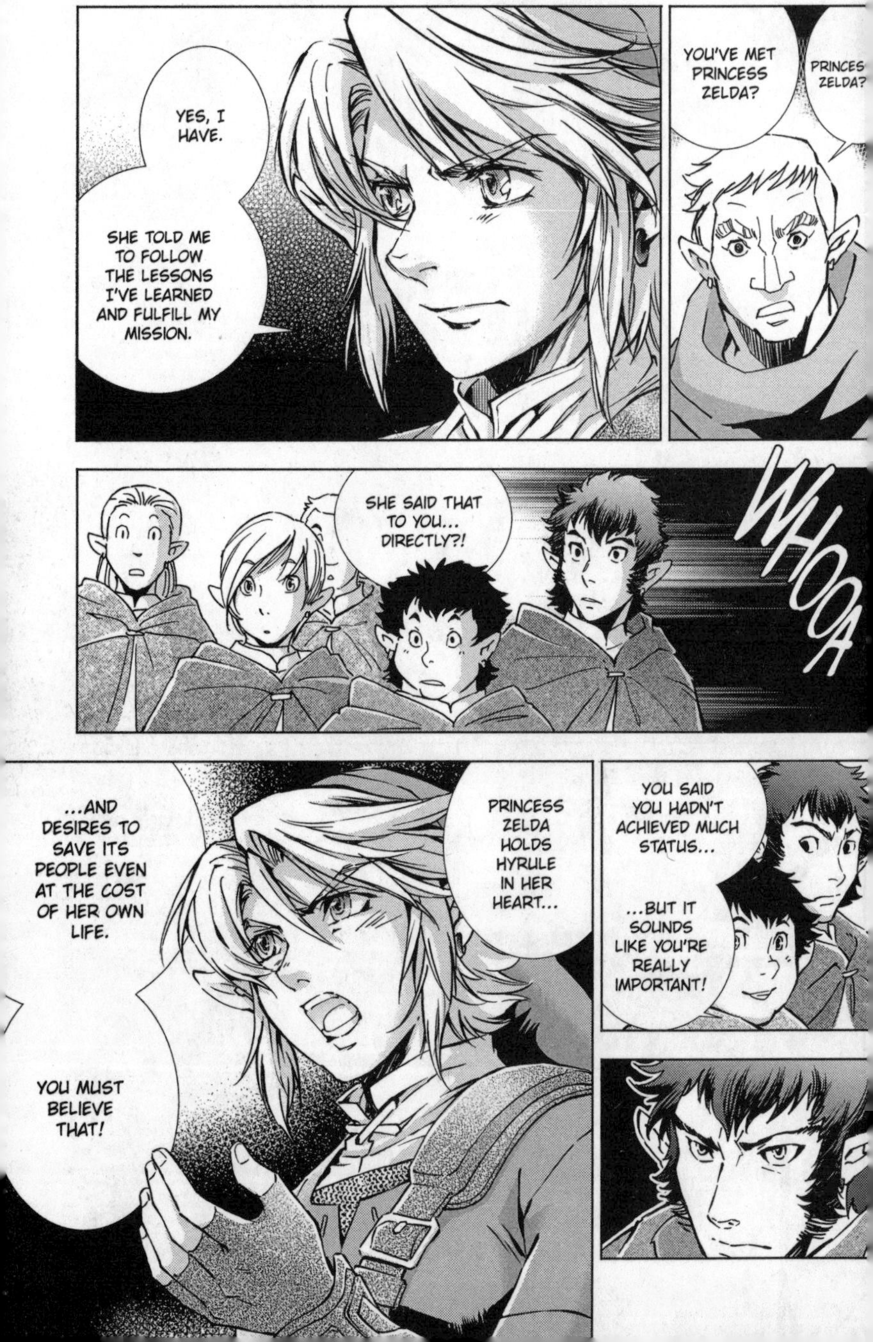
YOU'VE MET PRINCESS ZELDA?
PRINCES ZELDA?
YES, I HAVE.
SHE TOLD ME TO FOLLOW THE LESSONS I'VE LEARNED AND FULFILL MY MISSION.
WHOOA
SHE SAID THAT TO YOU... DIRECTLY?!
YOU SAID YOU HADN'T ACHIEVED MUCH STATUS...
...BUT IT SOUNDS LIKE YOU'RE REALLY IMPORTANT!
PRINCESS ZELDA HOLDS HYRULE IN HER HEART...
...AND DESIRES TO SAVE ITS PEOPLE EVEN AT THE COST OF HER OWN LIFE.
YOU MUST BELIEVE THAT!

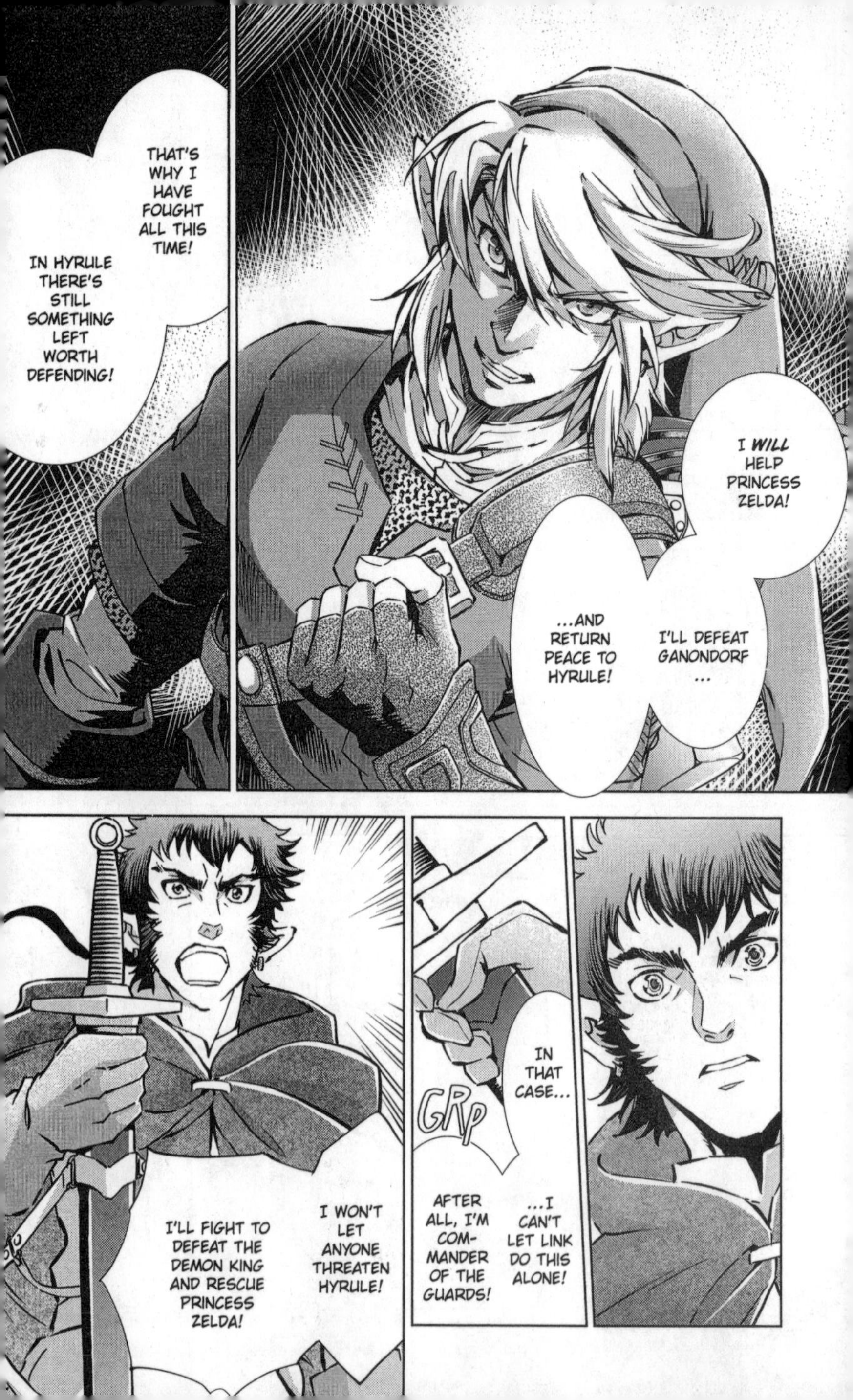
I WILL HELP PRINCESS ZELDA!
I'LL DEFEAT GANONDORF ...
...AND RETURN PEACE TO HYRULE!
THAT'S WHY I HAVE FOUGHT ALL THIS TIME!
IN HYRULE THERE'S STILL SOMETHING LEFT WORTH DEFENDING!
IN THAT CASE...
GRIP
...I CAN'T LET LINK DO THIS ALONE!
AFTER ALL, I'M COMMANDER OF THE GUARDS!
I WON'T LET ANYONE THREATEN HYRULE!
I'LL FIGHT TO DEFEAT THE DEMON KING AND RESCUE PRINCESS ZELDA!

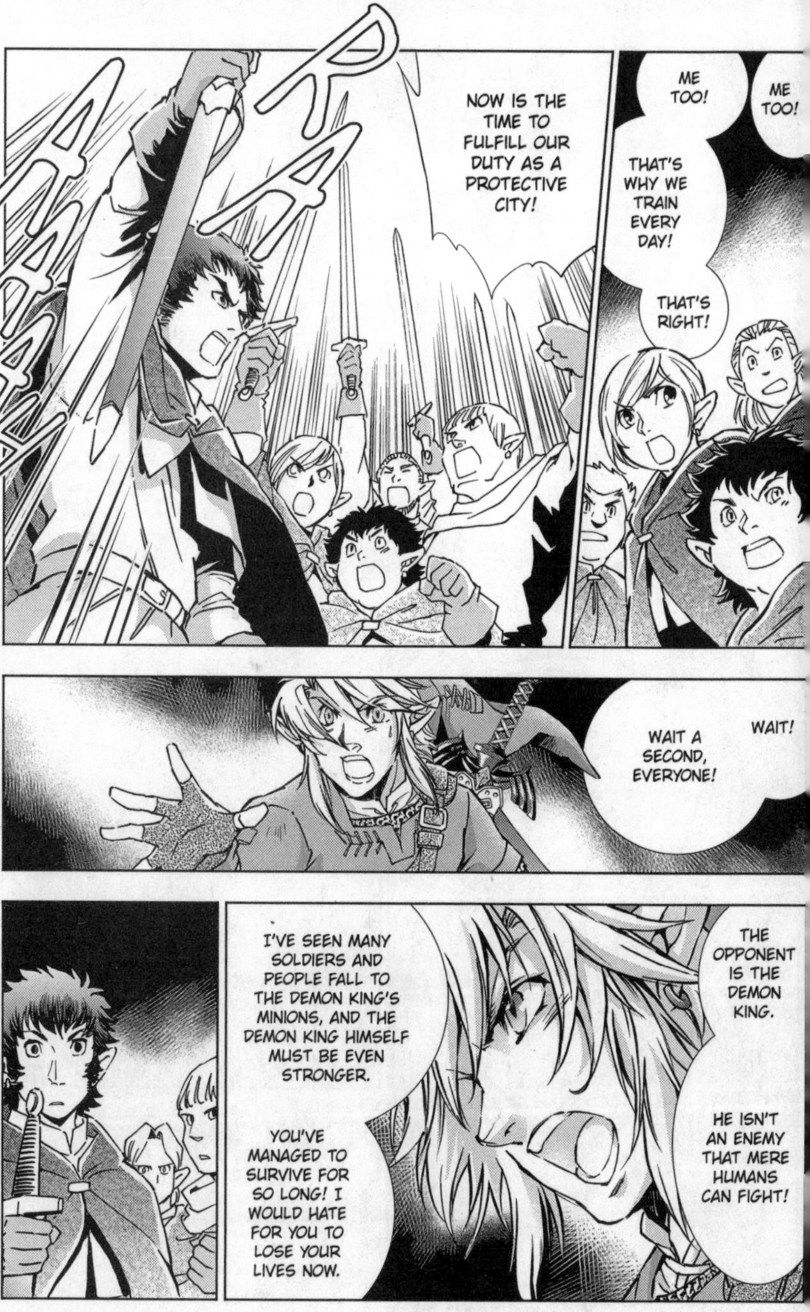
ME TOO!
ME TOO!
THAT'S WHY WE TRAIN EVERY DAY!
THAT'S RIGHT!
NOW IS THE TIME TO FULFILL OUR DUTY AS A PROTECTIVE CITY!
RAAAAAAH
WAIT!
WAIT A SECOND, EVERYONE!
THE OPPONENT IS THE DEMON KING.
HE ISN'T AN ENEMY THAT MERE HUMANS CAN FIGHT!
I'VE SEEN MANY SOLDIERS AND PEOPLE FALL TO THE DEMON KING'S MINIONS, AND THE DEMON KING HIMSELF MUST BE EVEN STRONGER.
YOU'VE MANAGED TO SURVIVE FOR SO LONG! I WOULD HATE FOR YOU TO LOSE YOUR LIVES NOW.

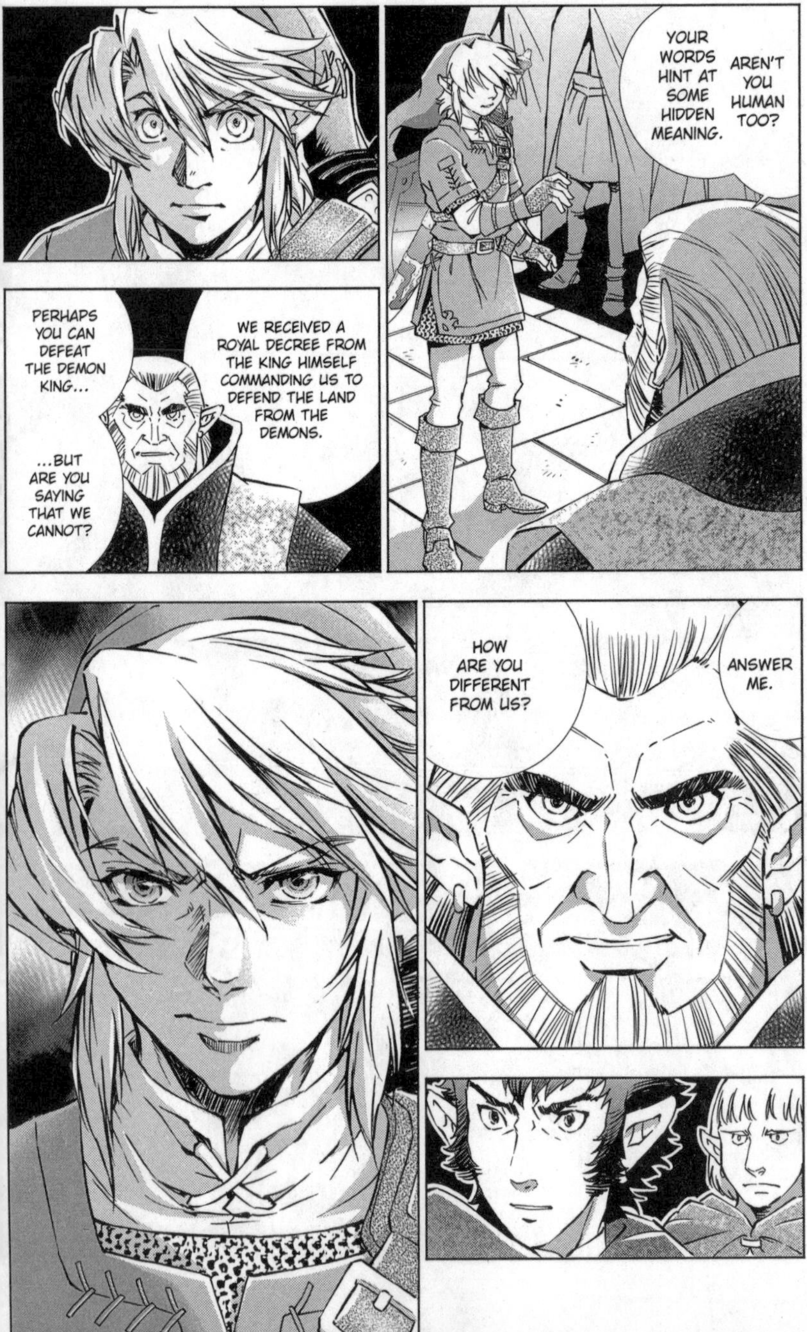
AREN'T YOU HUMAN TOO?
YOUR WORDS HINT AT SOME HIDDEN MEANING.
WE RECEIVED A ROYAL DECREE FROM THE KING HIMSELF COMMANDING US TO DEFEND THE LAND FROM THE DEMONS.
PERHAPS YOU CAN DEFEAT THE DEMON KING...
...BUT ARE YOU SAYING THAT WE CANNOT?
ANSWER ME.
HOW ARE YOU DIFFERENT FROM US?

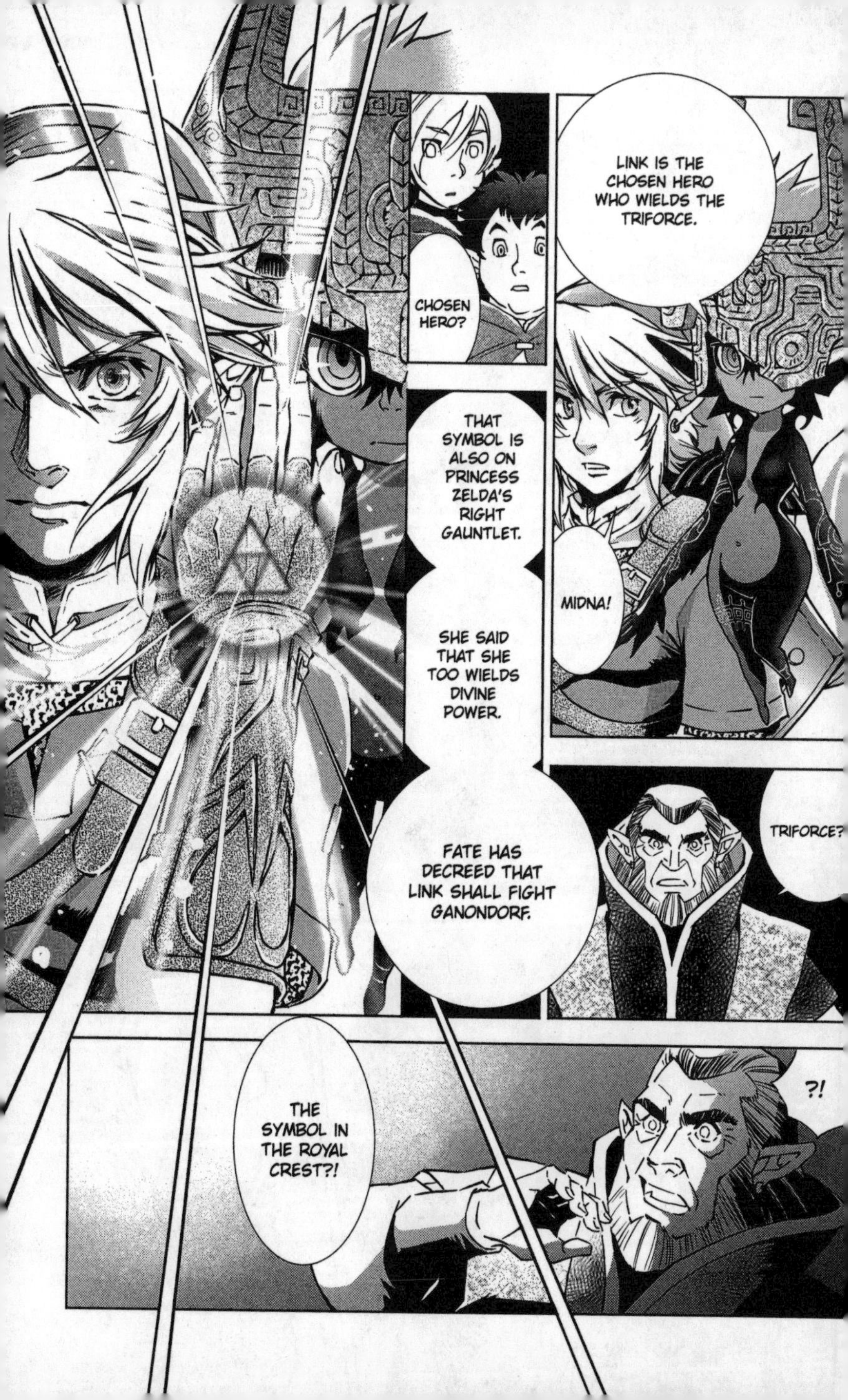
LINK IS THE CHOSEN HERO WHO WIELDS THE TRIFORCE.
CHOSEN HERO?
MIDNA!
THAT SYMBOL IS ALSO ON PRINCESS ZELDA'S RIGHT GAUNTLET.
SHE SAID THAT SHE TOO WIELDS DIVINE POWER.
TRIFORCE?
FATE HAS DECREED THAT LINK SHALL FIGHT GANONDORF.
?!
THE SYMBOL IN THE ROYAL CREST?!

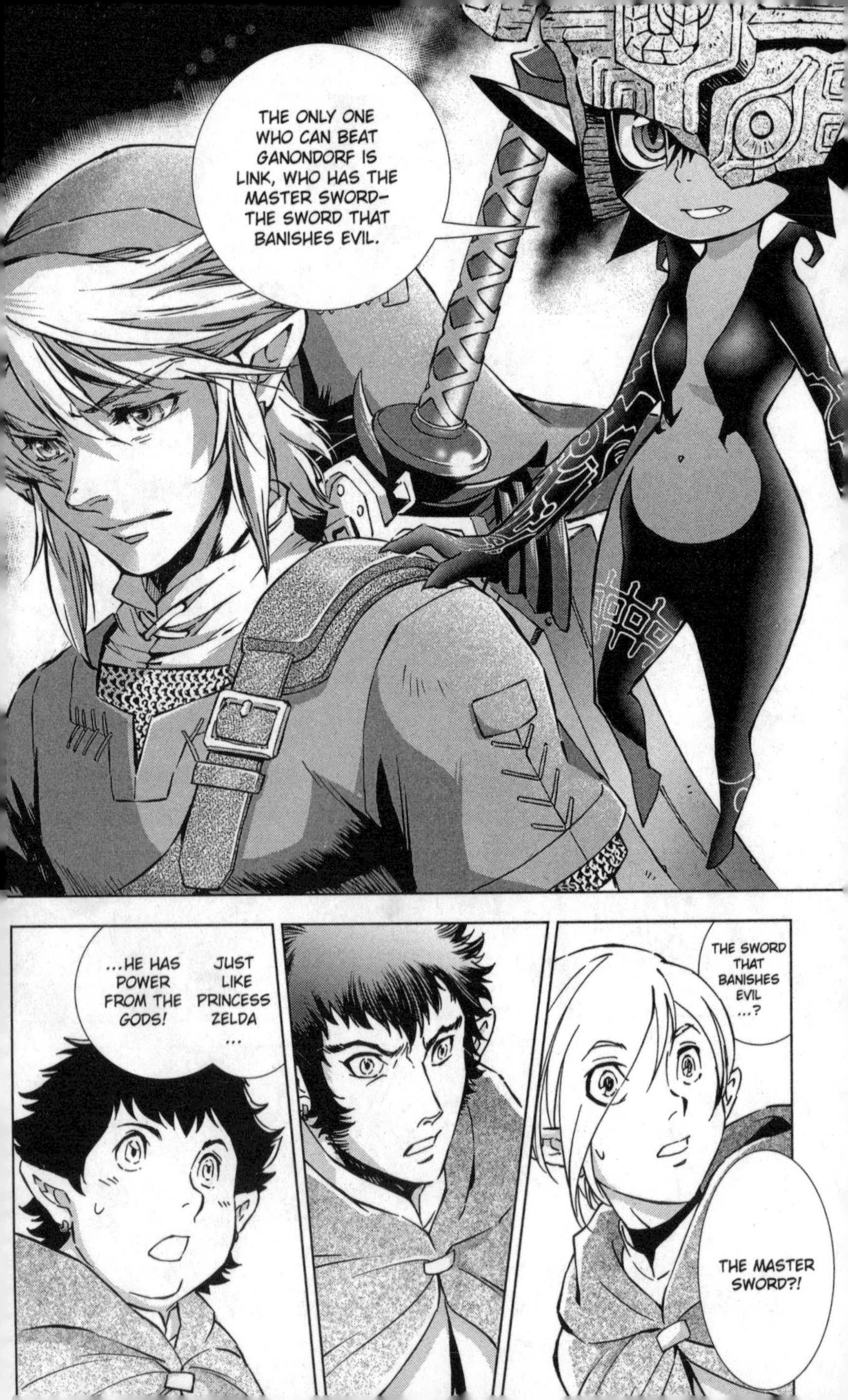
THE ONLY ONE WHO CAN BEAT GANONDORF IS LINK, WHO HAS THE MASTER SWORD– THE SWORD THAT BANISHES EVIL.
THE SWORD THAT BANISHES EVIL ...?
THE MASTER SWORD?!
JUST LIKE PRINCESS ZELDA ...
...HE HAS POWER FROM THE GODS!

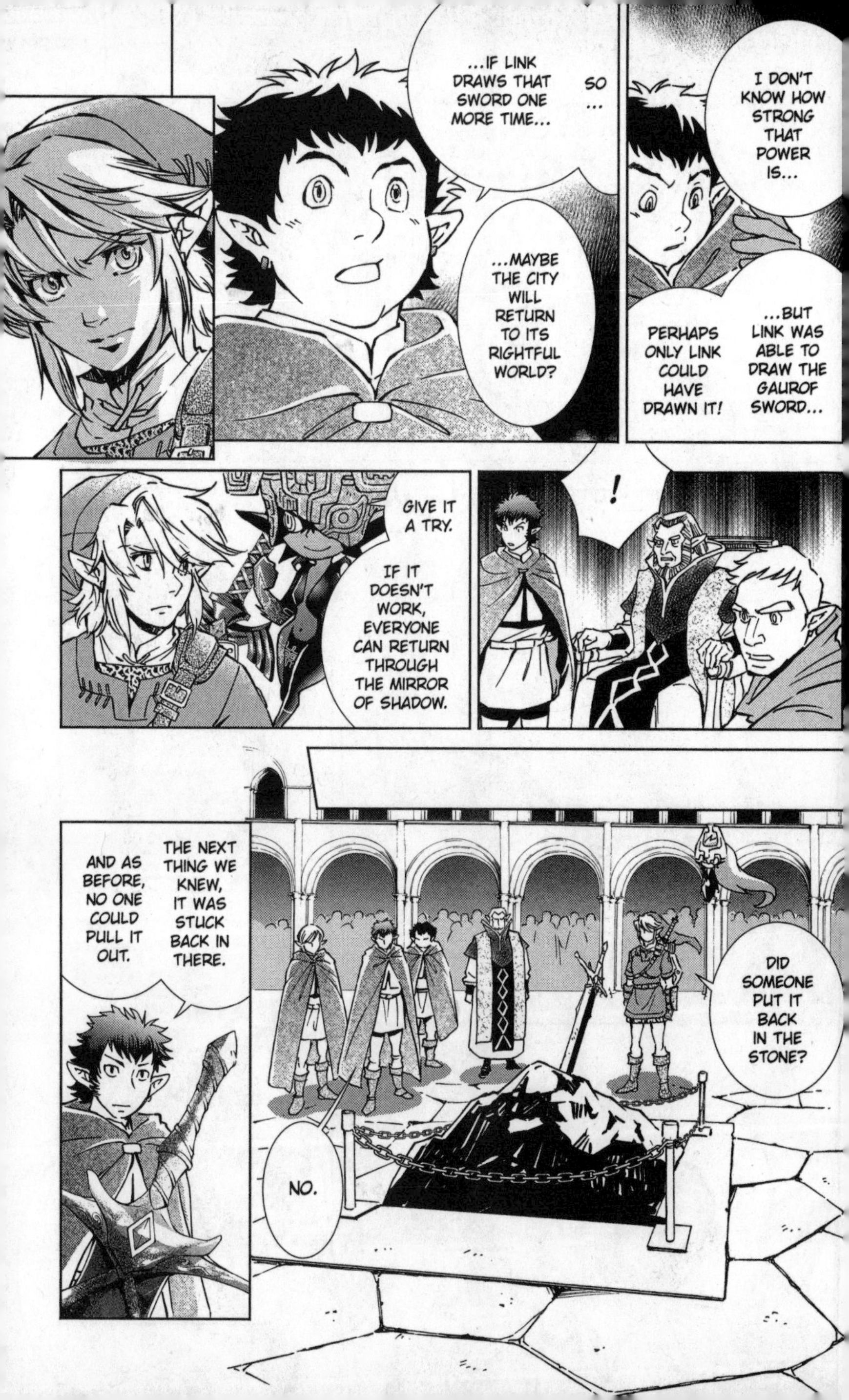
I DON'T KNOW HOW STRONG THAT POWER IS...
...BUT LINK WAS ABLE TO DRAW THE GAUROF SWORD...
PERHAPS ONLY LINK COULD HAVE DRAWN IT!
SO ...
...IF LINK DRAWS THAT SWORD ONE MORE TIME...
...MAYBE THE CITY WILL RETURN TO ITS RIGHTFUL WORLD?
!
GIVE IT A TRY.
IF IT DOESN'T WORK, EVERYONE CAN RETURN THROUGH THE MIRROR OF SHADOW.
DID SOMEONE PUT IT BACK IN THE STONE?
NO.
THE NEXT THING WE KNEW, IT WAS STUCK BACK IN THERE.
AND AS BEFORE, NO ONE COULD PULL IT OUT.

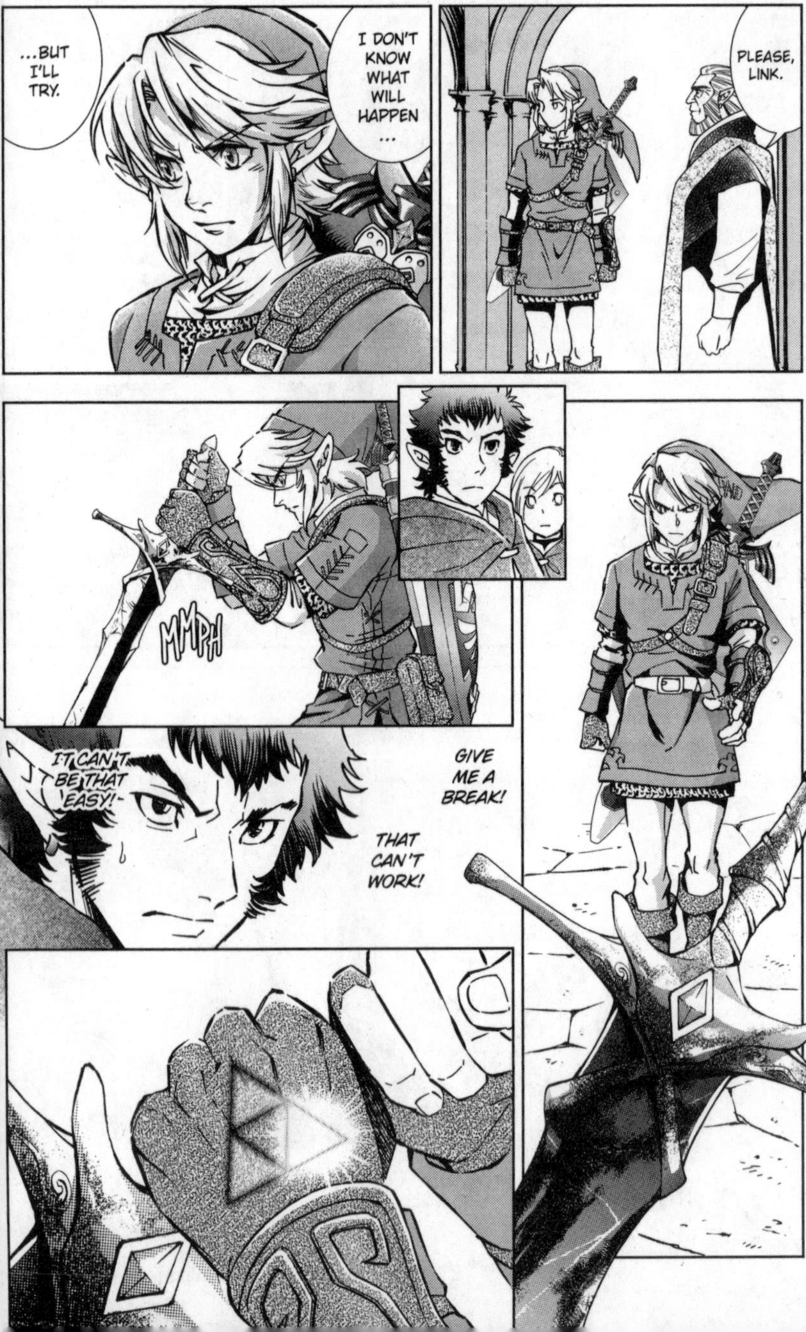
PLEASE, LINK.
I DON'T KNOW WHAT WILL HAPPEN ...
...BUT I'LL TRY.
MMPH
GIVE ME A BREAK!
IT CAN'T BE THAT EASY!
THAT CAN'T WORK!

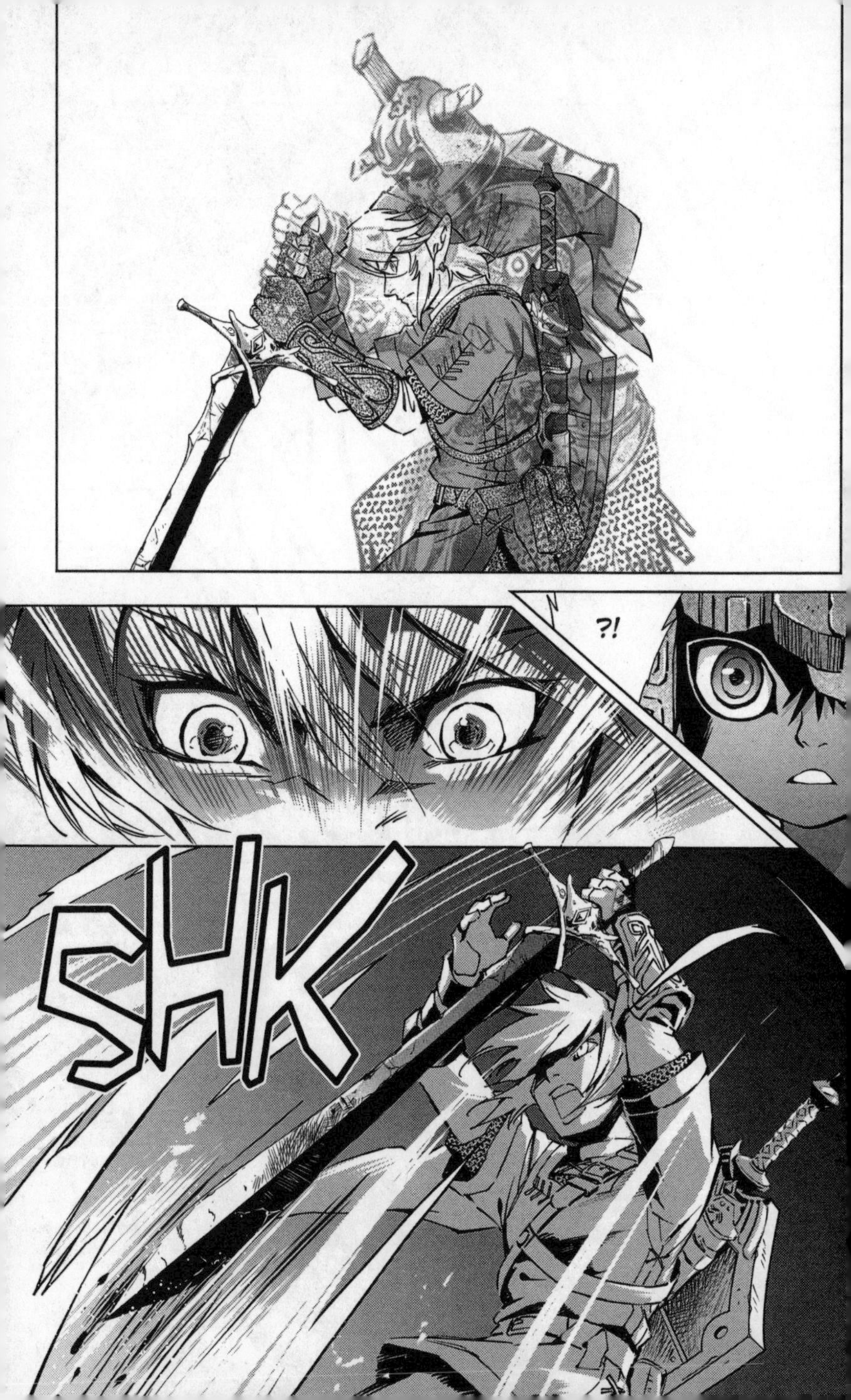
?!
SHK

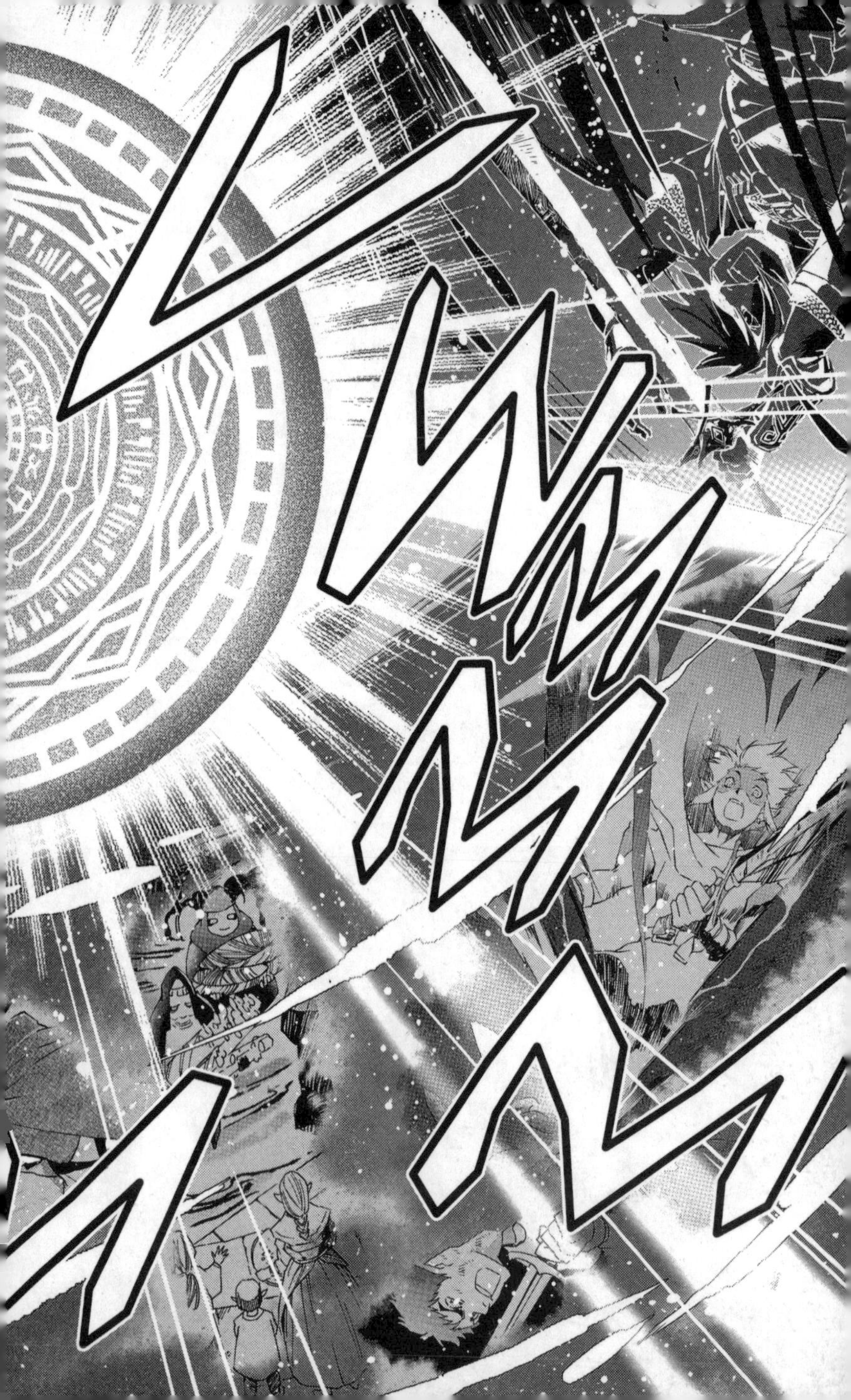

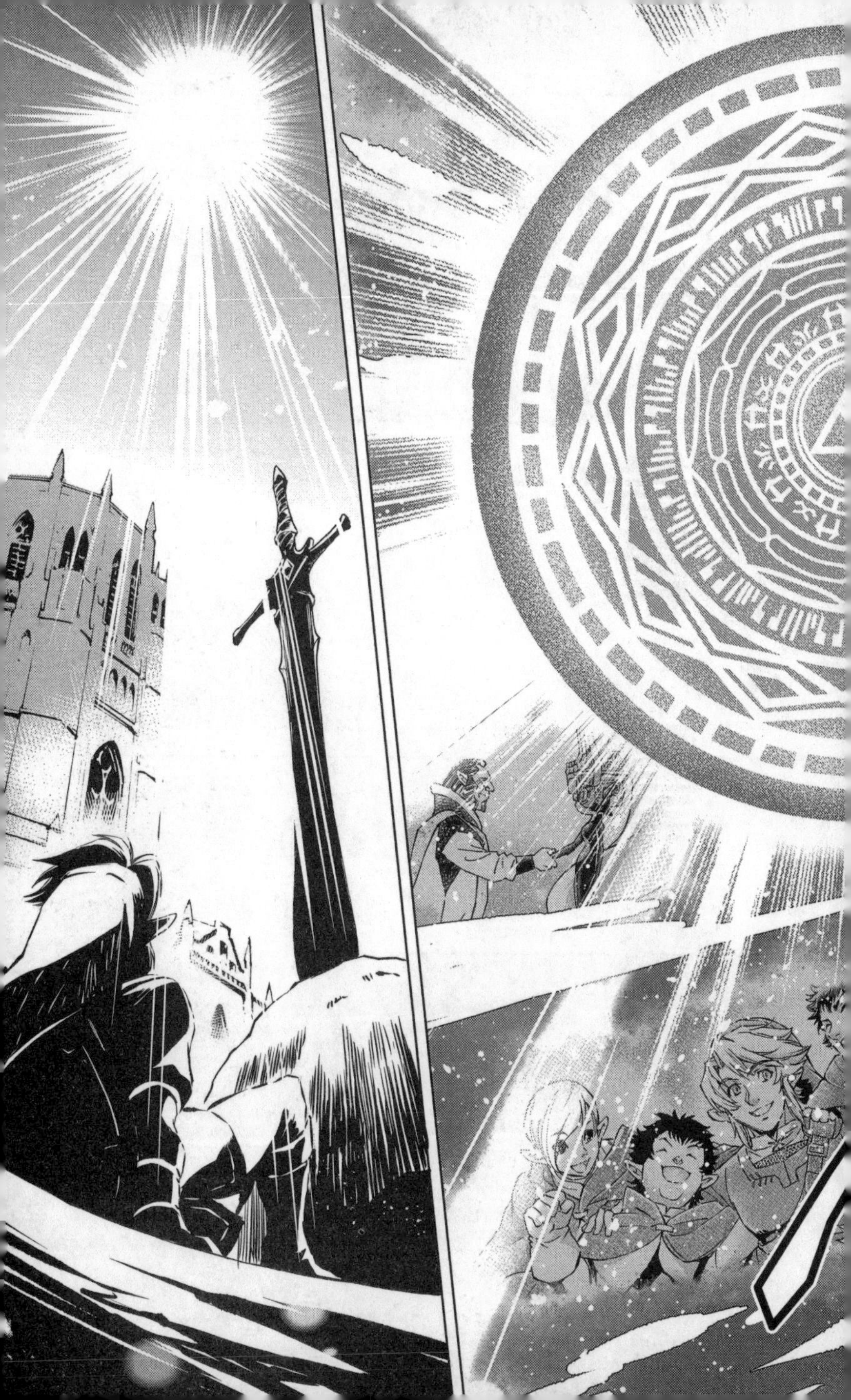

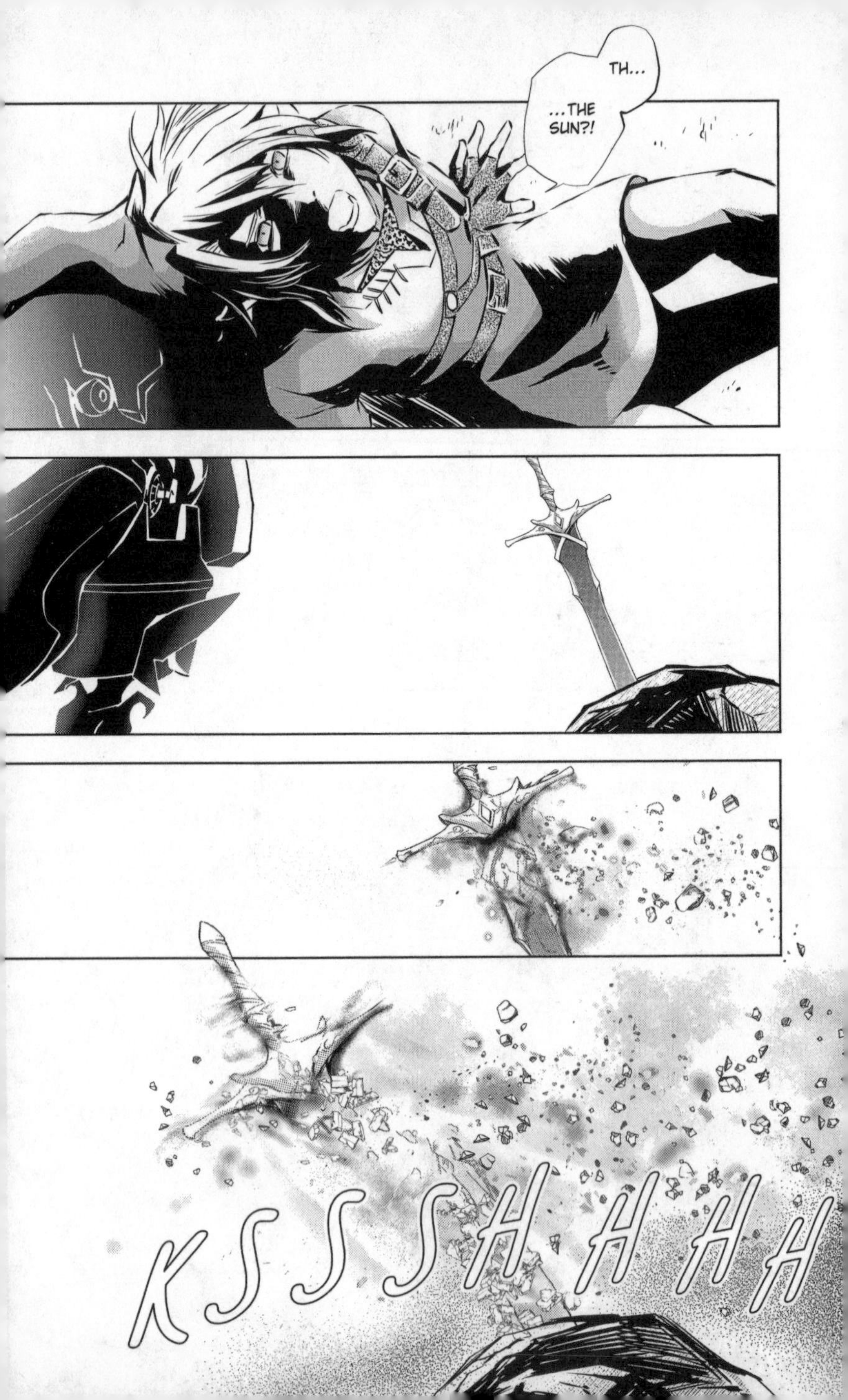
TH...
...THE SUN?!
KSSSHHHH

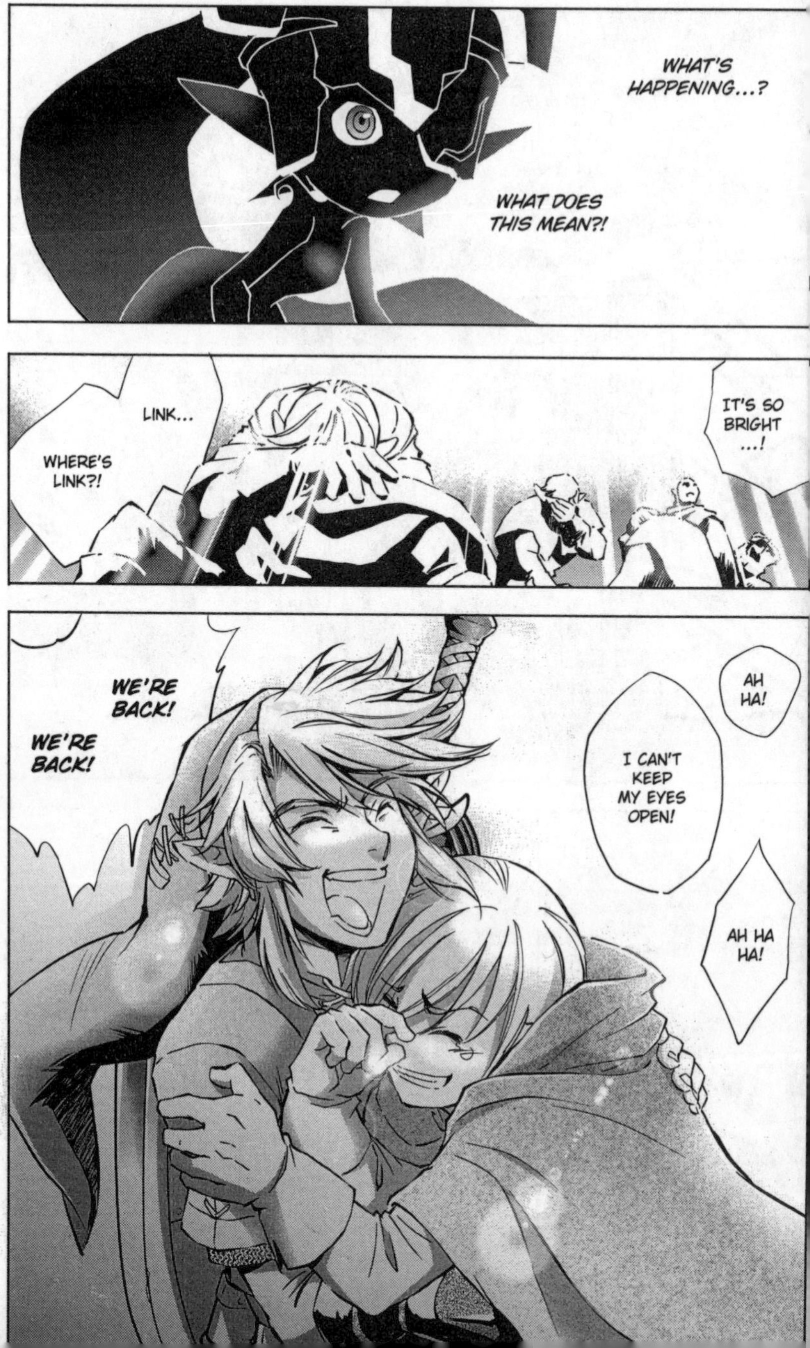
WHAT'S HAPPENING...?
WHAT DOES THIS MEAN?!
IT'S SO BRIGHT ...!
LINK...
WHERE'S LINK?!
AH HA!
I CAN'T KEEP MY EYES OPEN!
AH HA HA!
WE'RE BACK!
WE'RE BACK!

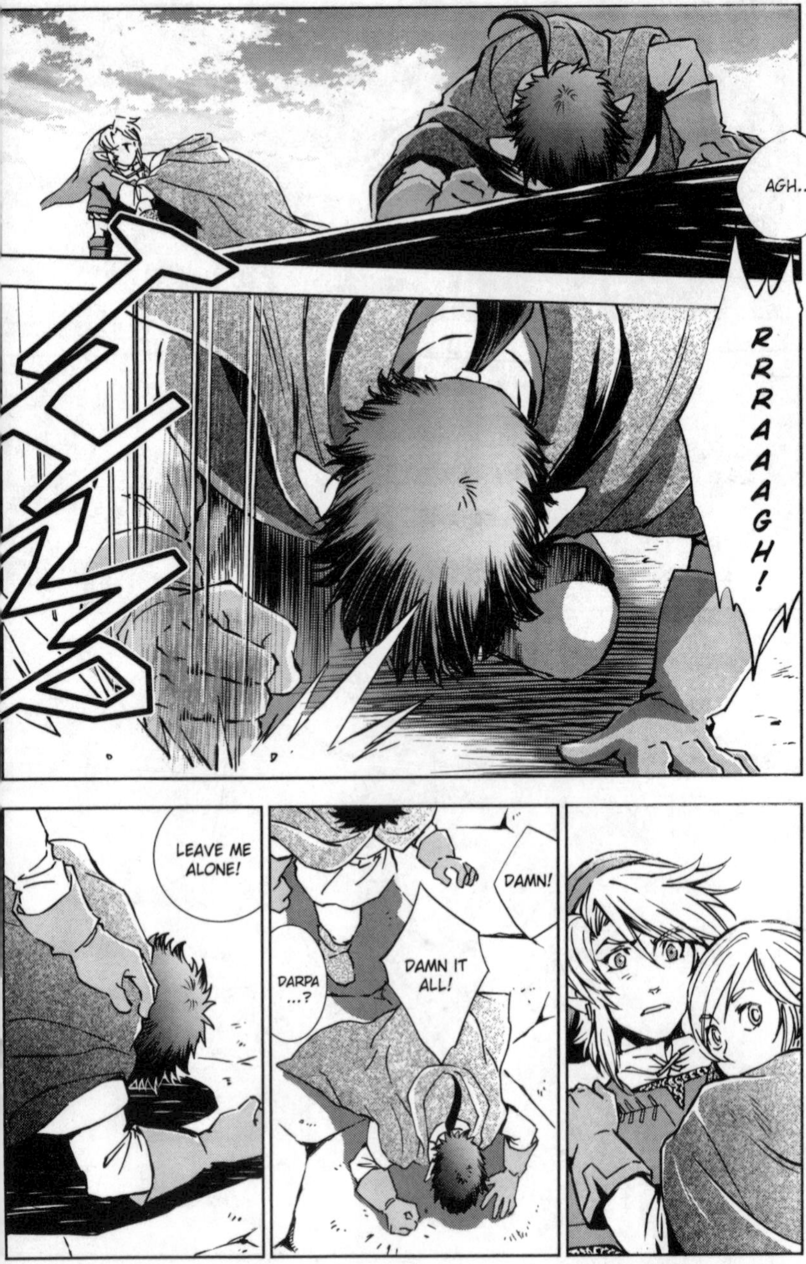
AGH...
RRRAAAAGH!
DAMN!
DAMN IT ALL!
DARPA ...?
LEAVE ME ALONE!

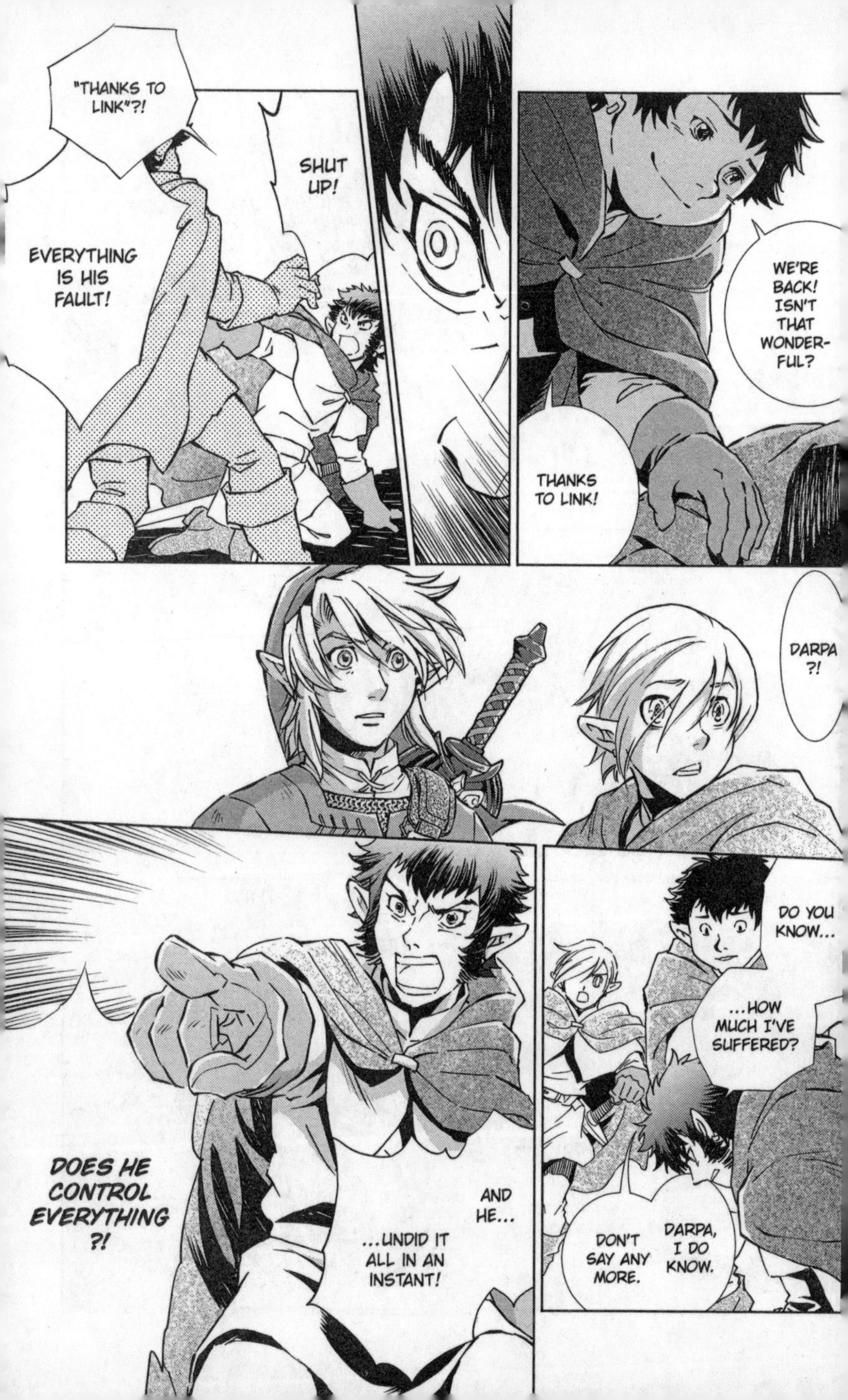
WE'RE BACK! ISN'T THAT WONDER-FUL?
THANKS TO LINK!
"THANKS TO LINK"?!
SHUT UP!
EVERYTHING IS HIS FAULT!
DARPA ?!
DO YOU KNOW...
...HOW MUCH I'VE SUFFERED?
DARPA, I DO KNOW.
DON'T SAY ANY MORE.
AND HE...
...UNDID IT ALL IN AN INSTANT!
DOES HE CONTROL EVERYTHING ?!

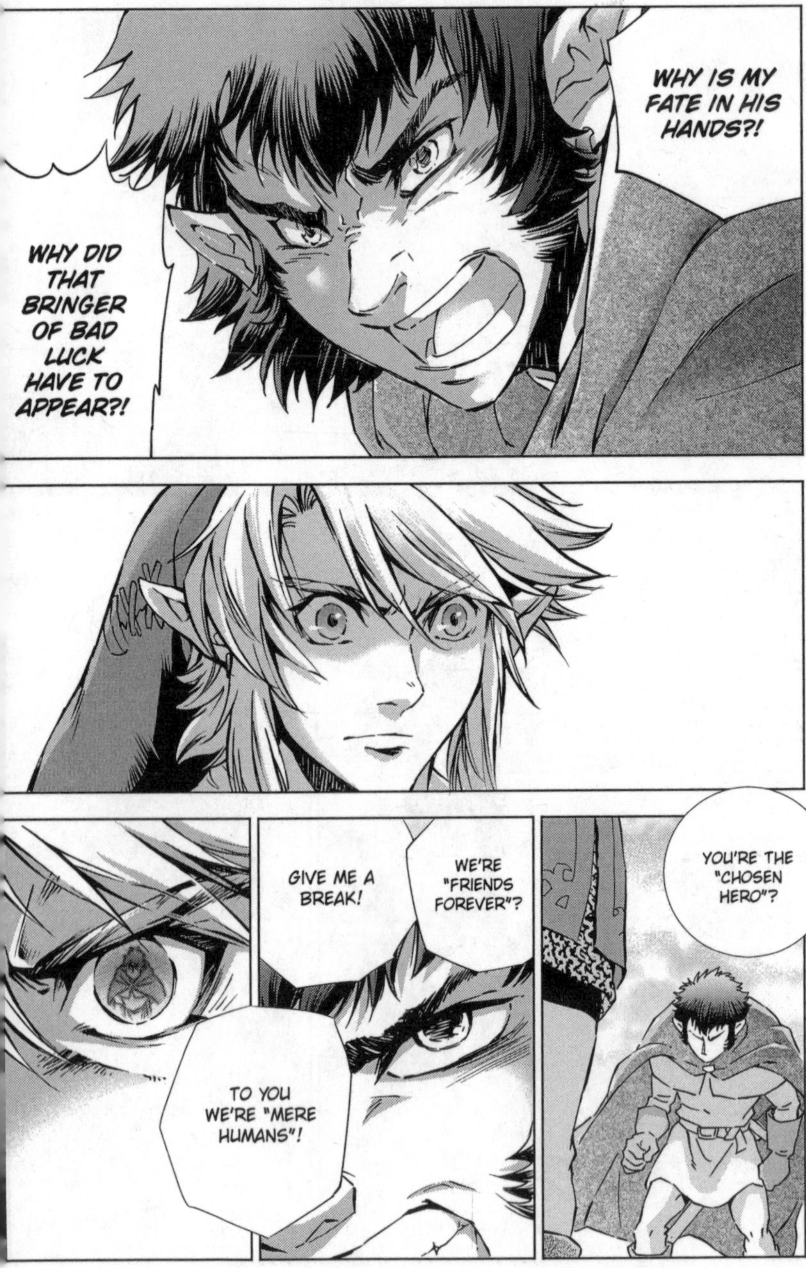
WHY IS MY FATE IN HIS HANDS?!
WHY DID THAT BRINGER OF BAD LUCK HAVE TO APPEAR?!
YOU'RE THE "CHOSEN HERO"?
WE'RE "FRIENDS FOREVER"?
GIVE ME A BREAK!
TO YOU WE'RE "MERE HUMANS"!

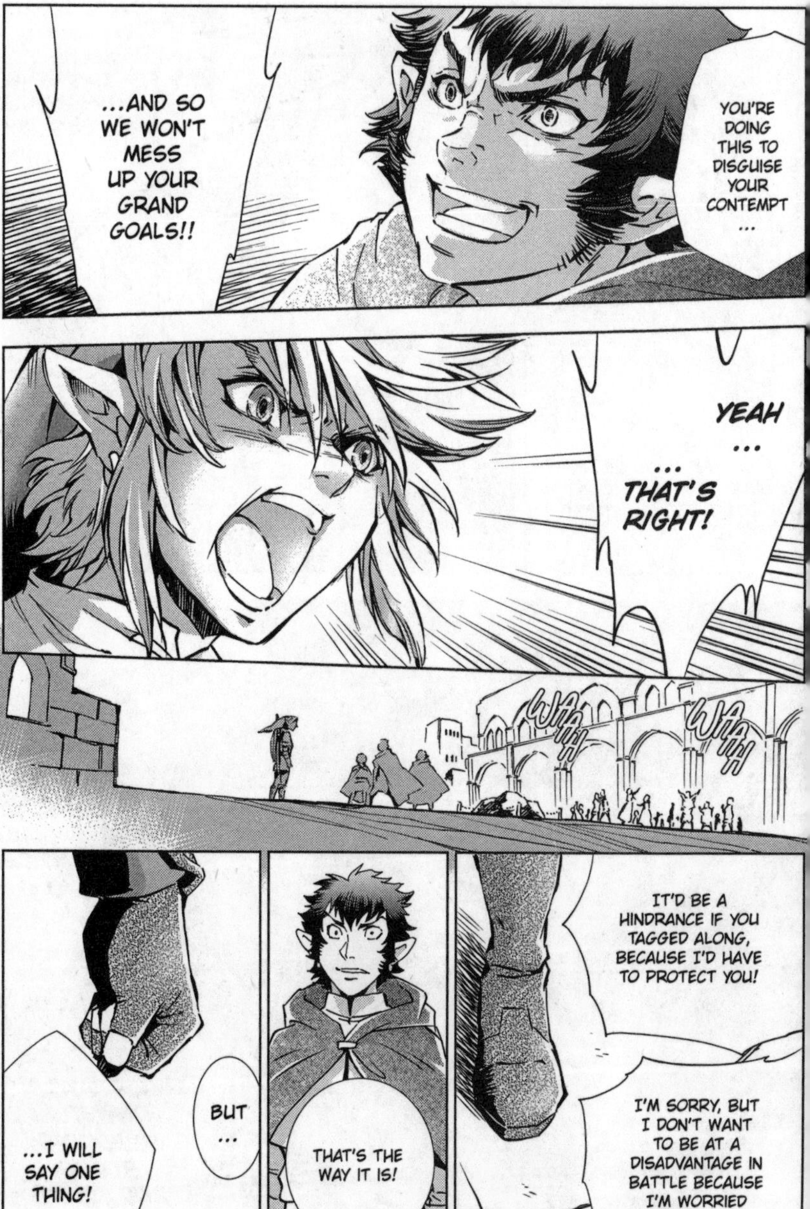
YOU'RE DOING THIS TO DISGUISE YOUR CONTEMPT ...
...AND SO WE WON'T MESS UP YOUR GRAND GOALS!!
YEAH ... ... THAT'S RIGHT!
WAAH
WAAH
IT'D BE A HINDRANCE IF YOU TAGGED ALONG, BECAUSE I'D HAVE TO PROTECT YOU!
I'M SORRY, BUT I DON'T WANT TO BE AT A DISADVANTAGE IN BATTLE BECAUSE I'M WORRIED ABOUT YOU PEOPLE!
THAT'S THE WAY IT IS!
BUT ...
...I WILL SAY ONE THING!

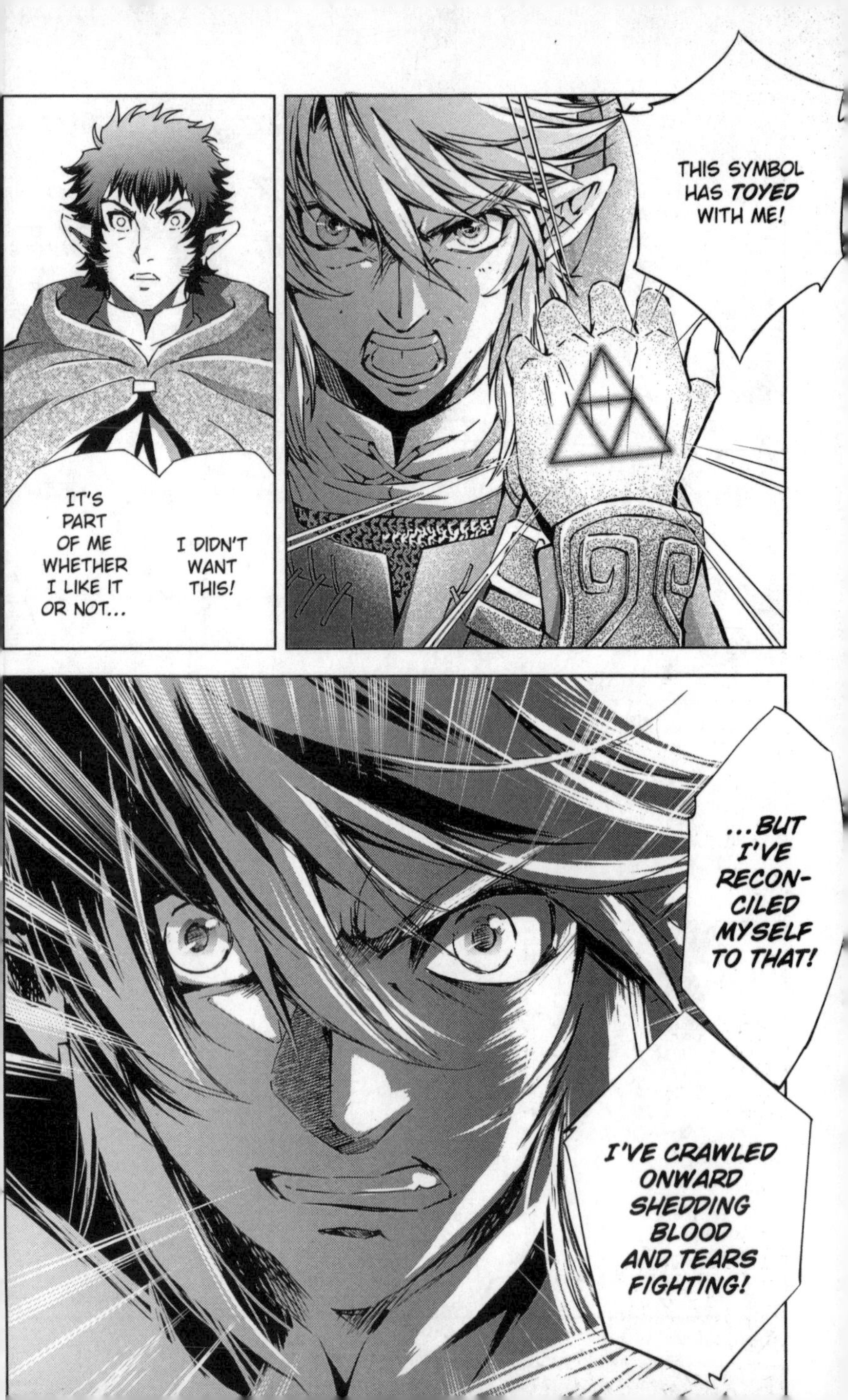
THIS SYMBOL HAS *TOYED* WITH ME!
I DIDN'T WANT THIS!
IT'S PART OF ME WHETHER I LIKE IT OR NOT...
...BUT I'VE RECON-CILED MYSELF TO THAT!
I'VE CRAWLED ONWARD SHEDDING BLOOD AND TEARS FIGHTING!

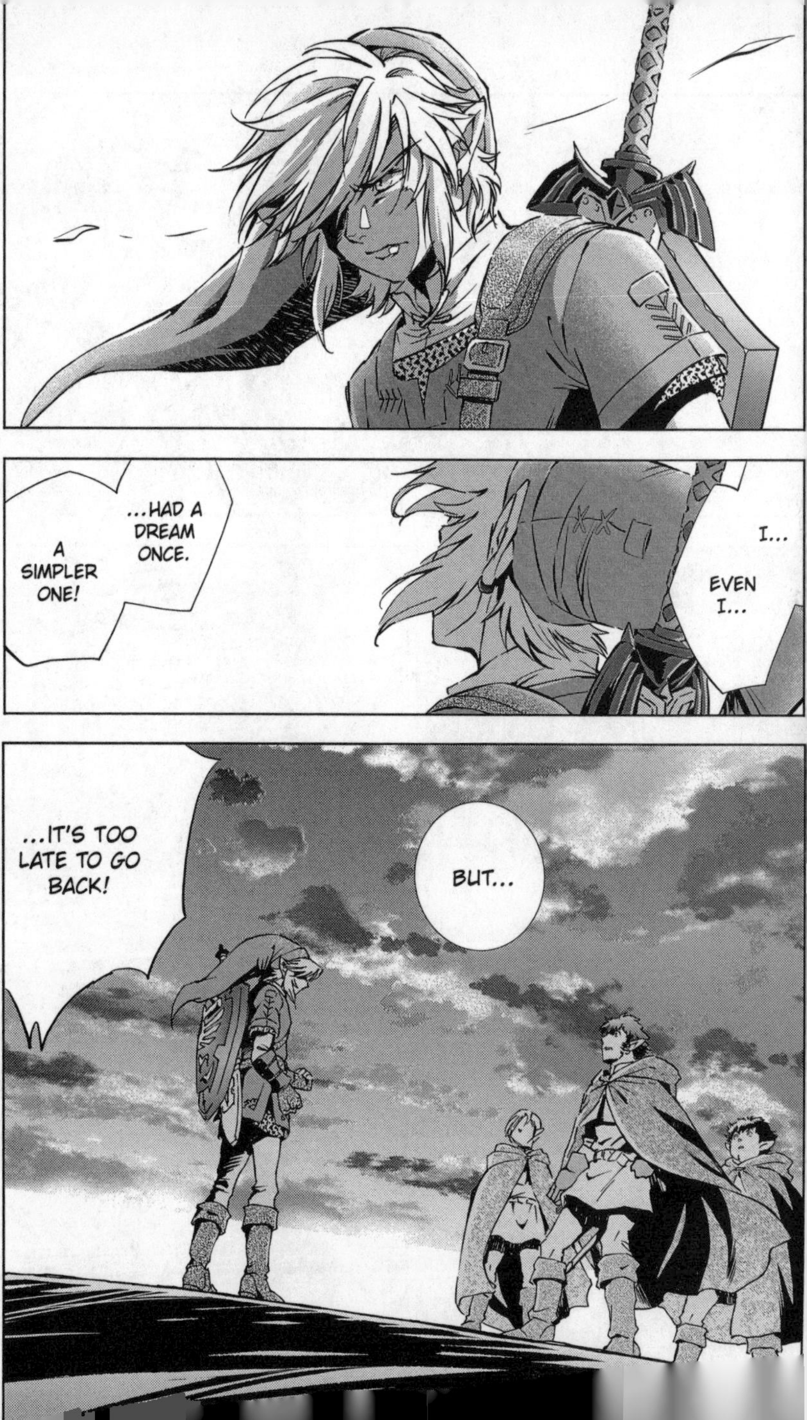
I...
EVEN I...
...HAD A DREAM ONCE.
A SIMPLER ONE!
BUT...
...IT'S TOO LATE TO GO BACK!

FAREWELL.

AND I'M GOING TO DEFEAT GANON-DORF!

I'M GOING TO HYRULE CASTLE.

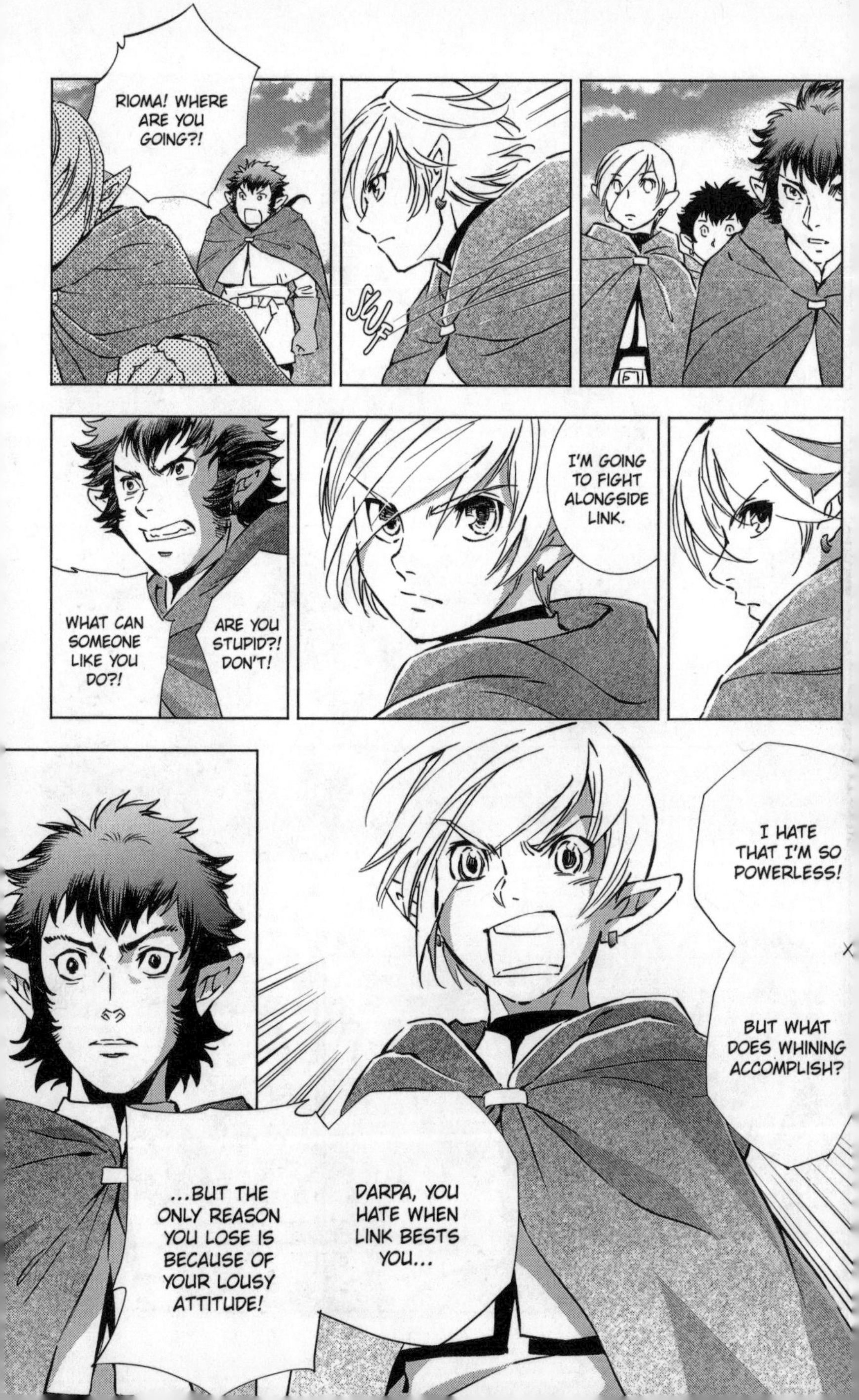
SWF
RIOMA! WHERE ARE YOU GOING?!
I'M GOING TO FIGHT ALONGSIDE LINK.
ARE YOU STUPID?! DON'T!
WHAT CAN SOMEONE LIKE YOU DO?!
I HATE THAT I'M SO POWERLESS!
BUT WHAT DOES WHINING ACCOMPLISH?
DARPA, YOU HATE WHEN LINK BESTS YOU...
...BUT THE ONLY REASON YOU LOSE IS BECAUSE OF YOUR LOUSY ATTITUDE!

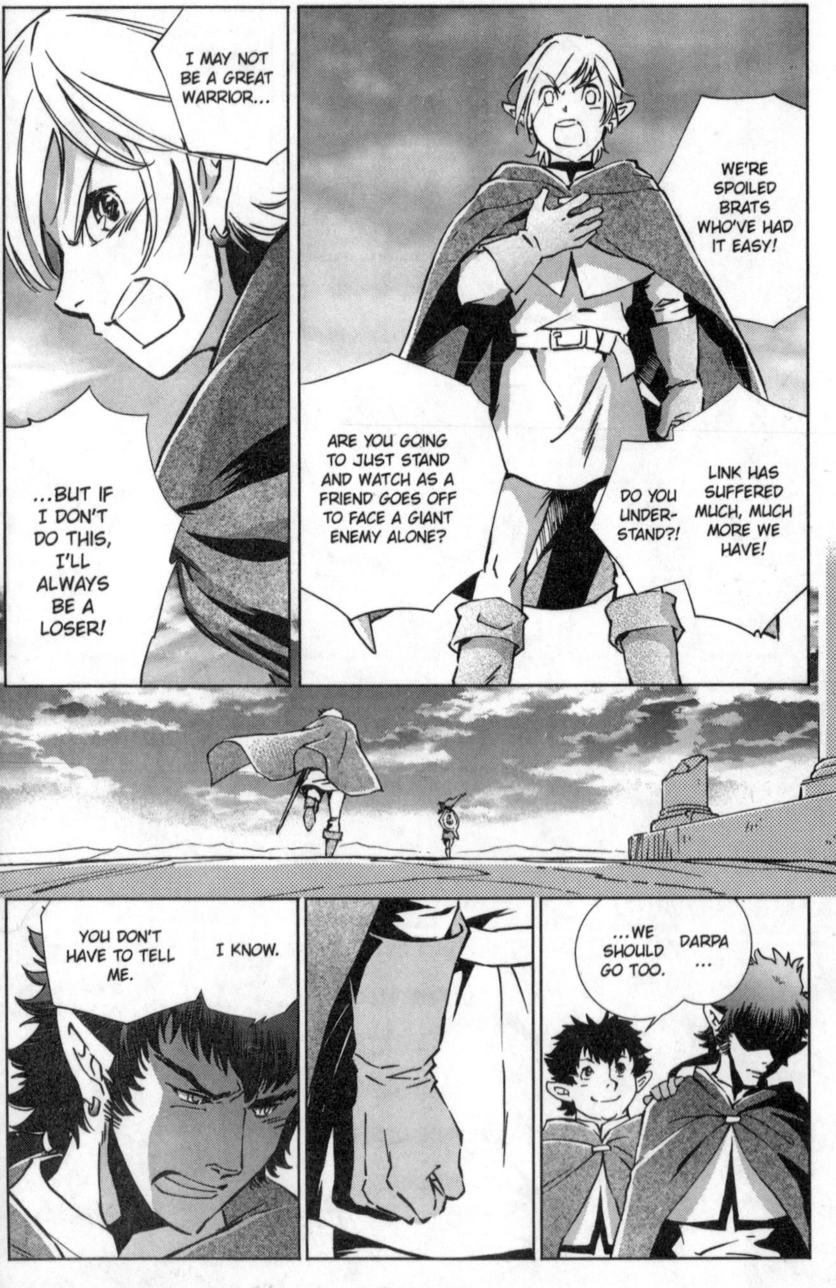
WE'RE SPOILED BRATS WHO'VE HAD IT EASY!
LINK HAS SUFFERED MUCH, MUCH MORE WE HAVE!
DO YOU UNDER-STAND?!
ARE YOU GOING TO JUST STAND AND WATCH AS A FRIEND GOES OFF TO FACE A GIANT ENEMY ALONE?
I MAY NOT BE A GREAT WARRIOR...
...BUT IF I DON'T DO THIS, I'LL ALWAYS BE A LOSER!
DARPA ...
...WE SHOULD GO TOO.
I KNOW.
YOU DON'T HAVE TO TELL ME.

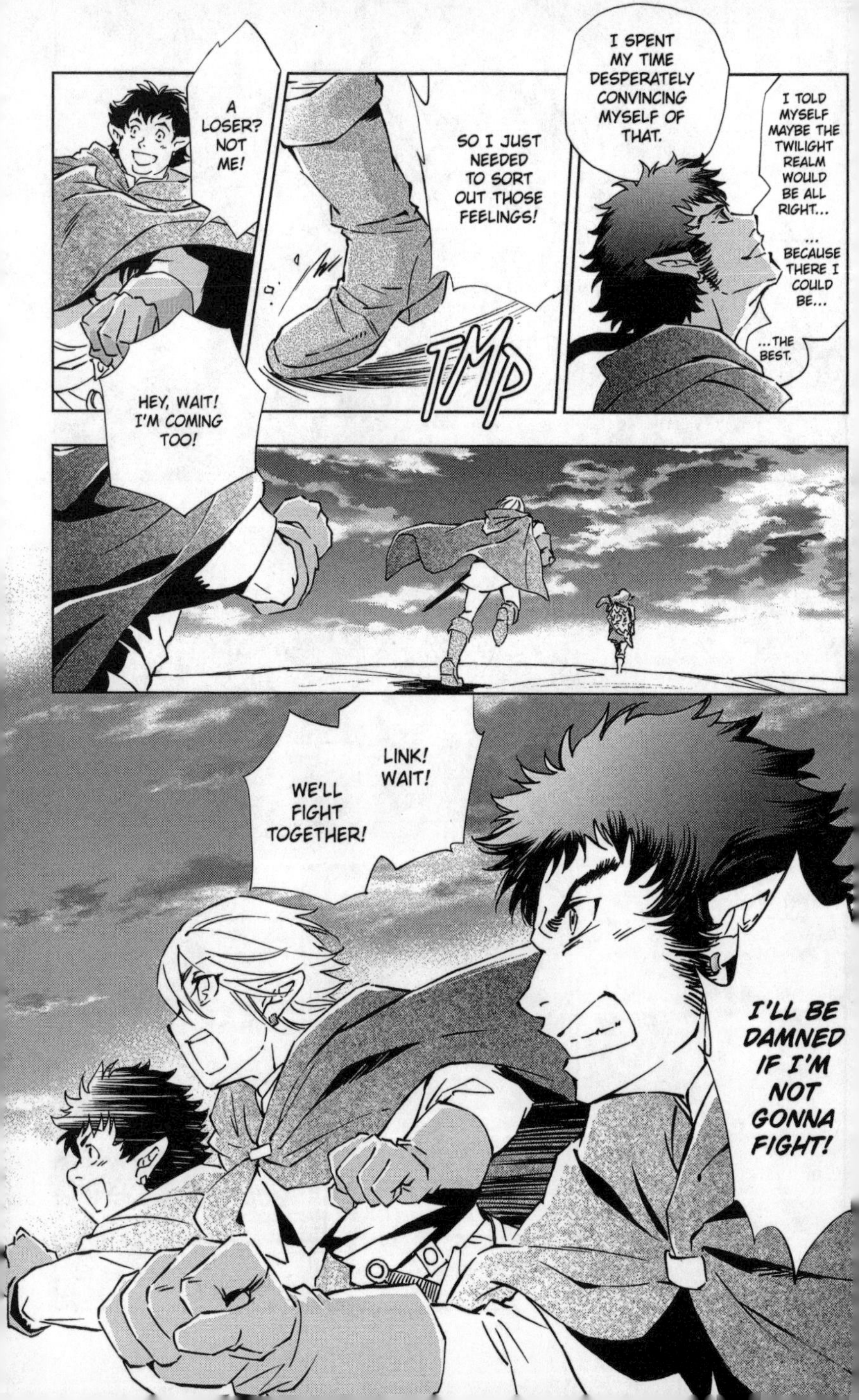

I TOLD MYSELF MAYBE THE TWILIGHT REALM WOULD BE ALL RIGHT...
...BECAUSE THERE I COULD BE...
...THE BEST.
I SPENT MY TIME DESPERATELY CONVINCING MYSELF OF THAT.
SO I JUST NEEDED TO SORT OUT THOSE FEELINGS!
TMP
A LOSER? NOT ME!
HEY, WAIT! I'M COMING TOO!
I'LL BE DAMNED IF I'M NOT GONNA FIGHT!
LINK! WAIT!
WE'LL FIGHT TOGETHER!

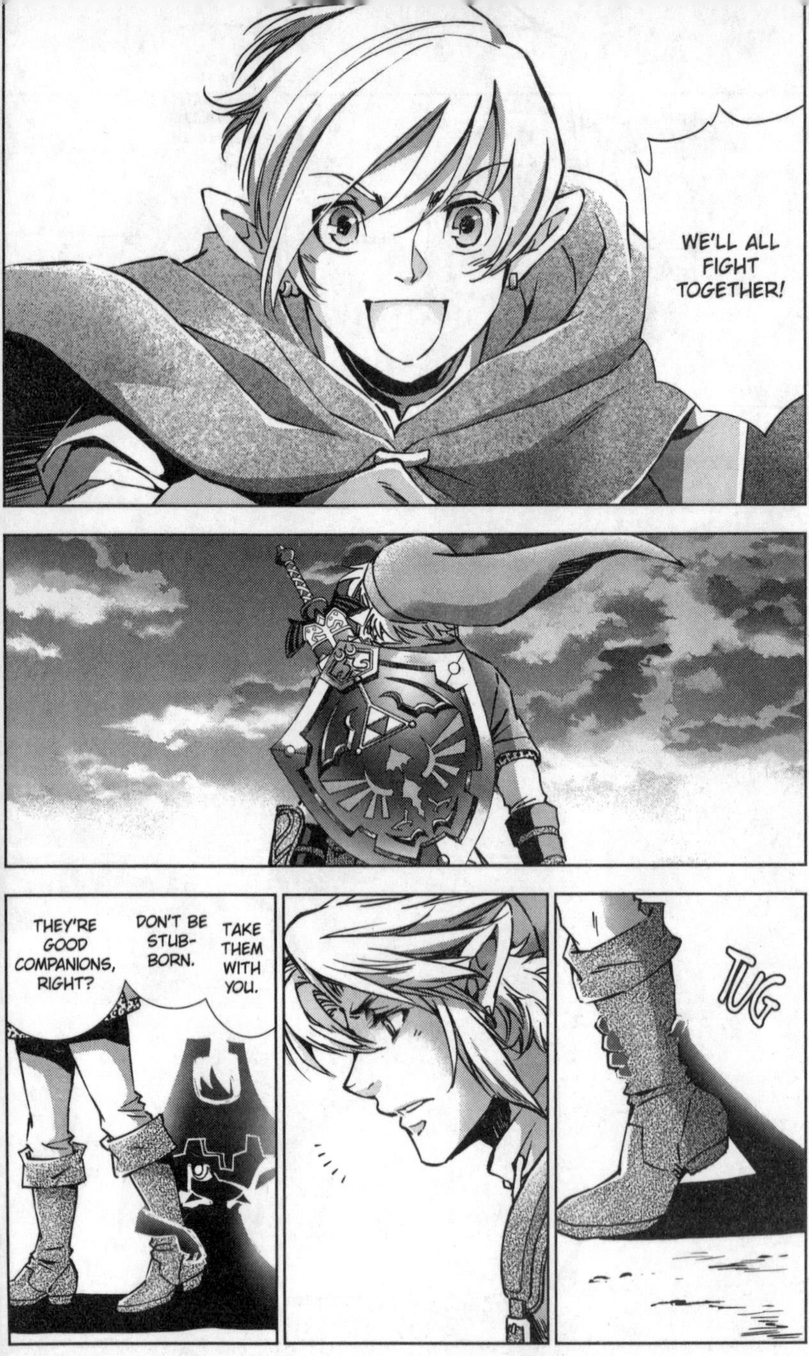

WE'LL ALL FIGHT TOGETHER!
TUG
TAKE THEM WITH YOU.
DON'T BE STUB-BORN.
THEY'RE GOOD COMPANIONS, RIGHT?

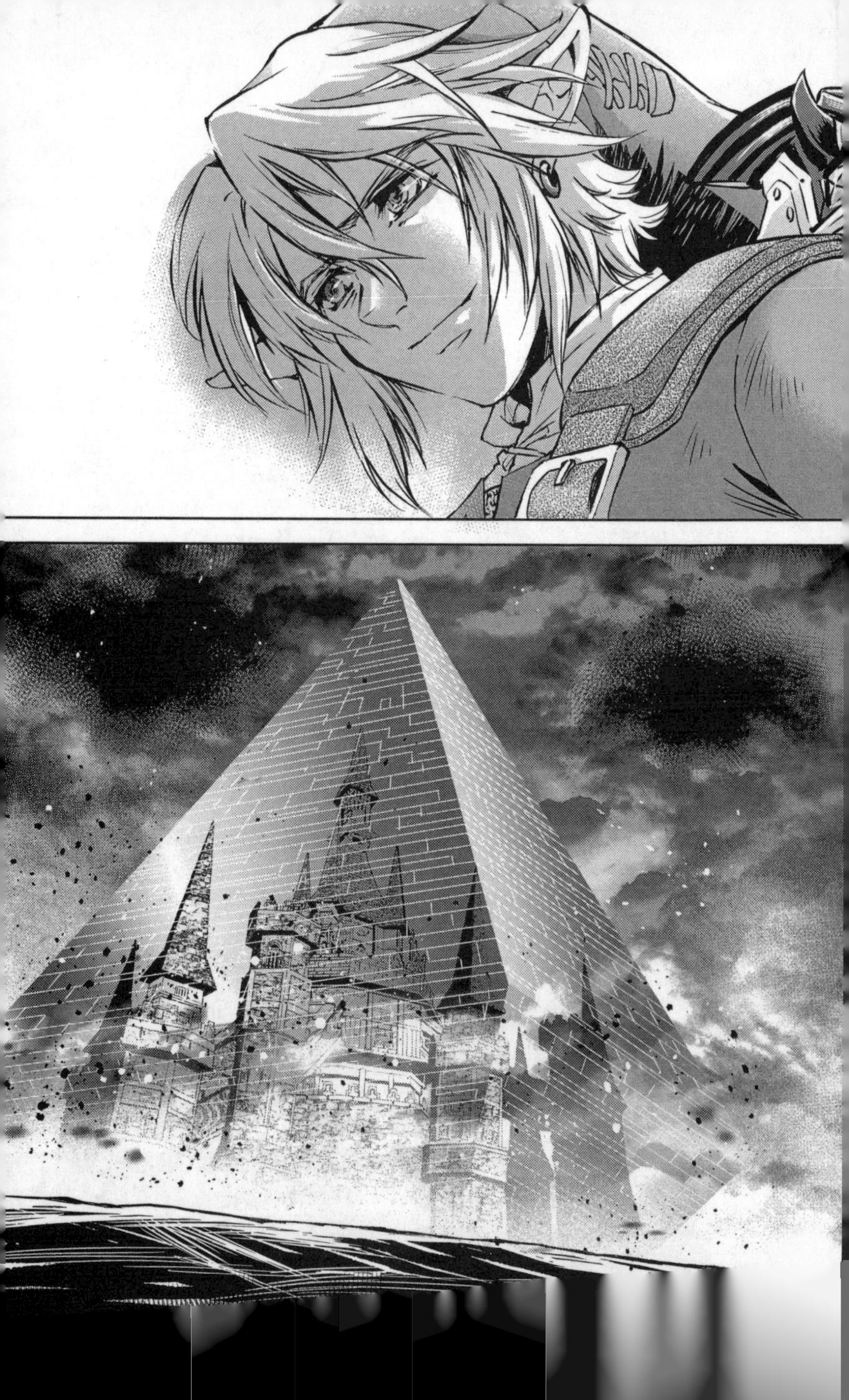

AUTHOR'S NOTE

We've entered the final stage, so Link's battle in *Twilight Princess* is coming up. Uncertain and suffering, Link has come this far by figuring out what he should do step-by-step and overcoming each difficulty that appears before him. Even as he questioned his right to be a hero, he has confronted those difficulties head-on to finally arrive at the final battle that fate has assigned him, and gained the will to fight.

This is the 15th year since the game this manga is based on first appeared in 2006. Even within the *Legend of Zelda* manga series, this series features many particularly hard and grueling ordeals. Link is large and realistic, with life-size proportions, and he transforms into a wolf. Midna is bewitching. Major enemies tend to have complex issues, shadowy beings hide in the light, and so on. Journeying alongside these very distinctive characters has been our own ordeal every day.

Before we knew it, it was volume 9, and five years had passed since we started working on the manga.

We hope we can keep doing our best and make it through the final battle to successfully complete this series. Keep rooting for us so we don't run out of power before the end.

Akira Himekawa is the collaboration of two women, A. Honda and S. Nagano. Together they have created ten manga adventures featuring Link and the popular video game world of The Legend of Zelda™. Their most recent work, The Legend of Zelda™: Twilight Princess, is serialized digitally on Shogakukan's MangaONE app in Japan.

THE LEGEND OF ZELDA™

·TWILIGHT PRINCESS·

Volume 9—VIZ Media Edition

STORY AND ART BY

Akira Himekawa

DRAWING STAFF **Akiko Mori / Sakiho Tsutsui**

TRANSLATION **John Werry**
ENGLISH ADAPTATION **Stan!**
TOUCH-UP ART & LETTERING **Evan Waldinger**
DESIGNER **Shawn Carrico**
EDITOR **Mike Montesa**

ZELDA NO DENSETSU TWILIGHT PRINCESS Vol. 9
by Akira HIMEKAWA
© 2016 Akira HIMEKAWA
All rights reserved.
Original Japanese edition published by SHOGAKUKAN.
English translation rights in the United States of America,
Canada, the United Kingdom, Ireland, Australia and
New Zealand arranged with SHOGAKUKAN.

Original design by Kazutada YOKOYAMA

The stories, characters and incidents mentioned
in this publication are entirely fictional.

Printed in the U.S.A.

Published by VIZ Media, LLC
P.O. Box 77010
San Francisco, CA 94107

10 9 8 7 6 5 4 3 2 1
First printing, September 2021

MEDIA
viz.com

THE LEGEND OF ZELDA™

LEGENDARY EDITION BOX SET

Story and Art by **Akira Himekawa**

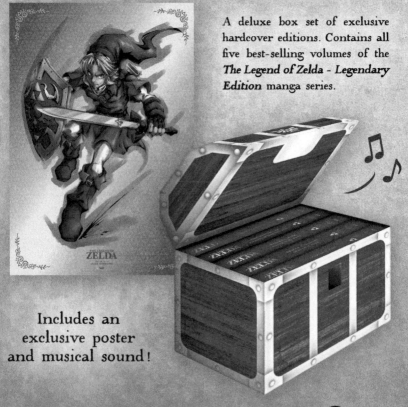

A deluxe box set of exclusive hardcover editions. Contains all five best-selling volumes of the *The Legend of Zelda - Legendary Edition* manga series.

Includes an exclusive poster and musical sound!

CELEBRATE more than **25 YEARS** of **KIRBY**, the popular pink hero of the best-selling series of video games from **NINTENDO**

KIRBY
ART & STYLE
COLLECTION

A stylish new collection of art and designs from the best-selling Kirby video games. Featuring twenty-five years worth of sketches, artwork, Japanese video game box art, and more. With exclusive notes from creators and artists who have brought Kirby to life throughout the years.

VIZ

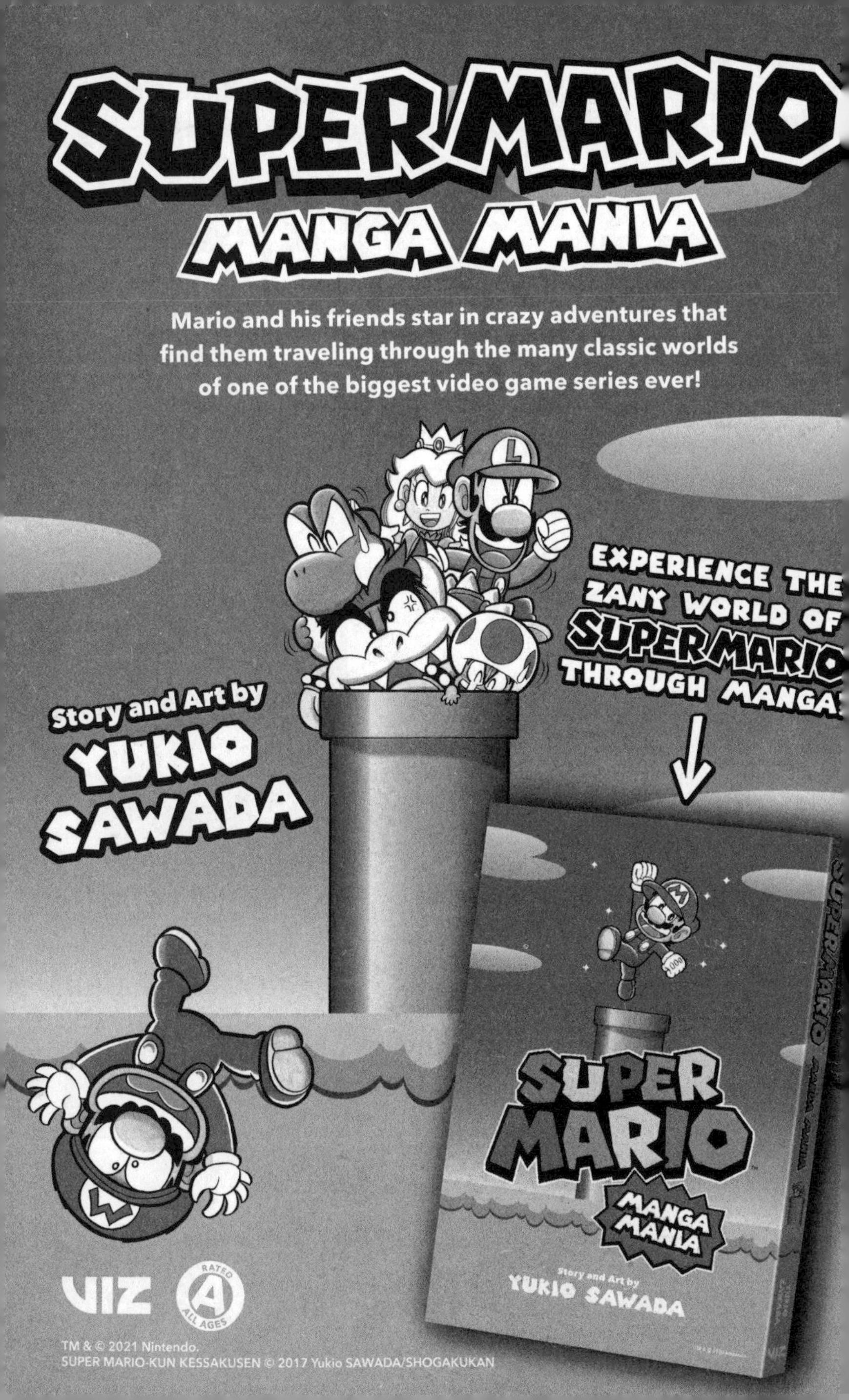
SUPER MARIO
MANGA MANIA
Mario and his friends star in crazy adventures that find them traveling through the many classic worlds of one of the biggest video game series ever!
EXPERIENCE THE ZANY WORLD OF SUPER MARIO THROUGH MANGA!
Story and Art by
YUKIO SAWADA
SUPER MARIO
MANGA MANIA
Story and Art by
YUKIO SAWADA
VIZ
RATED A ALL AGES
TM & © 2021 Nintendo.
SUPER MARIO-KUN KESSAKUSEN © 2017 Yukio SAWADA/SHOGAKUKAN

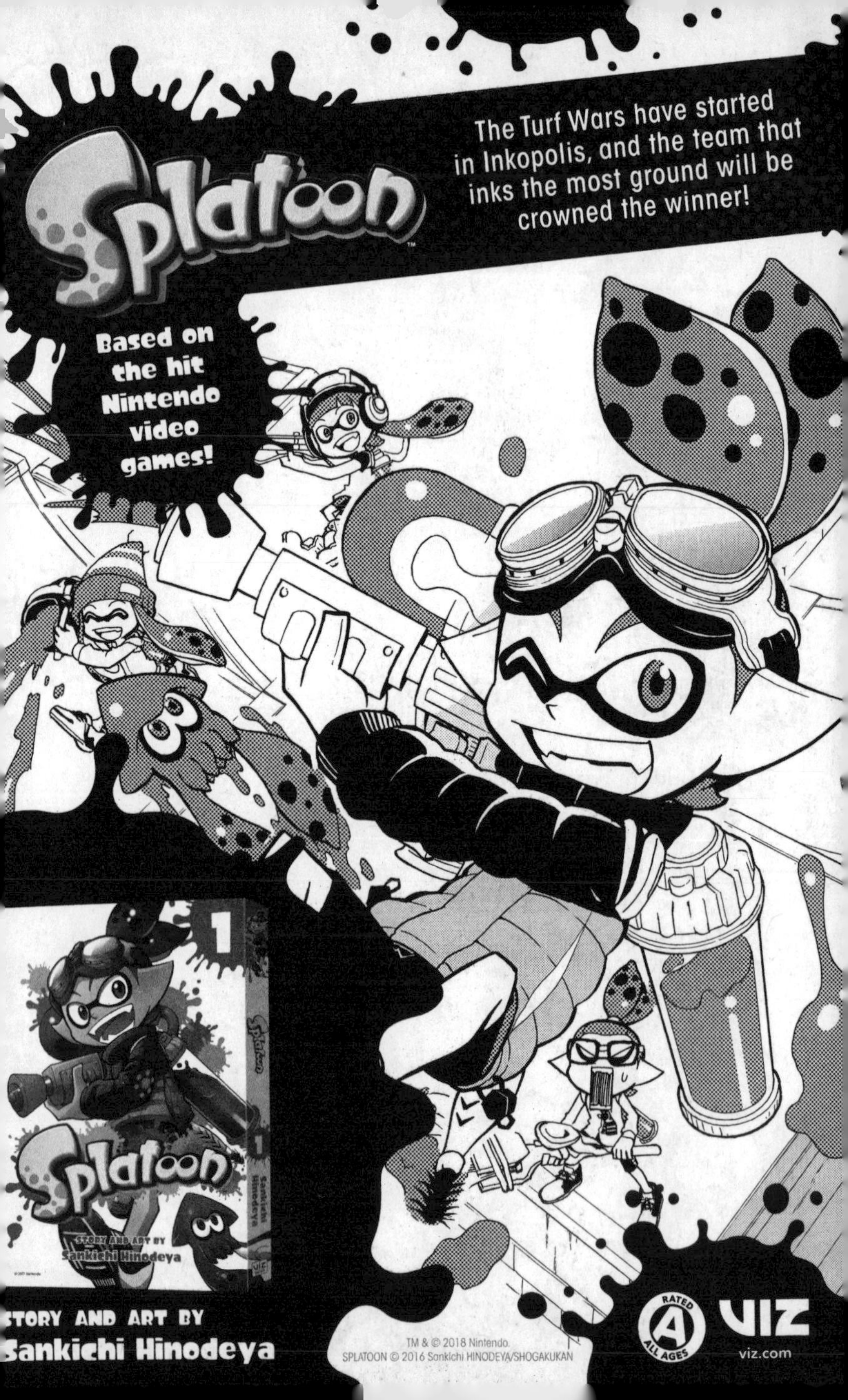
Splatoon
The Turf Wars have started in Inkopolis, and the team that inks the most ground will be crowned the winner!
Based on the hit Nintendo video games!
1
Splatoon
STORY AND ART BY
Sankichi Hinodeya
STORY AND ART BY
Sankichi Hinodeya
TM & © 2018 Nintendo.
SPLATOON © 2016 Sankichi HINODEYA/SHOGAKUKAN
RATED A ALL AGES
VIZ
viz.com

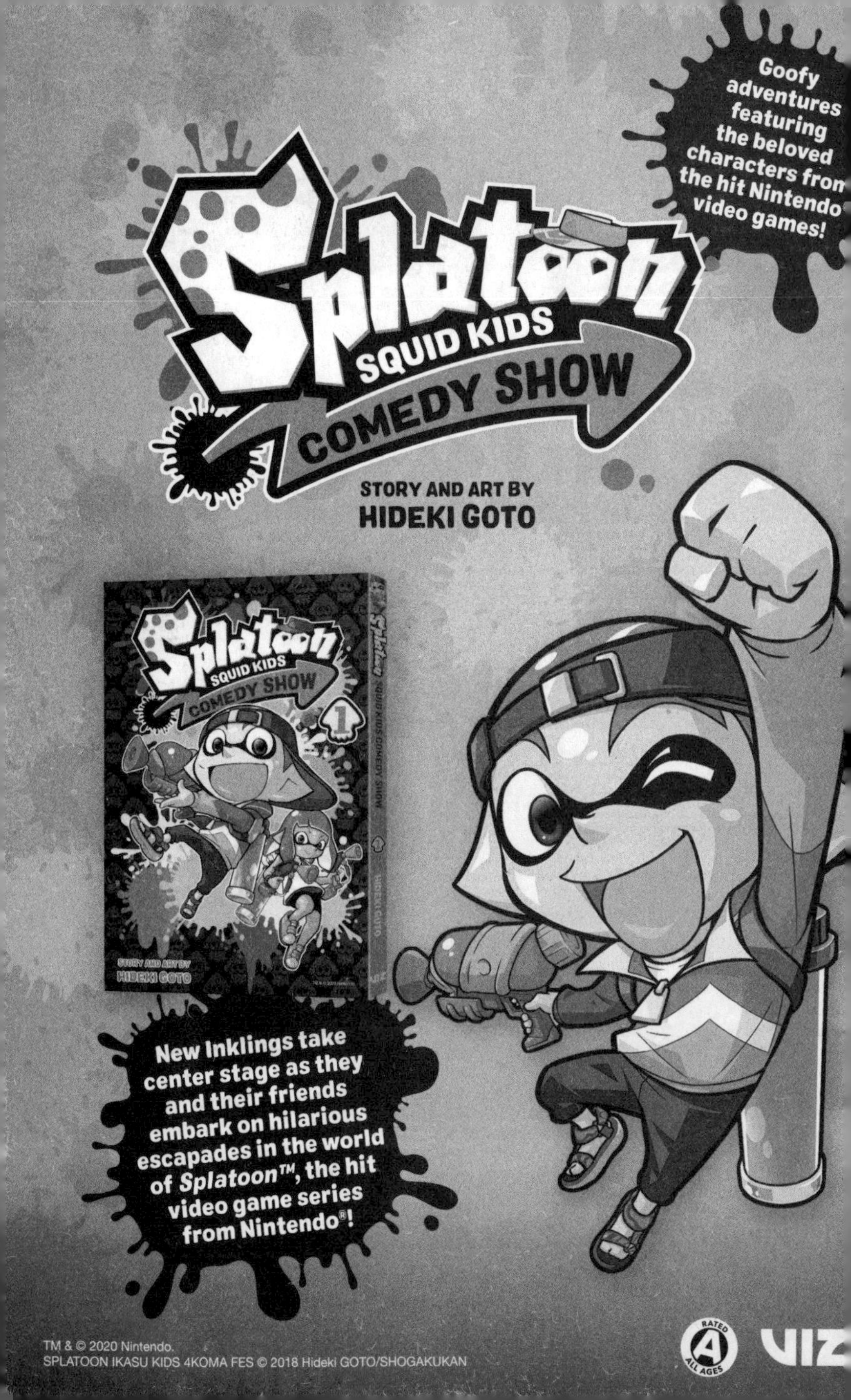
Goofy adventures featuring the beloved characters from the hit Nintendo video games!
Splatoon
SQUID KIDS
COMEDY SHOW
STORY AND ART BY
HIDEKI GOTO
New Inklings take center stage as they and their friends embark on hilarious escapades in the world of *Splatoon™*, the hit video game series from Nintendo®!
TM & © 2020 Nintendo.
SPLATOON IKASU KIDS 4KOMA FES © 2018 Hideki GOTO/SHOGAKUKAN
RATED A ALL AGES
VIZ

Hey! You're Reading in the Wrong Direction!

This is the **end** of this graphic novel!

To properly enjoy this VIZ graphic novel, please turn it around and begin reading from **right to left.** Unlike English, Japanese is read right to left, so Japanese comics are read in reverse order from the way English comics are typically read.

Follow the action this way

This book has been printed in the original Japanese format in order to preserve the orientation of the original artwork. Have fun with it!